Parliament, Politics and Policy in Britain and Ireland, c.1680–1832: Essays in Honour of D.W. Hayton

Professor David Hayton in the South of France, 2013

Parliament, Politics and Policy in Britain and Ireland, c.1680–1832: Essays in Honour of D.W. Hayton

Edited by
Clyve Jones and James Kelly

WILEY Blackwell

for

The Parliamentary History Yearbook Trust

John Wiley & Sons

Registered Office
John Wiley & Sons Ltd, The Atrium, Southern Gate, Chichester, West Sussex, PO19 8SQ, United Kingdom

Editorial Offices
350 Main Street, Malden, MA 02148-5020, USA
9600 Garsington Road, Oxford, OX4 2DQ, UK
The Atrium, Southern Gate, Chichester, West Sussex, PO19 8SQ, UK

For details of our global editorial offices, for customer services, and for information about how to apply for permission to reuse the copyright material in this book please see our website at www.wiley.com/wiley-blackwell.

Library of Congress Cataloging-in-Publication Data
Parliament, politics and policy in Britain and Ireland, c.1680-1832 : essays in honour of D.W. Hayton / edited by Clyve Jones and James Kelly.
    pages cm
  Includes bibliographical references and index.
  ISBN 978-1-118-81354-6 (alk. paper) 1. Great Britain–Politics and government–1603-1714. 2. Great Britain–Politics and government–18th century. 3. Great Britain. Parliament–History–17th century. 4. Great Britain. Parliament–History–18th century. 5. Ireland. Oireachtas–History–17th century. 6. Ireland. Oireachtas–History–18th century. I. Jones, Clyve, 1944- II. Kelly, James, 1959- III. Hayton, David, 1949- IV. Parliamentary History Yearbook Trust.
  DA445.P325 2014
  328.4109′03–dc23

                                2014002200

A catalogue record for this title is available from the British Library
Set in 10/12pt Bembo
by Toppan Best-set Premedia Limited
Printed and bound in Singapore
by Markono Print Media Pte Ltd

1   2014

Contents

LIST OF CONTRIBUTORS

Alex W. Barber is a lecturer in early modern British history at Durham University. His research focuses on the political and religious culture of 17th-century England, and he is particularly interested in the relationship between different forms of communication (scribal, print, oral) and religious and political participation. He is concerned with the nature of censorship and the differing ways in which books, newspapers and scribal newsletters could be restrained. He has published an article in *Parliamentary History* (June 2013) entitled 'It is Not Easy What to say of our Condition, Much Less to Write It'. He was a fellow of the Folger Shakespeare Library in 2012.

Toby Barnard is a fellow emeritus of Hertford College, Oxford. His main research interests are in the fields of the political, social and cultural histories of Ireland and England, c.1600–1800. Among his recent publications are: *A New Anatomy of Ireland* (New Haven, 2003); *Irish Protestant Ascents and Descents, 1641–1779* (Dublin, 2003); *The Kingdom of Ireland, 1641–1760* (Basingstoke, 2004); *Making the Grand Figure: Lives and Possessions in Ireland, 1641–1770* (New Haven, 2004); and *Improving Ireland? Projectors, Prophets and Profiteers, 1641–1786* (Dublin, 2008). He is currently working on a major history of Irish print.

John Beckett is professor of English regional history at the University of Nottingham, and was director of the Victoria County History, 2005–10. He studied at Lancaster University, where his supervisor was Professor Geoffrey Holmes. He has written extensively on English rural and urban history, and much of his work has involved the interaction of economic and social history with political history, including his book *The Aristocracy in England 1660–1914* (Oxford, 1986). His most recent books are *City Status in the British Isles, 1830–2002* (Aldershot, 2005), and *Writing Local History* (Manchester, 2007).

Robin Eagles is a senior research fellow on the House of Lords, 1660–1832 section of the History of Parliament. He has written on various aspects of parliament and the peerage in the 17th and 18th centuries. Previous publications include: *Francophilia in English Society 1748–1783* (Basingstoke, 2000); ' "No More to be Said"? Reactions to the Death of Frederick Lewis, Prince of Wales', *Historical Research*, lxxx (2007); and 'The House of Lords, 1660–1707', in *A Short History of Parliament*, ed. Clyve Jones (Woodbridge, 2009). He is currently working on an edition of the diaries of John Wilkes for the London Record Society.

Perry Gauci is the V.H.H. Green fellow in history at Lincoln College, Oxford. His work has largely centred on the social and political resonance of economic change in the late 17th and 18th centuries, concentrating on how merchants endeavoured to influence the political order at all levels of society. In this regard, he was particularly fortunate to have worked under the editorship of David Hayton in the House of Commons 1690–1715 section of the History of Parliament series. He has recently sought to expand his interests into more challenging imperial contexts, most notably with the publication of *William Beckford: First Prime Minister of the London Empire* (New Haven, 2013).

Richard A. Gaunt is associate professor in modern British history at the University of Nottingham, where he has worked since 2000. He is the author of *Sir Robert Peel: The Life and Legacy* (2010). His edition of the diaries of the 4th duke of Newcastle, between 1827 and 1838, was published in the Parliamentary History Records Series in 2006. A succeeding volume, covering the years 1839–50, is forthcoming in the Parliamentary History: Texts & Studies series. Since 2012, he has been joint editor of the journal *Parliamentary History*. He currently sits on the council of the Historical Association.

Clyve Jones is an honorary fellow of the Institute of Historical Research and has been the editor of the journal *Parliamentary History* since 1986. Previously he was reader in modern history in the University of London and collection development librarian in the Institute of Historical Research. He has published extensively on the history of the house of lords and of the peerage in the early 18th century. His main publications are editions of *The London Diaries of William Nicolson, Bishop of Carlisle, 1702–1718*, with Geoffrey Holmes (Oxford, 1985), and *Tory and Whig: The Parliamentary Papers of Edward Harley, Third Earl of Oxford, and William Hay, M.P. for Seaford, 1715–1754*, with Stephen Taylor (Woodbridge, 1998). He has also edited a *Festschrift* for his mentor, Geoffrey Holmes (1987), and essays in memory of his friends, Philip Lawson (Woodbridge, 1998), John A. Phillips (Edinburgh, 2005) and, again, Geoffrey Holmes (Oxford, 2009), and *A Short History of Parliament: England, Great Britain, United Kingdom, Scotland and Ireland* (Woodbridge, 2009; paperback, 2012).

James Kelly is Cregan professor of history, and head of the history department, at St Patrick's College, Dublin City University. He is a member of the Irish Manuscripts Commission. His publications include: *Poynings' Law and the Making of Law in Ireland, 1660–1800* (Dublin, 2007); *Proceedings of the Irish House of Lords, 1771–1800* (3 vols, Dublin, 2008); *Sir Richard Musgrave, 1746–1818: Ultra Protestant Ideologue* (Dublin, 2009); *Clubs and Societies in Eighteenth-Century Ireland*, ed. with Martyn Powell (Dublin, 2010); *Death and Dying in Ireland, Britain and Europe: Historical Perspectives*, ed. with Mary Ann Lyons (Sallins, Co. Kildare, 2013); and *The Proclamations of Ireland, 1660–1820*, ed. with Mary Ann Lyons (5 vols, Dublin, 2014).

Mark Knights is professor of history at the University of Warwick. He has published several monographs on later-Stuart political culture and is now working on a study of corruption in Britain from the Reformation to 19th-century reform. An earlier piece in this journal examines corruption and print culture. He is also contributing to a catalogue for the National Maritime Museum's forthcoming exhibition about Samuel Pepys.

Eoin Magennis is currently policy research manager in InterTradeIreland, the cross-border body responsible for trade and economic development. He is past editor of the journal *Eighteenth-Century Ireland*, author of *The Golden Age of the Undertakers: The Irish Political System 1740–65* (Dublin, 2000), and *Crowds in Ireland, c.1720–1920*, ed. with Peter Jupp (Basingstoke, 2000). The present article forms part of his current strand of research which focuses on the thinking, practice and operation of markets in 18th-century Ireland. He is the current president of the Eighteenth-Century Ireland Society.

Charles Ivar McGrath is a senior lecturer in Irish history in the school of history and archives, University College Dublin. He is the author of: *Ireland and Empire, 1692–1770* (2012); *The Making of the Eighteenth-Century Irish Constitution: Government, Parliament and the Revenue, 1692–1714* (Dublin, 2000); articles in *The English Historical Review*, *Irish Historical Studies*, *Parliamentary History*, *Eighteenth-Century Ireland*; and numerous edited collections and reference works. Other publications are *Converts and Conversion in Ireland, 1650–1850*, ed. with Michael Brown and Thomas P. Power (Dublin, 2005); *Money, Power and Print: Interdisciplinary Studies on the Financial Revolution in the British Isles*, ed. with Christopher Fauske (Newark, NJ, 2008); and *People, Politics and Power: Essays on Irish History, 1660–1850 in Honour of James I. McGuire*, ed. with James Kelly and John McCafferty (Dublin, 2009).

W.A. Speck is emeritus professor of modern history at the University of Leeds. His publications include: *Swift* (1968); *Tory and Whig: The Struggle in the Constituencies 1701–1715* (1970); *Stability and Strife: England 1714–1760* (1977); *The Butcher: The Duke of Cumberland and the Suppression of the '45* (Oxford, 1981; 2nd edn, Cardiff, 1995); *Society and Literature in England 1700–1760* (Dublin, 1983); *Reluctant Revolutionaries: Englishmen and the Revolution of 1688* (Oxford, 1988); *The Birth of Britain: A New Nation 1700–1710* (Oxford, 1994); *Literature and Society in Eighteenth-Century England: Ideology, Politics and Culture 1680–1820* (1998); *James II* (Harlow, 2002); *Robert Southey: Entire Man of Letters* (New Haven, 2006); *A Political Biography of Thomas Paine* (2013).

ABBREVIATIONS

BL = British Library
Bodl. = Bodleian Library
CJI = Journals of the Irish House of Commons
ed. = edited
HMC = Historical Manuscripts Commission
ILD = Irish Legislative Database
LJI = Journals of the Irish House of Lords
NAI = National Archives of Ireland
NLI = National Library of Ireland
np = no place
ODNB = Oxford Dictionary of National Biography
PA = Parliamentary Archives
PRONI = Public Record Office of Northern Ireland
RIA = Royal Irish Academy
RO = Record Office
TCD = Trinity College Dublin
TNA = The National Archives

Foreword

CLYVE JONES and
JAMES KELLY

No one who has read any of David Hayton's work will need to ponder for long on why he is the worthy recipient of a *Festschrift* on the occasion of his retirement from Queen's University, Belfast. The appreciation and bibliography of his publications that follow give a clear indication of why this volume has been published and why some of his friends and present and former colleagues did not hesitate to join in the project. The title of David's chair clearly attests to his mastery not only of modern British history but also of the modern history of Ireland. His period of speciality is the history of both countries in the Augustan era, from the Glorious Revolution of 1688–9 to the middle decades of the 18th century. One of David's contemporaries, W.A. Speck, has justly called him the natural successor to Geoffrey Holmes, for both men have transformed our understanding of the period through their research and publications. However, whereas Holmes confined his endeavour largely to England, David's research and publications have had a transformative effect on our comprehension not only of Great Britain but also of Ireland.

David's career has covered both aspects of modern historical scholarship: teaching, to which he arrived later than most of his contemporaries, and research and writing, which occupied his earlier career, particularly with the History of Parliament Trust. This culminated in his magisterial introduction to *The History of Parliament: The House of Commons, 1690–1715* (5 vols, 2002). Though the format of the *History* in some sense restricted David's analysis of the period, it can justly stand alongside Holmes's groundbreaking *British Politics in the Age of Anne* (1967) from the previous generation. His work on Ireland has proved equally groundbreaking. Though largely presented in articles during those decades in which he was employed by the History of Parliament Trust, the especial understanding of early-18th-century Irish history that he had achieved in the course of completing his DPhil 'Ireland and the English Ministers, 1707–16' (Oxford University, 1975) meant that he was uniquely well equipped to contribute to the reconstruction, for the first time, of an evidentially-tenable understanding not only of the Anglo-Irish nexus but also of the way in which Irish politics functioned. Indeed, it was apparent from the publication of the seminal essay 'The Beginnings of the "Undertaker System" ' in 1979 that he was in the vanguard of the generation of historians, which emerged in the 1970s and early 1980s, that was to replace the long ascendant nationalist and unionist narratives of 18th-century Irish political history with an evidentially-grounded reconstruction that was internally consistent. A veritable stream of careful, considered and convincing articles followed, the interpretative weight of which only became fully apparent with the publication in 2004 of *Ruling Ireland, 1685–1742: Politics, Politicians and Parties* and in 2012 of *The Anglo-Irish Experience, 1680–1730: Religion, Identity and Patriotism*. Combining, in each case, essays and studies, new and familiar, they illustrate vividly and lyrically the scale of David's redrawing of the Irish historical landscape at a crucial moment in the history of the island.

It might seem invidious to single out a single essay in this *oeuvre*, but his reconstruction of the politics and motivation of the court party in the second of the two volumes cited above is an exercise in forensic historical interpretation upon which superlatives can easily be bestowed. It bears witness not only to the precision of David Hayton's prose but to a refined historical sensibility honed by decades of careful archival sifting and deep thought. It is also built on his recognition of the value of producing accurate and reliable editions of texts and documents, in which he has also proven a master. *The Parliamentary Diary of Sir Richard Cocks, 1698–1702* (1996) may represent his most substantial achievement in that respect, but *Letters of Marmaduke Coghill, 1722–1738* (2005) is, arguably, still more revealing of the work of the men of political and parliamentary business that we overlook at our cost. Parallel with this, David has overseen (with James Kelly) the preparation of a database of the legislation of the Irish parliament, 1692–1800, that will (over time) facilitate an engagement with the work of parliament as comprehensive as that of the politics to which he has so productively devoted so much attention. The publication in 2010 of the collection *The Eighteenth-Century Composite State: Representative Institutions in Ireland and Europe, 1689–1800* was one of the first fruits of an exercise in historical scaffolding that will long pay rich dividends.

David's seemingly boundless energies also led him into the world of history journals. He was a superb joint editor of *Irish Historical Studies* from 1997 to 2007, when attention to detail and to high standards defined his tenure, and was one of the four original founders of *Parliamentary History* in 1982. He was the journal's first reviews' editor from 1982 to 1987 and, since 2010, has been chairman of The Parliamentary History Yearbook Trust, which owns and operates the journal. It is, thus, entirely fitting that it should publish a volume of essays in honour of such a distinguished exponent of parliamentary history.

David W. Hayton

W. A. SPECK

David William Hayton was born in Norfolk in 1949 and still retains a connection with the county, being a lifelong supporter of Norwich City FC. After graduating with a BA in history from Manchester University he went on to obtain a DPhil from Oxford. His doctoral thesis on 'Ireland and the English Ministers, 1707–16' established him as a historian of John Bull's other island. Approximately half of his many publications, as a glance at his extensive and impressive bibliography reveals, are on the history of Ireland or on Anglo–Irish relations in the 18th century. The first appeared in 1975, the year he obtained his doctorate, and dealt with political parties in County Cork in 1714. Several of his Irish articles were revised and republished, together with much new material, in *Ruling Ireland, 1685–1742: Politics, Politicians and Parties* (2004) and *The Anglo-Irish Experience, 1680–1730: Religion, Identity and Patriotism* (2012).

Ruling Ireland was not just a collection of essays for, as David explains in the preface, 'the intention is that they should coalesce into something approaching a coherent account of political developments in Ireland between the accession of King James II and the fall of Sir Robert Walpole'. The characteristically modest declaration of intent was more than fulfilled, making this his most substantial contribution to Irish political history, indispensable for anybody interested in Ireland under the later Stuarts and early Hanoverians. In the introduction he explains how, when he 'began research, over thirty years ago, this period was largely *terra incognita* as far as Irish historians were concerned'. He pioneered a trail which others have followed. 'The simple, and obvious, truth is that it is impossible to understand the way Ireland was governed in the first half of the eighteenth century without an appreciation of the nature of English political development.' It might be simple and obvious, but to do justice to it requires a formidable knowledge of the politics of both sides of the Irish Sea, which he demonstrates with considerable aplomb. Thus he shows how 'the power of the "Protestant Ascendancy" over Irish society may not have been challenged between 1691 and about 1740; nor was the Anglo-Irish constitutional relationship modified. Nonetheless, significant developments were taking place in Irish political life that influenced the way in which the country was governed'. The first was the rise of party which reflected that in England but was not just a mirror image of it. After the accession of the house of Hanover, the rhetoric of party was 'superseded as the common currency of parliamentary and political debate by the rhetoric of "patriotism" '.

Where in *Ruling Ireland*, as David explained, 'he had tried to describe and analyse the ways in which Ireland was governed and the ways in which Irish Protestants responded to government', *The Anglo–Irish Experience* is 'directed towards a different end; to understanding the political culture of the Irish governing class through relating it to the social background'. The opening essay 'From Barbarism to Burlesque' traces the English stereotype of the Irish over the 17th and 18th centuries. Oliver Cromwell summed up the

17th-century view with his observation that 'all the world knows their barbarism'. The 18th–century stereotype was captured in *The Irish Miscellany; Or Teagueland Jests*.[1] David concludes that, by about 1750, the Irish were 'no longer terrifying but contemptible'. He then goes on to consider 'shifting perceptions of national identity' in early modern Ireland. At the time of the Glorious Revolution the supporters of James II were dubbed 'the Irish', the Os and the Macs who were defeated along with the king. Their opponents in Ireland were Anglo–Irish, many having economic, political or family ties with England. Above all, perhaps, they were protestant by contrast with the Roman catholic natives. However, 'by the middle of the eighteenth century an Irish Protestant nation had emerged'. Three case studies of very different politicians, the 2nd duke of Ormond, the Brodricks and Henry Maxwell, illustrate the diverse strands of Irish politics in the period 1680 to 1730. Ormond, leader of the tory party in Ireland under Queen Anne, represented the last of the patricians who had dominated the country's political life under the Stuarts. His desertion to the jacobites on the death of Queen Anne accelerated an underlying trend towards bankruptcy brought about by his continually spending more than he earned. The Brodrick family represented the 'new men' who came to prominence in Irish politics after the Glorious Revolution. They 'may be regarded as classically Anglo-Irish, in that they were an English family who had made their fortune in Ireland but retained strong links with England'. Alan Brodrick was the leader of the Irish whigs in Anne's reign but lost out to William Conolly who became Speaker of the Irish parliament after the accession of George I. The contrast between the fate of the Brodrick interest, known as 'the Munster squadron', and that of the 'Castle party' led by Conolly, is symbolised in the state of their family seats. Ballyanna, the Brodrick mansion, is now a ruin, while Castletown House, Conolly's abode, is a showpiece of Georgian splendour. Henry Maxwell was a 'Commonwealthman', or classical republican. He began his political career as a Country whig connected to like-minded men in England such as the 3rd earl of Shaftesbury. But he gravitated towards the Castle party led by Conolly, and even became known as 'the Speaker's echo'.

Maxwell was also dubbed 'Don Dismallo', an appellation that was presumably known to Jonathan Swift, who applied it to the earl of Nottingham. Swift referred to the likes of Maxwell in George I's reign as 'paltry underlings of State'. The dean of St Patrick's Cathedral, Dublin, regarded them as 'hacks serving a turn rather than patriots serving their country'. David investigates this claim and concludes that, while some might have deserved Swift's censures, others 'seem to have prided themselves on the possession of a genuine concern for the improvement of their country and a coherent and realistic strategy for achieving it'. Like several of the essays in the volume, the investigation of Swift's critique of the Castle party first appeared in another publication. In most of them, however, David made significant changes. Thus an essay on charity schools in Ireland was initially published as 'Did Protestantism Fail in Early Eighteenth–Century Ireland?' whereas here it has the title 'Creating Industrious Protestants'. An essay on the Castle party began life in a collection of essays on Swift, who was used as a peg on which to hang it. In this collection it has been altered to address an issue in Irish political history more directly.

---

[1] *The Irish Miscellany; Or Teagueland Jests: Being a Compleat Collection of the Most Profound Puns, Learned Bulls, Elaborate Quibbles, of the Natives of Teagueland* (c.1680). In his *The Anglo-Irish Experience*, 11 n. 53, David says he used the 3rd edition (1749).

David's contributions to the history of Ireland make it seem natural, as well as appropriate, that he should spend an academic career at Queen's University, Belfast, where he was head of the school of history and anthropology for six years. He has served in the history department there since his appointment as a lecturer in 1994, being promoted to a readership in 1998 and to a chair in 2003. His contribution to the department's teaching as well as to its research output has been widely appreciated, one former student remarking that he 'can say from experience that David is a superb teacher – thorough, adaptable, amusing, and always prepared to go the extra mile for students'. He is also involved in the university's research activities, being a fellow in the Institute of Irish Studies at Queen's, while from 2004 to 2007 he was the director of a project on Irish legislation, 1690–1800, funded by the Leverhulme Trust. His eminent services to Irish history were recognized in 2008 when he became a member of the Royal Irish Academy.

Yet, like John Bull, David has another island. His title at Queen's is 'professor of modern Irish and British history'. This acknowledges his standing among historians of Britain as well as of Ireland, for he is rightly regarded as the leading authority on late-17th- and early-18th-century British politics. As with his publications on Ireland, those involved with Britain also span his career. His first substantial contribution to British history was a brilliant essay on 'The "Country" Interest and the Party System, c.1689–1720', published in 1984. This made political historians of the period sit up and pay attention, for it resolved a problem with which they had been wrestling for three decades, whether Court and Country or whig and tory represented the main dichotomy in post–revolution politics. David demonstrated how they interacted, and yet how the division between tories and whigs was the more significant. He followed this up with other contributions on the Country interest, notably the essay on Sir Richard Cocks published in 1988, based on Cocks's parliamentary diary which he later edited, and the article on moral reform and Country politics that appeared in *Past & Present*. The last was a particularly hard-hitting, even controversial, piece. It sought to explain the occasional outbursts of enthusiasm for Country measures in the house of commons during the 1690s. At the time, the conventional wisdom subscribed to J.G.A. Pocock's thesis that what he had dubbed 'neo–Harringtonianism' informed Country ideology. David's detailed investigation of the activities of MPs in the decade questioned the extent to which classical republicanism underpinned their beliefs. For one thing, the classical republicans were whigs whereas, increasingly, MPs who upheld Country measures tended to be tories. More to the point, they also got involved in campaigns for moral reform which begat the Society for Reformation of Manners, the Society for Promoting Christian Knowledge and the Society for the Propagation of the Gospel. David established a co-relation between members who supported these campaigns and those behind Country proposals in parliament. These reached a peak in the years 1697 to 1701, which saw a plethora of legislation against profanity, atheism and debauchery, amongst which the most notorious was the Blasphemy Act of 1698. They also witnessed the culmination of Country campaigns against the standing army and placemen. David concluded that 'over–emphasis on the influence of the Classical republican tradition has obscured the fact that most MPs seem to have understood the concept of corruption in narrow, simplistic terms, as failures of personal morality'. He acknowledged the invaluable help that access to the History of Parliament's biographies of members of parliament had provided, which enabled him to append lists of those who had been associated with the Country proposals.

In 1990, David became an editor of the History of Parliament Trust's projected volumes for the period 1690 to 1715, having previously been a research assistant there. He held the editorship until his appointment at Queen's. This resulted in *The History of Parliament: The House of Commons, 1690–1715* edited by Eveline Cruickshanks, Stuart Handley and himself, published in five volumes in 2002.

The first volume is devoted to an introductory survey which was written exclusively by David. Many regard this as his masterpiece. Its sheer range is remarkable. Like surveys of other periods in the History of Parliament, it covers such topics as sources, method, constituencies and elections, the members, the organisation of the House and the politics of the House. In addition, David added a section on the business of the House which deals with legislation, 'the grand inquest', regulation of membership, counselling the crown, the members at work and relations between the Lords and Commons. The subsection on the 'grand inquest' examines how the Commons went about 'remedying of individual grievances and keeping a jealous eye on the government of the country'. David's summary of the overall pattern of these activities displays an unrivalled grasp of the party alignments of the period:

> While the House never entirely relaxed its commitment to the investigation of grievances, the direction and emphasis of its inquiries shifted. The concerns of the 'Country party' in the early 1690s to subject government to what Robert Harley termed 'check, inspection, control [and] supervision', by means of the auditing of accounts and estimates, and close inquiry into complaints of official wrongdoing, seems to have given way by 1695 to a more overtly party-political campaign on the part of the Tories to hound their enemies from office by exposing corruption . . . In Anne's reign, however, there was a palpable slackening in the Commons' zeal. Under the Godolphin-Marlborough administration, and more particularly when the Whig Junto were back in power between 1705 and 1710, committees of inquiry became much more low-key, and their subject-matter much more specific . . . The Tory Parliaments of 1710–14 recovered something of their party's old enthusiasm for witch-hunts, though with publicity now their principal objective, and with less success than their predecessors had enjoyed a decade before.

This lines up the survey for the section on 'the Politics of the House'. It is a magisterial analysis of the political scene in the years 1690 to 1715 in which David demonstrates the same mastery of clarifying the complex politics of the 1690s as Geoffrey Holmes had done for the reign of Queen Anne. Where Holmes had felt himself to be writing in the shadow of Sir Lewis Namier, David paid his own tribute to him in an article that appeared in *Parliamentary History* in 2009, with the significant title 'In No One's Shadow'. Certainly the Namierite shades are swiftly dispatched at the outset of this crucial section of the introductory survey. Just as *British Politics in the Age of Anne* has become the received wisdom on the political scene in her reign, so 'The Politics of the House' looks fair to fixing the pattern of parliamentary politics during the years 1690 to 1715 for the foreseeable future.

David's hand can also be discerned in many of the constituency surveys and biographies of MPs which occupy the remaining volumes. Thus he wrote all the surveys of the Welsh constituencies and some of Scotland's. This demonstrates, as do his articles on Scottish history in scholarly journals, that he is truly a British, and not just an English, historian. (His credentials as a historian of Ireland are also reinforced with a discussion of Irish members and issues that concludes the section on the politics of the House.) Among the biographies which he contributes, mention must be made of that for Robert Harley, 'the most important parliamentarian of his day'. It is an outstanding achievement, bringing out the many facets of that complex and devious politician. It is also based on a formidable range of manuscript materials, including the voluminous papers which Harley himself hoarded. The appendices to the introductory survey include, for the first time, a bibliography of the principal manuscripts used in the compilation of this contribution to the History of Parliament.

David's long association with the History of Parliament Trust, which he first joined shortly after completing his DPhil, continues to inform his research. In 2007, he gave the annual History of Parliament lecture on the tercentenary of the Anglo-Scottish Union. His current major project is a biography of Sir Lewis Namier. One of the first fruits of this undertaking was an article published in *Parliamentary History* in 2013, 'Sir Lewis Namier, Sir John Neale and the Shaping of the *History of Parliament*'. Based on a wide range of archival evidence, including the papers of several historians, the article demonstrates how the editorial board of the History of Parliament set up in 1951 was dominated by Namier and Neale. These titans clashed over the aims of the project, Neale preferring a more narrative approach while Namier stressed the need for an analytical, 'sociological' model. Largely because Namier was more productive than Neale, the Namierite view prevailed, though it also held up the progress of the overall project as it necessitated far more input from the contributors. Delays led to criticism from politicians and, at one time, Harold Macmillan almost pulled the plug on the History. Namier's death in 1960 removed the blockage and led to the publication of successive volumes.

These include those which David edited along with Eveline Cruickshanks and Stuart Handley. It would be fascinating to have a similar 'fly on the wall' account of the interaction of this editorial team. David is uniquely placed to provide one, but so far has maintained a discreet silence. Yet something of the discussions that engaged them during his stint at the Trust echo in the volumes which cover the years 1690 to 1715. Dr Cruickshanks had played a prominent role in editing the previous volumes for the years 1715 to 1754 which were published as long ago as 1970. In them, she had insisted that the bulk of the tories who sat in the house of commons under George I and George II were jacobites actively committed to a Stuart restoration. The narrative of political history during the later Stuart era, published in the volumes that appeared in 2002, casts serious doubts on this assertion. Moreover, in the introductory survey David makes it clear that, if there is any discrepancy in the biographies of individual tories between the volumes for 1715 to 1754 and those for the earlier decades, the version that he helped edit is to be preferred. A comparison of the entries for tories in the two surveys reveals that many are described as jacobites in the later period, descriptions that for the earlier era are silently omitted. The discreet silence speaks volumes about David's scholarship and scholarly integrity.

© *The Parliamentary History Yearbook Trust 2014*

Bibliography of the Published Works of D.W. Hayton[*]

Compiled by
CLYVE JONES and
RICHARD A. GAUNT

(The place of publication of volumes is London unless otherwise stated.)

1975

'Tories and Whigs in County Cork, 1714', *Journal of the Cork Historical and Archaeological Society*, 2nd ser., lxxx, 84–8.

1976

Ireland After the Glorious Revolution, 1692–1715, ed. (Public Record Office of Northern Ireland, Education Facsimiles 221–40, Belfast) [booklet of 27 pp., plus 20 loose facsimiles, each with a text].

Review of F.G. James, *Ireland in the Empire, 1688–1770*, in *Studia Hibernica*, xvi, 182–6.

1979

Penal Era and Golden Age: Essays in Irish History, 1690–1800, ed. (with Thomas Bartlett) (Belfast), ix 232 pp.

A Register of Parliamentary Lists, 1660–1761, ed. (with Clyve Jones) (University of Leicester, Department of History, Occasional Publications 1, Leicester), xxvi, 168 pp.

'The Beginnings of the "Undertaker System" ', in *Penal Era and Golden Age*, 32–54 (revised and republished in *Ruling Ireland, 1685–1742* (2004), 106–30).

'The House of Commons Vote on the Transfer of the Crown, 5 February 1689' *Bulletin of the Institute of Historical Research*, lii, 37–47 (with Eveline Cruickshanks and John Ferris).

1980

'Divisions in the House of Lords on the Transfer of the Crown and other Issues 1689–94: Ten New Lists', *Bulletin of the Institute of Historical Research*, liii, 56–87 (with Eveline Cruickshanks and Clyve Jones).

'A Note on the Norfolk Election of 1702', *Norfolk Archaeology*, xxxvii, 320–4.

---

[*] The compilers would like to thank Bill Speck for drawing their attention to several of the publications listed.

Review of *Macartney in Ireland, 1768–72*, ed. Thomas Bartlett, in *History*, lxv, 310.

1981
'The Crisis in Ireland and the Disintegration of Queen Anne's Last Ministry', *Irish Historical Studies*, xxii, 193–215 (revised and republished in *Ruling Ireland, 1685–1742* (2004), 159–85).

1982
A Register of Parliamentary Lists, 1660–1761: A Supplement, ed. (with Clyve Jones) (University of Leicester, Department of History, Occasional Publications 2, Leicester), xii, 20 pp.

'Divisions in the Whig Junto in 1709: Some Irish Evidence', *Bulletin of the Institute of Historical Research*, lv, 206–14.

'An Irish Parliamentary Diary from the Reign of Queen Anne', *Analecta Hibernica*, xxx, 97–149.

1983
Review of Edward Gregg, *Queen Anne*, in *Irish Historical Studies*, xxiii, 90.

Review of *Parliament and Community: Historical Studies XIV*, ed. Art Cosgrove and J.I. McGuire, in *Studia Hibernica*, xxii–xxiii, 160–3.

1984
'Walpole and Ireland', in *Britain in the Age of Walpole*, ed. Jeremy Black, 95–119 (extensively revised and republished as ' "A Remote Part of the King's Dominions": Sir Robert Walpole's Administration and the Government of Ireland, c.1725–42', in *Ruling Ireland, 1685–1742* (2004), 237–75).

The "Country" Interest and the Party System, c.1689–1720', in *Party and Management in Parliament, 1660–1784*, ed. Clyve Jones (Leicester), 37–85.

Review of *London Politics, 1713–1717*, ed. Henry Horwitz, W.A.Speck and W.A. Gray, in *Journal of the Society of Archivists*, vii, 316–17.

Review of *The Manuscripts of the House of Lords, 1714–1718*, ed. D.J. Johnson, in *Archives*, xvi, 299–300.

1985
The Reorientation of Place Legislation in England in the 1690s', *Parliaments, Estates and Representation*, v, 103–8.

Ireland (1625–1783): Planters and Patriots', in *The Cambridge Historical Encyclopedia of Great Britain and Ireland*, ed. Christopher Haigh (Cambridge), 214–17.

'A Treasure-House Laid Open' [a review article on the Huntington Library's catalogue of British manuscripts], in *Parliamentary History*, iv, 205–8 (with Clyve Jones).

Review of J.G. Simms, *William Molyneux of Dublin*, in *Parliamentary History*, iv, 230–2.

1986

J.G. Simms, *War and Politics in Ireland, 1649–1730*, ed. (with Gerard O'Brien), xxi, 335 pp.

'Introduction: The Historical Writings of J.G. Simms (1904–79)', in *War and Politics in Ireland*, ix–xiv (with Gerard O'Brien).

'Selected Bibliography of J.G. Simms', in *War and Politics in Ireland*, xv–xxi (with Gerard O'Brien).

1987

'The Country Party in the House of Commons, 1698–1699: A Forecast of the Opposition to a Standing Army?', *Parliamentary History*, vi, 141–63.

'John Bull's Other Kingdoms: The English Government of Scotland and Ireland', in *Britain in the First Age of Party, 1680–1750: Essays Presented to Geoffrey Holmes*, ed. Clyve Jones, 241–80 (with Daniel Szechi).

'Debates in the House of Commons, 1697–1699', ed., in *Camden Miscellany XXIX* (Camden, 4th ser., xxxiv; Royal Historical Society), 343–407, 426–32.

'Anglo-Irish Attitudes: Changing Perceptions of National Identity among the Protestant Ascendancy in Ireland, ca.1690–1750', *Studies in Eighteenth-Century Culture*, xvii, 145–57 (revised and republished in *The Anglo-Irish Experience, 1680–1730* (2012), 25–48).

1988

'Sir Richard Cocks: The Political Anatomy of a Country Whig', *Albion*, xx, 220–46.

'From Barbarian to Burlesque: English Images of the Irish, c.1660–1750', *Irish Economic and Social History*, xv, 5–31 (revised and republished in *The Anglo-Irish Experience 1680–1730* (2012), 1–24).

The Blackwell Dictionary of Historians, ed. John Cannon (Oxford), contributed one biography (F.G. James).

Review of Gerard O'Brien, *Anglo-Irish Politics in the Age of Gratton and Pitt*, in *Irish Economic and Social History*, xv, 149.

1989

'Two Ballads on the County Westmeath By-Election of 1723', *Eighteenth-Century Ireland*, iv, 7–30.

'Robert Harley's "Middle Way": The Puritan Heritage in Augustan Politics', *British Library Journal*, xv, 158–72.

Review of *The Huguenots and Ireland: Anatomy of an Emigration*, ed. C.E.J. Caldicott, H. Gough and J.-P. Pittion, in *Irish Historical Studies*, xxvi, 414–15.

Review of *Colonial Identity in the Atlantic World, 1500–1800*, ed. Nicholas Canny and Anthony Pagden, in *Irish Economic and Social History*, xvi, 120–2.

Review of *The Gorgeous Mask: Dublin 1700–1850*, ed. David Dickson, in *Hermathena*, cxlvi, 90–3.

1990

'The Propaganda War', in *Kings in Conflict: The Revolutionary War in Ireland and its Aftermath, 1689–1750*, ed. W.A. Maguire (Belfast), 106–21.

'Moral Reform and Country Politics in the Late Seventeenth-Century House of Commons', *Past & Present*, No. 128, pp. 48–91.

Review of B.W. Hill, *Robert Harley: Speaker, Secretary of State, and Premier Minister*, in *Parliamentary History*, ix, 214–16.

Review of *Parliament, Politics and People: Essays in Eighteenth-Century Irish History*, ed. Gerard O'Brien, in *Parliamentary History*, ix, 379–81.

Review of Tim Harris, *London Crowds in the Reign of Charles II*, in *Bunyan Studies*, i, 86–8.

1991

The Williamite Revolution in Ireland, 1688–1691', in *The Anglo-Dutch Moment: Essays on the Glorious Revolution and its World Impact*, ed. Jonathan Israel (Cambridge), 185–213 revised and republished as 'Two Revolutions: Jacobite and Williamite', in *Ruling Ireland, 1685–1742* (2004), 8–34).

A Debate in the Irish House of Commons in 1703: A Whiff of Tory Grapeshot', *Parliamentary History*, x, 151–63.

Sir Charles Sedley's Prayer; or, The Repentant Rake', *Bunyan Studies*, iv, 66–9.

Review of *Council Book of the Corporation of Drogheda, Vol. 1*, ed. T. Gogarty, in *Irish Historical Studies*, xxvii, 374.

Review of P.K. Monod, *Jacobitism and the English People, 1688–1788*, in *The Scriblerian*, xxiii, 279–81.

1992
Review of *The Churches, Ireland and the Irish*, ed. W.J. Sheils and Diana Wood, in *Irish Historical Studies*, xviii, 96–7.

1993
The Dictionary of National Biography: Missing Persons, ed. C.S. Nicholls (Oxford), contributed four biographies (Sir Richard Cocks, Sir Rowland Gwynne, Sir Thomas Mansel, Sir John Philipps).

Review of *Corporation Book of Ennis*, ed. Brian Ó Dálaigh, in *Irish Historical Studies*, xxviii, 325–6.

Review of *Endurance and Emergence: Catholics in Ireland in the Eighteenth Century*, ed. T.P. Power and Kevin Whelan, in *Irish Historical Studies*, xxviii, 448–52.

1994
Review of R.E. Burns, *Irish Parliamentary Politics in the Eighteenth Century, Vol. 1*, in *Parliamentary History*, xiii, 249–50.

1995
British Parliamentary Lists, 1660–1800: A Register, ed. (with G.M. Ditchfield and Clyve Jones), xxi, 151 pp.

'Did Protestantism Fail in Early Eighteenth-Century Ireland? Charity Schools and the Enterprise of Religious and Social Reformation, c.1690–1730', in *As By Law Established: The Church of Ireland since the Reformation*, ed. Alan Ford, James McGuire and Kenneth Milne (Dublin), 166–86, 268–75 (revised and republished in *The Anglo-Irish Experience, 1680–1730* (2012), 149–73).

'Constitutional Experiments and Political Expediency, 1689–1725', in *Conquest and Union: Fashioning a British State, 1485–1725*, ed. Steven Ellis and Sarah Barber, 276–305.

Review of Patrick Fagan, *Dublin's Turbulent Priest: Cornelius Nary (1658–1738)*, in *Irish Historical Studies*, xxix, 124–5.

Review of Phil Kilroy, *Protestant Dissent and Controversy in Ireland, 1660–1714*, in *Irish Historical Studies*, xxix, 402–4.

Review of N.L. York, *Neither Kingdom nor Nation: The Irish Quest for Constitutional Rights, 1698–1800*, in *Parliamentary History*, xiv, 369–71.

1996
The Parliamentary Diary of Sir Richard Cocks, 1698–1702, ed. (Oxford), lxxvii, 345 pp.

'Traces of Party Politics in Early Eighteenth-Century Scottish Elections', *Parliamentary History*, xv, 74–99.

Review of F.G. James, *Lords of the Ascendancy: The Irish House of Lords and Its Members, 1600–1800*, in *Eighteenth-Century Ireland*, xi, 173–5.

Review of James Kelly, *'That Damn'd Thing Called Honour': Duelling in Ireland, 1570–1860*, in *Irish Economic and Social History*, xxiii, 164–6.

1997

'Exclusion, Conformity, and Parliamentary Representation: The Impact of the Sacramental Test on Irish Dissenting Politics', in *The Politics of Irish Dissent, 1650–1800*, ed. Kevin Herlihy (Dublin), 52–73 (revised and republished in *Ruling Ireland, 1685–1742* (2004), 186–208).

'Ulster Presbyterians and the Confessional State: The Sacramental Test as an Issue in Irish Politics, 1704–34', *Bulletin of the Presbyterian Historical Society of Ireland*, xxvi, 11–31.

Review of *The Synge Letters*, ed. Marie-Louise Legg, in *Irish Historical Studies*, xxx, 479–80.

Review of Tony Claydon, *William III and the Godly Revolution*, in *Parliamentary History*, xvi, 371–5.

1998

'The Stanhope/Sunderland Ministry and the Repudiation of Irish Parliamentary Independence', *English Historical Review*, cxiii, 610–36.

'The High Church Party in the Irish Convocation, 1703–1713', in *Reading Swift: Papers from The Third Münster Symposium on Jonathan Swift*, ed. Hermann Real and Helgard Stöver-Leidig (Munich), 117–40 (revised and republished as 'High Churchmen in the Irish Convocation', in *Ruling Ireland, 1685–1742* (2004), 131–58).

'British Whig Ministers and the Irish Question, 1714–1725', in *Hanoverian Britain and Empire: Essays in Memory of Philip Lawson*, ed. Stephen Taylor, Richard Connors and Clyve Jones (Woodbridge), 37–64 (revised and republished in *Ruling Ireland, 1685–1742* (2004), 209–36).

1999

Peers and Placemen: Lord Keeper Cowper's Notes on the Debate on the Place Clause in the Regency Bill, 31 January 1706', *Parliamentary History*, xviii, 65–79 (with Clyve Jones).

2000

Union with Scotland, ed. (vol. 4 of *The Works of Daniel Defoe: Political and Economic Writings*, ed. P.N. Furbank and W.R. Owens), vi, 398 pp.

Dependence, Clientage and Affinity: The Political Following of the Second Duke of Ormonde', in *The Dukes of Ormonde, 1610–1745*, ed. Toby Barnard and Jane Fenlon

(Woodbridge), 211–41 (revised and republished in *The Anglo-Irish Experience, 1680–1730* (2012), 49–75).

Review of Philip Woodfine, *Britannia's Glories: The Walpole Ministry and the 1739 War with Spain*, in *Parliamentary History*, xix, 301–3.

Review of Colin Kidd, *British Identities before Nationalism*, in *Economic History Review*, 2nd ser., liii, 360–1.

2001

The Irish Parliament in the Eighteenth-Century: The Long Apprenticeship, ed. (Edinburgh), xi, 156 pp. (also published as *Parliamentary History*, xx, pt 1).

'Introduction: The Long Apprenticeship', in *The Irish Parliament in the Eighteenth-Century*, 1–26.

'Ideas of Union in Anglo-Irish Political Discourse, 1692–1720: Meaning and Use', in *Political Discourse in Seventeenth- and Eighteenth-Century Ireland*, ed. D. George Boyce, Robert Eccleshall and Vincent Geoghegan (Basingstoke), 142–68.

Review of *Political Ideas in Eighteenth-Century Ireland*, ed. S.J. Connolly, in *English Historical Review*, cxvi, 417–18.

Review of *The Sieges of Derry*, ed. W.P. Kelly, in H-Net Book Reviews.

2002

The History of Parliament: The House of Commons, 1690–1715, ed. (with Eveline Cruickshanks and Stuart Handley) (5 vols, Cambridge), contributed 102 constituencies and 375 biographies.

'Introductory Survey, Appendices', volume 1 of *The House of Commons, 1680–1715*, xxix, 958 pp.

Daniel Defoe, *The History of the Union of Great Britain*, ed. (vols 7–8 of *Collected Writings of Daniel Defoe: Writings on Travel, Discovery and History*, ed. P.N. Furbank and W.R. Owens) (2 vols), vii, 389 pp; 346 pp.

'The History of Parliament', *History Scotland*, ii, pt 5, 19–23.

'The Development and Limitations of Protestant Ascendancy: The Church of Ireland Laity in Public Life, c.1660–1740', in *The Laity and the Church of Ireland, 1000–2000*, ed. Raymond Gillespie and W.G. Neely (Dublin), 104–32.

'Contested Kingdoms, 1688–1756', in *The Eighteenth Century, 1688–1815* (Short Oxford History of the British Isles), ed. Paul Langford (Oxford), 35–68.

2003

'Patriots and Legislators: Irishmen and their Parliaments, c.1689–c.1740', in *Parliaments, Nations and Identities in Britain and Ireland, 1660–1850*, ed. Julian Hoppit (Manchester), 103–23.

Review of *Irish History: A Research Yearbook, Vol. 1*, ed. Joost Augesteijn and Mary Ann Lyons, in *Irish Historical Studies*, xxxiii, 122–3.

Review of Jeremy Black, *Walpole in Power*, in *Parliamentary History*, xxii, 326–8.

Review of Éamonn Ó Ciardha, *Ireland and the Jacobite Cause, 1685–1766: A Fatal Attachment*, in *Eighteenth-Century Ireland*, xviii, 154–60.

2004

Ruling Ireland, 1685–1742: Politics, Politicians and Parties, (Woodbridge), xiii, 304 pp. (a collection of six revised, one largely rewritten, and one new paper, see below, and an introduction and conclusion)

'Anglo-Irish Politics, 1692–1704: The Rise of Party', in *Ruling Ireland, 1685–1742*, 35–105.

Opposition to the Statutory Establishment of Marsh's Library in 1707: A Case-Study in Irish Ecclesiastical Politics in the Reign of Queen Anne', in *The Making of Marsh's Library: Learning, Politics and Religion in Ireland, 1650–1750*, ed. Muriel McCarthy and Ann Simmons (Dublin), 163–86.

The Oxford Dictionary of National Biography, ed. H.C.G. Matthew and Brian Harrison (60 vols, Oxford), contributed 33 biographies (Arthur Annesley (5th earl of Anglesey), Francis Atterbury, Lewis Atterbury the younger, Sir John Barnard, John Berkeley (1st Baron Berkeley of Stratton), James Bonnell, Alan Brodrick (1st Viscount Midleton), Daniel Campbell, Sir John Cass, Sir Richard Cocks, Sir John Hynde Cotton, Sir John Cutler, Sir Gilbert Dolben, John Evans, Sir Ralph Gore, Sir Rowland Gwynne, Sir Thomas Hanmer, Francis Higgins, Sir William Hodges, Sir Elisha (Ellis) Leighton, Thomas Lindsay, John McBride, Thomas Mansel, Robert Molesworth, William Nicolson, Benjamin Overton, Sir John Phillips, Sir Constantine Phipps, Sir Edward Seymour, Edward Southwell, Charles Tottenham, Arthur Upton, Clotworthy Upton).

Review of *Archbishop William King and the Anglican Irish Context, 1688–1729*, ed. Christopher Fauske, in *Journal of Ecclesiastical History*, lv, 793–4.

Review of Patrick Griffin, *The People with No Name: Ireland's Ulster Scots, America's Scots Irish, and the Creation of a British Atlantic World*, in *Eighteenth-Century Ireland*, xix, 232–5.

2005

Letters of Marmaduke Coghill, 1722–1738, ed. (Irish Manuscripts Commission, Dublin), xiii, 198 pp.

'Voters, Patrons and Parties: Parliamentary Elections in Ireland, c.1692–1727', in *Partisan Politics, Principle and Reform in Parliament and the Constituencies, 1689–1880: Essays in Memory of John A. Phillips*, ed. Clyve Jones, Philip Salmon and Richard W. Davis (Edinburgh), 44–70 (also published as a supplement of *Parliamentary History*, xxiv).

Review of Eveline Cruickshanks and Howard Erskine-Hill, *The Atterbury Plot*, in *Parliamentary History*, xxiv, 392–5.

Review of David Dickson, *Old World Colony: Cork and South Munster, 1630–1830*, in *History Ireland*, xiii, no. 6, 58–9.

2006
Review of Sabine Baltes, *The Pamphlet Controversy about Wood's Halfpence (1722–25) and the Tradition of Irish Constitutional Nationalism*, in *Parliamentary History*, xxv, 283–5.

Review of Jeremy Black, *Parliament and Foreign Policy in the Eighteenth Century*, in *Journal of Modern History*, lxxviii, 405–6.

2007
'Henry Maxwell, MP, Author of "An Essay upon an Union of Ireland with England (1703)" ', *Eighteenth-Century Ireland*, xxii, 28–63 (revised and republished in *The Anglo-Irish Experience, 1680–1730* (2012), 104–23).

'The Personal and Political Contexts of Robert Molesworth's *Account of Denmark*', in *Northern Antiquities and National Identities: Perceptions of Denmark and the North in the Eighteenth Century*, ed. Knud Haakonssen and Henrick Horstbøll (Copenhagen), 41–67, 311–16.

2008
'Adjustment and Integration: The Scottish Representation in the British House o Commons, 1707–14', *Parliamentary History*, xxvii, 410–35.

2009
'In No One's Shadow: Geoffrey Holmes's *British Politics in the Age of Anne* and the Writing of the History of the House of Commons', *Parliamentary History*, xxviii, 1–1 (with a postscript by W.A. Speck).

'Bishops as Legislators: Marsh and his Contemporaries', in *Marsh's Library: A Mirror o the World. Law, Learning and Libraries*, ed. Muriel McCarthy and Ann Simmons (Dublin) 62–87.

The Dictionary of Irish Biography, ed. James McGuire and James Quinn (9 vols, Cam bridge), contributed six biographies (Alan Brodrick (1st Viscount Midleton), Jame

Butler (2nd duke of Ormond), George Philips, William Philips, Charles Talbot (duke of Shrewsbury), Charles Tottenham).

2010

The Eighteenth-Century Composite State: Representative Institutions in Ireland and Europe, 1689–1800, ed. (with James Kelly and John Bergin) (Basingstoke), xvii, 270 pp.

'Introduction: The Irish Parliament in a European Context: A Representative Institution in a Composite State', with James Kelly, in *The Eighteenth-Century Composite State*, 3–16.

'Parliament and the Established Church: Reform and Reaction', in *The Eighteenth-Century Composite State*, 78–106.

'Conclusion', with James Kelly, in *The Eighteenth-Century Composite State*, 244–53.

' "Paltry Underlings of State"? The Character and Aspirations of the "Castle" Party, 1715–1732', in *Politics and Literature in the Age of Swift: English and Irish Perspectives*, ed. Claude Rawson (Cambridge), 221–54 (revised and republished in *The Anglo-Irish Experience, 1680–1730* (2012), 124–48).

Review of A.I. Macinnes, *Union and Empire: The Making of the United Kingdom in 1707*, in *Parliamentary History*, xxix, 255–7.

2011

'Colonel Wedgwood and the Historians', *Historical Research*, lxxxiv, 328–55.

Review of *A Short History of Parliament: England, Great Britain, the United Kingdom, Ireland and Scotland*, ed. Clyve Jones, in *Irish Historical Studies*, xxxvii, 115–16.

Review of D.A. Fleming, *Politics and Provincial People: Sligo and Limerick, 1691–1761*, in *Irish Historical Studies*, xxxvii, 318–19.

2012

The Anglo-Irish Experience, 1680–1730: Religion, Identity and Patriotism (Woodbridge), xvii, 225 pp. (a collection of six revised and two new articles, see below).

'A Presence in the Country: The Brodricks and their Interest', in *The Anglo-Irish Experiences*, 77-103.

'A Question of Upbringing: Thomas Prior, Sir John Rawdon, 3rd Bt, and the Mentality and Ideology of "Improvement" ', in *The Anglo-Irish Experience*, 175-98. This article was also published in 2012, in *Irish Provincial Cultures in the Long Eighteenth Century: Essays for Toby Barnard*, ed. Raymond Gillespie and R.F. Foster (Dublin), 106–29.

'Irish Tories and Victims of Whig Persecution: Sacheverell Fever by Proxy', in *Faction Displayed: Reconstructing the Impeachment of Dr Henry Sacheverell*, ed. Mark Knights (Oxford), 80–98 (also published as *Parliamentary History*, xxxi, pt 1).

'Select Document: The Division in the Irish House of Commons on the "Tithe of Agistment", 18 Mar. 1736, and Swift's "Character . . . of the Legion Club" ', *Irish Historical Studies*, xxxviii, 304–21 (with Stephen Karian).

2013

'Accounts of Debates in the House of Commons, March–April 1731, Supplementary to the Diary of the First Earl of Egmont', *eBLJ* (*electronic British Library Journal*), Article 2, 40 pp.

'Sir Lewis Namier, Sir John Neale and the Shaping of the *History of Parliament*', *Parliamentary History*, xxxii, 187–211.

'Swift, the Church and the "Improvement of Ireland" ', in *Reading Swift: Papers from the Sixth Münster Symposium on Jonathan Swift*, ed. Kirsten Juhas, Hermann J. Real and Sandra Simon (Munich), 325–38.

'Preaching History', *Irish Historical Studies*, xxxviii, 523–7 (review article on Michael Bentley, *The Life and Thought of Herbert Butterfield: History, Science and God*).

Review of Jane Ohlmeyer, *Making Ireland English: The Irish Aristocracy in the Seventeenth Century*, in American Historical review, cxviii, 1597–9.

Internet Publication

The Irish Legislation Database (with James Kelly, John Bergin and Andrew Sneddon) (*http://www.qub.ac.uk/ild*).

Samuel Pepys and Corruption

MARK KNIGHTS

Picking up a theme that runs through David Hayton's work, this article examines corruption in the later Stuart period through a case study of Samuel Pepys. The latter's diary can be read alongside the public record of parliamentary inquiries and vilification in the press, allowing us a rare opportunity to study corruption simultaneously through the eyes of a perpetrator and his critics. Pepys reveals ambiguities in how corruption was defined and defended. At the same time as he criticized corruption in others, he took bribes and extorted favours but either lied about them when confronted, or excused them as lawful gifts from friends and those grateful for his services, arguing that his acceptance of them never worked against the king's interest. His critics, on the other hand, queried the compatibility of his private advantage and the public interest, and depicted him as greedy, hypocritical and unjust. Pepys thus illustrates contested notions of corrupt behaviour. The attack on Pepys also shows the political motives behind campaigns against corruption: the libel published against him was part of the murky world of popish plot intrigue, with clear overtones of both catholic and sexual misdemeanour. Popery and lust were associated with corrupt behaviour. Pepys's story was part of a larger one about long-term shifts in the nature of officeholding, state formation, the public interest, patronage and the culture of gift-giving that needs further exploration.

Keywords: Samuel Pepys; corruption; bribes; public interest; private interest; state formation; gift-giving; patronage; navy; restoration; popery; lust

1

Corruption is a theme which runs across David Hayton's work. His contributions to *The History of Parliament: The House of Commons, 1690–1715*, and especially his survey of constituencies and elections', frequently highlight the corrupt practices deployed at later Stuart polls.[1] His *Past & Present* article on moral reform and country politics was even more concerned with the issue of corruption. In it, he made the case for a correlation between Country and moral reforms: 'Both legislative programmes were essentially crusades against corruption: on the one hand the corruption of moral standards in society, on the other the corruption of political institutions.' Moreover, David offered an explanation for the neglect of this link: 'Over-emphasis on the influence of the classical republican tradition has obscured the fact that most M.P.s, many of them relatively unsophisticated country squires, seem to have understood the concept of corruption – and indeed diagnosed all major disorders in the body politic – in narrow,

---

[1] *The History of Parliament: The House of Commons, 1690–1715*, ed. Eveline Cruickshanks, Stuart Handley and D.W. Hayton (5 vols, Cambridge, 2002), i, 36–261.

simplistic terms, as failures of personal morality.'[2] Although this article does not see issues of personal morality as either narrow or simplistic, it does seek to build on this central insight about the broad definition of corruption by examining different conceptions of corruption in the later Stuart period. It uses a case study of Samuel Pepys in order to point to important ambiguities in how contemporaries defined corrupt behaviour, as well as how they defended, exposed and attacked it. This article is also a foretaste of a longer project, since I plan to address such questions in a more systematic way and over a much longer time frame, in a study of pre-modern corruption, from reformation to reform. At the moment we lack such an overview. Although we have many excellent case studies of particular moments or scandals or types of corruption, there has not yet been a systematic attempt to synthesise such material and make the links across it.[3]

Because we have both the private Pepys of the diary and the public record of Pepys as controversial naval administrator, we are able to recover, to a degree that is often difficult to achieve with other subjects of scandal, both a private and public perspective

[2] David Hayton, 'Moral Reform and Country Politics in the Late Seventeenth-Century House o Commons', *Past & Present*, No. 128 (1990), 48–91.

[3] Joel Hurstfield, *Freedom, Corruption and Government in Elizabethan England* (Harvard, 1973); Linda Levy Peck, *Court Patronage and Corruption in Early Stuart England* (1990); Pauline Croft, 'Patronage and Corruption Parliament and Liberty in Seventeenth-Century England', *Historical Journal*, xxxvi (1993), 415–21; Alan Stewart, 'Bribery, Buggery, and the Fall of Lord Chancellor Bacon', in *Rhetoric and Law in Early Moder Europe*, ed. Victoria Kahn and Lorna Hutson (New Haven, 2001); Nieves Matthews, *Francis Bacon: The Histor of a Character Assassination* (New Haven, 1996); David Hebb, 'Profiting from Misfortune: Corruption and the Admiralty under the Early Stuarts', in *Politics, Religion and Popularity in Early Stuart England*, ed. Tom Cogswel Richard Cust and Peter Lake (Cambridge, 2002); John Pocock, *The Machiavellian Moment* (Princeton, NJ 1971); John Pocock, *Virtue, History and Commerce* (Cambridge, 1985); Anna Clark, *Scandal: The Sexual Politi of the British Constitution* (Princeton, NJ, 2005); Howard Tomlinson, 'Place and Profit: An Examination of th Ordnance Office, 1660–1714', *Transactions of the Royal Historical Society*, 5th ser., xxv (1975), 55–75; Faramer Dabhoiwala, 'Sex and the Societies for Moral Reform, 1688–1800', *Journal of British Studies*, xlvi (2007 290–319; Mark Knights, 'Parliament, Print and Corruption in Later Stuart Britain', *Parliamentary History*, xx (2007), 49–61; Wilfred Prest, 'Judicial Corruption in Early Modern England', *Past & Present*, No. 133 (1991 67–95; Clayton Roberts, 'Party and Patronage in Later Stuart England', in *England's Rise to Greatne 1660–1763*, ed. Stephen Baxter (Berkeley, CA, 1983); Aaron Graham, 'Partisan Politics and the Britis Fiscal-Military State, 1689–1713', University of Oxford PhD, 2011; Thomas Horne, 'Politics in a Corru Society: William Arnall's Defense of Robert Walpole', *Journal of the History of Ideas*, xli (1980), 601–14; Car Howard, 'Wollstonecraft's Thoughts on Slavery and Corruption', *The Eighteenth Century*, xlv (2004), 61–10 Isaac Kramnick, 'Corruption in Eighteenth Century English and American Political Discourse', in *Virtu Corruption and Self Interest: Political Values in the Eighteenth Century*, ed. Richard K. Matthews (Bethlehem, P 1994); John Noonan, *Bribes* (New York, 1984); Nicholas Dirks, *The Scandal of Empire: India and the Creatio of Imperial Britain* (Boston, MA, 2006); Philip Stern, 'Corporate Virtue: The Language of Empire in Ear Modern British Asia', *Renaissance Studies*, xxvi (2012), 510–30; Andrew Fitzmaurice, 'American Corruptior in *The Monarchical Republic of Early Modern England*, ed. John F. McDiarmid (Farnham, 2007); Brian Smi 'Edmund Burke, The Warren Hastings Trial and the Moral Dimension of Corruption', *Polity*, xl (2008 70–94; Eckhart Hellmuth, 'Why Does Corruption Matter? Reforms and Reform Movements in Britain a Germany in the Second Half of the Eighteenth Century', *Proceedings of the British Academy*, c (1999), 5–24; Lawson and J. Phillips, ' "Our Execrable Banditti": Perceptions of Nabobs in Mid-Eighteenth Centu Britain', *Albion*, xvi (1984), 225–41; Philip Harling, *The Waning of 'Old Corruption': The Politics of Economi Reform in Britain, 1779–1846* (Cambridge, 1996); Philip Harling, 'Rethinking Old Corruption', *Past & Prese* No. 147 (1995), 127–58; William D. Rubinstein, 'The End of "Old Corruption" in Britain 1780–1860', *P & Present*, No. 101 (1983), 55–86; Gerald Aylmer, 'From Office-Holding to Civil Service: The Genesis Modern Bureaucracy', *Transactions of the Royal Historical Society*, 5th ser., xxx (1980), 91–108; *Corrupt Histor* ed. Emmanuel Kreike and William Chester Jordan (Rochester, NY, 2004). For a comparative analysis s Jean-Claude Waquet, *Corruption: Ethics and Power in Florence 1600–1770*, trans. Linda McCall (Cambrid 1991); Patricia Bonomi, *The Lord Cornbury Scandal: The Politics of Reputation in British America* (1998).

on corruption. Pepys's simultaneous condemnation of corrupt behaviour in others and his justification or legitimisation of his own corrupt behaviour sheds interesting light on how corruption was defined and, in particular, on the uncertain boundaries between presents or gifts and bribery, and the similarly blurred boundaries of public and private interests. Pepys developed interesting ideas about the need to provide private incentives in order to maximise efficiency that was in the king's interest and hence to develop a notion that private and public interests could be made to coincide. The public revelation of his profiteering also highlights the role of print in exposing and defining corrupt behaviour and the ways in which the charge of corruption was used as a political weapon against rivals and enemies. Moreover, Pepys's sexual indiscretions also highlight, as David Hayton sought to do, the link between sexual immorality and other forms of immoral conduct in office, and hence the extent to which personal failings were necessarily related to public ones. Finally, Pepys raises the issue of whether attention paid to corrupt individuals might mask more systematic corruption and how far Pepys's corrupt behaviour was symptomatic of a climate of corruption induced by the growing reaches of the state and its capacity to raise money.

Historians have generally been kind to Samuel Pepys, who, because of the extraordinary richness of his diary, has generally been hailed as something of a lovable rogue, whose foibles humanise him and can be forgiven because of his tireless work to reform the navy. Pepys has a reputation as reformer, not someone who himself needed reform. Arthur Bryant's subtitle of the third volume of his biographical trilogy, 'The Saviour of the Navy', is a view accepted by his most recent biographer, Claire Tomalin: 'Pepys is regarded as one of the most important naval administrators in England's history'.[4] Latham and Matthews, despite having outlined the ways in which he profited from his office, nevertheless suggest, apparently without irony, that Pepys 'mastered the useful art of receiving gifts without becoming corrupt'.[5] Amidst the admiration there have, nevertheless, been some more discordant voices. Henry Roseveare's short entry on Pepys's finances in the *Companion* to Latham and Matthew's edition of the diary concludes that Pepys's income was composed of 'fees, perquisites, gratuities and downright bribes'.[6] But it is really only the American legal scholar, John Noonan, in his massive survey of bribery from ancient Egypt to the modern day, who has considered Pepys's corruption in any depth. Noonan devotes a chapter to showing how Pepys's diary, 'rich as it is in many other aspects, is also the confession of a grafter'.[7] Noonan expertly highlights some of the 'complexity' of Pepys's consciousness about his actions. This will be explored further here and linked to some greater contextual discussion than Noonan was able to achieve in a work that covers 4,000 years.

As Noonan points out: 'the man who began his career as a clerk in 1660 with 25 pounds liquid capital . . . became a man possessing over 7,000 pounds by the end of 1667', an increase of almost 30,000%.[8] Since his official salary was £350, this wealth

---

[4] Arthur Bryant, *Pepys: Saviour of the Navy* (Cambridge, 1938); Claire Tomalin, *Samuel Pepys. The unequalled Self* (2002), p. xxxvi.

[5] *The Diary of Samuel Pepys*, ed. Robert Latham and William Matthews (10 vols, 1970–6), i, pp. cxxiii–iv.

[6] *The Diary of Samuel Pepys*, ed. Latham and Matthews, x, 131, 133.

[7] Noonan, *Bribes*, 387.

[8] Noonan, *Bribes*, 385.

could only have come from unofficial sources. Pepys's diary reveals that he secured a number of payments, gifts and favours as a result of the office he held: animals, clothing, food, furniture, silverware, cash and sex. The money came from suppliers to the navy who wished to secure a contract; those who wished to secure a post; and those for whom Pepys could get bills paid or accounts settled. Pepys had a particularly close relationship with Sir William Warren, who supplied the navy with masts and used bribes to sweeten his deals: he sent Pepys gloves and a 'fair State-dish of Silver and cup with my armes ready-cut upon them';[9] and then another pair of gloves 'wrapped up in paper' so that the '40 pieces in good gold' were not visible.[10] In September 1664, Warren brought Pepys £100 'in a bag', secretly handed over in a tavern when the two men were alone.[11] Pepys records how he made even more out of the Tangier victuallers. About the time when Warren handed him the bag of money, Pepys also received £105 from a group of merchants tendering for the contract; and the money kept flowing from that deal 'for my particular share of the profits'.[12] Pepys's own testimony thus shows the extent of his corruption. It also chronicles Pepys's sense of sheer excitement at receiving these bribes. When the 40 pieces of gold fell out of the gloves, Pepys records, it 'did so cheer my heart that I could eat no victuals almost for dinner for joy'.[13] When he received a gift of two flagons 'with a merry heart, I looked up on them' and they made 'a fine sight and better than ever I did hope to see of my own'.[14] Similarly he was 'not a little proud' when he rode 'a very pretty Mare' he had been given.[15]

The diary is thus useful for revealing what was normally kept hidden: the routine ways in which an official salary could be enlarged. But it is even more useful for showing Pepys's contradictory and ambiguous attitude to bribery and corruption. A paradox stands out: Pepys seemed to have a very clear idea of what corruption was, but increasingly justified, even to himself, the money he was making on the side. This paradox, not unique to Pepys, is worth exploring further.

At precisely the time when he was receiving his bribes, Pepys wrote entries about 'abuses' in the navy office and used the word 'corruption' to describe them.[16] Thus he was deeply aware of what he called 'Sir W[illiam] Batten's corruption and underhand dealing';[17] and noted in a condemnatory manner: 'that hardly anybody goes to sea or hath anything done by Sir W Batten but it comes with a bribe'.[18] Indeed, he perceived that 'the corruptions of the Navy are of so many kinds that it is endless to look after them – especially while such a one as Sir W Batten discourages every man that i

---

[9] I have used *The Diary of Samuel Pepys MA, FRS*, ed. Henry Wheatley (10 vols, 1893–9) [hereafter cite as Diary, with date of entry], since it is the basis for an online edition (at *http://www.pepysdiary.com/*) that readily accessible. The text is reasonably reliable when compared with *The Diary of Samuel Pepys*, ed. Latham and Matthews, though the latter's notes are superior. *Diary*, 2 Oct. 1663.

[10] *Diary*, 2 Feb. 1664.

[11] *Diary*, 16 Sept. 1664.

[12] *Diary*, 4 Feb. 1667.

[13] *Diary*, 2 Feb. 1664.

[14] *Diary*, 21 July, 9 Sept. 1664.

[15] *Diary*, 5 Aug. 1664.

[16] The word 'corruption' had many meanings but its religious, moral and medical ones were supplemente as here, by a notion of malpractice in office.

[17] *Diary*, 13 June 1664.

[18] *Diary*, 27 June 1663. On 15 Nov. 1665 he called him a 'lazy, corrupt, doating rogue'.

honest'.[19] In 1668, MP Matthew Wren talked to Pepys 'of the corruption of the Court, and how unfit it is for ingenious men, and himself particularly, to live in it, where a man cannot live but he must spend, and cannot get suitably, without breach of his honour'.[20] Pepys also seemed shocked by Richard Cooling, the earl of Arlington's secretary, who boasted that 'his horse was a bribe, and his boots a bribe and told us he was made up of bribes and that he makes every sort of tradesman to bribe him; and invited me home to his house to taste of his bribe-wine. I never heard so much vanity from a man in my life.'[21] Pepys also thought it 'a very odd thing' that his patron, the earl of Sandwich, profited from the Tangier contract to the tune of £1,500.[22] Pepys certainly had a concept of corrupt behaviour and condemned it where he found it.

Moreover, Pepys records his own uneasiness about accepting bribes and the lengths he went to keep them hidden for fear of how he might be made to answer for them. In 1663, on receiving one of his first bribes, he did not open the package in which the money was contained until he returned home: 'and there I broke it open, not looking into it till all the money was out, that I might say I saw no money in the paper if ever I should be questioned about it'.[23] Pepys was sensitive to the possibility of being questioned about corrupt activity and took careful precautions to avoid being ensnared. He was, thus, annoyed when his wife acknowledged receipt of a 'neat silver watch' from a potential client, presumably since it meant that witnesses could be questioned; no wonder that Pepys resolved 'to do the man a kindnesse'.[24] Even his own diary entries were part of his attempt to cover his tracks. He carefully recorded that although he accepted 50 pieces of gold from Warren in 1667: 'I never did to this day demand any thing of him', and refused the money twice before finally accepting it; Warren promised him more if Pepys would get his bills paid, prompting Pepys to declare that he would 'do my utmost for nothing to do him that justice' – but all this was for show: Pepys confessed that he wrote in his diary 'at large for my justification if anything of this should be hereafter enquired after'.[25]

This fear of discovery was not fanciful and his awareness of corruption was no doubt heightened by several parliamentary investigations and prosecutions. In 1663, an attempt was made to impeach Charles II's chief minister, the earl of Clarendon, on charges of having been 'bribed' to make a disadvantageous peace with the Dutch.[26] In 1666, Pepys was put 'into a great pain' by a 'wild motion made in the House of Lords by the Duke of Buckingham for all men that had cheated the King to be declared traitors and felons, and that my Lord Sandwich was named'.[27] And, in 1668, Pepys even had to justify his own actions to the commissioners of accounts, prompting him to 'prepare' those summoned to be interrogated 'about what presents I had from them, that they may not

---

[19] *Diary*, 17 June 1664; cf. 22 May 1664.
[20] *Diary*, 27 Sept. 1668.
[21] *Diary*, 30 July 1667.
[22] *Diary*, 27 Dec. 1667.
[23] *Diary*, 3 Apr. 1663.
[24] *Diary*, 17 Apr. 1665.
[25] *Diary*, 25 Nov. 1667.
[26] *Diary*, 10 July 1663.
[27] *Diary*, 5 Oct. 1666.

publish them'.[28] Pepys and his colleagues were accused of having 'corruptly preferred and postponed payments' and he resolved 'to declare plainly, and, once for all, the truth of the whole, and what my profit hath been'.[29] Yet in the winter of 1669–70, Pepys was, again, called to account, this time to the Brooke House commissioners, and responded by protesting that he never did 'directly or indirectly . . . demand or express any expectation of fee, gratuity or reward from any person for any service' and deliberately underestimated the amount he was now worth by £6,000.[30] Pepys's diary shows that he understood what a bribe was, expressed his shock at the bribes taken by others, was uneasy that his own conduct might be discovered and sought to cover his tracks through outright denials of culpability.

Despite these clear signs that he knew what constituted corrupt behaviour and the risks involved in being caught, Pepys increasingly justified, even to himself, the money he was making on the side. He had a number of strategies for doing this. One was to think of, and describe, the bribes as gifts, presents, compliments, acknowledgements, kindnesses and loans. Thus Pepys refers to 'a very noble present' and, a year later, 'a good present' given to him.[31] The language of presents was mirrored by one of 'kindnesses' being properly recognized, or 'obligations' being requited.[32] This was the language of friendship. Talking with Warren about a mutually-beneficial contract, Pepys noted that he had 'a prospect of just advantage by his friendship'.[33] Indeed, Pepys described Warren as 'the best friend I have ever had in this office'.[34] By deploying such terms, Pepys could accommodate his actions within ambiguous, but accepted, notions of how friends behaved to one another. Even the anglican divine, Jeremy Taylor's popular advice about friendship, first published in 1657 and reprinted three times before 1671, urged that one friend was not to refuse the 'kindnesses' of another nor despise 'the impropriety of them. . . . A gift (saith Solomon) fastneth friendships . . . so must the love of friends sometimes be refreshed with material and low Caresses; lest by striving to be *too divine* it becomes *less humane*: It must be allowed its share of *both*.'[35] Even when he does not use the language of friendship, Pepys carefully distinguished between a bribe and a civil acknowledgement for services rendered. Thus, when being offered £200 for help in securing a patent, he declared: 'that as I would not by anything be bribed to be unjust in my proceedings, so I was not so squeamish as not to take people's

---

[28] *Diary*, 2 Mar. 1668. The examinations of 1668–70 are explored in C.S. Knighton, *Pepys and the Navy* (Stroud, 2003), ch. 5.

[29] *Diary*, 11 Feb. 1668. See also Anchitell Grey, *Debates of the House of Commons* (10 vols, 1769), 15 Feb. 1668 [accessible online via British History Online, at *http://www.british-history.ac.uk*].

[30] *The Letters of Samuel Pepys: 1656–1703*, ed. Guy De la Bédoyère (2006), 80–1: Pepys to the Brooke House commissioners, 6 Jan. 1670; Noonan, *Bribes*, 380. For a fuller defence of the accusations of corruption see the journal Pepys made of his interactions with the Brooke House, published in *Pepys's Later Diaries*, ed. C.S. Knighton (Stroud, 2004), 12–40. This records the moment when, having challenged the commissioner to produce a single ticket that showed a fraudulent payment to himself, they promptly did so.

[31] *Diary*, 10 Feb. 1663; 2 Mar. 1664.

[32] *Diary*, 12 Feb., 18 July 1664.

[33] *Diary*, 17 Oct. 1664.

[34] *Diary*, 5 Dec. 1664.

[35] Jeremy Taylor, *A Discourse of the Nature, Offices, and Measures of Friendship with Rules of Conducting* (1657), 100–1.

acknowledgement where I have the good fortune by my pains to do them good and just offices'.[36] This lack of squeamishness diminished further over time.

As the last quotation suggests, reward for 'good and just offices' for others became a way of legitimising self-interest, especially if the greater good was that of the king as well as of the client. Thus, although Pepys accepted money from one contractor, he noted that: 'there is not the least word or deed I have yet been guilty of in his behalf but what I am sure hath been to the King's advantage and profit of the service, nor ever will I'.[37] Pepys insisted that the king's interest always came above his own and, indeed, that the public good was actually being furthered through the sweetened deals he struck. Thus, when Warren came to repay a 'kindness', Pepys notes that: 'I must also remember [it] was a service to the King.'[38] When he was offered a bribe to go against the public interest, he contemplated returning it: 'I [went] to the office and there had a difference with Sir W. Batten about Mr. Bowyer's tarr, which I am resolved to cross, though he sent me last night, as a bribe, a barrel of sturgeon, which, it may be, I shall send back, for I will not have the King abused so abominably in the price of what we buy, by Sir W. Batten's corruption and underhand dealing.'[39]

Moreover, Pepys argues, his actions always fell within the law. When negotiating a share of the profits from one contract, he calls this 'lawfull profit'.[40] Even when faced with parliamentary scrutiny of the £500 'profit' he had made on prize goods, he still thought that: 'there is nothing of crime can be laid to my charge'.[41] The 'lawful' nature of such bribes derived in no small measure from their customary nature and ubiquity, in turn a reflection of the low pay of many state offices. Right at the start of his career Pepys's patron, Sandwich, had told him: 'that it was not the salary of any place that did make a man rich, but the opportunities of getting money while he is in the place';[42] and Sir William Warren told Pepys that 'everybody must live by their places'.[43] The system in which Pepys found himself operating was, thus, built around a tacit acceptance that an office was a means to an end as well as an end in itself. And it was a system in which others lacked the knowledge to expose abuse of office or even to fully understand how the system could be abused. In 1663, Pepys drew up a contract for £3,000 worth of masts and noted: 'good God, to see what a man might do were I a knave – the whole business, from beginning to the end, being done by me out of the office'.[44]

The strategies adopted in the diary to legitimise his bribe-taking were the same as those that Pepys used in public when cornered. He made an appeal to a notion of bribes as voluntary gifts, fair rewards for services rendered, of always working in the king's and the public's interest when, in 1670, Pepys explicitly and publicly denied the bribes that

---

[36] *Diary*, 12 Dec. 1663.

[37] *Diary*, 5 Jan. 1664.

[38] *Diary*, 25 Nov. 1667 – also noting that: 'I never did to this day demand any thing of him'.

[39] *Diary*, 13 June 1663.

[40] *Diary*, 5 Mar. 1663.

[41] *Diary*, 3 Feb. 1668.

[42] *Diary*, 16 Aug. 1660 and he later learned that Lord Sandwich had received £1,500 on one contract (27 Dec. 1667).

[43] *Diary*, 2 Aug. 1664.

[44] *Diary*, 10 Sept. 1663.

his own diary reveals that he took. He affirmed his 'diligence' and 'integrity to my master and fair dealing towards those whom his service hath led me to have to do with'. Indeed, he protested: 'from the first hour of my serving his Majesty in this employment I did never to this day directly or indirectly demand or express any expectation of fee, gratuity or reward from any person for any service therein by me done or to be done them . . . no gratuity, though voluntarily offered, hath ever met with my acceptance where I found not the affair to which it did relate accompanied with the doing right or advantage to his Majesty'. He had been so solicitous of the public interest that he 'f[ou]nd not my estate at this day bettered by one thousand pounds' since his admission to office. He was ready 'to justify the same not only by oath but by a double retribution of every penny or pennyworth of advantage I shall be found to have received'. Pepys thus pleaded that he placed public over private interest: 'no concernments relating to my private fortune, pleasure or health did at any time (even under the terror of the Plague itself) divide me one day and night from my attendance on the business of the place', which had cost him his good eyesight.[45]

In his earlier speech to MPs, Pepys had also defended what seemed corrupt by pleading necessity, utility, custom and humanity. The system of paying sailors by tickets was both useful and necessary, he explained, when there was 'not ready money' to pay them; 'nor can that be called irregular that never was regular'; and although he admitted that the practice 'may be extremely abused if not well looked to', he argued that the 'irregularity' in the order in which sailors were paid was due to the 'discretion' exercised in the sailors' favour: the navy office was 'not to be condemned if the pitiful necessity of some have been relieved before others out of the strict order'. Pepys denied 'any indirect or partial paying by tickets, but only where mere necessity did compel them'.[46] Administrative irregularity was thus inevitable because of the irregularity of government finance to pay sailors and was actually in the sailors' interest.

Moreover, Pepys was convinced that incentives of private profit improved the public service. In 1666, he wrote a paper for Sir William Coventry about victualling, in which he set down the maxim that 'my work is likeliest to be best done by him whose profit is increased by the well doing of it without increase of charge to me that employs him'.[47] Greasing the machine, he claimed, actually improved its efficiency: pursers would have an incentive to keep their ships at sea for longer if by doing so they stood to gain, and this, in turn, would give them 'a plain and unbeholden subsistence and thereby be delivered from the necessity of studying new and practising old artifices'.[48] The conspiracies of embezzlement and fraud practised by pursers and commanders would, Pepys was convinced, stop. As things currently stood, he suggested, 'it is not the purser's corruption but necessity must be thought able to tempt him to such unthrifty ways of profit'[49] – but change the system to increase the private profit and the public would be better served not least because the motives for corruption would be removed. This

[45] *Letters of Samuel Pepys*, ed. De la Bédoyère, 80–2.
[46] *The Diary of John Milward, Esq. Member of Parliament for Derbyshire September 1666 to May 1668*, ed. C. Robbins (1938), 207–9.
[47] *The Further Correspondence of Samuel Pepys 1662–1679*, ed. J.R. Tanner (1928), 93–111, quotation at 105.
[48] *Further Correspondence of Samuel Pepys*, ed. Tanner, 109.
[49] *Further Correspondence of Samuel Pepys*, ed. Tanner, 98.

philosophy also seems to capture Pepys's attitude to his own profits, which he consistently argued were not only compatible with, but actually furthered, the king's interest.

Pepys thus argued, both to himself and to those who questioned him, that the bribes he accepted were lawful, freely-given gifts, that either justly rewarded his effort or furthered the king's interest, and even made it more humane for those employed at the sharp end. If Pepys's defence was right, then corruption could, at worst, be the inevitable outcome of not paying state officials adequately, or, at best, actually beneficial to the state. The trouble with this interpretation is, first, that Pepys had to lie to legitimise his behaviour and, second, that a very different construction could be, and was, put on Pepys's actions by his critics. Far from working in the public interest, Pepys was accused of pursuing his private interest; instead of 'friendship', Pepys was depicted as abusing social relationships for profit; and where Pepys saw self-restraint and legality, others saw rapaciousness and illegality. The ambiguity inherent in Pepys's own views about corruption show that different and clashing definitions of corruption also existed in the public sphere.

2

Pepys was the subject, in 1679, of a parliamentary enquiry that landed him in the Tower and of a vitriolic pamphlet. Both are instructive about public attitudes to corruption.

That Pepys became a victim of the Popish Plot is well known.[50] One of the witnesses, William Bedloe, alleged that Samuel Atkins, one of Pepys's servants, was present at the murder of Sir Edmund Berry Godfrey, whose death in suspicious circumstances triggered the anti-popish alarm.[51] Pepys may have been the intended target of the accusation, saved by the fact that he had a cast-iron alibi, since he was away from London on the night in question. Nevertheless, pressure on Pepys persisted. A parliamentary enquiry investigating the 'miscarriages of the navy' heard information, orchestrated by the colourful intriguer, Colonel Scott, that Pepys was a traitor and popishly inclined.[52] The evidence against Pepys was provided by his former butler, John James, who harboured a grudge after his dismissal for having been caught in bed with his master's housekeeper.[53] James told MPs that the Pepys household included a 'jesuit', the Portuguese musician, Morelli, who participated in catholic masses in Somerset House; that the two men sang psalms together; and that Pepys commended catholics 'for their constancy in Religion'.[54] Pepys was ordered to be arrested, despite his vehement protest that he was 'as good a son of the Church of England as any man' and hence 'far from

---

[50] James Long and Ben Long, *The Plot against Pepys: Detection and Intrigue in Seventeenth Century London* (2007).

[51] For Atkins, see John H. Wilson, *The Ordeal of Mr Pepys's Clerk* (Columbus, OH, 1972).

[52] On 25 Oct. 1668, his wife revealed that she was a catholic.

[53] Pepys told MPs that James had the 'ill luck to fall into an amour with my house-keeper, and, as fortune was, *Morello* overheard their intrigues, and catched them together at an unseasonable time of the night. It was *Sunday*, three o'clock in the morning (the better day the better deed.) I turned him away, and he was never in my House since; but I had cause of suspicion that *James* came within my House at a window, and robbed me': Grey, *Debates*, 20 May 1679.

[54] Grey, *Debates*, 20 May 1679. For a fuller list of the accusations made by James see his testimony at Bodl., MS Rawlinson, A 173, ff. 178–9.

suspicion of Popery'.[55] As Sir Francis Rolle sarcastically noted, Pepys 'has been very unfortunate in his Servants; one accused to be in the Plot (*Atkins* his Secretary!) another, his best maid, found in bed with his Butler! another accused to be a *Jesuit!* very unfortunate!'[56]

The chair of the parliamentary enquiry, Sir William Harbord, also noted that this was not the first time that Pepys's protestantism had been questioned. In 1673 Pepys became MP for Castle Rising, one of the notoriously corrupt pocket boroughs that had only about 30 voters (amongst whom Pepys spent over £600) and where, during the Restoration, the catholic, Henry Howard, had a strong influence because the family held the lordship of the manor.[57] Indeed, a letter of recommendation from Howard was the subject of a complaint to the Commons and, in February 1674, during the subsequent investigation, Pepys's religion became the focus of parliamentary attention. Rumours that he had an altar and a crucifix in his house, and even that he had said protestantism 'came out of *Henry* the eighth's codpiece', were repeated in the Commons, forcing him to give a speech defending himself 'as a good Protestant and a good Churchman, and the best sort of Protestant'.[58] He declared that he had assiduously attended church; taken communion; qualified himself according to the Test Act; and had ensured that there were no catholic chaplains on any navy ship. He protested that he 'had not been once in his life at Mass', a lie according to the testimony of his own diary where, on 19 May 1661, he records hearing not one but two masses at York House, the Spanish ambassador's residence, and that was clearly not the first occasion he had done so, nor the last.[59] The affair finally blew over when the charges against him could not be fully substantiated, but clearly suspicions lingered.[60]

Popery played a significant role in early modern ideas about corruption. Anti-popery drew a good deal of its force in the 16th and earlier 17th centuries from an association between the corruption of the true word of God and the corruption of money. That correlation was repeated in the accusations made against Pepys. In parliament, the catholic duke of York's control of the navy translated into fiscal mismanagement. As Sir Francis Winnington put it, £600,000 had been granted for the building of ships and Pepys had told MPs that 'they would be built in a year'; but 'there was 600,000*l*. gone, for they got the money and prorogued the Parliament'.[61] This was symptomatic of a more general alliance between fiscal corruption and the favouring of popery. Lord Treasurer Danby, Winnington said, had 'exhausted the Treasure of the Crown, by acquiring a great estate to himself, &c. and endeavoured to stifle the discovery of the Plot, when it was just coming to light'. Danby and popery rose together. Also Danby had systematically attempted to use state money to bribe MPs to become supporters of

[55] Grey, *Debates*, 14 Apr. 1679.

[56] Grey, *Debates*, 20 May 1679.

[57] *The History of Parliament: The House of Commons, 1660–1690*, ed. B.D. Henning (3 vols, 1983) [hereafter cited as *HPC, 1660–90*], i, 323–4.

[58] Grey, *Debates*, 10, 16 Feb. 1674.

[59] See also, Diary, 10 May 1663.

[60] For an excellent discussion of Pepys's religious beliefs, see Kate Loveman, 'Samuel Pepys and "Discourse touching Religion" under James II', *English Historical Review*, cxxvii (2012), 46–82.

[61] Grey, *Debates*, 22 Mar. 1679.

the Court.[62] Two days after Pepys was interrogated in parliament about his religion, MPs investigated the abuse of secret service money which had been paid to 27 of their colleagues.[63] An intrinsic part of 'popery and arbitrary government' was, thus, the misspending of state resources to subvert parliament.

The association of popery and corruption was also made in a two-part pamphlet, *A Hue and Cry after P and H.*, which had *Plain Truth, or a Private Discourse between P. and H.* appended to it.[64] The tract satirised Pepys and his friend, Will Hewer, accusing both of favouring catholics 'so far as to promote them to be Captains, or Lieutenants, or Mid-Ship-Men extraordinary' and ridiculed Pepys for his ostentatiously-painted coach, imagining that it was decorated with 'your Jesuite M[orelli] Playing upon his Lute, and Singing a Holy Song'.[65] The tract's charge of popery followed immediately on from a damning indictment of the two men's corrupt behaviour, demanding that they:

> refund all the money they have unjustly taken for Permissions & Protections, to their Merchants or Owners of all such Ships as were fitted out for the last Imbargo. And also give satisfaction for your extraordinary Gain made to your selves in buying of Timber, for Building the New Ships of war. P & H you must also Refund those before-hand Guinies or Broadpieces; and also the Jars of Oyl, and Boxes of Chocolett and Chests of Greek Wines, and Chests of Syracusa Wines, and Pots of Anchovies and Quarter-Casks of old Malago, and Butts of Sherry & Westphalia hams & Bolonia Sauceges & Barrels of Pickel'd Oysters and Jars of Ollives, and Jars of Tent, & Parmosant Cheeses, & Chests of Florence Wine and Boxes of Orange Flower Water; And all those dry'd Cods and Lings, and Hogsheads of Claret, White-Wines, Champaynes, and Dozens of Syder: And also all those Mocos, Parrotts and Parakeets, Virginia Nightingales and Turtledoves, and those Fatt Turkeys and Pigs, and all those Turkish Sheep, Barbery Horses, and Lyons, Tygers, and Beares; and all those fine Spanish Matts. All which were received from Sea-Captains, Consuls, Lieutenants, Masters, Boatswains, Gunners, Carpenters and Pursers; or from their Wives or Sons or Daughters; Or from Some of the Officers in the Dock Yards; as Master Ship-Wrights, Master of Attendance, or Clerk of the Cheques, and Storekeeprs &c And more especially those great Lumps taken of Sir D G Victualler.[66]

This rich, almost lyrical, passage, cataloguing the sumptuous goods becoming available during the Restoration, publicly exposed the bribes and inducements privately recorded in the diary.

Indeed, the tract played on the public unveiling of the private. It thus promised 'plain truth' by publishing an allegedly 'private discourse' between Pepys and Hewer, using the dialogue format to reveal their secret calculations about moneymaking. The pamphlet

---

[62] For Pepys's support of this, see *HPC, 1660–90*, iii, 226: in the face of the discipline of opposition forces, 'we must be sure to bribe voices enough'.

[63] Grey, *Debates*, 23 May 1679.

[64] The Early English Books Online copy has *Plain Truth* first, but it is paginated first at p. 5, with *A Hue and Cry*, paginated at pp. 1–4. The pamphlet as a whole will be referred to as *A Hue and Cry* because of the continuous pagination.

[65] *A Hue and Cry*, 3.

[66] *A Hue and Cry*, 1–2. The reference at the end is probably to Sir Denis Gauden, a navy victualler. I am grateful to Kate Loveman for spotting this.

makes an extended play on how Hewer and Pepys had sought to keep their corruption away from the public gaze. Hewer reveals that he would only bring commissions to be signed for which he already had received money, ironically so that 'it is impossible, that ever [Pepys] should be brought in question' for them and Hewer promised to keep both men 'clear enough, let the World pry never so close into our business' – yet the tract itself publicly catalogues and exposes that hidden corruption.[67] Similarly, the two men discuss extorting money for promotions within the navy service, which Pepys declares is 'very discreetly done, and it is impossible that ever it shou'd be discover'd so', yet the tract does very clearly 'discover' their corruption.[68] The two men had come 'within the Reach of the Printing Press' which, the tract declares, 'squeezes you both very hard, with Matter of Truth'.[69]

The tract thus puts forward a very different view of the 'friendly favours' and lawful 'gratifications' referred to in the diary, and of the notion that a culture of venality in office justified rapacity in all. Pepys and Hewer are depicted as conspiring how best to rake off money from the preparations for war against France: 'we ought to think of getting as much as we can, in our Imploys, as well as others in the like have done . . . And what will the World say, if we do not? That we are all Fools.' But the justification that they were simply doing what everyone else did was here delegitimised, for their corrupt behaviour is shown as a cruel twisting of proper social relationships and far from victimless: the men had committed a 'great Robbery' by extorting money from cripples and maimed sailors who had been 'squeazed so cruelly' and 'forc'd to stand a whole day in Snow and Rain, in the Corners of the Streets, and beg for it'.[70] Moreover, the discrepancy between Pepys's public persona and his private corruption exposed him to be a hypocrite: the mock painting described in the tract as embellishing Pepys's ostentatious carriage showed cripples receiving 'his Charity' which was, in reality, never given.

The pamphlet further publicly exposed Pepys and Hewer's private corruption and their victims through allegations that they used their office to abuse women.[71] Pepys and Hewer were said to have extorted gifts and money from 'wives' and 'daughters' as well as their menfolk. And the tract ended with a mock 'hue and cry' (significantly in a larger font) referring to 'a Lady in Lincolns-Inn-Fields, or to a Lady at her Country House in Chelsey; or to another at her House near the Exchequer; or to two Merchants Daughters in London; they being well known to these Two Persons; especially P[epys]'.[72] These women may well be more of those wronged by extortions of money along the lines of the abused woman discussed in the tract's previous paragraph;[73] but there is also a clear hint of sexual impropriety. Pepys's long-time but unmarried

---

[67] *A Hue and Cry*, 6.

[68] *A Hue and Cry*, 7.

[69] *A Hue and Cry*, 2. For print as a means of correcting victualling abuses see Knights, 'Parliament, Print and Corruption'.

[70] *A Hue and Cry*, 2, 7.

[71] *A Hue and Cry*, 3.

[72] *A Hue and Cry*, 4. Cf. C.S. Knighton's observation 'that he was never denounced for immorality by his political opponents'; *ODNB* (entry on Samuel Pepys).

[73] That paragraph refers to John Walbanke, clerk to the navy and another of Pepys's friends: Bodl., MS Rawlinson, A 173. ff. 180–3: ms tract.

companion, Mary Skinner, who was 'well known' to Pepys in more senses than one, was the daughter of a merchant and may well be one of the women being referred to.[74] The diary, of course, provides evidence that Pepys did seek sex by advancing husbands to better positions in the navy. Pepys received and, indeed, aggressively pursued sexual favours in return for his patronage. The diary records, for example, how he deliberately sought out the 'pretty' and 'virtuous modest' wife of a carpenter, Bagwell. Initially he resolved to help the man without offering any 'courtship' to her (she is never given a first name in the diary), but he found that impossible: he began first with caresses and found 'her every day more and more coming with good words and promises of getting her husband a place'. Then, having dined at Bagwell's home, 'je tentais a faire ce que je voudrais et contre sa force je le faisais biens que passe a mon contentment'. Pepys kept his side of the bargain and furthered Bagwell's career; as a further reward 'en fin j'avais ma volont d'elle'.[75]

The printed insinuations about Pepys's behaviour towards women could have been the response to allegations made by him about the immorality of his former butler, John James. James and Pepys were trying to smear each other's reputation and creditworthiness.[76] It is significant that Pepys tried to counter the corruption charges against him by claiming that James had himself received money to lay false charges and to write the printed tract.[77] We can discover a good deal about the tract's genesis as a result of Pepys's characteristically methodical attempt to get to the bottom of the affair. James had been prompted to write the mock dialogue by Colonel Roderick Mansell (himself the intended victim of the Meal Tub Plot, which was to have planted incriminating evidence of a presbyterian plot) and received payment for it.[78] As James explained, Mansell wanted to publish another piece 'drawne by way of Narrative of Proceedings betweene me and Mr Pepys & the usages I had from him' but James had refused to let it be printed. So the *Hue and Cry* section of the published tract was written (depending

[74] Mary's 'steady friendship and Assistances' for the last 33 years of Pepys's life was rewarded in his will with a bequest of £200 per annum: James H. Hanford, 'Pepys and the Skinner Family', *Review of English Studies*, vii (1931), 257–70.

[75] Diary, 9, 17 July, 7 Aug. 1663; 31 May, 20 Oct., 20 Dec. 1664; 23 Jan., 20 Feb. 1665; 1 July 1666; 1 Feb., 4 Mar. 1667. The passages translate as 'I tried to do what I would with her and, against her struggles, did it well although not to my contentment'; 'at last I had my way'.

[76] In the period of the diary we see something similar when James Carkesse was removed as a clerk in the navy office in 1666 for corrupt irregularities, but got himself reappointed: he went on to accuse Pepys and his colleagues of paying a privateer in their ownership rather than the sailors of a royal navy ship: *Letters of Samuel Pepys*, ed. De la Bédoyère, 79.

[77] Bodl., MS Rawlinson, A 173, ff. 178–9: testimony of John James; A 175, ff. 210-14: information of Felix Donlius about James receiving money; ff. 215–17: declaration of John James. James admitted receiving about £12 from Harbord but also the promise of preferment. Further details are to be found in the journal Pepys kept about his dealings with James, published in *Pepys's Later Diaries*, ed. Knighton, 82–117, which make it clear that Harbord extracted a confession from James denying that he had bribed him to accuse Pepys. Long and Long, *Plot against Pepys*. See also Peter Hinds, '*The Horrid Popish Plot': Roger L'Estrange and the Circulation of Political Discourse in Late Seventeenth-Century London* (Oxford, 2010). The tract is considered by Arthur Bryant but James's allegations are described as 'rather puerile': Arthur Bryant, *Samuel Pepys: The Years of Peril* (1967), 212.

[78] Bodl., MS Rawlinson, A 175, ff. 215–17: declaration by John James, as he lay sick and dying. The copy of the dialogue written by James, retrieved from Francis Smith who 'corrected it', is at Bodl., MS Rawlinson, A 173, ff. 180-3. James's declaration also makes clear that he received 20s. for the pamphlet from the dissenting bookseller and publisher, Benjamin Harris.

on which version of the story Pepys chose to believe) either by Mansell or by 'Narrative' Smith or by Felix Donlius (also known as Lewes).[79]

Such details are important because they suggest larger political motives behind the accusations of corruption against Pepys. According to Alexander Harris, a messenger of the admiralty who had temporarily fallen out with Pepys (he suspected the latter of blocking payments to him), Colonel Mansell was 'ye Principll Enemy of Mr Pepys, a Person very intimate with and employ'd by ye Earle of Shaftesbury and ye greatest Stickler in the carrying on of this Business'.[80] As the duke of York's creature, Pepys was damned by association and so naturally became a target for those in the house of commons seeking to attack James, who included Sir William Harbord and Shaftesbury.[81] Moreover, although the earl's biographer largely discounts allegations that Shaftesbury had himself accepted bribes,[82] it seems likely that Pepys knew that he did: his diary records him admiring 'how prettily this cunning Lord can be partial and dissemble it in this case, being privy to the bribe he is to receive'.[83] The two men, it seems, had both been accepting backhanders from the same man, but neither let on. Whether Shaftesbury feared that Pepys had proof against him or, more probably, disliked Pepys because of his closeness to the duke of York, it is no surprise to find Shaftesbury deliberately smearing Pepys over the allegations of popery in 1674 (he was the named source of the rumours against Pepys) or that Pepys was convinced that Shaftesbury was behind much of the attack in 1679. Allegations of corruption, therefore, were intensely political.

3

What, then, does a case study of Pepys tell us about the culture of corruption in the later Stuart period or about pre-modern corruption more generally?

One important theme is the ambiguity, capaciousness and contested nature of the definition of corruption.[84] Pepys could at once both condemn others for corruption and engage in it himself by redefining what was corrupt, so that the bribes he took became, for him at least, lawful rewards or friendly gifts for favours and exertion, and were never done at the expense of the crown's interests. Indeed, he could even construct a case in which irregularities had virtue, usefully and humanely meeting the necessities of a system that was otherwise incapable of ensuring regular payments to sailors. Pepys constructed a notion of himself as a man of integrity and even that his rise in fortunes was a

---

[79] Bodl., MS Rawlinson, A 175, ff. 215–7; ff. 220–1: the testimony of the cleric Adam Littleton; A 179, f. 48: Felix Donlius to Hewer, 6 Feb. 1688.

[80] Bodl., MS Rawlinson, A 175, f. 224: information of Alex Harris, 24 Mar. 1679[/80]; *Pepys's Later Diaries*, ed. Knighton, 104.

[81] James claimed that he had been given money by Harbord when he had sent him the 'libel' about Pepys and Hewer: *Pepys's Later Diaries*, ed. Knighton, 102.

[82] K.H.D. Hailey, *The First Earl of Shaftesbury* (1968), 154–6.

[83] *Diary*, 23 Sept. 1667.

[84] For a helpful discussion see Mark Philp, 'Defining Political Corruption', *Political Studies*, xlv (1997), 436–62 – which discusses Pepys at p. 443.

reflection of God's providence.[85] Yet the public attacks on Pepys constructed a very different picture which turned Pepys's defence on its head: accepting bribes was rapacious and wrong, and it did harm because it preyed on those, including the vulnerable and weak, who needed his help.[86] In this reading, Pepys deserved a 'hue and cry' after him.

Pepys, thus, helps us to construct two concurrent, but rival, interpretations of officeholding. One recognized offices as poorly paid, administering an emerging 'fiscal-military state' that was full of inefficiency and which, therefore, needed the enterprise of men who could deliver core services and make them more efficient even if that meant incentivising them through deals that promoted their private interest.[87] This interpretation of office saw gifts and rewards as voluntary marks of friendship or lawful and just acknowledgements of services not only rendered but done with special speed, care or assistance. And it recognized that such gifts were everyday practice, without which an officeholder would remain relatively poor, and that they could be beneficial to the state: private profit yielded public benefit. The alternative construction stressed vice rather than virtue, viewing such behaviour as immoral and illegitimate, hypocritical and full of pride and greed; the acceptance of bribes signified a lack of justice, integrity and honesty. Such corruption involved a comprehensive immorality that encompassed religious belief, sexual behaviour and a wide range of vices.[88] This second construction also stressed the need to expose what remained hidden and secretive; and for friendship to be based on more than mutual self-gratification. Finally, it depicted the scheming intelligence of the officeholder as very far from being harnessed to the interests of the public or even the state: private profit was self-serving vice.

A number of things flow from this duality. First, corruption lay in the eye of the beholder and was something that others did rather than oneself; but, because the allegation was an emotive one that impugned public spiritedness, it could also be used as part of a political game to delegitimise an opponent or rival. The accusation of corruption was often one intrinsically about hypocrisy: a private vice masquerading as a public benefit needed to be exposed and punished. Second, corruption explored the boundaries of friendship, and the relationship between patron and client. Pepys used the language of friendship for the man who offered him most bribes, Sir William Warren, and the friendship between Pepys and Hewer was symbolised in the printed dialogue between them when they pause to 'hugg and kiss one another';[89] but these could be

---

[85] Noonan, *Bribes*, 377. Later in his career Pepys even sought to expose and correct, through a series of printed pamphlets, what he saw as mismanagement, unaccounted outgoings and 'self-interest' at Christ's Hospital: *Mr. Pepys to the President and Governours of Christ-Hospital upon the present state of the said hospital* (1698), paper V. For a discussion of the tracts, see Kate Loveman, 'Pepys in Print, 1660–1703', Oxford Handbooks Online (forthcoming), and I am grateful to her for drawing these tracts to my attention.

[86] Bryant, *Years of Peril*, 213.

[87] For the development of the fiscal-military state see John Brewer, *The Sinews of Power: War, Money and the English State, 1688–1783* (1989).

[88] Pepys himself used corruption in a number of different but compatible ways. Thus, as well as castigating the corruption of Batten and the court, he used the verb 'corrupt' to mean leading astray: one maid endeavoured 'to corrupt our cook maid' (Diary, 9 Apr. 1663), and he was annoyed at his servant 'Will's corrupting the mayds with his idle talke and carriage' (Diary, 31 Oct. 1663).

[89] *A Hue and Cry*, 6.

characterised as self-interested friendships in which legitimate gift-giving or service between friends was abused. We need to know much more about such uncertain boundaries, how contemporaries sought to negotiate them, how they were viewed and how they changed over time.[90] Aaron Graham has recently argued that such informal networks, rather than an emerging bureaucracy, were intrinsic to the emergence of the fiscal-military state because they supplied the necessary trust needed to raise capital and because they were the more effective in delivering services. 'Corruption', if it merits that term, might thus have been a price worth paying.[91] But whilst it is true that credit was built on personal networks, we also need to factor public perceptions of exploitative corrupt behaviour into this calculation and the significant cost of lost trust in the structures of politics.[92]

Such public mistrust was not new. In the late 16th and early 17th centuries, as Linda Levy Peck has shown, an increasing anxiety about corruption pervaded the political and literary discourse and the cause was, in part, structural: 'Early Stuart England was governed by a personal monarchy which ruled through a patrimonial bureaucracy organised within a hierarchical society structured by patron-client relationships.'[93] Such relationships were often monetarised. One text, written in the 16th century but translated and published during the time Pepys was writing his diary, argued for a deeply-instrumental view of the patron-client relationship. Giovanni della Casa's *The arts of grandeur and submission, or, A discourse concerning the behaviour of great men towards their inferiours, and of inferiour personages towards men of greater quality* (1665) claimed that clients approached patrons '*principally*, or *only*' from motives of '*either profit, or pleasure*' not from 'True and Ideated Friendship' of virtuous persons.[94] Since 'Riches and Power' were the principal motives for the relationship, virtues that might be prized elsewhere were out of place: 'that *modesty* which becomes a *Virgin* in a *Cloyster*, is criminall in a *Curtesan*'.[95] 'Utility' was thus the proper bond:

Thus it is manifest, that in these kindes of associations, such onely are comprehended as are *different in power and riches*: and the *bonds* of them are not a *particular* affection and *love* each have for others, but *utility*. From whence also it is concluded (which was before asserted) that they are *much mistaken*, who think that this sort of friendship hath *any affinity* with, or ought to be managed according to the principles of *true and exact friendship*.[96]

---

[90] For literature on friendship and gift-giving, see Illana Ben Amos, *The Culture of Giving in Early Modern England* (Cambridge, 2008); *The Culture of the Gift in Eighteenth Century England*, ed. Cynthia Klekar and Linda Zionowski (Basingstoke, 2009); Felicity Heal, 'Food Gifts, The Household and the Politics of Exchange in Early Modern England', *Past & Present*, No. 199 (2008), 41–70; Sarah Haggarty, *Blake's Gifts: Poetry and the Politics of Exchange* (Cambridge, 2010). For patronage, see Peck, *Court Patronage*.

[91] Graham, 'Partisan Politics and the British Fiscal-Military State', *passim*.

[92] For a helpful discussion of the social and cultural manufacture of credit, see Craig Muldrew, *The Economy of Obligation: The Culture of Credit and Social Relations in Early Modern England* (New York, 1998).

[93] Peck, *Court Patronage*, 4.

[94] Giovanni della Casa, *The Arts of Grandeur* (1665), 6, trans. Henry Stubbe.

[95] Della Casa, *Arts of Grandeur*, 12–13.

[96] Della Casa, *Arts of Grandeur*, 14.

Clients should not 'perplexe themselves with *scruples* out of *Divinity, Morallity*, or *Politicks*'.[97] Thus, although della Casa believed that a client ought not to be enslaved by his patron, for the latter 'The *world* is but a *great market*, in which every thing is *sold*'.[98] The publication of such works in the early Restoration, together with Pepys's behaviour, suggests that such views were not uncommon. Gerald Aylmer suggested long ago that early modern officeholding was seen 'as a private right or interest, rather than as a public service'. Aylmer even quotes a tract of 1702 which, significantly in light of the previous discussion, depicts a dialogue over naval mismanagement in which 'Fudg', an Admiralty official, deflects talk of private interest by referring to 'the King's interest'.[99] Yet Aylmer also sensed that the pressure of war in the later Stuart period was putting significant pressure on what constituted private and public interests, a tension that was to play out for much of the 18th century.

Charting the shift of attitudes to public and private interests, friendship, gift-giving and patronage requires a broad chronological treatment, stretching into the early 19th century, and an attempt to relate state formation to ideas and practices of officeholding.[100] Such a survey would also need to examine the *rise* of 'old corruption' – the term given to the system of parasites who fed off the state through sinecures, pensions, rewards, government contracts and so on, and, in turn, filled parliament, as Pepys did, by buying corrupt boroughs or unduly influencing elections with money, bribes and lavish entertainments – as well as its decline. As the study of Pepys suggests, and as David Hayton's work also urges, we might challenge the association of 'old corruption' with the long regime of Robert Walpole and 'whig oligarchy' after 1715.[101] Such an interpretation obscures larger trends that pre-date Walpole's premiership and ignores ways in which Walpole reflected, as well as caused, cultural shifts.

---

[97] Della Casa, *Arts of Grandeur*, 49.

[98] Della Casa, *Arts of Grandeur*, 17.

[99] Aylmer, 'From Office-Holding to Civil Service', 92–4. The tract is *The Present Condition of the English Navy Set Forth in a Dialogue* (1702), and the discussion of public and private interests occurs at pp. 3–4.

[100] Harling, *Waning of 'Old Corruption'*; Philip Harling, 'Parliament, the State, and "Old Corruption": Conceptualising Reform, c.1790–1832', in *Rethinking the Age of Reform*, ed. A. Burns and J. Innes (Cambridge, 2003); Harling, 'Rethinking Old Corruption', 127–58; Rubinstein, 'The End of "Old Corruption" in Britain', 55–86.

[101] Roberts, 'Party and Patronage', 185–212.

The Glorious Revolution, Parliament, and the Making of the First Industrial Nation

JOHN BECKETT

Historians have traditionally viewed the Glorious Revolution as essentially a political event, but in recent decades the growing recognition of just how extensively it impacted on British society has led to various reappraisals of its significance. This article argues that the structure of post-1689 parliamentary activity encouraged both MPs and peers to take a greater interest in the concerns of their constituencies and constituents. In turn, this led to the promotion of private legislation, and these developments together provided the conditions for underpinning the infrastructural developments needed to encourage investment in industrial processes. Thus, the legacy of the Glorious Revolution in relation to parliamentary proceedings was of great importance to the establishment of the circumstances in which industrialisation could flourish, conditions which did not exist prior to 1689 but which subsequently enabled Britain to become the first industrial nation.

Keywords: Glorious Revolution; legislation; parliament; MPs; Lancashire; Cumbria; Nottingham; industrial revolution

1

The Glorious Revolution of 1688–9 has traditionally been viewed as, first and foremost, a political event. It was more-or-less bloodless, it was conservative and it is perhaps best characterised as a *coup d'etat* in which one monarch, King James II, was replaced by another, King William III. Only with time did it become clear that these apparently straightforward events had wider ramifications, and that the seemingly low-key events of 1688–9 had served to bring about a radical alteration in the structure of government in Great Britain, by putting it on to a modernising path through the creation of parliamentary democracy. Since celebrations of the 300th anniversary of the Glorious Revolution, new questions have been asked, and new interpretations offered. Most recently, Steven Pincus has proposed that the Glorious Revolution was a European event, not simply a minor dispute over the crown conducted between Britain and the Low Countries.[1] This article is not primarily concerned with the Glorious Revolution as an event, but with some of the political and longer-term economic consequences; in particular, the relationship between regular parliamentary sessions and the legislative underpinning which helped to create the first industrial nation. The first part (part 2, below), examines the importance for economic confidence of the shift from the monarch to parliament as the source of 'power' in the context of projecting and

[1] S. Pincus, *1688: The First Modern Revolution* (New Haven, 2009).

promoting economic activity. This was reflected in a growing interest and concern in parliament with issues affecting the economy, the subject of part 3. Part 4 of the article examines the extent to which this broad-brush interest was subsequently reflected in local and private legislation helped through parliament by MPs and peers. The fifth part of the article examines how this interest in economic matters provided the context in which the economy was able to flourish. The article concludes that the changed role of parliament within the post-1688 constitution inadvertently provided a forum in which property rights were protected and the confidence that this generated enabled entre-preneurs to invest with confidence, preparing the way for Britain to become the first industrial nation.

2

This part of the article examines the importance for economic confidence of the post-1689 relationship between crown and parliament. It looks at the shifting balance of power away from the monarch towards parliament, and at how this helped to secure property rights. In turn, this security was vital for projecting and promoting economic activity.

Before 1688, the monarch was head of state and head of government, with the right to call and dismiss parliament. During the 17th century, long periods went by when parliament was less than effective, including the years of personal rule by Charles I in the 1630s. The 1640s and 1650s were decades of political disruption and, during the reign of Charles II, parliamentary sessions were shorter than they would become after 1689. They were also subject to sudden adjournments and prorogations which interrupted business. In the Cavalier Parliament, nine of the 16 sessions lasted for less than three months, and in 1672 and 1676 there were no sittings at all. Between 1680 and 1688 parliament sat for only 20 weeks in total. Unpredictability on this scale seriously curtailed the business which parliament could conduct. In the 1680–1 session, for example, only one private bill reached the statute book.

When it was in session, parliament was primarily concerned with taxation, foreign policy and, occasionally, home affairs. It was only called when the monarch needed funds, and then only when all other mechanisms, including customs revenues, forced loans and monopolies, had been exhausted.[2] With the crown desperate to persuade parliament to increase the flow of funding and with parliament frequently dissolved because no agreement could be reached with the crown, there was little, or no, opportunity for developing any programme of domestic improvement, nor was there any attempt to monitor or direct the activities of local government. Local communities were left to their own initiative, except in rare cases such as the 1601 poor law legislation, which outlined the role of parish government in relation to the poor. In the longer term, this pointed to a Westminster-directed shift in local responsibility away from manorial courts towards elected officers of the parish operating under conditions laid down and overseen by the state.

---

[2] Robert Ashton, *The Crown and the Money Market, 1603–1649* (1960); Richard Cust, *The Forced Loans and English Politics* (1987).

Two mechanisms for promoting local matters developed in the course of the 17th century: crown patents, and acts of parliament. Projectors, or promoters, of enterprises needed some sort of legal protection in order to raise capital, and to recover their costs. In the early 17th century, they were likely to turn to the crown for their legal underpinning, perhaps in the form of a patent or similar type of royal privilege to undertake a specific project and collect tolls in perpetuity.

The alternative was to seek parliamentary legislation. As an example, in 1604, legislation reached the statute book empowering 18 commissioners from Oxfordshire, Berkshire, Wiltshire and Gloucestershire to take measures to reopen the River Thames to water-borne traffic between Burcot and Oxford. The legislation gave them powers to raise funds to engage labourers and engineers and agree compensation. The work went on sporadically, but a further act in 1623 set up what proved to be a more efficient commission of eight. The first three-gated pound-locks on the Thames were set up at Culham, Iffley and Sandford under their supervision.[3] This was all well and good but an act of parliament required the Commons and Lords to be in session long enough to see the proposed legislation through all its stages in both Houses as well as to gain the royal assent. This could not happen during the years of King Charles I's personal rule (1629–41) and, subsequently, even when parliament was called it was often dissolved with business still incomplete. Nine of the 23 initiatives to parliament from Lancashire between 1660 and 1688 did not reach the statute book. This failure rate of 40% can be compared with the 40 years after 1689 when it fell to just 16%.[4]

By contrast, a crown patent could be obtained at any time, and it is no surprise to find Charles I issuing many royal patents and other privileges to would-be river improvement undertakers during the 1630s. After the failure of an improvement bill for the River Lark in 1629, Henry Lambe successfully obtained a patent in 1635. After the civil wars, the security of patentees' rights was less certain. With the abolition of the monarchy in 1649, it was not clear if their rights would be maintained since regulatory authority passed to the house of commons. Beyond 1660, most rights were initiated through legislation, but the king still exercised significant influence. The dual system of regulatory activity was inadequate, in many ways, with improvement rights difficult to obtain and, crucially, not always protected when they were acquired. The crown retained a veto over parliamentary bills, but it lacked the same extent of control as it enjoyed when issuing patents.[5]

For its part, parliament concentrated on securing property rights. It is no real surprise to find parliament acting in defence of individual property rights because this was, after all, a parliament composed largely of landowners, either in possession (the house of lords) or in reversion (the house of commons). It was not going to vote for measures which might be perceived as potentially undermining property rights, and tension between the crown and parliament was always likely when monarchs exercised royal power in a way which was perceived to be eroding property rights. This, in turn, explains the evolution of the strict

---

[3] Simon Townley, *Henley-on-Thames: Town, Trade and River* (2009), 64; Dan Bogart, 'Did the Glorious Revolution Contribute to the Transport Revolution? Evidence from Investment in Roads and Rivers', *Economic History Review*, lxiv (2011), 1079.

[4] Stuart Handley, 'Local Legislative Initiatives for Economic and Social Development in Lancashire, 1689–1731', *Parliamentary History*, ix (1990), 14–37.

[5] Bogart, 'Transport Revolution', 1078–84.

settlement from the 1660s, designed to protect landed property. Much later, private legislation was promoted, partly to unravel complex settlements which proved to be hindrances to the promotion of economic initiatives, but in the 1660s, a combination of the arbitrary rule of Charles I, and the confiscatory activities of parliament through the 1640s and 1650s, encouraged parliament to tie up estates as firmly as it could.[6] As North and Weingast have expressed it: 'for economic growth to occur the sovereign or government must not merely establish the relevant set of [property] rights, but must make a credible commitment to them'. The perceived willingness of parliament to secure private rights, in contrast to the apparent threat to them from the monarch, increased the security of private rights and placated worried investors.[7]

3

In the wake of the Glorious Revolution, parliament met more regularly. It sat for just 20 weeks from 1680 to 1688, but from 1689 to 1697 it sat for 53.5 *months*. The reasons for this change were constitutional and financial, because the revolution settlement secured parliamentary supremacy, a permanent role in government underpinned by a central role in financial matters. If this came about partly for practical financial reasons connected with raising funds to fight a major European war, it also meant that the frequency, timing and duration of sessions became more predictable. And since the monarch could no longer bypass parliament or interfere in the judiciary, private property rights became fundamentally more secure. Once it was clear that parliamentary government meant financial agreements would be honoured and property rights secured, much else followed. The commercial and financial revolutions brought new problems in the organisation of overseas trade and the mechanisms of public credit, and arising from these concerns came a succession of bills to establish merchant companies, restrict the import of foreign luxuries, regulate the market in stocks, and improve the law in relation to the collection of debt, the declaration of bankruptcy and the pursuit of small claims. Parliament was now a forum in which MPs could debate issues of substance, often with a bearing on their constituencies, in the context of legislation.[8] It is hardly surprising to find a rapid increase in legislative initiatives post-1689.[9]

Parliament, in other words, was called primarily to deal with the affairs of state, but simply because it was in session for longer it began to take an interest in a wide range

---

[6] J.V. Beckett, 'The Pattern of Landownership in England and Wales, 1660–1880', *Economic History Review*, xxxvii (1984), 1–22; John Habakkuk, *Marriage, Debt and the Estates System: English Landownership 1650–1950* 1994); Eileen Spring, *Law, Land, and Family: Aristocratic Inheritance in England, 1300–1800* (1993); Barbara English and John Saville, *Strict Settlement: A Guide for Historians* (1983).

[7] D.C. North and B.R. Weingast, 'Constitutions and Commitment, the Evolution of Institutions Governing Public Choice in Seventeenth-Century England', *Journal of Economic History*, xlix (1989), 803–4; Dan Bogart and Gary Richardson, 'Making Property Productive: Reorganizing Rights to Real and Equitable Estates in Britain, 1660–1830', *European Review of Economic History*, xiii (2008), 3–30; Dan Bogart and Gary Richardson, 'Estate Acts, 1600 to 1830: A New Source for British History', *National Bureau of Economic Research*, Working Paper 14393: *http://www.nber.org/papers/w14393* (2008).

[8] *The History of Parliament: The House of Commons 1690–1715*, ed. Eveline Cruickshanks, Stuart Handley and D.W. Hayton (5 vols, Cambridge, 2002) [hereafter cited as *HPC, 1690–1715*], i, 389–90.

[9] *HPC, 1690–1715*, i, 383–94.

of issues, some of which related to the growth of the economy. Initial interest was soon translated into legislation, at least, in part, because of growing pressure for public bills to be passed which had a local, or particular, rather than a national impact. In turn, interest groups developed lobbying techniques which involved petitioning parliament and the distribution of manuscript or printed briefs, the employment of legal agents and solicitors, increasingly professional lobbying groups, and the engagement of individual MPs to promote particular causes in the House. Robert Harper was a parliamentary agent who, between 1717 and 1767, drew up 613 bills. Between 1732 and 1762 he drafted 37% of the private acts that received the royal assent. Harper specialised in estate and enclosure bills, while other solicitors were engaged with turnpike and navigation bills.[10]

Organised lobbying on behalf of borough corporations, City of London interests, provincial trading companies, *ad hoc* associations of manufacturers and merchants, and many other groups and individuals, grew up in the wake of these changes. Some bills involved mass petitioning by large and well-co-ordinated groups: various representatives of the leather industry presented over 150 petitions from more than 100 different locations (1697–9) in a campaign to have the leather duties repealed. The duties were not renewed in 1699. Other campaigns were led by the woollen manufacturers in the west country, East Anglia and Yorkshire, keen to resist competition from Ireland and East India imports. Counter-petitioning was used to try to frustrate or amend legislation, most notoriously in 1713 when there was widespread, co-ordinated mercantile lobbying against the French commercial treaty.[11]

In these circumstances, parliament became, in part, a debating chamber for considering the great economic questions of the day, and many of these issues were inevitably contentious. Edmund Burke told the electors of Bristol in 1774:

> Parliament is not a *congress* of ambassadors from different and hostile interests, which interests each must maintain, as an agent and advocate, against other agents and advocates; but Parliament is a *deliberative* assembly of *one* nation, with *one* interest, that of the whole – where not local purposes, not local prejudices, ought to guide, but the general good, resulting from the general reason of the whole. You choose a member, indeed; but when you have chosen him, he is not member of Bristol, but he is a Member of *Parliament*. If the local constituent should have an interest or should form an hasty opinion evidently opposite to the real good of the rest of the community, the member for that place ought to be as far as any other from any endeavour to give it effect.[12]

[10] Sheila Lambert, *Bills and Acts: Legislative Procedure in Eighteenth-Century England* (1971), 11 and Appendix 1. Lambert's work showed that agency in this form long preceded the assumption that it began only in the mid 18th century, as in the work of O.Cyprian Williams, *The Historical Development of Private Bill Procedure and Standing Orders in the House of Commons* (2 vols, 1948). D.L. Rydz, *The Parliamentary Agents: A History* (1979), 27–41, considers parliamentary agency to be a 19th-century profession while accepting that it had many precedents in the 18th century.

[11] John Brewer, *The Sinews of Power: War, Money and the English State, 1688–1783* (1989), 231–49.

[12] Edmund Burke, 'To the Electors of Bristol on Being Declared by the Sheriffs, Duly Elected One of the Representatives of Parliament for that City' [1774]: *The Works of the Right Honourable Edmund Burke*, vol. 2 (1887): *http://www.gutenberg.org/files/15198/15198-h/15198-h.htm#ELECTORS_OF_BRISTO* (accessed 30 Apr. 2013); David Eastwood, 'Parliament and Locality: Representation and Responsibility in Late-Hanoverian England', in *Parliament and Locality 1660–1939*, ed. David Dean and Clyve Jones (Edinburgh, 1998), 68–81.

1 theory this may have been so, but in practice the business of the house meant that
many MPs – particularly those sitting for boroughs – found that they were drawn ever
more tightly into constituency affairs. The object of petitioning was to secure parliamentary interest in what might be considered to be regional or local concerns about
general legislation.

Between 1689 and 1731, petitions relating to general legislation sent to parliament
from Lancashire, were almost always reactions to bills under active consideration, or
more explicit criticisms of existing statutes – 34 petitions related to the textile industries,
reflecting the importance of cloth manufacture within the local community, 13 to the
leather trade, nine concerned local opposition to the chartered trading companies, six
related to developments in the salt industry, four to the tobacco trade, and three each
to the pewter industry, and wire and pin manufacture. This was important for an area
such as south Lancashire, which was already experiencing the early stages of industrialisation. Between 1689 and 1731, various petitions were submitted from this area, for
leave to bring in bills relating to economic concerns such as harbour development, dock
construction, and turnpike roads.[13]

General, public bills were often responses to grievances pressed by local or vested
interests. Increasingly, they were willing to employ legal agents and solicitors, and to
engage personally with individual MPs to promote their cause in the Commons.[14]
Merchants and manufacturers saw parliament as the forum in which solutions could be
developed to commercial issues, if necessary by passing legislation which was really little
more than an attempt to protect, and sometimes to encourage, commercial policy which
was in their interest.[15] In turn, this could lead to parliament fudging issues in order not
to alienate particular groups. A notable example of such behaviour was with the gin
legislation of the 1730s, when a compromise had to be found to keep happy both the
moralists who wanted to outlaw gin drinking and the distilling industry which had every
reason to continue with its promotion.[16]

Lobbyists needed MPs to act on their behalf, not only presenting petitions but also
serving on the committees set up to consider them. When parliament agreed to set up
a committee it normally expected the petitioner to act as its chairman. Lancashire MPs
were invariably to be found serving on the committees convened to consider petitions
which were deemed to have a bearing on the county's industrial interests, or even issues
such as coal where there might be no petitions directly from Lancashire but in which
the county clearly had an interest.

Annual sessions of parliament after 1688 provided the localities with a parliament
which was capable of responding to local demands and helping to legitimise the changes
taking place in the 18th-century economy. Debates in the two Houses were followed
with growing interest in the localities, particularly by economic interest groups looking

[13] Stuart Handley, 'Provincial Influence on General Legislation: The Case of Lancashire, 1689–1731',
Parliamentary History, xvi (1997), 171–84.

[14] *HPC, 1690–1715*, i, 390–3; Lambert, *Bills and Acts*, ch. 2; Brewer, *Sinews of Power*, 236–9.

[15] Tim Keirn, 'Parliament, Legislation and the Regulation of English Textile Industries, 1689–1714', in
Stilling the Grumbling Hive: The Response to Social and Economic Problems in England, 1689–1750, ed. Lee
Davison, Tim Hitchcock, Tim Keirn and Robert Shoemaker (Stroud, 1992), 1–24.

[16] Lee Davison, 'Experiments in the Social Regulation of Industry: Gin Legislation, 1729–1751', in *Stilling
the Grumbling Hive*, ed. Davison *et al.*, 25–48.

to their MPs to try, wherever possible, to obtain concessions or to alter bills before they became law.[17]

By the mid 18th century, the whig corporation of Nottingham took it to be axiomatic that it had the right to advise the town's MPs, even when the men involved were tories by political persuasion. In 1768, the burgesses sent a petition to the sitting MPs, John Plumptre and William How, in which they claimed to be exercising 'an undoubted right as your constituents to give you instructions', in this case in relation to placemen in the house of commons.[18] In 1783, the corporation resolved to instruct its MPs to 'join the City of London in their intended Motion in Parliament for the Repeal of the late Act of Parliament for a Tax on Receipts'.[19] In 1785, the sitting MPs were asked to oppose a bill that was thought likely to prejudice Sir Thomas White's charity estate in Nottingham.[20]

There were plenty of other examples, but MPs did not necessarily follow the advice that they were given. Some perceived it to be their duty or obligation to present any petition from a constituent, but others either would not present at all, or would obstruct the presentation of petitions of which they disapproved.[21] Of course, this could lead to difficulties at future elections. Daniel Parker Coke's failure to oppose the war with France to the satisfaction of Nottingham Corporation led to his being dropped as a candidate in 1802.[22] It was this capacity to dismiss, or drop, an MP, which in the longer run gave the electors the upper hand, and by the 1860s, MPs took it for granted that they were at Westminster as representatives.[23]

4

As a result of the regular meeting of parliament, MPs grew increasingly involved in a wide range of issues relating to the economy, and in doing so they came to recognize the power of legislation in shaping economic affairs. At the same time, they became involved with the promotion of local and private legislation, much of it concerned with the economic matters specific to their constituency or to the locality in which their constituency was to be found.

An important effect of parliament meeting regularly from 1689 was that it did more. In absolute terms, the volume of business going through parliament increased substantially in the 25 or so years following the Glorious Revolution. Some of this took the form of

---

[17] Handley, 'Provincial Influence', 171–84.

[18] BL, Add. MS 33063, f. 219.

[19] *Records of the Borough of Nottingham*, ed W.H. Stevenson *et al.* (9 vols, 1882–1956) [hereafter cited a *RBN*], vii, 204.

[20] *RBN*, vii, 210.

[21] Brewer, *Sinews of Power*, 233.

[22] John Beckett, 'Responses to War: Nottingham in the French Revolutionary and Napoleonic Wars 1793–1815', *Midland History*, xxii (1997), 71–84; John Beckett, 'Parliament and the Localities: The Borough of Nottingham', in *Parliament and Locality*, ed. Dean and Jones, 58–67.

[23] Maurice Cowling, *1867: Disraeli, Gladstone and Revolution* (Cambridge, 1967); Angus Hawkins, ' "Parliamentary Government" and Victorian Political Parties, c.1830–c.1880', *English Historical Review*, civ (1989), 638–69. I am grateful to Richard Gaunt for this last reference.

public general acts, but, increasingly, it was private or local legislation which occupied the time of both Houses. The acts were divided in the statute book into 'local and personal acts', and 'private acts'. A petition would be presented, usually from a local body, the promoters of a company, or even an individual. It would be considered by a committee, and then go forward into parliament as a bill. To become an act, each bill had to pass through both houses, and to comply with standing orders. It was a measure of the importance of this type of legislation after 1689, that between 1690 and 1715, 32 new standing orders were introduced, of which seven (all between 1690 and 1708) related to private bills. In an attempt to bring order into an area that was distinctly disorderly, a provision was introduced in 1699 whereby each reading of a private bill should take place at least three days apart. In 1705, it was agreed that all private bills should be printed before being introduced into parliament, and in 1708, the three-day provision was increased to 30 days, largely to allow for better scrutiny.[24] In 1706, a standing order laid down that each petition for private legislation involving the levying of tolls should be referred to a select committee before leave was given to introduce a bill. These safeguards grew ever more numerous as promoters became both more knowledgeable and more skilful in assessing the economic benefits to be gained from private legislation.[25]

The emphasis here on private bills reflected the fact that much legislation relating to local matters went through parliament in this manner. 'Local acts' were not formally distinguished as such until 1798. Until then, acts were separated into two categories, private and public, although particular acts were not assigned to either of these in a consistent fashion. The first canal acts passed as private acts, and enclosure acts were invariably private acts. Local and general bills were handled slightly differently by parliament. Local bills had to be inaugurated by petition, but general bills did not, although petitions were sometimes submitted. Private bills were more likely to be the subject of supportive or counter-petitioning, but the primary difference between the two was their geographical scope.[26]

Despite these difficulties, there is no shortage of evidence of a rapid increase in the number of private bills introduced into parliament, many of them originating in the upper House. Some of these bills subsequently became public, rather than private, initiatives, but they represented a substantial slice of the growing business of parliament.[27] Increasingly, it proved vital to employ an experienced solicitor, or parliamentary agent, to draft the bill. If it was contentious, the bill was likely to be referred to a select committee, and counsel had to be briefed to argue cases. Both Houses came to operate an 'open' committee system for private bills. Any member could attend and vote, or even come in at the last moment to vote, having heard nothing of the previous

[24] *HPC, 1690–1715*, i, 364, 381–94.

[25] Handley, 'Local Legislative Initiatives'; Michael McCahill, 'Estate Acts of Parliament, 1740–1800', in *Institutional Practice and Memory: Parliamentary People, Records and Histories: Essays in Honour of Sir John Sainty*, ed. Clyve Jones (Oxford, 2013), suggests that 'some have argued that parliamentary scrutiny of personal and local acts involved little more than the ratification of agreements made at the local level or by the individual parties to an act' (165–6), a point with which he disagrees.

[26] Joanna Innes, 'The Local Acts of a National Parliament: Parliament's Role in Sanctioning Local Action Eighteenth-Century Britain', *Parliamentary History*, xvii (1998), 23–47.

[27] Julian Hoppit and Joanna Innes, 'Introduction', in *Failed Legislation, 1660–1800*, ed. Julian Hoppit 997), 1–40.

discussion.[28] Trouble could brew at any stage, as, for example, if the officials of the two Houses were not given their due, since they had many opportunities to promote or frustrate private bills.[29]

What, precisely, was the role played by MPs? Their major task was to sponsor legislation and to see it through the lower House. Sometimes they would do this alone. In the early 18th century, John Harpur, MP for Derby, helped to promote bills relating to the River Derwent navigation scheme, as well as estate bills on behalf of his Derbyshire neighbours. Sir John Barnard felt obliged to present a constituent's petition regardless of its content.[30] In other cases, whole groups of MPs worked together to promote local interests: legislation designed to protect textile makers against the incursions of foreign imports was often promoted by a caucus of 25–30 MPs, mainly motivated by local interests, and coming generally from the woollen producing areas, who were invariably appointed to relevant committees over the period 1689–1714.[31] Whether alone or in a group, MPs were expected to protect what were perceived to be the interests of their constituents in relation to private legislation. David Hayton has estimated that well over one-fifth of members were 'active' in the early years of the 18th century, some particularly so in procuring private legislation.[32]

Whether this was a good or bad thing is more problematic. As Paul Langford observed:

> The object of local, *ad hoc* legislation was to meet the stated needs of particular communities. But highly localised legislation could harm the interests of other communities. In a sense much of it was meant to. Many improvements were designed to gain an advantage, at the expense of some other locality, even when they were manifestly of public benefit.[33]

The whole business escalated with time. The growth of parliamentary solicitors and other forms of agency meant that MPs did not personally draft bills. In 1709, the Yorkshire MP, Cyril Arthington, saw through the Commons a bill relating to broadcloths. He relied on the clothiers to sort out its terms, working with a parliamentary solicitor.[34] Other MPs were less amenable. Some disagreed with the legislation they were being asked to promote, and some actively tried to obstruct petitions of which they disapproved. Of course this could spell danger in future elections, especially during the rage of party during Queen Anne's reign.

For those MPs willing to undertake the work involved, much depended on their knowledge of procedures and their ability to operate them to the advantage of peti

---

[28] John Prest, *Liberty and Locality* (1990), 5; Lambert, *Bills and Acts*, 84–109; C.T. Ellis, *The Solicitor Instructor in Parliament Concerning Estate and Enclosure Bills* (1799); C.T. Ellis, *Practical Remarks, and Precedents Proceedings in Parliament* (1802).

[29] Frederick Clifford, *A History of Private Bill Procedure* (2 vols, 1885–7); Williams, *Historical Developmen*, Rydz, *Parliamentary Agents.*

[30] *HPC, 1690–1715*, i, 421, Brewer, *Sinews of Power*, 233.

[31] *HPC, 1690–1715*, i, 422. See also *Stilling the Grumbling Hive*, ed. Davison *et al.*, esp. the essays by Keir and Davison.

[32] *HPC, 1690–1715*, i, 417.

[33] Paul Langford, *Public Life and the Propertied Englishman, 1689–1798* (1991), 180.

[34] *HPC, 1690–1715*, i, 423.

tioners. James Lowther was returned to the Commons in 1694, when he was just 21 years old, partly so that he would be on hand if any legislation came into the Commons which might be beneficial or detrimental to his family's farming and mining activities in West Cumberland. He quickly got to know the business of the House, frequently acted as teller, was often appointed to committees, and claimed, in 1701, that Lord Carlisle supported his candidature at Carlisle, 'particularly for my great application to the business of the House'.[35] As he told his father, Sir John Lowther, he was well thought of in the Commons, 'for my diligence and knowledge of the orders, and judgement I was able to make of the proceedings of the house . . . they have a great regard for me'.[36] He strongly supported measures which he and his father regarded as important for the prosperity of West Cumberland, arguing, in 1699, in favour of Whitehaven being named as one of the ports open for the importation of Irish wool, and speaking against a bill relating to tobacco imports.[37]

James Lowther's position was much more problematic when, in late 1705, Thomas Lamplugh, MP for Cockermouth, introduced a petition to promote a harbour at Parton on the West Cumberland coast. The Lowthers believed that such a harbour would threaten the family's commercial interests in the area, so their opposition was entirely self-motivated. Neither father (unwell, and by now permanently domiciled in Whitehaven) nor son, was in parliament. Sir John stood down in 1699 on health grounds, and James Lowther did not stand in 1702 due to his doubts about whether being in the Commons was compatible with holding a government post in the ordnance.[38] Now, drawing on his knowledge of procedures, but without a seat, he found himself struggling to make sure that Lamplugh's petition was thrown out. Writing to his father on 6 December 1705, he outlined the measures he was taking. He was waiting 'in the gallery' when Lamplugh presented the petition. Next: 'I took care to have a great number of my friends named' on the committee appointed by the House to consider the petition. 'On Tuesday morning I added to the committee about sixteen of my particular friends, and attended about the House all day, and engaged about 25 sure friends to come to the committee yesterday morning.' Not trusting them to turn up without prompting, Lowther 'sent to a great many of their lodgings to desire them to come before 10 o'clock . . . then we being about 17 to their 4 I got a particular Friend of mine put into the Chair'.[39] To Lowther's annoyance, Lamplugh refused to back down in the face of such odds, but he was sure of their friends: 'I have no manner of fear of the success . . . I have spoke to at least three-quarters of the House of Commons.'[40] His optimism was presumably for his father's benefit because four days later, on 29 December, he admitted that both of the Cumberland MPs were backing Lamplugh, and he was now considering 'what terms we might give way to in case of necessity'.[41] In the end

[35] Cumbria RO [hereafter cited as CRO], D/Lons/W2/2: James Lowther to Sir John Lowther, 15 Nov. 1701.

[36] CRO, D/Lons/W2/2: James Lowther to Sir John Lowther, 8 Jan. 1702.

[37] CRO, D/Lons/W2/2: James Lowther to Sir John Lowther, 15 Apr., 2 May 1699.

[38] *HPC, 1690–1715*, ii, 113–19; iv, 685–6.

[39] J.V. Beckett, *Coal and Tobacco: The Lowthers and the Development of West Cumberland, 1660–1750* (1981), 59–61; CRO, D/Lons/W2/2: James Lowther to Sir John Lowther, 6 Dec. 1705.

[40] CRO, D/Lons/W2/2: James Lowther to Sir John Lowther, 25 Dec. 1705.

[41] CRO, D/Lons/W2/2: James Lowther to Sir John Lowther, 29 Dec. 1705.

it was all to no avail, since Sir John Lowther died early in 1706 and James Lowther returned home to Whitehaven. The petition was allowed, a bill was introduced, and legislation ensued.

Lowther did not repeat the mistake. In 1708, he made sure he was returned as MP for Cumberland, and he remained in the house until his death in 1755. He regularly attended the Commons, although he spoke only infrequently and then usually on general matters he thought likely to have an adverse impact on his West Cumberland business interests. In 1713, he presented a petition from the Whitehaven merchants opposing clauses in the Anglo-French treaty of commerce relating to the woollen trade, in April 1739, he spoke in the House during a debate about the state of the coal trade, and in the 1740s, he opposed government attempts to introduce the registration of seamen, because he regarded such a move as likely to exacerbate Whitehaven's acute shortage of labour.[42] During the 1740s, he presented further merchant petitions relating to the state of the Whitehaven tobacco trade.[43]

The jockeying for position referred to here can be found in many other private bills. In 1721, for example, the Mersey-Irwell Navigation Bill came to the Commons on 1 February from Manchester and Salford. Seven petitions were presented in favour, five against, and one for an extension of the route, which was lost in the committee stage. Two of the petitions in favour were introduced to nullify a petition against the bill from the JPs of Lancashire and Cheshire. All six were referred to the select committee appointed after the second reading, but it is clear from the legislation that followed, that the petitions against the bill were to see it amended, not to see it rejected; in other words, the final act was the result of much negotiation following from the petitioning, both inside and outside parliament, to protect interested parties. The act was a compromise in which parliament was used to gain statutory protection and compensation for rights and property.[44]

James Lowther was also active in promoting private legislation on behalf of constituents and his own business interests. In 1752, when attending Carlisle assizes, he let it be known that he was willing to steer through parliament any turnpike bills relating to roads in Cumberland, and to provide one-sixth of the required working capital (as one of the six sitting MPs for the three Cumberland constituencies). The following year, a a direct result, he was responsible for steering six turnpike bills through the Commons. By the time they reached the statute book, Lowther claimed that 'hardly any other members attend so much as I do because of these six turnpike bills'.[45] He was just approaching his 80th birthday and was in poor health.

Of course, not all MPs were like Lowther. Jasper Maudit, returned for his native Liverpool in 1695, was nominated to a vast number of select committees during his three years in the Commons, but seems to have done very little actual work.[46]

---

[42] CRO, D/Lons/W2: Sir James Lowther to John Spedding, 19 Feb., 13, 15 Mar. 1740; 3 Mar. 1741; Apr. 1744.

[43] CRO, D/Lons/W2: Sir James Lowther to John Spedding, 23 Mar. 1745; 29 Dec. 1748; 27 Apr. 174■

[44] Handley, 'Local Legislative Initiatives', 14–37.

[45] CRO, D/Lons/W2: Sir James Lowther to John Spedding, 20 Jan., 24, 27 Feb., 3, 6 Mar. 1753; Joh■ Beckett, 'A Back-Bench MP in the Eighteenth Century: Sir James Lowther of Whitehaven', *Parliamenta■ History*, i (1982), 79–97.

[46] *HPC, 1690–1715*, i, 416.

Who was the more typical, Lowther or Maudit? Our difficulty here is to assess what the MPs were actually doing. The *Commons Journal* and the *Lords Journal* seldom if ever give names of MPs or peers undertaking business, and the names that are given – of committees appointed to examine bills – are not usually of either MPs or peers with local connections.[47] Even so, it is hard to believe that local MPs were not called upon for their support when locally-significant legislation was under consideration. Daniel Parker Coke certainly took the initiative in regard to the Sneinton Enclosure Bill of 1796. Discussions during 1795 revealed that John Musters and Charles Pierrepont, the two main landowners in Sneinton, which adjoins the east side of Nottingham only a few hundred yards from the town centre, were both anxious to see the parish enclosed. Musters had enlisted the support of John Manners Sutton, MP for Newark, to introduce the bill into parliament, and Parker Coke thought his own services would be superfluous. He made clear that he was ready to 'come forward very willingly to render every assistance . . . few things would give me more pleasure than being able to render any service'.[48] Doubtless, many MPs must have expressed similar views.

The work of MPs on behalf of their constituencies and constituents was not the result of a coherent strategy. It happened because parliament was meeting regularly, and was able to develop its role in government, but there was more to it than this. Parliament, as a body, remained focused on affairs of state through the 18th century. Legislation which was unconnected with the affairs of the country was usually considered in the form of private bills and, while these may not have made the headlines, they contributed greatly to the sum of legislation. Between 1750 and 1850, parliament passed more than 4,000 enclosure bills, over 900 turnpike bills, 427 canal bills and, from the 1830s, railway bills by the score, together with naturalisation bills and divorce bills. These all required the attention of MPs, very often local MPs.[49] Simultaneously, numerous estate bills were also going through parliament, often because owners needed to release parts of their estate from strict settlement. Between 1660 and 1685, 77 private estate acts were passed relating to estates, but from 1689 to 1714, no fewer than 262 acts were added to the statute book.[50]

5

How did all this activity translate into the promotion of the economy more generally? How, in other words, do we link these developments in procedure and representation resulting from the constitutional changes following the Glorious Revolution, to the state of the economy? The answer, in simple terms, was confidence, and confidence began with property rights. Regular meetings of parliament, and longer legislative sessions, allowed time to deal with local issues. Fewer bills failed, and promoters grew in

---

[47] Possibly the manuscript minutes of house of lords committees, now in the Parliamentary Archives, will throw some light on the activities of local peers in respect of local bills.

[48] University of Nottingham Library, Manuscripts and Special Collections, M.3319/19: Daniel Parker Coke Charles Pierrepont, 17 Aug. 1795.

[49] Handley, 'Provincial Influence'.

[50] *HPC, 1690–1715*, i, 381–94.

confidence so that the number of petitions and bills increased rapidly.[51] To handle the work, parliament developed ways of dealing successfully with an expansion in the number of requests for legislation.[52] Confidence was also generated by the constitutional supremacy of parliament, because parliament was clearly the arbiter of law and, through the legislation that it passed, the protector of property rights.[53] Once property rights were seen to be protected, entrepreneurs could invest confidently, knowing that their investment would not be subject to political interference.

When historians have discussed political change and economic development in Britain they have tended to focus on government or private borrowing, taxation, the stock market and the financial revolution, and the commercial revolution.[54] Within a story which is largely about progress, the defence of property rights, notably through the impact of the strict settlement, has sometimes been seen in a negative light, as protecting property against the instincts of entrepreneurs by artificially constraining the market in land. It is undeniable that property transfer *was* restricted, but it was not prevented. Land could be released from settlement by legislation, often in the form of an estate act, and the defence of property was not sectional: all property rights were now protected. Had would-be innovators remained dependent on charters, patents, monopolies or other forms of approval coming from the crown, the confidence needed to generate invest-ment may well have remained elusive. The property rights of landowners may have been protected and the strict settlement may, in certain regards, have constrained market forces, but the same political conditions ensured that undertakers were also protected simply because the law applied to all property and not just land.

We can demonstrate the impact of confidence in a number of ways, via estate acts, enclosure acts, and infrastructure legislation, to show how the emerging industrial economy was underpinned by legislation which provided confidence for investors and entrepreneurs. This does not constitute a simplistic 'explanation' of why Britain was first; rather, it points to the underlying conditions without which the industrial revo-lution would have been hampered. With parliament established as the sole regulatory authority, the rights of undertakers and entrepreneurs were protected. In turn, they could increase their investment with confidence and without fear of it being lost.[5] Between 1690 and 1697, government demand 'crowded out' private borrowing but with the return of peace, government borrowing retrenched and the new political climate seems to have been such as to stimulate demand for loanable funds – a sure indication of confidence.[56]

The strict settlement has been widely viewed as artificially constricting the land market in favour of protecting the landowners rather than encouraging the free flow of land. Consequently, the limitations caused by settlement inhibited economic innovation and improved management. This appears, ostensibly, to make sense, but there is another

---

[51] *Failed Legislation*, ed. Hoppit, 1–40.

[52] Innes, 'Local Acts', 47.

[53] Innes, 'Local Acts', 32.

[54] Bogart, 'Transport Revolution', 1073 n. 6; J.V. Beckett, 'Land Tax or Excise: The Levying of Taxation in Seventeenth and Eighteenth Century England', *English Historical Review*, c (1985), 285–308.

[55] Bogart, 'Transport Revolution', 1100.

[56] Stephen Quinn, 'The Glorious Revolution's Effect on English Private Finance: A Microhistory', *Journal of Economic History*, lci (2001), 593–615.

way of viewing it, which is that landowners who knew they could tie up their land over long periods of time were more likely to invest in future development, just as they engaged in planting and in garden layout designed for forthcoming generations rather than for their own benefit. Once landowners could see that their property rights were protected, they could gather confidence to take part in long-term park, woodland and garden management and, where they had appropriate resources, industrial developments both through direct activities such as coal and iron mining, and infrastructure improvements for transport. In their role as parliamentarians, they played a positive part in promoting the legislation on which so much now depended.[57]

Unfortunately, there is a danger here of moving from one perspective in which landowners were seen to be the villains of the peace for self-interestedly protecting their property against the potential impact of spendthrift generations to come, to another in which their fortuitous decision making in the 17th century made them all potential entrepreneurs. Bogart and Richardson have argued that, by liberating owners from a 'rigid system', estate acts were instrumental in promoting Britain's economic development during the late 18th and early 19th centuries.[58] The result was not just that landowners played a significant part in promoting industrial and urban development, but that in the period 1760–1830, numerous estate acts authorised sales and leases. They suggest that acts authorising long-term leases (15% of all estate acts) typically described the projects such as the opening of mines or construction of residences, that the leases were intended to facilitate.[59]

The problem with this argument is that it is over optimistic. The fact that landowners could, and did, apply for acts to exploit their resources, or to raise mortgages to finance improvements, or to proceed with the consolidation of their properties, is certainly evidence that they made positive contributions to the growth and diversification of the economy in the 18th century. Without recourse to an estate act they would have had to rely on the courts, which may have been slow and costly. Yet the fact remains that more than half of the sample of estate acts assembled by Bogart and Richardson were simply to release land for sale, presumably to pay debts, because so many families engaged in self-indulgent and unproductive expenditure.[60]

The protection of property simply as an end in itself would not necessarily have promoted an industrial revolution. Its importance lay in the fact that it protected the property owner in the context of what he might do with his land. Since landed families did not normally sell their land, given their protective ethos in terms of 'family', they would be less likely to exploit their land if they feared for their property rights. Would they have willingly risked letting land to colliery developers if they could not be sure that their ownership was protected? (This was how most mining worked.[61]) Or, perhaps more importantly in this context, how would they have responded to the important structural changes for which they are often considered to have played a key role, such

---

[57] John Beckett, *The Aristocracy in England* (1986), chs 4–9.

[58] Bogart and Richardson, 'Making Property Productive', 3–30.

[59] Bogart and Richardson, 'Estate Acts'.

[60] McCahill, 'Estate Acts'; Julian Hoppit, 'The Landed Interest and the National Interest', in *Parliaments, Nations, and Identities in Britain and Ireland, 1660–1850*, ed. J. Hoppit (2003), 85–6.

[61] Beckett, *Aristocracy*, ch. 6.

as post-1750 enclosure in terms of maximising the efficiency of their land, of schemes
for river navigation, turnpike roads, canals and, eventually railways, all of which were
critical for laying the base upon which the economic growth of the nation depended?
When they had to give up land for canals and railways, they could be sure that they
would be adequately compensated, and this encouraged them to act positively. In turn,
this ensured that entrepreneurs could invest, knowing that the infrastructure would be
in place to enable them to move their goods.

Landowners, as peers and MPs, were aware of the need for legislation to underpin
economic development. A good example of their acceptance of this position, in an area
which was well known to them, related to enclosure legislation. The enclosing of land
to change or develop the agriculture which was practised, was the subject of an act of
parliament as early as 1604, but the majority of enclosure in the 17th century was by
'agreement', sometimes confirmed in the courts to provide legal backing. Between 1750
and 1850, parliament passed more than 4,000 enclosure acts, all of them designed with
agricultural improvement (and, for landowners, rental increases) in a countryside that
was being challenged to meet the food requirements of an increasing (and increasingly-
urbanised) population. Leaving aside the possible social costs of enclosure, the evidence
strongly suggests that it brought not only rental increases for landowners, but productivity improvements. Enclosure might have happened without parliamentary legislation,
but acts were sought because they confirmed property rights and provided the legal
context for reorganising the land.[62]

Parliament also legislated in favour of infrastructure improvements, notably in terms
of water and road transport and, in the 1840s and beyond, railways. Landowners
supported, and sometimes invested in, turnpike roads, which were important in creating
an improved infrastructure for the movement of people and goods. Turnpikes were run
by trusts, which raised funds to improve the highway, and then charged tolls for usage.
Although the first turnpike act was in 1663, they were not a regular feature of
parliamentary business until the 1690s and beyond, peaking in the 1750s and 1760s with
the passage of over 300 bills covering 10,000 miles of roads. By the 1830s, there were
more than 900 trusts, each established by legislation, managing approximately 20,000
miles or 17% of the entire road network.[63] The network was densest near to towns in
the north and west, some of which were undergoing the early stages of industrial
change, including Birmingham, Manchester, and Sheffield, while in the south-east, the
network mainly served London.[64] The rapid rate of growth in Lancashire and Cheshire
can be contrasted with much lower levels in Hertfordshire and Buckinghamshire.[65]
Turnpikes contributed to higher property income through the growth of manufacturing
because so many were established in areas that already had manufacturing and, because

---

[62] M.E. Turner, J.V. Beckett and B. Afton, *Farm Production in England 1700–1914* (2001); M.E. Turner, *English Parliamentary Enclosure* (1980).

[63] W. Albert, *The Turnpike Road System in England, 1663–1840* (Cambridge, 1972), 20–3; E. Pawson, *Transport and Economy: The Turnpike Roads of Eighteenth Century Britain* (New York, 1977), 281–2; D. Gerhold, 'Productivity Change in Road Transport before and after Turnpiking, 1690–1840', *Economic History Review*, xxxix (1996), 491–515.

[64] Pawson, *Transport and Economy*, 151.

[65] Bogart and Richardson, 'Estate Acts', 29, 35.

they had greater access to markets, may have encouraged more firms to locate in these areas. It will not have been lost on landowners that the value of their land also increased and, therefore, we can conclude that turnpike trusts made a significant contribution to economic growth in England.[66]

Water transport was improved by a combination of means, including both legislation and patents in the 17th century, as we have seen, but after 1690 almost entirely by act of parliament. After 1688, only one river improvement proposal (1693) was made directly to the crown between 1689 and 1727, compared with more than 100 bills introduced into parliament. This was a clear and distinctive shift in which parliament became the main forum for initiating and maintaining transport developments, partly because it was seen as the guardian of undertakers' rights. The only case in which it appeared to violate pre-existing undertakers' rights was when they failed to complete a navigation scheme.[67] Legislation created river navigation authorities and they raised capital which was repaid through tolls. A similar method, with some additional engineering, worked for canals, so the regulatory environment became more favourable for undertakers after 1690, with their rights better protected. It cannot be a coincidence that investment in improving rivers, as well as roads, increased substantially in the mid 1690s.[68]

Between them, river navigation authorities and turnpike trustees contributed to lowering transport costs and generating social savings equalling several percentage points of gross domestic product by the early 19th century. The work of improving the transport network was not work for which a government, largely concerned with foreign policy, was equipped to undertake, so parliament, by empowering individuals and local groups through legislation, offered a successful alternative approach to raising investment. The Glorious Revolution provided a political foundation supporting greater investment in transport infrastructure.

6

The changed role of parliament within the post-1688 constitution inadvertently provided a forum in which property rights were protected and confidence was generated which enabled entrepreneurs to invest, preparing the way for Britain to become the first industrial nation. The post-1689 legislative framework was such as to be beneficial to the promotion of the economy.[69] If parliament had not been reformed in the wake of the Glorious Revolution, it is much less likely that the conditions described in this article would have come into being, which led to the promotion of legislation concerned with food supply (enclosure), and transport infrastructure (rivers, canals, roads). The improvement of roads was vital to the industrial revolution, and rivers and canals

[66] Dan Bogart, 'Turnpike Trusts and Property Income: New Evidence on the Effects of Transport Improvements and Legislation in Eighteenth-Century England', *Economic History Review*, lxii (2009), 134, 146, 149.

[67] Bogart, 'Transport Revolution', 1084–9.

[68] Bogart, 'Transport Revolution', 1100.

[69] Bogart, 'Transport Revolution', 1073.

were the arteries along which ran the coal which powered industry. An unintended consequence of parliament's new role beyond 1688 was to make it possible to pass legislation, in the form of a private or local bill, which protected private property rights and was, in the long term, responsible for creating conditions which were vital to the making of the first industrial nation.[70]

As Acemoglu and Robinson have argued, the success and failure of nations is about institutions. 'Economic institutions', they suggest, 'are critical for determining whether a country is poor or prosperous, [but] it is politics and political institutions that determine what economic institutions a country has.' As they would see it, the key to economic success lies with democracy, innovation and free markets, not narrow 'extractive' institutions which cream off power and wealth for a tiny minority. On this general basis, they have suggested that the Glorious Revolution pioneered a new order based on pluralism and property rights and that these developments provided the infrastructure on to which the first industrial nation was bolted.[71] As an argument it is simplistic, but it does emphasize how the Glorious Revolution played a key role in providing conditions which helped Britain to be first: as Bogart has commented: 'the finding suggests that acts changing property rights and the financing of infrastructure were a contributing factor to English economic growth during the eighteenth century'.[72]

The Glorious Revolution fundamentally altered constitutional arrangements. Crown action, such a dominant feature of the 17th century, was rapidly supplemented and then replaced by parliamentary action. Annual meetings of parliament, and longer sessions, made it much easier for acts to reach the statute book, and by the early 18th century there was a greater sense of what would pass and what would not, as well as the development of new mechanisms to facilitate legislation.[73] Undertakers could take time and spend resources obtaining rights from parliament in the anticipation of having these rights affirmed. They could then invest confidently, hence the increase in the annual investment in roads and rivers from the mid-1690s, and the number of petitions and acts for improving roads and rivers.[74] The greater protection of rights 'effectively raised the demand for acts among individuals and local communities'.[75] The opportunity to obtain local legislation, authorising actions that would not otherwise have been legal, or putting the coercive force of the law behind local projects, represented one of the most powerful resources available to those striving to exercise that initiative.[76]

It has to be said that this was not immediately clear in 1688–9. In the post-Glorious Revolution political environment, it was not obvious that the rights of existing

---

[70] Bogart, 'Transport Revolution', 1073–112; Dan Bogart, 'Did Turnpike Trusts Increase Transport Investment in Eighteenth-Century England?', *Journal of Economic History*, lxv (2005), 439–68; Bogart, 'Turnpike Trusts', 128–52; Dan Bogart and G. Richardson, 'Property Rights and Parliament in Industrialising Britain', *Journal of Law and Economics*, liv (2011), 241–74.

[71] Daron Acemoglu and James A. Robinson, *Why Nations Fail: The Origins of Power, Prosperity and Poverty* (2012).

[72] Bogart, 'Turnpike Trusts', 129.

[73] Innes, 'Local Acts', 31–4.

[74] T.S. Willan, *River Navigation in England, 1600–1750* (2nd edn, 1964), 24–30; Albert, *Turnpike Road System*, 20–6; Pawson, *Transport and Economy*; J.R. Ward, *The Finance of Canal Building in Eighteenth-Century England* (Oxford, 1974); Bogart, 'Transport Revolution', 1075.

[75] Bogart, 'Transport Revolution', 1076; Bogart and Richardson, 'Estate Acts', figs 1, 2, tables 3, 4.

[76] Innes, 'Local Acts', 23–47.

undertakers would be protected. It was the fact that parliament did not generally violate pre-existing undertakers' rights that helped to build confidence. When this was added to regular meetings of parliament and longer legislative sessions allowing for more time to deal with local issues, and a decline in the failure rate for bills, the role of parliament evolved positively in terms of the interests and concerns of MPs, perhaps particularly for those representing the newly-emerging industrial areas of the country.

It should be said that not all scholars accept this view. Some are sceptical as to whether property rights were more secure after 1689, and whether – if so – this actually fostered economic growth. Others have questioned whether the post-1689 regime may have hampered financial development and international trade.[77] Yet others have asked why only Britain seems to have benefited when property rights were well developed in other states such as France? The answer would seem to be that countries such as France and the Low Countries did not have active parliaments involved with both protecting property rights and making sure development could occur, and it was these conditions which gave Britain a positional advantage, particularly in the capacity to facilitate the creation of the infrastructure.[78] Apart from the Dutch republic, where similar legislation was passed at provincial level in the 17th century, European states lacked both the machinery, and the political will, to develop their economies in this manner. Consequently, an understanding of how, and why, legislation came to be used as a way of facilitating improvements in the economy is a way of resolving the larger question of why Britain was the first industrial nation.[79]

It is not, perhaps, going too far to suggest that an indirect impact of the Glorious Revolution was the creation of conditions which helped to drive forward the British economy. This was as a result not of the short-term political processes surrounding events in 1688–9 but of long-term constitutional and governmental implications which gave much greater responsibilities to MPs in terms of their constituencies and their constituents, as well as the power of parliament through legislation, which could not have been foreseen when William of Orange was crowned King William III in April 1689. It did not make Britain the first industrial nation – that depended on invention, technology, labour and a host of other significant factors – but it did provide the context in which it could occur.[80]

---

[77] Patrick O'Brien, 'Central Government and the Economy, 1688–1815', in *The Cambridge Economic History of Britain since 1700*, ed. R. Floud and P. Johnson (2nd edn, 3 vols, 2003–4), i, 205–41; G. Clark, 'The Political Foundations of Modern Economic Growth: England, 1540–1800', *Journal of Interdisciplinary History*, xvi (1996), 563–88.

[78] J.V. Beckett and Michael Turner, 'Taxation and Economic Growth in Eighteenth-Century England', *Economic History Review*, xliii (1990), 377–403.

[79] Bogart, 'Turnpike Trusts', 150.

[80] R.C. Allen, 'Why the Industrial Revolution was British: Commerce, Induced Invention, and the Scientific Revolution', *Economic History Review*, lxvi (2011), 357–84; Robert C. Allen, *The British Industrial Revolution in Global Perspective* (Cambridge, 2009), 4–5.

The Irish Parliament and the Regulatory Impulse, 1692–1800: The Case of the Coal Trade★

EOIN MAGENNIS

The legislative activity of the 18th-century Irish parliament has become clearer in recent decades. So, too, has the regulatory impulse and how this impacted upon markets and the economy in Britain and Ireland. Recent research on the regulation of Britain's economy between 1650 and 1850 has identified four areas in which the legislature and executive intervened: import/export trade; manufacturing production; labour markets and the domestic/internal market. This article aims to explore what such a regulatory impulse meant in the 18th-century Irish parliament. The article focuses on the 18th-century Irish coal trade as a case study, one which shows the influences of the belief in the possibilities for the economic improvement of Ireland, the concerns about high prices in a necessity of life for the urban poor and the residual anglophobia that such subjects could raise.

Keywords: regulation; legislation; coal; parliament; Ireland; markets; moral economy; 18th century; hoarding; price-fixing

1

The legislative activity of the 18th-century Irish parliament has become clearer in recent decades thanks, in large part, to David Hayton's research. His earliest work focused on English ministerial policy towards Ireland and how this was received, engaged with and occasionally, resisted. His approach to this subject was informed by the Namierite approach with its emphasis on the structure of Irish politics, and it was consonant with the work he did while in the History of Parliament project in London. The result was a series of articles that have transformed the historical understanding of the 1690–1740 period in terms of party politics, the management of Irish politics and the nature of patriotism.[1]

★ An earlier version of this article was presented at the 'Making Money in Dublin, 1500–2000: Commerce in the City of Dublin over Five Centuries' seminar in May 2012. I would like to thank Lesa Ní Mhunghaile, Ivar McGrath, Patrick Walsh, John Bergin and James Kelly for their encouragement and assistance, whilst also acknowledging the huge debt owed to Louis Cullen's research.

[1] See, e.g., D.W. Hayton, 'The Beginnings of the "Undertaker" System', in *Penal Era and Golden Age: Essays in Irish History, 1690–1800*, ed. Thomas Bartlett and D.W. Hayton (Belfast, 1979), 32–54; D.W. Hayton, 'The Crisis in Ireland and the Disintegration of Queen Anne's Last Ministry', *Irish Historical Studies* xxii (1981), 193–215; D.W. Hayton, 'Walpole and Ireland', in *Britain in the Age of Walpole*, ed. Jeremy Black (1984), 95–119; D.W. Hayton, 'The Stanhope/Sunderland Ministry and the Repudiation of Irish Parliamentary Independence', *English Historical Review*, cxiii (1998), 610–36. A continuing interest in patriotism can be found in articles collected in D.W. Hayton, *The Anglo-Irish Experience, 1680–1730: Religion, Identity and Patriotism* (Woodbridge, 2012).

However, the subject matter of this contribution to a *Festschrift* for David Hayton reflects a more recent focus of his research – parliament. It can be suggested that there have been two factors which have guided this change in focus from the nature of parliamentary politics and management to the activity of the institution. The publication, in 2002, of the *History of the Irish Parliament, 1692–1800* by Edith Johnston-Liik was a significant moment in Irish historiography; first and foremost a biographical dictionary of the membership of the house of commons, the first volume included a 200-page survey and summary of the legislation of the Irish parliament under 17 broad subject areas and a chronological list of the 1,962 Commons' statutes passed between 1692 and 1800.[2] One reviewer properly identified this feature of Professor Johnston-Liik's monumental reference work as important, commenting that the author 'should be warmly commended for her decision to include such an analysis of the statutes passed by the parliament whose principal function, after all, was to enact legislation'.[3] Soon after, David Hayton was the principal investigator on the Irish Legislation Database (ILD) project, launched in 2007, which as well as permitting easier access, has facilitated the identification and analysis of the patterns, content and significance of parliamentary legislation in 18th-century Ireland.[4]

A second factor encouraging David Hayton to focus his attention on legislation has been the Leverhulme Trust-funded project, co-ordinated by Julian Hoppit, which explored the legislation that failed to make it to the statute book of the Westminster parliament between 1660 and 1800. It makes the important point that 'much still remains to be learnt . . . especially in relation to parliament's legislative and judicial activity'.[5] The influence of the 'Failed Legislation' project can be seen, not only in the detailed categories for legislation that it and the ILD share, but also in an important pair of articles in which Hayton has compared the patterns of legislation in Dublin and Westminster.[6]

2

This line of research has proven to be very fruitful, not only for David Hayton but also for those Irish historians who have followed the advice of Hoppit and Joanna Innes, not just to look at specific bills and acts but to explore legislative activity in the round. An essential preface to this work has been the identification and clarification of the major points of difference between the Irish and British parliaments – specifically the constitutional constraints upon the legislative activity of the Irish parliament imposed by

[2] Edith Mary Johnston-Liik, *History of the Irish Parliament, 1692–1800* (6 vols, Belfast, 2002), i, 209–404 introductory survey) and 405–583 (statutes).

[3] Paddy McNally, 'The Eighteenth-Century Irish House of Commons', *Parliamentary History*, xxiii (2004), 390.

[4] See the ILD website at *http://www.qub.ac.uk/ild/*

[5] Julian Hoppit and Joanna Innes, 'Introduction', in *Failed Legislation, 1660–1800*, ed. Julian Hoppit (1997), ; Julian Hoppit, 'Patterns of Parliamentary Legislation, 1660–1800', *Historical Journal*, xxxix (1996), 109–31.

[6] The subject categories used on the ILD website are listed in *Failed Legislation*, ed. Hoppit, 30–3. For the relevant articles, see D.W. Hayton, 'Introduction: The Long Apprenticeship', *Parliamentary History*, xx (2001), –15; D.W. Hayton, 'Patriots and Legislators: Irishmen and their Parliaments, c.1689–c.1740', in *Parliaments, Nations and Identities in Britain and Ireland, 1660–1850*, ed. Julian Hoppit (Manchester, 2003), 103–23.

Poynings' Law (1494) and the Declaratory Act (1720). In practice, the second of these, which declared the right of Westminster to legislate for Ireland, confirmed the subservient position of the Irish parliament *vis-à-vis* Westminster, and the fact that London was generally more interested in asserting its rights than in exercising them, while the first, which shaped the deliberations and procedures of the Irish parliament, was a constant reminder of dependency.[7] In February 1761, during one serious dispute over the operation of Poynings' Law in relation to calling a new parliament, Lord Chancellor Bowes commented that Irish MPs 'have considered your house [of Commons at Westminster] as the model and in general think themselves injured in the instances wherein theirs upon legal constitution must differ'.[8]

Historians have begun to piece together the circumstances, considerations, and influences that resulted in the enactment of some of the 2,247 statutes passed by the Irish parliament between 1692 and 1800. This work began decades ago, in the case of the most contentious legislation, the penal laws, which targeted Irish catholics and, to a lesser extent, protestant dissenters.[9] Ongoing research into the penal laws has provided something of a model to follow, in terms of identifying the origins of legislation, the personnel involved, the motivations of those responsible, the way in which the 'heads of bills' negotiated the cumbersome legislative process, the influence of the interventions of external forces (lobbies, interest groups, the press or the crowd), and its changing content over time.[10] More recently, a series of publications has engaged with the legislation appertaining to finance,[11] crime,[12] the army and militia,[13]

---

[7] Isolde Victory, 'The Making of the 1720 Declaratory Act', in *Parliament, Politics and People: Essays in Eighteenth-Century Irish History*, ed. Gerard O'Brien (Dublin, 1986), 8–21; Hayton, 'Stanhope/Sunderland Ministry', *passim*; C.I. McGrath, 'Government, Parliament and the Constitution: The Reinterpretation of Poynings' Law, 1692–1714', *Irish Historical Studies*, xxxviii (2006), 160–172; James Kelly, 'Monitoring the Constitution: The Operation of Poynings' Law in the 1760s', *Parliamentary History*, xx (2001), 87–106; James Kelly, *Poynings' Law and the Making of Law in Ireland, 1660–1800* (Dublin, 2007).

[8] Cited in S.J. Connolly, *Divided Kingdom: Ireland, 1630–1800* (Oxford, 2008), 389: John Bowes to George Dodington, 5 Feb. 1761.

[9] J.G Simms, 'The Making of a Penal Law (2 Anne, c. 6), 1703–4', *Irish Historical Studies*, xii (1960) 105–18; J.G. Simms, 'The Bishops' Banishment Act, 1697', *Irish Historical Studies*, xvii (1970), 185–99; S.C Connolly, 'The Penal Laws', in *Kings in Conflict: The Revolutionary War in Ireland and its Aftermath, 1689–1750* ed. W.A. Maguire (Belfast, 1990), 157–72.

[10] C.I. McGrath, 'Securing the Protestant Interest: The Origins and Purpose of the Penal Laws of 1695' *Irish Historical Studies*, xxx (1996), 25–46; James Kelly, 'Sustaining a Confessional State: The Irish Parliament and Catholicism', in *The Eighteenth-Century Composite State: Representative Institutions in Ireland and Europe 1689–1800*, ed. D.W. Hayton, James Kelly and John Bergin (Basingstoke, 2010), 44–77.

[11] C.I. McGrath, 'Central Aspects of the Eighteenth-Century Constitutional Framework in Ireland: The Government Supply Bill and Biennial Parliamentary Sessions, 1715–82', *Eighteenth-Century Ireland/Iris a dá chultúr*, xvi (2001), 9–34; Philip O'Regan, 'Accountability and Final Control as "Patriotic" Strategies Accomptants and the Public Accounts Committee in Late-Seventeenth- and Early-Eighteenth-Century Ireland', *Accounting Historians Journal*, xxx (2003), 105–31; C.I. McGrath, 'Money, Politics and Power: The Financial Legislation of the Irish Parliament', in *The Eighteenth-Century Composite State*, ed. Hayton *et al* 21–43.

[12] Neal Garnham, 'Criminal Legislation in the Irish Parliament, 1692–1760', *Parliamentary History*, x (2001), 55–70; Neal Garnham, 'Riot Acts, Popular Protest, and Protestant Mentalities in Eighteenth-Century Ireland', *Historical Journal*, xlix (2006), 403–23.

[13] Neal Garnham, 'Defending the Kingdom and Preserving the Constitution: Irish Militia Legislation 1692–1793', in *The Eighteenth-Century Composite State*, ed. Hayton *et al.*, 107–35.

divorce,[14] medicine,[15] the established Church[16] and the role of individual lobby groups.[17]

Of more immediate relevance to the regulatory impulse addressed here are the smaller number of publications which explore the role of the Irish parliament in improving the economy and infrastructure or regulating internal markets.[18] As David Hayton would point out, research on this subject in Ireland has been influenced by the approach and findings of historians who have engaged with the subject of improvement in Great Britain.[19] For Ireland, Andrew Sneddon has used the ILD to establish the dimensions of improving legislation; 1,200 'heads of bills', or over a quarter of all legislative initiatives proposed between 1692 and 1800. Improving legislation was comparatively under-represented until the 1720s, but did not suffer the same mid-century slump and replicated the increase in economic activity from the 1760s onwards.[20] This might signify a pragmatic accommodation to imperial realities from the 1720s onwards or, more plausibly, a channelling of energy into economic patriotism that, as well as legislation, could, and did, generate limited bursts of anger at the metropolitan author-ities at several points later in the century.[21]

The thrust of the research into the nature and operation of the 18th-century Irish parliament sustains an impression of an institution that was constrained by the pro-cedures which governed how it functioned, but which was permitted by reason of the fact that it met in regular session, controlled the supply of taxation, was possessed of a body of active legislators and was subject to calls from 'out of doors' for inter-vention in many areas, to offer more than most other representative or colonial

[14] John Bergin, 'Irish Private Divorce Bills and Acts of the Eighteenth Century', in *People, Politics and Power: Essays on Irish History, 1660–1850, in Honour of James I. McGuire*, ed. James Kelly, John McCafferty and C.I. McGrath (Dublin, 2009), 94–122.

[15] Andrew Sneddon, 'Institutional Medicine and State Intervention in Eighteenth-Century Ireland', in *Ireland and Medicine in the Seventeenth and Eighteenth Centuries*, ed. James Kelly and Fiona Clark (Farnham, 2010), 137–62.

[16] D.W. Hayton, 'Parliament and the Established Church: Reform and Reaction', in *The Eighteenth-Century Composite State*, ed. Hayton *et al.*, 78–106.

[17] E.g., see John Bergin, 'The Quaker Lobby and its Influence on Irish Legislation, 1692–1705', *Eighteenth-Century Ireland/Iris an dá chultúr*, xix (2004), 9–36.

[18] Eoin Magennis, 'Coal, Corn and Canals: The Dispersal of Public Moneys, 1695–1772', *Parliamentary History*, xx (2001), 71–86; Eoin Magennis, 'Regulating the Market: Parliament, Corn and Bread in Eighteenth-Century Ireland', in *The Law and Other Legalities in Ireland, 1689–1850*, ed. Michael Brown and Seán Donlan (Aldershot, 2011), 209–30; Andrew Sneddon, 'Legislating for Economic Development: Irish Fisheries as a Case Study in the Limitations of "Improvement" ', in *The Eighteenth-Century Composite State*, ed. Hayton *et al.*, 136–59; Sneddon, 'Institutional Medicine and State Intervention'; Andrew Sneddon, 'State Intervention and Provincial Health Care: The County Infirmary System in Late-Eighteenth-Century Ulster', *Irish Historical Studies*, cxlix (2012), 5–21.

[19] P.J. Jupp, *The Governing of Britain, 1688–1848* (2006); Paul Langford, *Public Life and the Propertied Englishman, 1689–1798* (Oxford, 1991); Joanna Innes, *Inferior Politics: Social Problems and Social Policies in Eighteenth-Century England* (Oxford, 2009).

[20] Sneddon, 'Legislating for Economic Development', 138, 141–5.

[21] See J.G. McCoy, 'Local Political Culture in the Hanoverian Empire: The Case of the Anglo-Irish', University of Oxford DPhil, 1994; S.C. Connolly, 'Precedent and Principle: The Patriots and their Critics', in *Political Ideas in Eighteenth-Century Ireland*, ed. S.J. Connolly (Dublin, 2000), 130–58; Hayton, 'Patriots and Legislators', *passim*; Stephen Small, *Political Thought in Ireland, 1776–1800* (Oxford, 2002), 30, 65–74.

assemblies.[22] The aim of this article is to explore further what a regulatory impulse could mean in the 18th-century Irish parliament. This will be done through looking at the coal trade as a case study, since it well illustrates the belief in the possibilities for the economic improvement of Ireland, concerns about high prices in respect of a necessity of life for the urban poor, and the residual anglophobia that such subjects could raise.

3

How can this regulatory impulse be described? While regulations are often declaimed as 'red tape' or a burden on business, the regulatory impulse can equally emerge as a consequence of lobbying by one interest seeking to gain an advantage over a rival, while the results (such as product standards) may be of benefit both to businesses and consumers. The balance between regulation and deregulation has varied over time, depending on the needs of the state.[23] These needs have been characterised by the desire to promote order in local areas, to collect higher levels of taxation, support employment in domestic manufacturing, and increase the volume of external trade.[24]

In terms of what was regulated in the 18th century, recent research has identified four areas in which the legislature and executive in Britain (and Ireland) intervened in the period 1660–1850.[25] The first was the import/export trade between Britain and its colonies or continental markets; this trade was regulated by tariffs and legislation, which prohibited the export of certain goods from either Ireland (for example, woollens) or the American colonies. The second area was that of production, where export bounties and import prohibitions were intended to encourage new forms of manufacturing, and to protect older forms, including, to a lesser extent, agriculture. A third area was the labour market where wages, apprenticeships and mobility of workers were all regulated. The fourth and final economic area is internal trade; here, regulation was intended to assist with the emergence of larger internal markets (for example, through better infrastructure), with the provision of necessary goods/services (such as bread and coal) and with credit and debt issues. A fifth area was corporate governance, although there was limited activity in this area in 18th-century Ireland.[26]

---

[22] Michael Watson, 'The British West Indian Legislatures in the Seventeenth and Eighteenth Centuries: An Historiographical Introduction', *Parliamentary History*, xiv (1995), 89–98; *The Eighteenth-Century Composite State*, ed. Hayton *et al.*, 251 n. 34.

[23] Joyce Appleby, *Economic Thought and Ideology in Seventeenth Century England* (Princeton, NJ, 1978); Steve Pincus, 'Rethinking Mercantilism: Political Economy, the British Empire, and the Atlantic World in the Seventeenth and Eighteenth Centuries', *William and Mary Quarterly*, 3rd ser., lxix (2012), 3–34.

[24] Tim Keirn, 'Parliament, Legislation and the Regulation of English Textile Industries, 1689–1714', in *Stilling the Grumbling Hive: The Response to Social and Economic Problems in England, 1689–1750*, ed. Lee Davison, Tim Hitchcock, Tim Keirn and Robert Shoemaker (New York, 1992), 4.

[25] *Regulating the British Economy, 1660–1850*, ed. Perry Gauci (Aldershot, 2011), 12–18; Jupp, *Governing of Britain*, 166–74. Case studies can be found in Stuart Handley, 'Local Legislative Initiatives for Economic and Social Development in Lancashire, 1689–1731', *Parliamentary History*, ix (1990), 14–37; Raymond Sickinger 'Regulation or Ruination: Parliament's Consistent Pattern of Mercantilist Regulation of the English Textile Trade, 1660–1800', *Parliamentary History*, xix (2000), 211–32.

[26] *Shareholder Democracies? Corporate Governance in Britain and Ireland before 1850*, ed. Mark Freeman, Robin Pearson and James Taylor (Chicago, 2012). My thanks to Dr Patrick Walsh for this reference.

These areas of regulation also obtained in Ireland even if the extent of the regulation engaged in, its timing and enforcement, all differed from Britain. In Ireland, the initiation and implementation of economic regulations was broadly shared between four groups. The first, and that highlighted in this article, was the central executive in Dublin Castle and the parliament in College Green. A shift, similar to that which took place in Great Britain, from privy council or royal proclamation to parliamentary statute, occurred in Ireland. However, there was a time lag as the Irish parliament only began to meet in regular (biennial) session in the reign of Anne. The Irish parliament did regulate each of the areas noted above, although the regulation of external trade could be a source of conflict with Britain.[27] Finally, with regard to central government, the fast-growing Irish revenue service was crucial in the enforcement of regulations, especially those that involved the paying of customs and excise.[28]

The second group involved in the regulatory process consisted of those active in local government, such as justices of the peace, members of urban corporations and of county grand juries.[29] They sometimes instigated new legislation by petition to parliament and were also the enforcers of regulations, because they possessed an inspection and/or judicial role, in respect of internal trade and the labour market. A third group was businesses themselves; these were often organised on a collective basis either in the form of guilds or chambers of commerce. Self-regulation had its origins in the role performed by medieval guilds in policing the quality and price of goods and in controlling labour mobility. This survived into the 18th century, as we shall see, in the case of the coal trade. The final, important, group of regulators was the crowd, which sought to enforce certain regulations when it perceived that government or self-regulation had failed. This group's interest centred on the internal market, the world of work, and the protection of manufacturing industries, such as textiles.[30]

A final introductory point to make is that there were other areas of social policy where regulation was deemed acceptable and necessary in the 18th century. These included, in the words of Joanna Innes: 'the relief and regulation of the poor, the repression of vice (variously conceived), the handling of insolvent (and therefore perhaps imprisoned) debtors, and the prevention and punishment of crime'.[31] These regulatory categories are equally pertinent in the case of Ireland; using the ILD, one can identify 236 enactments and 301 failed bills (approximately 11% of the total) between 1690 and 1800.

[27] James Kelly, 'The Irish Trade Dispute with Portugal, 1780–7', *Studia Hibernica*, xxv (1989–90), 8–48; James Kelly, 'The Anglo-French Treaty of 1786: The Irish Dimension', *Eighteenth-Century Ireland/Iris an dá Chultur*, iv (1989), 93–112.

[28] Patrick Walsh, ' "The Sin of With-Holding Tribute": Contemporary Pamphlets and the Professionalization of the Irish Revenue Service in the Early Eighteenth Century', *Eighteenth-Century Ireland/ Iris an dá Chultur*, xxi (2006), 48–65.

[29] Jacqueline Hill, *From Patriots to Unionists: Dublin Civic Politics and Irish Protestant Patriotism 1660–1840* (Oxford, 1997), chs 2–4; Neal Garnham, 'Local Élite Creation in Early Hanoverian Ireland: The Case of the County Grand Jury', *Historical Journal*, xlii (1999), 623–42.

[30] Maurice O'Connell, 'Class Conflict in a Pre-Industrial City: Dublin in 1780', *Irish Ecclesiastical Record*, ciii (1965), 93–106; Eoin Magennis, 'In Search of the "Moral Economy": Food Scarcity in 1756–57 and the Crowd', in *Crowds in Ireland, c.1720–1920*, ed. Peter Jupp and Eoin Magennis (Basingstoke, 2000), 189–211; John Cunningham, ' "Compelled to their Bad Acts by Hunger": Three Irish Urban Crowds, 1817–45', *Eire-Ireland*, xliv (2010), 128–51.

[31] Innes, *Inferior Politics*, 21.

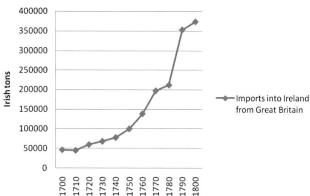

Figure 1: *Coal Imports into Ireland from Great Britain, 1700–1800*
Source: L.M. Cullen, *Anglo-Irish Trade, 1660–1800* (Manchester, 1968), 79.

4

Before turning to parliament's attempts to regulate the coal trade, it is necessary to provide some detail on the operation and peculiarities of the trade in Ireland.[32] The first point to note is that there was very little indigenous supply of coal in Ireland. Despite the hopes of some, and the oft-quoted call by Jonathan Swift to 'burn everything English except their coal', Ireland never discovered its own rich seams of coal as geology was against the country.[33] The Irish parliament did try, through various legislative efforts, to develop Irish coal (and other) mines. However, the efforts came to little, and were occasionally to elicit accusations of jobbery against the projectors.

Given the absence of sufficient coal resources within Ireland, the vast bulk of the coal burned in the kingdom was imported, as it had been since the 1660s, largely from the north-west of England.[34] Coal imports trebled in the course of the 18th century (see Figure 1) to 372,999 tons in 1800, and it increased further to over half a million tons in 1810.[35] The sharpest rise occurred in the second half of the century, when Dublin was the primary domestic market, though its share fell from 77% of total imports in 1750 to 49% in 1800.[36] Most Irish cities and towns sustained a strong demand for coal, as it was the main domestic fuel in urban areas and the key source of energy of expanding industries such as breweries. Galway and Limerick, with access to local turf supplies, were the only ports to import small volumes of coal in 1800.

Cumberland was the main source of coal destined for the Irish market, and it was shipped primarily from the port of Whitehaven to Dublin and Cork. Whitehaven

---

[32] For more detail, see L.M. Cullen, *Anglo-Irish Trade, 1660–1800* (Manchester, 1968), 122–30.

[33] Those enthusiastic about Ireland's mineral prospects sometimes also argued that an absence of coal should not prevent industrialisation. For the debate, see Cormac Ó Gráda, *Ireland: A New Economic History, 1780–1939* (Oxford, 1994), 315–21.

[34] D.A. Chart, *An Economic History of Ireland* (Dublin, 1920), 82.

[35] Cullen, *Anglo-Irish Trade*, 52.

[36] Cullen, *Anglo-Irish Trade*, 81.

continued to supply the vast majority of Irish coal throughout the century, although Liverpool and Swansea assumed a greater share of the trade after 1770. In terms of the origins of coal, Whitehaven's collieries increasingly had to share the market with the Workington and Harrington pits.[37] The Irish coal trade was organised in such a way that the pit owners, such as the Lowthers of Cumberland, sold their produce to the masters of ships in the colliery ports on credit, which was redeemed on their return to port. Since these masters had little correspondence with Ireland, their knowledge of market conditions there was dependent on the information they gleaned from visits to the kingdom. Another difficulty was that, in wartime, press gangs targeted the crews of colliers for impressment into the navy. In February 1726, the lord mayor of Dublin asked the viceroy, Lord Carteret, to intervene and request the suspension of the ongoing press as it deterred the coal ships from going to sea, and stoked fear in the city of an imminent shortage as there were then only two weeks of fuel left.[38]

In Dublin and other ports, the masters had to decide whether or not to sell some, or all, of their consignment to a local coal merchant or factor, who would take it to a coalyard from which it would be sold to customers. One consideration that guided captains in this decision was the time they spent (up to six weeks in the case of Dublin) downriver awaiting a quayside berth. During this time, a captain had to cover his costs and hope that coal prices did not fall from what they were when the ship arrived off the port. At one point in the late 17th century, masters transferred coal onto flat-bottomed craft to permit it to be brought upriver to Dublin, but this was criticized in the Irish parliament and it ceased. Generally, masters brought their ships to the quayside and sold the coal directly from the vessel to factors and individual customers. The regulations provided that coal could be brought to a coalyard for sale or sold directly from the ship either by the captain or by a coal factor or coal factors who bought the shipment. In both places, the prices were to be visible to customers who could then decide – depending on the price and their need – whether or not to make a purchase. In practice, only industrial and wealthy consumers could afford to buy up and store stocks of coal. In the event that a decision to buy was made, and the volume and price was agreed upon, the coal was bagged and carted to the customer's house by one of the porters who worked on the quays; there was an additional carriage cost for destinations removed from the port.

In theory, this seems like a transparent market where prices were displayed, coals were sold by weight and measure, and the customer could obtain the fuel required for their business or household. However, this flatters to deceive. It was, L.M. Cullen has observed, a somewhat chaotic trade, which was prone to provide a low return due to a lack of market information and to seasonal gluts, the consequences of which were borne by the masters.[39] He concludes that: 'the organisation of the coal trade remained confused . . . and was at the mercy of recurrent changes in supply and demand:

---

[37] W.H Makey, 'The Place of Whitehaven in the Irish Coal Trade, 1600–1750', University of London MA, 1952. For Cork's trade with Wales and, increasingly, Cumberland and Belfast's with the Scottish coalfields, see David Dickson, *Old World Colony: Cork and South Munster, 1630–1830* (Cork, 2005), 154; George Benn, *History of Belfast* (2nd edn, 2 vols, Belfast, 2008), i, 254.

[38] TNA, ADM 3990: Carteret to lords of the admiralty, 25 Feb. 1726. My thanks to Dr Patrick Walsh for this reference.

[39] Cullen, *Anglo-Irish Trade*, 122.

imbalance was reflected alternately in excessively high or unduly low prices'.[40] The trade was also subject to consistent criticism because of the origins of the coal, its quality, the prices charged and the general lack of transparency. Indeed, the coal trade resembled the trade in bread, since, like the factors, bakers were subjected to the allegation that they sold bad goods or charged too much for their goods.[41] Such criticisms prompted two contrasting responses: the provision of incentives to promote the development of Irish collieries and the associated infrastructure; and the ratification of legislation in an attempt to ensure that the coal trade (in Dublin, particularly) functioned fairly and was not burdened by abuses.

5

There was considerable support for the development of Irish coalfields on the grounds that if this 'infant industry' could successfully be encouraged it would save the country between £150,000 and £450,000 per annum, which was the order of the sum spent on imported English, Scottish and Welsh coal. With this object in view, high hopes were entertained that significant coalfields might be developed in Ballintoy, Coalisland and Kilkenny, the last for anthracite deposits. The conviction that it was only infrastructural deficiencies, such as canals (like the Newry Canal built from the 1740s) and ports (at locations like Ballycastle where work began in the 1720s), that prevented an indigenous supply of coal being exploited fully proved persuasive. This prompted a disbursement of public monies – more than £50,000 in parliamentary grants between 1728 and 1771 alone – to assist with the opening of mines and the development of the necessary infrastructure.[42] The Irish parliament also passed an act in 1757 providing bounties for coal production along the lines of the corn bounties, which were agreed simultaneously.

In addition to the public money that was made available to assist with the development of collieries and of a related communications infrastructure, there were 13 legislative attempts to encourage the development of mines (coal and otherwise). Eight (61.5%) of these bills received the royal assent, which was significantly above the success rate for all bills. Figure 2 reveals that, one failed attempt in 1692 apart, there was little before the first successful measure of this kind in 1723. There was greater activity in parliament in the 1740s and 1750s, perhaps sparked by the high hopes for the Tyrone and Antrim collieries. This was followed by a break of almost 40 years before a second phase of legislation ensued in the 1790s, which was designed to encourage, through raising subscriptions, the opening of mines in County Wicklow and better infrastructure to take County Kilkenny coal to market.

The legislation to encourage the development of Irish collieries can be assigned to three categories.[43] The first sought to encourage landowners to facilitate exploration for coal (and other minerals) on their lands. The methods indicated in the 1723 act included allowing the clergy and guardians of the mentally ill to grant leases in order to encourage

[40] Cullen, *Anglo-Irish Trade*, 128.

[41] Magennis, 'Regulating the Market', 210–2.

[42] Magennis, 'Coal, Corn and Canals', *passim*.

[43] All of the subsequent detail about the passage of legislation comes from ILD.

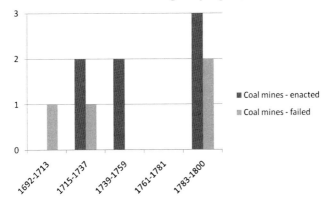

Figure 2: *Legislation for Development of Coal and Other Mines in the Irish Parliament, 1690–1800*
Source: Irish Legislation Database (ILD).

the finding of coal.[44] Two refinements of this piece of legislation followed in 1741 and 1749; the second provided incentives by allowing 41-year leases and by protecting those who were described as 'finders and discoverers'.[45] The remaining measure in this category, which was approved in 1727, was initiated with the same intention as the 1723 act but the regulation that made it to the statute book made the destruction of mining equipment a felony. Interestingly, many of the promoters of the 1720s initiatives – including John Beauchamp (MP for Old Leighlin), Sir Thomas Taylor (MP for Kells), and Agmondisham and William Vesey (MPs for Tuam) – were tories; so, too, was Robert Cope (MP for County Armagh), who was the architect of the 1741 act, which was his only piece of legislation in almost 30 years in parliament.[46] By contrast, John Bourke (MP for Naas), who steered the 1749 measure into law, was a solid government supporter, a revenue commissioner for 31 years (1749–80), and a promoter of many different pieces of legislation. Like Taylor, Bourke was a founder member of the Dublin Society in 1731 and many of his and Beauchamp's bills were devoted to economic improvement (linen, canals and tillage). Bourke also provides a link to the legislation that sought to regulate the coal trade as an advocate of the enforcement and tightening of regulations appertaining to the assize of bread.[47]

The second category of legislation was targeted at encouraging the development of coalmines in Ulster. The background was provided by the food shortages and high fuel prices of the severe winter of 1756–7. This prompted a chorus of attacks on the 'combinations' of factors and masters that, it was alleged, ran the Dublin coal trade, and calls for imports from locations other than Whitehaven and Workington.[48] The MP

[44] 10 Geo. I, c. 5 (1724).
[45] 15 Geo. II, c. 10 (1742); 23 Geo. II, c. 9 (1750).
[46] Johnston-Liik, *Irish Parliament*, iii, 148–9, 505–6; vi, 380–1, 468–9, 473.
[47] Johnston-Liik, *Irish Parliament*, iii, 226–8.
[48] Magennis, ' "Moral Economy" ', 198–201. For a flavour of these attacks, see *Universal Advertiser*, 26 Dec. 1756; 1, 18, 29 Jan., 1, 5 Feb. 1757.

behind two bills presented in 1757 was William Richardson, who represented County Armagh, who was assisted by Redmond Morres, the MP for Thomastown, who was a supporter of the Ponsonbys.[49] Richardson was a solid government supporter during the early 1750s, closely attached to Archbishop Stone, and heavily involved in both the Tillage and Linen Boards.[50] His first attempt to introduce a bill (which both sought to encourage collieries and prevent combinations in Dublin's trade) foundered shortly after Morres and he were given leave on 21 November 1757 to bring the heads of a bill before the Commons, and the import figures for 1755–7 were laid before MPs.[51] Leave was subsequently granted on 6 December to both to bring in a second bill, for the sole purpose of encouraging Irish collieries, which was read and committed a week later and forwarded to the viceroy.[52] The bill's key clause authorised a 2s. per ton bounty on coal produced by Irish collieries and transported to Dublin.[53] A petition from the lord mayor and Dublin's corporation presented to the British privy council did not hurt the bill's prospects. The measure was substantially amended in London, but the bounty provision survived, although it did not have the much-hoped-for effect of generating the indigenous supply of coal that would diminish reliance on exports from Whitehaven.[54]

The third category of mining legislation, dating from the 1790s, can be dealt with quickly. Comprising three acts and two bills, the common object of these measures was to establish a statutory framework for companies to raise funds by subscription in order 'to open and work mines'.[55] Prompted by the discovery in the 1790s of gold in the Wicklow mountains, the priority of the measure was precious metals rather than coal,[56] and the companies that were facilitated to raise share capital of up to £50,000 were the Royal Mining Company, the Hibernian Mining Company and the Associated Irish Mines Company.[57] One additional notable element of the 1792 act that does echo earlier legislation was the inclusion of a provision to open a harbour in Arklow and a canal to Glenmalure to serve the mines of County Wicklow and the anthracite collieries of Castlecomer in County Kilkenny.[58]

The MPs involved in promoting the latter legislation comprised a politically-mixed group of active parliamentarians, which included Sir John Blaquiere, the former chief secretary, who was behind the 1791 act. The 1792 act supporting the Hibernian Mining Company was the work of the patriot Robert Day (MP for Ardfert), and the independent Samuel Hayes (MP for Maryborough), while Isaac Corry (MP for Newry and

---

[49] Johnston-Liik, *Irish Parliament*, v, 321–3.

[50] Johnston-Liik, *Irish Parliament*, vi, 159–60.

[51] *CJI*, x, 335, 341.

[52] *CJI*, x, 373–4, 402, 434.

[53] Magennis, 'Coal, Corn and Canals', 82. For the argument that British bounties were 'often assessed by political and imperial contexts', see Julian Hoppit, 'Bounties, the Economy and the State in Britain, 1689–1800', in *Regulating the British Economy*, ed. Gauci, 160.

[54] TNA, PC2/106, ff. 74, 102.

[55] 31 Geo. III, c. 39 (1791); 32 Geo. III, c. 24 (1792); 38 Geo. III, c. 40 (1798).

[56] Timothy Alborn, 'An Irish El Dorado: Recovering Gold in County Wicklow', *Journal of British Studies*, l (2011), 359–80; Des Cowman, 'The Mining Community at Avoca, 1780–1880', in *Wicklow: History and Society*, ed. Ken Hannigan and William Nolan (Dublin, 1994), 760–79.

[57] John Morris, 'The Battle of the Tokens, 1789–1799: The Hibernian Mining Company vs the Associated Irish Mines Company', *Journal of the Mining Heritage Trust of Ireland*, iii (2003), 42–7.

[58] 32 Geo. III, c. 24 (1792).

chancellor of the exchequer) reported on the 1798 act supporting the rival Associated Irish Mining Company.[59] All four were members of the Dublin Society, Hayes being an active member. Blaquiere and he possessed a shared interest in promoting improving legislation embracing such areas as protecting foundling children in Dublin, better paving and lighting, and the regulation of gaols.[60] The unsuccessful 1792 bill was presented by Charles Osborne (MP for Carysfort) and the 1798 act by Henry Brooke Parnell (MP for Maryborough), both first-time legislators; Parnell enjoyed a long career in Westminster after the union.[61] Another MP involved in the legislation of the 1790s provides a link to the regulatory bills that will be addressed next; Annesley Stewart, MP for Charlemont, reported on Blaquiere's 1791 act. However, he was still more actively engaged in the same year with a measure that sought to reduce the price of imported coal.

6

Alongside the economic patriotism that inspired the various legislative initiatives targeted at the promotion of mining, there was a second category of regulation, prompted by the conviction that the prices paid for coal in Dublin were inflated by the hoarding, forestalling or engrossing practices pursued singly, or together, by colliers in Whitehaven, masters on board ship, and coal factors in Dublin. Accusations abounded, and they were readily to be encountered in the press and in parliament where they were included in petitions presented by the public or in the evidence given to committees. Ships were said to lay up outside Dublin bay until such times as prices rose, while cartels were believed to be endemic in the realms of the masters and the coal factor.[62] It was alleged, in addition, that fraudulent weights were made up by the addition of coal dust to bags filled on the ships at the quays out of the sight of customers. Then there were the abuses perpetrated by porters, who were accused of demanding a fee, called the 'old man', for bringing customers to certain ships or who sought extra payment if they were required to carry bags. Other colourful allegations include claims that masters met to fix prices at taverns, and that porters not only combined but secured themselves against prosecution by threatening any legal figure that sought to prevent them abusing their position.[63]

Regulation by commercial interests, local government and the crowd, aimed to combat these and other abuses, which those involved in the trade strongly denied. Both the corporation and the Merchants' Guild were possessed of a regulatory role in the capital. In 1640, the guild appointed the first inspector of master porters with the responsibility of licensing master porters and enforcing 'ordinances of ancient custom'.

---

[59] Johnston-Liik, *Irish Parliament*, iii, 202–4, 511–5; iv, 33–4, 388–90.

[60] Blaquiere was also behind a 1796 act (37 Geo. III, c. 14) to reduce the price of sugar in Ireland.

[61] Johnston-Liik, *Irish Parliament*, v, 421–2; vi, 14–6.

[62] A rare piece of evidence of a combination in 1728–9 comes from Whitehaven where the masters attempted to combine to stop sailings in order to push up prices in Dublin; see Edward Hughes, *North Country Life in the Eighteenth Century: Cumberland and Westmoreland, 1730–1800* (1965), 187–8.

[63] NAI, M1A.46.46: minute books of the parliamentary committees on the coal trade, 1757–1796, books 3 (1777–8), 6 (1793) and 7 (1796).

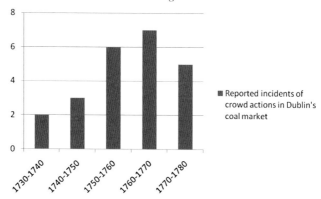

Figure 3: *Incidents of Disorder in Dublin Related to the Coal Trade, 1730–1780*
Source: Newspapers, including *Pue's Occurrences, Faulkner's Dublin Journal* and *Freeman's Journal.*

The inspector was also authorised to assist the master porters to stamp out abuses by porters, who had a reputation for rowdiness.[64] This is an interesting example of regulation from above by one commercial group over another. Meanwhile, the corporation contrived to ensure that factors were licensed by the lord mayor, though the cost of this licence was itself a cause of controversy.[65] The existence of this hierarchy in the coal trade in Dublin supports the conclusion of Louis Cullen that those involved in the coal trade (as in baking) were not deemed to belong to the important trades or to hold a high station within the metropolitan merchant community.[66]

Still further regulation came in the form of crowd intervention to enforce 'fair prices'. This made the coal trade a potential public order matter and is one of the primary reasons that it came to the attention of legislators.[67] Based on incidents reported in the Dublin press between 1730 and 1780, a total of 23 incidents of crowd action have been identified at the quayside markets, in the coalyards operated by merchants, and against coal porters. The press reports cannot be regarded as a wholly reliable source in respect of such matters, but an average of nearly one disturbance every two years would have been hard to ignore, especially by MPs representing Dublin City (see Figure 3).

The public interest in the operation and regulation of the coal trade, particularly in Dublin, is displayed in the petitions that prompted the appointment of parliamentary committees or the leave granted for bills to be introduced. These petitions came from the members of Dublin's corporation, the Merchants' Guild, and the wider public. For

[64] Dublin Public Library, Gilbert Collection [hereafter cited as DPL, GC], MS 78: charters and documents of the Guild of the Holy Trinity or Merchants' Guild, 1438–1824, vol. 1, ff. 23–4, 26, 164; vol. 2, ff. 245–6, 288; NAI, M1A.46.46: minute book 7 (1796).

[65] NAI, M1A.46.46: minute books 5 (1790) and 7 (1796).

[66] Communication from Louis Cullen to the author, 7 Apr. 2012. In line with this, the Dublin committee of merchants in the 1760s and 1770s never debated the coal trade; see Royal Irish Academy, MS 12.D.29: committee of merchants minute book, 1767–1781.

[67] Neal Garnham, 'Police and Public Order in Eighteenth-Century Dublin', in *Two Capitals: London and Dublin, 1500–1840*, ed. Peter Clark and Raymond Gillespie (Oxford, 2001), 81–92.

example, in November 1761, three petitions came before MPs. The first was a petition from the lord mayor of Dublin seeking legislative redress against abuses in the coal trade; it was followed by two more from separate individuals arguing that there was evidence of collusion between coal merchants. The end result was the act that brought public coalyards to Dublin.[68] However, petitions did not guarantee legislative success. In November 1777, the 'citizens of the Meath Liberty' petitioned parliament requesting the establishment of a public coalyard in that area of Dublin and a committee was appointed under Luke Gardiner to hear evidence. This resulted in Sir Edward Newenham being given leave to introduce a bill to amend the 1761 act. However, Newenham's attempt was quickly sidelined. As a result, the same petition came before another parliamentary committee in February 1778 and a second unsuccessful bill, whose purport was to establish new yards that would buy coal at fixed prices, also failed to negotiate the Commons.[69] Alongside the petitioning went the press coverage which was generally, but not always, in favour of greater regulation. There was also an occasional pamphlet. One of these, dating from 1738, was modelled on Jonathan Swift's satirical style; it attacked the Whitehaven masters who had appointed an agent and claimed they were making the coal trade fairer than relying on Dublin's factors. A second, in 1761, was addressed to MPs and asked them to emulate the recent effort that had resulted in the provision of 'bread at a cheap price'.[70]

As a result of this attention, the coal trade was a frequent subject for discussion in parliament between 1690 and 1800 and at least 15 committees were established with this purpose from 1757. Minute books for seven of these parliamentary committees survived the destruction of the Public Record Office of Ireland in 1922. These contain a great deal of information on Dublin's coal trade from a variety of informed witnesses (masters, factors and porters) as well as detail of the regulation undertaken by Dublin corporation and the Merchants' Guild. The evidence supplied could be contradictory, but it does offer an insight into what MPs heard, as well as how they responded, since the committee's recommendations and the legislation that ensued are also available.

Twenty-six bills were introduced between 1703 and 1798 with the purpose of regulating the coal trade. Of the 26 bills, 15 (or 58%) received the royal assent in order better to regulate the coal trade, to prevent 'excessive high prices', to prevent combinations in the trade, and to establish public coalyards in Dublin and Cork. Figure 4 illustrates the pattern of increasing legislative activity and the improving success rate over the century.

The 26 bills can be divided into two groups: 22 consisted of measures to regulate the coal trade through the prevention of combinations among actors within the trade or the provision of public coalyards; and four proposed using income from the imports of coal (by adding a duty on every ton) to pay for the widening of streets in the capital. The first bill in the first group dates from 1703; it was initiated by the Irish privy council in

[68] *CJI*, xii, 239, 287, 297; 1 Geo. III, c. 10 (1761).

[69] NAI, M1A.46.46: minute books 3 (1777–8) and 4 (miscellaneous papers). One patriot newspaper was full of praise for the 'gentlemen who devoted themselves to the public good': *Freeman's Journal*, 7 Apr. 1778.

[70] *Dublin Newsletter*, 11 Feb. 1737; *Belfast Newsletter*, 1 Jan. 1757; *Freeman's Journal*, 4 July, 19 Oct. 1782; *Reflections on the coal trade with remarks on English pursers, in a letter to the people of Ireland* (Dublin, 1738); *Some considerations relative to the coal trade in Dublin* (Dublin, 1761), 12.

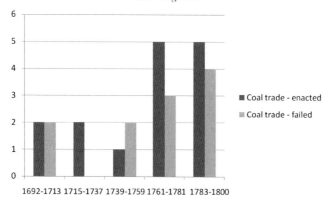

Figure 4: *Legislation for Regulating the Coal Trade in the Irish Parliament, 1690–1800*
Source: Irish Legislation Database (ILD).

a vain attempt to prevent the engrossing (or the buying up of large quantities for resale) of coal. Until the 1760s, the focus of the legislation was the licensing of the growing number of coal factors (the fees increased as time went on), the attempt to compel coal factors to admit to ownership of coal ships, the fixing of prices to the masts of ships or the gates of the coalyards selling coal, a ban on gabbards taking coal upriver to sell, fines for not weighing in clear view of the customer using scales, and fines or loss of wages for porters charging the 'old man'.[71] Although these elements continued to feature in legislation until 1796, they were overtaken by the idea of establishing public coalyards, which emerged out of the 1761–2 session. It first arose in a Commons' committee and was authorised, first for Dublin, in 1762, and next for Cork in 1764, on the suggestion of the MP for Cork City, John Hely-Hutchinson.[72] As Louis Cullen has pointed out, private coalyards, whether owned by coal factors or masters, had been in existence since the early 18th century. These offered their owners protection against price volatility but they also attracted criticism. Two acts, one approved in 1711 and another in 1719, limited the tonnage of coal that yards could hold to 1,000 and then 1,500 tons in order to prevent a factor from monopolising supply.[73] The public coalyards for Dublin were stocked using £10,000 of public funds initially and they were required to sell coal at a 1s. per ton profit to the deserving poor, as determined by corporation officials. Cork City did likewise and, although amending legislation in 1778, 1781, 1791 and 1793 sought to improve the operation of yards and to extend their number, they could not make them efficient; they generally ran at a loss because of their small size and problems generated by what amounted to speculative purchasing.[74] To encourage economies of

---

[71] 4 Anne, c. 8 (1705); 11 Anne, c. 4 (1712); 6 Geo. I, c. 2 (1720); 1 Geo. II, c. 21 (1728); 31 Geo. II, c. 15 (1758); 11 Geo. III, c. 5 (1771); 33 Geo. III, c. 40 (1793).

[72] 1 Geo. III, c. 10 (1762); 3 Geo. III, c. 17 (1764).

[73] Cullen, *Anglo-Irish Trade*, 124–5; 11 Anne, c. 4 (1712); 6 Geo. I, c. 2 (1720).

[74] 31 Geo. III, c. 33 (1791); 33 Geo. III, c. 40 (1793); 33 Geo. III, c. 47 (1793).

scale, the 1793 act introduced both a 1s. per ton bounty for yarding over 4,000 tons and public funds to pay up to £800 rent for yards selling more than 8,000 tons per annum.[75]

As Figure 4 shows, more than half of the 22 coal bills failed to secure the royal assent. Bills fell in 1703, 1710, 1750, 1756, two bills in 1778, 1781, 1792, and two in 1796. Although masters of ships petitioned the British privy council (unsuccessfully) against legislation on several occasions (1720 and 1728), the procedures provided for in accordance with Poynings' Law did work to the disadvantage of some bills. In 1710, a bill to regulate the coal trade and 11 others were simply deemed 'not fit for her Majesty's approbation' (possibly due to their originating with whig MPs) and, in 1750, the law officers in London recommended that the current coal bill should be rejected on the doubtful grounds that it 'may effect the exportation of coals from England to Ireland' at a time of economic distress in England.[76] The 1756 bill was passed by the Irish parliament but dropped in the Irish privy council, possibly because of the dislike of its sponsor, Edmond Sexten Pery.[77]

Interestingly, the MPs active in the promotion of coal bills formed a more varied group than those who promoted legislation to encourage mines. In the period to 1750, they were often on the side of the Irish administration and included Sir Richard Levinge (MP for Longford borough), law officer and moderate tory; the prominent whig lawyer and later prime serjeant, William Caulfield (MP for Tulsk); Stephen Ludlow (MP for Dunleer), revenue commissioner and tory; Sir John Rogerson (MP for Dublin City), recorder for Dublin, Ludlow's son-in-law and a moderate whig who was a very active legislator in George I's reign before he was made lord chief justice in 1727; and Sir Charles Burton (MP for Dublin City), who was an alderman on Dublin corporation for over 30 years and a government supporter.[78] After 1750, the MPs behind the coal trade legislation were more likely to be encountered on the opposition benches, with the possible exceptions of Edmond Sexten Pery and John Hely-Hutchinson who might be called 'ministerial patriots'. Pery (MP for Wicklow borough and then Limerick City) sponsored a bill in 1756 and two acts, in 1758 and 1771, specifically targeting the coal factors and masters as the architects of cartels in the trade, for which he was granted the freedom of Dublin City in 1760, while Hely-Hutchinson (MP for Cork City) promoted four acts (in 1762, two in 1764 and 1793) supporting the erection and better management of public coalyards in both Dublin and Cork.[79]

The other MPs behind coal legislation between 1778 and 1796 embraced a number with Dublin political connections. They included Sir Edward Newenham (MP for County Dublin), Sir Samuel Bradstreet (MP for and Recorder of Dublin City) and Henry Grattan (MP for Dublin City), and allies of Grattan, such as Robert Graydon

---

[75] NAI, M1A.46.46: minute book 6 (1793); 33 George III, c. 40 (1793).

[76] TNA, PC2/83, f. 36: committee on Irish bills, 28 July 1710; f. 383: committee on Irish bills report, 3 Sep. 1719; PC1/4/68, f. 1: petition of coal merchants of Great Britain, 3 Apr. 1728; PC1/6/18, f. 1: committee on Irish Bills report, 13 Mar. 1750. The references come from the ILD.

[77] E. Magennis, *The Irish Political System, 1740–1765* (Dublin, 2000), 108–9.

[78] Johnston-Liik, *Irish Parliament*, iii, 321–2, 392–3; v, 89–91, 138–40; vi, 186–9.

[79] For both MPs, see *Dictionary of Irish Biography* [http://dib.cambridge.org, accessed 19 Mar. 2013].

(MP for Kildare borough) and Sir Annesley Stewart.[80] All of these were usually in opposition and all sought to curry favour with the Dublin electorate by advancing regulations which were intended to reduce coal prices; indeed, Newenham actually went further and enquired of the freeholders if they agreed with his bill.[81] Popular or not, only a third of their bills were successful, and the fact that most fell in the Commons is revealing of the isolation of the majority of these individuals. There is one exception, Sir Jonah Barrington (MP for Tuam), who sided with the administration in parliament until he opposed the Act of Union. He worked with Grattan on the parliamentary committee in 1796, which also dealt with forestalling, but the bill did not progress, possibly because it ran out of time.[82]

Though the Commons manifested its willingness not to proceed with bills to regulate the coal trade that were deficient or unsuitable in 1778 (twice), 1781, 1792 and in 1796 (twice), the debate in the Lords in 1792 may provide a good reason as to why this was happening. Addressing the subject, the lord chancellor, John FitzGibbon, expressed his personal unease at an 'extraordinary' situation where 'regulations in trade could not be adopted but by the application to penalties and summary jurisdictions'. FitzGibbon articulated the mounting dislike of this sort of measure and the Lords' amendments were enough to kill the bill in the Commons.[83] Although a coal bill negotiated the Lords without amendment in 1793, FitzGibbon, again, unburdened himself of his opinion that high coal prices could only be prevented by 'repealing every law existing for the regulation of the trade, to suffer the trade to be perfectly free, and force its own step'.[84] Certainly, some MPs, peers and others outside parliament no longer believed that regulation was the key to improving the coal trade in Dublin or Cork.[85] Comparable opinions were expressed by others. One of Dublin's leading merchants, Travers Hartley, described combinations as a cause of high prices at a parliamentary committee in 1796.[86] Given this context, it is no surprise that a 1782 act contained a clause, the purpose of which was to deregulate the coal trade by allowing everyone to 'be at liberty to buy and sell coals at such times, in such manners and quantities and from such persons as he, she or they shall choose'.[87] This was followed by similar measures (two acts and one bill), the intention of which was to impose a duty on coal imports to pay for the widening of the capital's streets. However, this provision seems to have been ahead of Irish opinion, since most contemporary comment on the 1782 act and the 1798 bill reflected the belief that the duty would be passed on to consumers, rich and poor.[88]

[80] For Bradstreet and Graydon, see Johnston-Liik, *Irish Parliament*, iii, 258–9; iv, 312–3; see also J. Kelly, *Sir Edward Newenham, MP, 1734–1814: Defender of the Protestant Constitution* (Dublin, 2004), ch. 4; R.B. McDowell, *Grattan a Life* (Dublin, 2001).

[81] *Freeman's Journal*, 31 Jan. 1778.

[82] *Dictionary of Irish Biography*; *CJI*, xvi, 176, 228, 233, 270, 272.

[83] *Proceedings of the Irish House of Lords, 1771–1800*, ed. James Kelly (3 vols, Dublin, 2008), ii, 291.

[84] *Proceedings*, ed. Kelly ii, 474.

[85] For the point that 'if combinations existed the act of throwing open the trade to all who choose to deal in coals, cut combinations up by the roots', see *Freeman's Journal*, 4 July 1782.

[86] NAI, M1A.46.46: minute book 7 (1796).

[87] 21 & 22 Geo. III, c. 17, section xi.

[88] *Freeman's Journal*, 7 Jan. 1783; *Proceedings*, ed. Kelly iii, 326–30.

Most of the MPs involved in the four bills, like David La Touche (MP for Longford borough), John Foster (MP for County Louth), Sir John Parnell (MP for Queen's County) and John Claudius Beresford (MP for Swords), were members of the Commission for Wide Streets, for whom such an obvious income-raising scheme seemed entirely appropriate. Others, including Robert Johnson (MP for Hillsborough) and George Shee (MP for Knocktopher), were associates of the Beresfords through the Revenue Commission and Treasury.[89] It is also clear that many of the commissioners maintained close links with the leaders of commercial life in Dublin, like the bankers, La Touche and Beresford, while other prominent figures, such as John Foster and Sir John Parnell, were close to the mercantile community. They were not uniformly supportive of free trade, however. Beresford also sponsored an unsuccessful bill in 1797, the object of which was to strengthen certain regulations against factors whilst loosening others on masters, and he was thanked by the Merchants' Guild for his efforts.[90]

7

The regulatory attitude towards the coal trade in the Irish parliament was closer to that adopted with respect to London's coal trade than the economic patriotism of James II's 'Patriot Parliament'.[91] The legislation of that parliament, which met in 1689, was declared null and void by Westminster in 1690, but it did deal with coal in a singular manner. One of its acts banned imports of coal from England, Scotland and Wales in order to promote demand for indigenous coal and turf, which the jacobite MPs believed was plentiful. To prevent exploitation by the Irish mine-owners, the price of coal was fixed at 9*d.* a barrel. However, reports from Ireland in the winter of 1689 of a lack of fuel, discouraged this autarkic approach and it was not pursued in the 18th century.[92]

The nature of the legislation enacted to regulate the coal trade invites the question as to whether economic regulation changed in the course of the 18th century from a position in which the state and the crowd intervened actively to regulate the internal trade to one where free trade ideas began to take hold. There does appear to have been some change, if we compare the attitude of the press to the coal trade in the 1780s and the 1820s. In the earlier decade, the belief that prices were being forced up by cartels was generally accepted, particularly in the patriot press. It was one of the factors that encouraged investment in promoting coal mining and infrastructural projects, as it generated the expectation that, when complete: 'we will have this necessary of life in a great abundance, free from the combinations, the frauds, the monopolies, the exactions of colliers, coal factors, and engrossers, and save the sending out of the kingdom so large

[89] For these MPs, see Johnston-Liik, *Irish Parliament*, iii, 166–7; iv, 494–5; v, 62–4; vi, 18–21, 266; A.P.W. Malcomson, *John Foster (1740–1828): The Politics of Improvement and Prosperity* (Dublin, 2011).

[90] DPL, GC, MS 79, f. 313: minutes of the Merchants' Guild.

[91] 'Coal Trade: Introduction', *Journal of the House of Lords: volume 62: 1830*, 1435–1437 [*http://www.british-history.ac.uk/report.aspx?compid=16568*, accessed 13 Mar. 2013].

[92] J.G. Simms, *Jacobite Ireland, 1685–1691* (Dublin, 2000), 91–2. My thanks to Dr John Bergin for this reference.

a sum annually in specie'.[93] However, by the 1820s, there was a sharp debate as to whether intervention in the coal trade might not be counterproductive and questions were raised about the role of the Merchants' Guild.[94] As a result, when it was decided, in 1832, to repeal the various regulations covering the coal trade, it provoked little, or no, response. However, the goals of 'just prices' and of public coalyards did not disappear in the 1830s. While the prospect of regulating the coal trade disappeared from the realm of practical politics, the aspiration left its mark and it was fondly, if perhaps inaccurately, remembered as an efficient form of consumer protection. Some Dublin merchants, such as Heitons, who made money in the coal trade, embraced coal charity in their philanthropic endeavour in the 19th century.[95]

It is important, in conclusion, to put this exploration of the regulatory impulse in perspective. The 39 legislative initiatives covering the development of collieries and the regulation of the coal trade in Dublin and Cork account for less than 1% of the total number of bills brought before the Irish parliament between 1690 and 1800. While not the most urgent matter addressed by the legislature, it was returned to time and again because it was perceived as an issue that not only stymied industrial development but was also a cause of hardship, through high prices, for the urban poor. This was true not only in the cities but of smaller towns, such as Bandon, as well. In November 1792: 'In consequence of the uncommon scarcity and high price of turf in the winter of 1792 and the great hardship that the poor of the town of Bandon suffered thereby, a meeting of the principal inhabitants was held in the court house . . . and a liberal subscription was entered into . . . for the purpose of procuring coals by the cargo and selling them out in small quantities to the poor.' The *ad hoc* purchase of three small cargoes was followed in July 1793 by the corporation of the town granting a piece of ground for a permanent public coalyard. A subscription of £765 7s. 11d. was raised to build and stock the yard, with the duke of Devonshire at its head and 69 other subscribers following his example. During the winters that followed, the yard opened between one and three days weekly and cargoes were purchased in the summer when prices were at their lowest. Things continued in that vein until the 1820s, by which time interest had lapsed; when the yard finally closed in 1873, it is recorded that the poor were then supported by private philanthropy.[96] By the mid-Victorian era, the strong impulse to regulate that defined the 18th century had well and truly dissipated.

---

[93] *Freeman's Journal*, 17 Mar. 1781.

[94] The debate was as much to do with the 'unconstitutional action' of the attorney general as about the utility of the regulatory system; see DPL, GC, MS 78: 'Charters of the . . . Merchants' Guild', ii, ff. 354–6

[95] Tony Farmar, *Heitons in the Irish Coal, Iron and Building Markets, 1818–1996* (Dublin, 1996), 187.

[96] NLI, MS 34,218: account book of the Bandon coalyard, 1793–1873.

The Private Bill Legislation of the Irish Parliament, 1692–1800

JAMES KELLY

Between 1692 and 1800, 485 private bills and heads of private bills were initiated in Ireland, of which 313 (or 65%) received the royal assent. Initially, most private bills were admitted to the political process through the medium of the Irish privy council, but once the house of commons had asserted its primacy as the place of origin of Irish law, private bills increasingly took their rise as heads of private bills at that forum, in accordance with the requirements of Poynings' Law. While this meant that private bills were subject to the same close scrutiny that was accorded public bills at both the English/British and Irish privy councils, the fact that such bills sought to modify family settlements obliged both Houses of the Irish parliament and both councils to establish particular procedures that are at once revealing of the operation of these bodies, of the procedural innovations required to make private legislation, and of the privileged position it gave to the elite who could appeal to parliament. Indeed, though the manner in which private legislation was made changed with legislative independence, private bills continued to be authorised by the Irish parliament until the Act of Union.

Keywords: Irish parliament; procedure; private bills; transmisses; Poynings' Law; petitions; Irish bills committee; Irish privy council; English/British privy council

1

The enactment of private legislation was a function of the Irish parliament that is at once revealing of the operation of that legislature, of the centrality of Poynings' Law to the definition and management of the Anglo-Irish nexus between the inauguration of regular sessions of parliament in 1692 and its abolition in 1800, and of the financial and other private concerns of the Anglo-Irish elite to which recourse was made to parliament. As such, the fact that it has been all but ignored by historians of the Irish parliament may be perceived as a missed opportunity. This need no longer be the case. The availability of the Irish Legislation Database (ILD), assembled under the direction of David Hayton and the present author,[1] facilitates the analysis of Irish legislation, whilst publication, in the past decade, of studies of the membership and key aspects of

[1] ILD, which is available on the website of Queen's University, Belfast, is a product of The Irish Legislation Project, which was funded by the Leverhulme Trust and undertaken at the school of history and anthropology, Queen's University, Belfast, between 2004 and 2007. The principal investigator was David Hayton and the co-investigator, James Kelly.

Table 1: *Legislation of the Irish Parliament, 1692–1800*

Monarch	Public acts	Private acts	Total	Number of sessions	Average number of bills per session	Average number of private bills per session
William and Mary, 1692–4; William III 1695–9	62	23	85	3[1]	28.3	7.7
Anne 1703–13	87	42	129	7	18.4	6.0
George I 1715–26	95	36	131	6	21.8	6.0
George II 1727–59	325	58	383	17	22.5	3.4
George III 1761–82	415	73	488	13	37.5	5.6
George III 1783–1800	976	81	1057	18	58.7	4.5
Total	1960	313	2273	64	35.5	4.9

Note: [1] Calculated on the basis that the meetings of parliament held in 1695 and 1697 constitute one session.
Sources: *The Irish Statutes* (rev. edn, 1885); Irish Legislation Database (ILD).

the operation of that parliament has provided a secure context in which it can be located.[2]

Between 1692 and 1800, 313 private acts were approved by the Irish parliament. This constituted 13.8% of the total (see Table 1). However, because the average number of private bills enacted per session was less than five, and the regnal average oscillated between a high of 7.7 per session achieved during the reign of William and Mary (1689–1702) and a low of 3.4 during the reign of George II, one could be excused for concluding that private legislation was not only a statistically-minor but also peripheral element of that legislature's work. This certainly was the attitude of the compilers of the statutes at large of the Irish parliament, since they confined what is commonly perceived as the definitive edition of the legislation of the Irish parliament to public statutes, and other, more selective editions that have ensued, have followed their lead.[3] Since private acts, by definition, appertain to the concerns of individuals and their families rather than the general public, the prioritisation of public statutes possessed an obvious rationale. I

[2] See Charles Ivar McGrath, *The Making of the Eighteenth-Century Irish Constitution: Government, Parliament and the Revenue, 1692–1714* (Dublin, 2000); *The Irish Parliament in the Eighteenth Century: The Long Apprenticeship*, ed. D.W. Hayton (Edinburgh, 2001); Edith Mary Johnston-Liik, *History of the Irish Parliament 1692–1800* (6 vols, Belfast, 2002); James Kelly, *Poynings' Law and the Making of Law in Ireland, 1660–1800* (Dublin, 2007); *The Eighteenth-Century Composite State: Representative Institutions in Ireland and Europe, 1689–1800*, ed. D.W. Hayton, James Kelly and John Bergin (Basingstoke, 2010).

[3] *The Statutes at Large Passed in the Parliaments Held in Ireland, 1310–1800* (20 vols, Dublin, 1789–1800); *Statutes Passed in the Parliaments Held in Ireland* (12 vols, Dublin, 1794–1801); *The Irish Statutes* (rev. edn, 1885).

was also influenced by the fact that the Irish edition followed the British precedent.[4] Yet there is a contrary perspective to which one can appeal in favour of a more inclusive approach. Private bills were an integral aspect of the business of parliament and were regarded as such by peers and MPs, and scrutinised no differently by the judges and law officers in both kingdoms who were charged with ensuring that all legislation was properly drawn, legally correct, and fair and reasonable in its provisions. Moreover, the proportion of such measures to receive the royal assent between 1703 and 1800 (68%) did not greatly exceed the percentage of public bills (58%) that did likewise. The fact that the number of private bills admitted to the statute book per session ranged from zero to 14, and that private bills took their rise variously in the Irish privy council, in the house of commons, and in the house of lords, also means that they are a useful measure of the relative weights of these three bodies in the making of Irish law across the 18th century and, with the English/British privy council, of their impact on the Irish statute book. In addition, because the regulations and procedures that applied to private bills were subject to periodic revision, they possess a particular history that ought not to be elided because the compilers of the most commonly-resorted-to edition of the statutes of the Irish parliament did not deem them worthy of inclusion.

2. *Establishing a Pattern: Private Bills in the Irish Parliament, 1691–1714*

Though the first meeting of the Irish parliament convened after the Williamites's triumph over the forces of James II lasted for less than a calendar month and added a mere four acts (all public) to the statute book, the fact that three of the 25 putative measures initiated in the lead-up to, and during, that short session were private bills is noteworthy.[5] It is still more so since one of these measures, whose purpose was to secure the protestant creditors of John Browne, embarked on the long odyssey that was to culminate in the royal assent in 1695 as a 'clause' in a (public) bill 'relating to the lawyers and physicians who are within the benefit of the Articles of Galway'. This bill was not deemed appropriate to become law (because it was incompatible with a relevant act approved at Westminster) when the measure was scrutinised at the English privy council, pursuant to the 1494 enactment – 'An act that no parliament be holden in this land until the acts be certified into England' (or 'Poynings' Law') – which, as it was then applied and interpreted, provided that all legislation presented for ratification by the Irish parliament must first be approved at the Irish and English council boards.[6] Curiously, in the light of the concerns they were later to express on this very point, officials were untroubled by the presence of a private clause in a public bill, as they made clear by recommending that the clause should be 'inserted in another act as you shall judge proper'. However, their intervention obliged the Irish council to reconsider how the matter might best be dealt with, and to conclude that Browne's 'protestant creditors' would be better served if the issue was addressed in a 'particular bill', which was

---

[4] Owen Ruffhead, *The statutes at large . . . of the parliament of England, afterwards of Great Britain from Magna Charta to the Union of Great Britain and Ireland* (18 vols, 1663–1800).

[5] See James I. McGuire, 'The Irish Parliament in 1692', in *Penal Era and Golden Age: Essays in Irish History, 1690–1800*, ed. D.W. Hayton and Thomas Bartlett (Belfast, 1979), 1–31.

[6] See Kelly, *Poynings' Law, passim*, esp. ch. 1.

prepared and forwarded to London in late September 1692. Though it is apparent from the lord lieutenant's earnest request that the new bill should be returned promptly that the Irish executive's priority was to appease the 'considerable number of the Protestants of this kingdom, who are concerned therein', rather than establish a rule that private matters should be reserved for private bills, this is what it did. The distinction between what was public and private was not rigidly drawn from this point, but it did make it clear that there was a material difference that legislators ought to observe.[7]

This is not to suggest that the Irish parliament had not previously engaged with what were manifestly private matters or approved legislation that fits this definition. At least eight of the 54 enactments authorised by the so-called 'Restoration parliament', which met in Dublin over five sessions between 1661 and 1666, were designated private, but the distinction between public and private bills was far from clearly drawn, and a number of what were denominated public bills might equally have been categorised as private.[8] If, as this implies, there was some ambiguity in the 1660s as to what constituted a private bill, the fact that measures of this ilk were obliged to negotiate the same hurdles as bills that were explicitly and unambiguously public was a tangible indication of the resolve of all parties in the making of Irish law to ensure that they were subject to equivalent processes and procedures.[9] This resolve was further evidenced by the manner in which the three private bills initiated in 1692 were proceeded with, though the early prorogation of the session ensured that MPs and peers dispersed before a developed procedure for private bills could be put in place.[10]

This was, to be sure, a relatively minor matter at the time, since the failure of the Irish parliament in 1692 to live up to the expectations of officials and representatives on both sides of the Irish Sea might have meant that this embryonic experiment in parliamentary government was still born if the king and his advisors could have raised the money required to pay for the government of Ireland and to finance the army by other means. But impelled by financial necessity and by a belief in the merits of a constitutional monarchy, which was echoed by those Irish protestants who were adamant that they were entitled to the same constitutional and political rights as English subjects of the crown, they were persuaded by the lord deputy, Henry, Baron Capell (1638–96), of the wisdom of a 'compromise' which would allow them a direct input into the making of Irish law in return for their approval of financial legislation. This 'compromise' necessitated a retreat by both Irish protestants, who were obliged in practice to ease up on their previous insistence that it was their 'sole right' to initiate financial legislation, and the crown-appointed Irish executive, backed by the government in London, which favoured an active application of Poynings' Law which must have meant, if it had continued to be employed in the manner in which it was invoked in the run-up to the 1692 session, that the Irish parliament would have been obliged to accede to a passive role in the making of law for the kingdom of Ireland.

---

[7] *CSPD, 1692*, pp. 199, 208: Sydney to Nottingham, 9, 29 Sept. 1692; TNA, SP67/1, f. 216: Nottingham to Sydney, 13 Sept. 1692.

[8] For a detailed engagement with the legislative history of the Restoration parliament, see Kelly, *Poynings' Law*, ch. 1.

[9] Kelly, *Poynings' Law*, 33.

[10] See, e.g., TNA, PC2/75, ff. 6–7, 21; *CSPD, 1691–2*, p. 478.

Instead, the compromise reached in 1695 permitted both Houses of the Irish parliament, but specifically the Commons, to assume an active role in the initiation of legislation through the medium of 'heads of bills'[11] in return for their approval of financial legislation that provided the Irish administration with sufficient funds to govern the kingdom.[12] It was a mutually-beneficial solution that paved the way for the assumption by the house of commons of the initiative in the making of Irish law, and its emergence, following the precedent established at Westminster, as the primary locus of law-making authority. This was a prolonged process extending over a number of decades, as a result of which the Irish legislature not only took the lead in the initiation of the crucial money bills, but also contrived to reduce the privy council's role in the initiation of legislation to no more than symbolic proportion.[13] The manner in which private legislation was implemented followed logically, and inevitably, the same pattern, and it is equally revealing, *mutatis mutandis*, of the same trends and tendencies. However, it was also possessed of its own particular significance, since it provided the elite, who perceived a private act as the optimal way to resolve certain familial, financial and personal difficulties, with the opportunity to pursue a bespoke solution in their own legislature. It was certainly more convenient and (generally) less costly than the most obvious alternative, which some of the better connected or more politically compromised pursued, of seeking a private act of parliament at Westminster, and more advantageous than pursuing a case through the courts, either because the point at issue was not suitable to a judicial resolution or because a favourable outcome was less assured.[14]

In keeping with the spirit of the compromise of 1695, the volume of legislation, both public and private, that was proffered for ratification in 1695 and when the session resumed in 1697, was greatly in excess of that suggested three years earlier. Indeed, it exceeded the capacity not only of the legislature to deal with, but also of the English privy council to process. Matters were not assisted, to be sure, by the lack of procedural specificity manifest in the faintly *ad hoc* manner in which the privy council referred bills to its law officers (primarily the attorney general) for consideration. The law officers were instructed on occasion to report 'with all convenient speed', but these words were uttered in hope rather than confident anticipation, and the system did not always produce the expeditious outcome that was desired. This may be attributed, in part at least, to the absence of a designated committee to oversee the management of Irish bills, but the failure to require a written report in respect of each and every bill, and to record both its receipt and content in the minutes of the council, is emblematical of the lack

[11] Heads of bills were fully drafted measures, which required the authorisation of both the Irish and English/British privy councils before they could be presented as bills to the Irish parliament for approval, whereupon they received the royal assent, or rejection: see Kelly, *Poynings' Law*, chs 1 and 2, for the evolution of the heads of bills process.

[12] McGrath, *The Making of the Eighteenth-Century Irish Constitution*, ch. 3; C.I. McGrath, *Ireland and Empire, 1692–1770* (2012), part 2.

[13] Kelly, *Poynings' Law*, 126–33, 204–09; C.I. McGrath, 'Central Aspects of the Eighteenth-Century Constitutional Framework in Ireland: The Government Supply Bill and Biennial Parliamentary Sessions, 1715–82', *Eighteenth-Century Ireland*, xvi (2001), 9–34.

[14] See John Bergin, 'Irish Private Divorce Bills and Acts of the Eighteenth Century', in *People, Politics and Power: Essays on Irish History 1660–1850 in Honour of James I. McGuire*, ed. James Kelly, John McCafferty and Charles Ivar McGrath (Dublin, 2009), 94–121.

of bureaucratic formality that then obtained.[15] These procedural and administrative deficiencies contributed to the fact that only a fraction of the private bills forwarded from Ireland in 1695 made it to the statute book that year, and that as many as ten, which were then designated as 'depending', lay unreported when preparations commenced for the resumption of the session in 1697.[16] However, matters improved significantly in 1697, and while there were still obvious administrative weaknesses, the system worked sufficiently well not only to ensure that those outstanding bills transmitted in 1695, but also the substantial additional transmisses of private bills conveyed in 1697, were processed satisfactorily. It is difficult, because of the embryonic nature of certain procedures, and because so many private bills and heads of bills that had their rise in 1695 were not proceeded with until 1697, to provide a clear statistical perspective on the fortunes of private legislation at this formative moment. However, if we treat the meetings of parliament in 1695 and 1697 as one session, as we are entitled to do, it is apparent from the number of private measures that were initiated, and the number enacted, that the mid 1690s firmly established private acts as a distinct, definable category of Irish legislation, and as a real option for those members of the elite seeking a way out of complex financial and familial problems.

In all, 40 private bills were initiated in Ireland in the course of the overlapping 1695 and 1697 sessions. The number was high because a striking proportion, such as the Jephson Act ratified in 1697, or the act for 'securing the debts owing to the Protestant creditors of Colonel John Browne' ratified in 1695, were prompted by problems 'contracted in the late troubles'.[17] Significantly, and illustrative of the elevation of the house of commons as a source of legislation following the 1695 'compromise', they took their rise almost equally in the privy council (21), which had previously assumed that this was its function, and in the Irish house of commons (19). Because it possessed the authority to prepare and to forward bills, and to amend and to respite bills received from both Houses of the legislature, the privy council exercised great influence in the making of legislation, and private legislation in particular, but it is not possible, in the absence of pertinent records,[18] to establish the manner in which it went about this task, the total number of measures it considered, and the proportion it deemed suitable to forward. It was, as mentioned above, responsible for a majority (52.5%) of the private bills initiated in Ireland in the mid 1690s, and it underlined its ascendancy by respiting the heads of two private bills forwarded from the house of commons. This is in keeping with the impression it cultivated that it closely scrutinised legislation forwarded from both houses of parliament, and amended and respited heads of bills as it deemed appropriate.

In any event, an unprecedented 37 private measures, with an accompanying letter briefly explaining their purpose and purport, and the view of the Irish administration, were received at the English council board in the course of 1695 and 1697. Since the power to scrutinise (and if necessary to veto and amend as required) Irish bills was

---

[15] Kelly, *Poynings' Law*, 79–94.

[16] TNA, PC2/77, f. 6.

[17] 7 Will. III, c. 2 (Browne Act); 9 Will. III, c. 5 (Jephson Act).

[18] The relevant records were destroyed in a fire in 1711.

[19] *CSPD, 1697*, p. 279; HMC, *Buccleuch MSS*, ii, 517: Galway to Shrewsbury, 3 Aug. 1697.

the key power provided by Poynings' Law 'to keep that kingdom dependent upon the crown of England', members of the English council were equally conscious not only that theirs was an important role, but also that it placed them under an obligation to ensure that no bill was returned to Ireland for ratification until it had been thoroughly examined and formally approved.[20] The size and unfamiliarity of the task may have been factors in explaining why Irish bills were not always processed with optimal efficiency in the mid 1690s, but the council's procedures were sufficiently administratively robust to ensure that no bill that had not previously been subject to thorough scrutiny was sent for engrossment and to pass under the great seal, in order that it might be returned to Ireland with a commission authorising the lord lieutenant, lord deputy or lords justices to grant the royal assent, should it negotiate both Houses of the Irish parliament.[21] What this meant in practice was that any political, commercial, legal or administrative feature of a bill to which exception was taken, or any factual or drafting error that was detected, was amended or deleted. In cases in which the transgression was more serious, or the bill was judged seriously defective or deficient on other grounds, it was ordered to be respited and not returned.[22] Because private bills engaged in a large proportion of instances with issues of succession, inheritance rights, family settlements, divorce and allied matters, the range of identifiable concerns raised with respect to such legislation was narrower than was the case with public bills. As a result, a larger percentage of private than public bills was returned to Ireland, but the fact that nine (or 24%) of the 37 private bills received in 1695–7 were either not reported or formally respited offers the most compelling evidence that private bills were subject to equivalently close scrutiny. Indicatively, only eight bills (22%) were authorised to proceed without amendment, while the largest category, comprising 20 measures (54% of the total), were approved with amendments. The nature of the amendments varied greatly. A substantial proportion were syntactical corrections, which were introduced to correct minor errors. They were equalled by the requirement for technical amendments, such as arose when a bill was delayed, to accommodate a different date of implementation, or some such matter. However, a large number of bills required substantial amendment, either because they were transmitted in a defective condition or, and this was more likely, because, in their eagerness to address a particular problem, they advanced a partial, or partisan, solution to which objection was made by other parties.

Though there was provision in the rules of both Houses of the Irish parliament, and in the procedures employed by the Irish privy council, to receive and hear petitions from interested parties, there is little evidence to suggest that this tactic was resorted to with any frequency, if at all, in the 1690s. By contrast, it was resorted to frequently and successfully at the English council board. The first identified instance dates from the autumn of 1692, when a number of Irish catholics resident in England petitioned the privy council 'on behalf of themselves and the rest of their majesties subjects of that persuasion'. Their primary focus was a public bill – a bill of indemnity – but they were equally bothered by the presence in the 'lawyers of Galway' measure of the provision for

---

[20] TNA, SP67/3, ff. 200–1: Sunderland to Wharton, 12 June 1709; *The Marlborough-Godolphin Correspondence*, ed. H.L. Synder (3 vols, Oxford, 1975), iii, 134–6: Godolphin to Marlborough, [16 Aug. 1709].

[21] For an example of this instruction in the case of the Ormesby Bill, see TNA, PC2/76, f. 323.

[22] See Kelly, *Poynings' Law*, 81–5, 140–52, 210–36, for a full discussion of this process.

the protestant creditors of John Browne 'whereby severall of the said Roman Catholiques estates are charged with a great sum of money'. In order that they might prepare their case, they requested 'copies of the said bills and reasonable time by the aid of council to make their necessary observations', which was agreed.[23] This was an important concession, albeit one that was consistent with the council's *modus operandi*, since it provided petitioners with an opportunity, not then always provided in Ireland, to make clear their reservations with individual measures.

Though it was perhaps inevitable, given the ratio of public to private bills, that more petitions were presented by institutions and organisations in respect of public than private bills, individuals were equally entitled to do so, and they did not hesitate to take this step in those instances in which they perceived that a private enactment pursued by a family member or relation was misjudged or unjust. The first case of this kind occurred in the spring of 1693, when Francis Stafford of Portclone, County Antrim, petitioned the council to be heard against a bill presented on behalf of his son, Edmund, who sought to protect his right of inheritance by restraining his father from making provision for his (second) wife and eight children. It was not an untypical family difference, and the council board set an important precedent when it acceded to the petitioner's request to hear counsel on his behalf. Since parliament was not then in session, the matter was not proceeded with at this point, with the result that it had to be revisited in 1695 when a new bill was presented. Once again family concerns were high, and a further important precedent was established when, on foot of another petition from Francis Stafford, both he and his son were invited to meet with the attorney general, and provided with a copy of the bill so that he (Francis) could isolate the key issues. The resulting meeting seems to have served a useful purpose, as a slightly amended bill was forwarded thereafter to make its way onto the statute book.[24] It was one of eight instances in which petitions were presented at the English council and, as it turned out, one of the more straightforward. It was certainly less replete with political implications than the petition presented by Colonel Thomas Dongan and three others also in 1695, 'humbly praying that a saving clause of their rights may be inserted in the bill lately sent from Ireland for confirming his majesty's grant to [Godard van Reede] the Earl of Athlone'. The eminence of the parties may have contributed to the keen interest taken in the case, but it did not determine the outcome. The petitioners were given a copy of the bill and afforded an opportunity to present their case in person, as a result of which an additional clause was introduced into the bill safeguarding Thomas Dongan's entitlement to pursue his claim to the estate of William Dongan (1630–98), the first earl of Limerick, who had been attainted for jacobitism in 1691.[25] This was a striking outcome, since it exemplified the commitment, manifest in the response to other petitions, both to be seen to do right by those who felt they had a demonstrable grievance, and to ensure that the legislation that was returned to Ireland was properly

---

[23] TNA, PC2/75, ff. 6–7, 8.

[24] ILD; TNA, PC2/76, ff. 117, 120, 123, 135; 7 Will. III, c. 4.

[25] TNA, PC2/76, ff. 117, 125, 134–5; BL, Trumbull Papers, Add. MS 72566 (unfoliated): Trumbull notes on privy council meeting, 24 Oct. 1695; privy council memoranda 1660–1708, Add. MS 35707, 21–4: notes and minutes of evidence on behalf of Colonel Dongan, 31 Oct. 1695; 7 Will. III, c. 3.

drafted and equitable in its terms and provisions.[26] This did not always mean that bills against which petitions were presented were appropriately amended and ushered forward to become law. Measures for the relief of Dame Ann Yolanda Sera Court and Anna Margaretta Wall, which met with strong resistance by various members of the Wall family, and for the relief of Charles Lambart, third earl of Cavan, and 'his family against fraudulent purchasers', were respited in 1695 at least in part because of the strength of the case that the petitioners presented.[27]

Such experiences, and the realization that private acts could, if not fairly, carefully and accurately crafted, disadvantage individuals with genuine interests, also encouraged the inclusion, when appropriate, of a 'saving clause' whose purpose was to safeguard the interest of other parties who were not explicitly mentioned in the bill. In the case of the Jephson Bill, the discovery in the course of the hearings prompted by the presentation of a petition by Jephson's agent that both William Jephson and his wife were alive (when the contrary had been assumed) prompted the English privy council to authorise a sweeping saving clause, which ran as follows:

> Provided also that nothing in this act conteyned shall any waies prejudice the right, title, interest, claim or demand of any person or persons whatsoever to the above mentioned premises, or any part thereof, other than the persons who derive their right, title or interest by or from the above mentioned settlement, anything herein conteyned to the contrary notwithstanding.[28]

Because of the obvious usefulness of a saving clause in safeguarding the rights of parties who were either unaware of proceedings or whose material interests might be affected thereby, the Irish parliament sought to insist on the inclusion of such a clause in private measures where and when appropriate. The Irish position on this matter was made explicit in 1697 when the executive 'sent back' a bill that *inter alia*, sought to confirm 'several grants' of land to the former lord lieutenant, Henry Sydney, earl of Romney, on the grounds 'that there is no saving therein for the legall right of any person that might be thereby prejudiced'.[29] Further amendments were made to the bill on foot of this request but, despite the addition of an explicit saving clause, it was never presented to parliament.[30] Though it may reasonably be assumed that considerations other than the wording of the 'saving clause' were responsible for the loss of this bill, the absence of an appropriate clause was a matter upon which Irish sensitivities remained acute, and the rejection in 1699 of a measure empowering William O'Brien, third earl of Inchiquin,

---

[26] Petitions were presented and appropriate amendments introduced into the Waller Bill (7 Will. III, c. 6; TNA, PC2/76, ff. 126–7, 135); the Jephson Bill (9 Will. III, c. 5; TNA, PC2/76, ff. 126–7; PC2/77, ff. 6, 10, 15–6); the Delamer Bill (9 Will. III, c. 6; TNA, PC2/76, ff. 126–7, 130; PC2/77, ff. 6, 21–2).

[27] ILD; TNA, PC2/76, ff. 126–7, 130 (Court and Wall Bill); PC2/76, ff. 138, 144; PC2/77, ff. 6, 10.

[28] TNA, PC2/77, ff. 10, 15–16.

[29] NAI, May-Blathwayt correspondence, 1697–8, MS 3070; May to Blathwayt, 6 Nov. 1697.

[30] TNA, PC2/77, ff. 65–6; NAI, May-Blathwayt correspondence, 1697–8, MS 3070: May to Blathwayt, Dec. 1697.

to make leases for lives 'because there was no general saving in it' is evidence that the commitment to ensure that private bills were drafted in a manner that was fair was shared on both sides of the Irish Sea.[31]

The rejection in Ireland of the Inchiquin private bill demonstrated that, even when a measure had negotiated the testing hurdle that was the English privy council, and returned to Ireland, its enactment was not guaranteed. A total of 34 private bills (or 72% of the total) were passed under the great seal and returned to Ireland as appropriate to receive the royal assent in the 1690s. A striking 32% (11 bills) of those returned did not make it to the statute book and, while their number is somewhat inflated by the fact that the prorogation of the 1692 session ensured that no private bill was presented to the Irish parliament for approval, the fact that eight (out of 28) or 29% failed in 1695–7 and two of five (40%) failed in 1698–9, is a measure of the stern test that awaited certain bills on their return. Moreover, there was no single cause, for while the Irish authorities chose, or were obliged by reason of the prorogation, in 1692 not to present three bills, five of the remainder were formally rejected by the house of commons and three by the house of lords.

Though the manner in which private bills were processed in the 1690s and the procedural and administrative innovations that were made both contributed to the greater regularity that one can identify in the way in which both private and public law was made as the 17th century drew to a close, it would be wrong to give the impression that this was a story only of achievement. There were embarrassing failures also, notably in 1695 when three bills (two private and one public) that were retransmitted from the English council board were inadvertently 'lost' in the chief secretary's office. No satisfactory explanation was ever forthcoming as to how this happened (other than a vague reference to 'misfortune'), but it obliged the lord justices at the head of the Irish administration to swallow their pride and appeal to the English council board that 'the same may be reingrossed and passed under the great seal in order to their being retransmitted to Ireland'.[32] Both bills finally made it into the statute book in 1697, two years later than they might have ordinarily, but this was of less consequence than the administrative deficiencies the episode revealed. They might have been still more visible. Adverting to Irish administrative practices in the context of the missing bills, the lord chancellor, John Methuen, expressed no surprise because, he observed, 'everything here is in the same manner'.[33]

Another error, this time perpetrated at the English council board, occurred in respect of the Barry Bill, which was returned to Ireland in 1695 with a 'small mistake' that was not identified until the bill was presented to the house of lords. Unable to introduce a correction, because of prohibition on the Irish parliament amending bills that had passed under the great seal, it was necessary to reject the bill, and prepare a new, corrected version which made its way promptly through all stages. This, too, was awkward, but there was no recrimination because officials and politicians on both sides of the Irish Sea

---

[31] TCD, King Papers, MS 750/2/1, f. 64: King to Annesley, 2 Feb. 1699; TNA, PC2/77, ff. 128–9.

[32] TNA, PC2/77, ff. 37–8. The bills at issue were the Ponsonby Settlement Bill (9 Will. III, c. 8) and the Eustace Bill (9 Will. III, c. 12).

[33] *CSPD, 1697*, p. 283: Methuen to Vernon, 3 Aug. 1697.

were disposed to be realistic and to address, rather than to exploit such lapses for partisan purposes.[34] However, there were those who felt that more could be done to streamline the manner in which private bills were initiated and progressed. The secretary of state for the southern department, the duke of Shrewsbury, suggested in 1697 that matters would be improved if those who pursued the private legislation route were required to observe 'the ancient custom . . . to first petition the King in Council for leave to offer such a bill'. The wisdom of proceeding in this manner, Shrewsbury advised, was that 'by this means time is given to all parties to apply, and not to be too surprised by too hasty proceedings'. The secretary of state acknowledged that there was little to be gained thereby if no private bill was proceeded with at the Irish council 'without first hearing all the parties concerned', but since this was not Irish practice at this point, and the 'ancient custom' to which reference was made had never obtained in Ireland, the point was moot. An instruction was subsequently issued that parties 'desiring a private bill here must first make application in England', but this was not taken up, and matters were left in this essentially unsatisfactory situation.[35]

Moreover, in so far as the weight of Irish protestant opinion was concerned, this was an intrinsically-peripheral issue by comparison with the major grievance that was Poynings' Law. One of the sharpest critics of the restraints under which the Irish parliament functioned, Archbishop William King, made an acerbic observation in 1689 that the business of the Irish parliament 'is not to make good laws, but to hinder ill ones [since this] is all that is left to us by Poinings Act'; this statement pithily encapsulated the resentment that was felt by some in Ireland at the manner in which the legislature was required to share its authority to make law with the Irish and English privy councils.[36] Such sentiment was largely kept in check during the mid 1690s, when the majority of the 23 private bills that received the royal assent during the reign of William III were being addressed, and when the process of law-making assumed a definable and effective form. The fact that such opinions were more visible during the 1698–9 session had more to do with the fallout and ill feeling generated by the decision of the Westminster parliament to confine Ireland's right to export woollen cloth than with the specific procedures that were developed to ensure that the legislative deliberations of the Irish parliament were kept within familiar bounds.[37] Yet one cannot simply dismiss the expressions of irritation as emotional or ill-informed, and it was, thus, probably fortuitous that it was not deemed necessary to convene an Irish parliament for the final years of William's reign (he died on 8 March 1702) or for more than four-and-a-half years following its adjournment on 26 January 1699, since it provided time for certain emotions to cool. As a result, when MPs and peers assembled in September 1703, for the first time in Queen Anne's reign, they did so with a more accepting attitude towards Poynings' Law, and the recognition that the heads of bill process provided them with

[34] TNA, PC2/76, ff. 126–7, 130, 135–6; PC2/77, ff. 27, 32; PC4/1, f. 253; ILD; TNA, SP63/359, f. 67; *JI*, i, 657; *CJI*, ii, 210; 9 Will. III, c. 13.

[35] TNA, SP67/2, ff. 88–9: Shrewsbury to lords justices of Ireland, 3 Aug. 1697; *CSPD, 1697*, p. 315: minutes of proceedings of the lords justices, 17 Aug. 1697.

[36] TCD, King Papers, MS 750/2/1, f. 59: King to Annesley, 2 Feb. 1699.

[37] For the politics of the Woollen Act, see Patrick Kelly, 'The Irish Woollen Export Prohibition Act of 1699: Kearney Revisited', *Irish Economic and Social History*, vii (1980), 22–44.

an opportunity to play an active part in the making of law, of which the entitlement to propose private bills was a significant aspect.

By comparison with the formative environment of the 1690s, when the task of devising a workable procedure was both a challenge – and an achievement – of some measure, the enactment of private bill legislation during the 12 years that Anne was on the throne, 1702–14, was pursued in a more structured fashion. This can be attributed, in the first instance, to the fact that the *modus operandi* developed in the 1690s was essentially solidly grounded. It was not that it was beyond improvement, and that refinements were not made. The inauguration, in 1709, of an Irish bills committee to manage and oversee the administration of Irish legislation at the British council board was of particular consequence in regularising the way that Irish bills were addressed at that forum. It certainly ensured that the transmisses of bills received from Ireland thereafter were dealt with efficiently and expeditiously, which was a tangible improvement on the situation that had obtained in the mid 1690s.[38] It was also a logical procedural development on the fact that, prior to the emergence of the Irish bills committee, the reign of Anne had witnessed the effective cessation of the practice (common in the 1690s) of not formally reporting on bills that were deemed unsuitable.[39]

Second, the assumption by the Irish parliament, and specifically of the house of commons, of the dominant role in the initiation of private bills (57% rose there as against 39% at the privy council and 4% in the house of lords, in the decade 1703–13), meant not only that a higher proportion of measures took the form of heads of bills, but also that a higher proportion of what were, one may plausibly assume, less than clearly worked out or defective proposals, were not allowed to proceed. The evidence for this is statistical; more than four times the number of heads of private bills that took their rise with MPs and peers during the reign of Anne did not proceed to the privy council, compared with the number that fell at this hurdle in the 1690s (Table 2). Moreover, in an implicit acknowledgement that the concerns expressed at Whitehall in the 1690s at the limitations of Irish procedural practices were not without foundation, the Irish house of commons had greater recourse to the provision, employed occasionally in the 1690s, of requiring those seeking the protection offered by a private bill to petition parliament for leave to present, and of referring the petition to a committee of MPs for a report before authorisation was forthcoming.[40] In addition, both petitions from, and requests to be heard by, interested parties were acceded to and sent to committees for consideration, which also provided an opportunity to correct weaknesses and errors in private bills.[41] As a result, during the reign of Anne, some 40% of heads of private bills that were proposed and presented failed to proceed out of the legislature, and in 18% of cases for

---

[38] Kelly, *Poynings' Law*, 138–43.

[39] E.g., the Wall Bill and the Power Bill, 1703–4 (TNA, PC2/79, ff. 484–7); Gormanston Bill, 1707 (TNA, PC2/81, f. 442). The language employed to indicate that a bill was not to proceed varied. It was signalled by the employment of the term 'rejected' in 1703–4 and 1707; 'refused' in 1705; 'layd (or "laid" aside' in 1709 and 1710; and by recourse to the phrases the 'advice . . . is not to pass the bill' or the bill was 'not fitt for her majesty's approbation' in 1709, 1710 and 1711 (TNA, PC2/80, ff. 49, 55, 361; PC2/81, f. 453; PC2/82, ff. 350, 397; PC2/83, f. 36).

[40] *CJI*, ii, 75, 114, 438, 440, 450, 452; iii, 62. For later examples, indicating that this practice continued see *CJI*, iii, 271, 283, 359; iv, 175, 489; vi, 163; vii, 250, 253, 254, 272; viii, 78; x, 332; xi, 127.

[41] *CJI*, ii, 75, 114, 438, and for examples outside the reign of Anne, *CJI*, iii, 60, 279, 191.

Table 2: The Private Bill Legislation of the Irish Parliament, 1692–1800

	Ireland							England						Ireland			
	Origin of (heads of) bills			Lost heads of bills/bills				Privy council bills and heads of bills at the privy council						Bills at the Irish parliament			
				House of commons											Rejected		
Years	Privy council bills	House of commons	House of lords	Leave only	Rejected	House of lords	Privy council	Received	Respited[1]/ postponed	Amendments	No amendments	Petitions against	Approved	Not re-presented	House of commons	House of lords	Receive royal assent
1692–9	32	24	–	4	1	–	2	49	15	23	12	14	34	3	5	3	23
1703–13	35	52	4	10	10	2	2	67	18	36	13	8	49	1	6	–	42
1715–26	9	42	7	5	1	1	8	43	6	33	4	5	37	–	1	–	36
1727–60	6	61	14	1	4	–	6	70	12	46	12	6	58	–	–	–	58
1761–82	–	90	11	5	5	–	13	78	4	27	47	2	74	–	1	–	73
1783–1800	–	24	74	–	2	15	–	81	–	6[2]	–	1	81	–	–	–	81
Total	82	293	110	25	23	18	31	388	55	171	88	36	333	4	13	3	313

Notes: [1] Theoretically, objectionable or poorly-drafted bills transmitted from Ireland were not vetoed but respited (i.e., postponed for further consideration) at the privy council board; in practice very few were ever afforded a reconsideration unless transmitted anew.
[2] As a result of the amendment of Poynings' Law in 1782, the British privy council did not possess the entitlement to amend legislation received from Ireland, but it could, and did, register reservations with bills that were ill-drawn; these bills are included under this heading.
Sources: TNA, privy council registers, PC2/1; privy council papers, PC1; CJI; LJI: Irish Legislation Database (ILD).

which leave was given a bill did not materialise.[42] This also served to ensure that the number of heads of private bills arising in either the Commons or the Lords that failed to negotiate the Irish privy council remained low (less than 4%) (Table 2).

In common with the English council and the Irish parliament, the Irish privy council may also have engaged in procedural reforms, with equivalently-beneficial consequences, though the archival problems previously referred to continue to obscure the workings of that body. Be that as it may, it may be significant that when James Stopford, the MP for Wexford, was frustrated by the rejection (at the English council board) of his initial attempt in July 1703 to vest 'certain lands and hereditaments' in trustees in order that they might be sold for the payment of debts, he appealed to his political connections, which enabled him to push a revised measure through the Irish council and personally to present 'full answers to the objections' that were raised. This was unusual, but it worked to Stopford's advantage, for though his bill was extensively amended at the English council board, its passage into law was not further delayed.[43]

If the increase by one-third in the number of private bills transmitted from Ireland to the English (from 1707 British) privy council during the reign of Anne is consistent with the conclusion that procedural improvements introduced in Ireland had positive consequences for the manner in which private bills were prepared, this assessment receives further support from that fact that the scale and extent of amendments made to Irish bills at that forum during the reign of Anne was less than that made in the 1690s. Significantly, the percentage of private bills that were amended (54%) was significantly less than the percentage of public bills (69%) that were subject to modification.[44] This did not mean that bills, such as that 'for the relief of Charles Plunkett' (1709),[45] or the 1710 measure to remedy deficiencies in the bill providing for the payment of the debts of the duke of Ormond, were not subject to major redrafting; the alterations required in the case of the Ormond Bill extended over 25 elephant folios and necessitated the rewriting of the vast majority of the bill.[46] This was exceptional, to be sure, but in common with the readiness to approve alterations to bills in those instances in which petitioners proved their case, it attested to the continuing commitment to ensure that legislation was as fairly and properly drawn as circumstances permitted.[47] It also guaranteed that there was no relaxation in the readiness of councillors to respite those bills that were deemed inappropriate. Indeed, the percentage of private bills lost at the English/British council board (27%) was nearly double the percentage of public bills (15%).[48]

These percentages are high, and consistent with the conclusion that the English/British council maintained a strongly-interventionist attitude to Irish legislation. Yet they are only marginally different from those produced in the 1690s and that were to be sustained for many decades thereafter. Moreover, the determination of the law officers

---

[42] See Table 2; *CJI*, ii, 359, 363, 403.

[43] ILD; TNA, PC2/79, ff. 413, 470, 477–8; *CSPD, 1703–4*, p. 142: Ormonde to Nottingham, 2 Oct 1703; *CJI*, ii, 393, 394, 395, 397, 406, 414.

[44] Figures are calculated from Table 2 and Kelly, *Poynings' Law*, 146.

[45] TNA, PC2/82, f. 366; 8 Anne, c. 5.

[46] *LJI*, ii, 349; TNA, PC2/83, ff. 50–76; *CJI*, ii, 679, 680, 685.

[47] See Kelly, *Poynings' Law*, 151–2.

[48] Figures are calculated from Table 2 and Kelly, *Poynings' Law*, 145.

and, following their lead, of the minority of active councillors, to be seen to perform their responsibilities diligently did not falter. Indeed, there is evidence to suggest that prejudice and partisan sentiment was more visible in respect of private bills in Ireland than it was in England. It was certainly manifest in the Irish parliament in 1703–4 when a total of six bills (or half the total during the whole reign) were denied the royal assent. Indicatively, they included a bill for the reversal of the outlawry of Walter Butler, which was rejected because, Edward Southwell noted, MPs 'had no mind to encourage anyone bred up in arms in foreign service'.[49] Such manifestations of partisanship notwithstanding, the number of private bills admitted to the statute book during the reign of Anne (42) was almost double what it had been in the 1690s (23). A significantly larger proportion of private as opposed to public bills continued to take their rise at the privy council (an average of 4–5 per session), but the fact that the percentage emanating from that forum had fallen to 39% (down from 57% during the 1690s) was in keeping with the broader trend, which was that the house of commons continued to consolidate its dominant position in the Irish legislative triad of Commons, Lords and privy council (Table 2). It also confirmed that private legislation was a distinct, and significant, aspect of the legislation of the Irish parliament.

3. Making Private Legislation, 1715–82

The successful inauguration of the Hanoverian dynasty in 1714 ensured that the ratification of private legislation between the assembly of the first parliament of the Georgian era in November 1715 and the achievement of legislative independence in 1782 followed the pattern established during the preceding two reigns. The most obvious manifestation of this is that the average number of private bills per session approved during the reign of George I remained at the level achieved during the reign of Anne (6). Both the number, and average, declined appreciably during the reign of George II, as the legacy of financial and other difficulties created by the crisis years of James II's reign was finally cleared and the country embarked on an era of economic growth that, for a time, prompted a reduced recourse to private legislation. However, there were always landed families with complex financial and dynastic problems seeking legislative resolution and the growth of the economy gave rise to new issues, in the banking sector particularly, that did likewise. As a consequence, the number of private bills increased appreciably in the late 1750s. This was sustained through the 1760s and 1770s, with the result that the number of heads of private bills presented and private acts approved during the first 22 years of the reign of George III climbed back towards the sessional average of the reigns of Anne and George I (Table 1). In specific terms, this meant that the number of private bills proposed per session, which averaged 13.0 in the reign of Anne, fell to 9.7 in the reign of George I. It reached its nadir of 4.8 during the reign of George II, before climbing back to 7.8 during the early decades of George III's reign (Table 2).

---

[49] For the Burke Bill, see *LJI*, ii, 67; TNA, PC2/79, ff. 484–7, 497–507; *CJI*, ii, 402, 412. Other bills that may be placed in this category include the Conway Bill (TNA, PC2/80, f. 70).

Besides the decline in the number of private bill initiatives, the other striking change to private bill legislation to take place during the 18th century was the almost complete marginalisation of the Irish privy council as the place where private acts took their legislative rise. A modest nine private bills were forwarded from that body to the British privy council during the reign of George I; this fell to six during the reign of George II and none was forwarded during the reign of George III.[50] In keeping with the trend already underway, the house of commons consolidated its place as the preferred place in which to introduce private legislation with 72% of such measures during the reign of George I (up from 57% during the reign of Anne); and it subsequently reinforced its position as the jurisdiction of choice for private as well as public bills by giving leave to 75% during the reign of George II and an imposing 89% between 1761 and 1782.[51] With the effective eclipse of the privy council as a source of private bill legislation, a space was created for the house of lords, which admitted 12% (7) of primary bills during the reign of George I (up from 4.4% during the reign of Anne). This increased further to 17% (14) during the reign of George II and, while this percentage fell back during the eventful first two decades of the reign of George III, when the Lords admitted 11% (11) of the heads of private bills, the house of peers was, by then, firmly established as the only alternative to the house of commons for those who pursued private legislation (Table 2).

Though more than one-fifth of the heads of bills for which leave was sought in the Irish parliament between 1715 and 1782 either did not make it out of their House of origin (10%) or were respited at the Irish privy council (12%),[52] a total of 191 private measures were transmitted to the British council. Once received, they were promptly entrusted to the Irish bills committee, which invariably referred them to the crown's law officers to determine whether the measure was proper to proceed, or, if all was not in order, whether it should be respited or returned in an amended form. Significantly, the proportion of private bills that fell at this hurdle fell from more than a quarter, which was where it stood during the 1690s and the reign of Anne, to a less forbidding 11.5% (22) between 1715 and 1782. Indicatively, no private bill was respited during 23 of the 36 sessions of parliament convened during this time. Since this included 11 of the 13 sessions convened between 1761 and 1782, and the percentage of private bills respited during these years was a modest 5%, one can reasonably link the high success rate registered to the heightened resentment manifested in Ireland during the 1760s, 1770s and early 1780s with Poynings' Law.[53] It was not the only consideration, however, improvements in the drafting and processing of private bills must also be taken into account, as evidenced by the decline in the percentage of private measures subject to amendment at the British council board, which fell from 77% (33 in all) during the reign of George I to 66% (46 out of 70) during the reign of his successor. It is also notable that the number of bills that proceeded without amendment exceeded the number

---

[50] Kelly, *Poynings' Law*, Table 7, p. 242.

[51] Kelly, *Poynings' Law*, Table 7, p. 242.

[52] Of the private measures proposed in Ireland that were not forwarded to the British privy council, 45% did not emerge out of parliament, 55% were lost at the privy council.

[53] For the politics of Poynings' Law, see Kelly, *Poynings' Law*, 316–36.

respited by a factor of three[54] and that the number of petitions lodged against private bills also declined (Table 2).

The proportion of private bills subject to amendment manifested considerable variation, as these figures imply. The fact that it was well above the 50% level (which is where it stood between 1692 and 1715) during the reigns of George I and George II is consistent with the pattern identified for the 1690s, when the members of the English privy council who examined Irish private bills manifested their preparedness to use the power available to them to amend as well as to respite. Indeed, they played an important part in ensuring that Irish private acts were properly drafted, by detecting and correcting syntactical, orthographical, factual and legal errors. Similar concerns guided them in their engagement with petitioners, for though the number of petitions presented fell away over time, those petitioners who made a persuasive case could generally anticipate a positive response. Indicatively, four of the six private bills that failed to negotiate the British council during George I's reign, and seven of the 18 lost between 1715 and 1760, were subject to petitions presented by interested parties objecting to the bill at issue. Petitions were not always sufficient in, and of, themselves to prevent a bill proceeding, as instanced by the four petitions presented over two different sessions against a measure 'for the relief of the creditors of James Leathley' and others, in which it was alleged that they asserted claims against the estate of the controversial deputy vice-treasurer, Sir William Robinson, 'contrary to law'; however, in the latter instance, they raised sufficient doubt for the council to conclude that the bill was 'not fitt for . . . royall approbation'.[55] A similar judgment was arrived at in respect of a private bill 'to enable John Bingham . . . to pay his debts', which was the subject of a petition from Richard Fitzwilliam. In this instance, the absence 'both of certainty and proof' was sufficient to warrant the decision that the bill was 'not fit to be approved'.[56] The privy council was well capable of arriving at such judgments in the absence of a petition,[57] but they were more likely to do so when it was demonstrated that the material interests of spouses, children, siblings or other interested parties would be adversely affected, or where there was some doubt about the legality or *bona fides* of the facts on which a bill was based.[58] In such cases, the eagerness of councillors and the law officers to do nothing that could be construed in any way 'to barr the right of any person' without due and adequate compensation, or that might

---

[54] Sixty-three private bills (33%) were forwarded without amendment at the British privy council between 1715 and 1782 compared with the 22 respited during the same period (see Table 2).

[55] TNA, PC2/87, ff. 423, 438, 444–5, 471; PC2/88, ff. 391, 440, 446–7; SP63/382: Irish council letter, 22 Nov. 1723.

[56] TNA, PC2/88, ff. 375, 392, 411.

[57] TNA, PC2/88, ff. 416, 440, 446–7 (Kelly Bill); PC2/88, ff. 392, 440, 446–7 (Mervyn Bill); PC2/91, ff. 582, 595–6 (Moore Bill); PC2/92, ff. 347–8, 440; PC1/5/22–3: law officers' report, 2 Apr. 1734 (Maynard Bill); PC2/95, ff. 516, 639, 659 (Strafford Bill); PC2/99, ff. 423, 427, 437 (Fitzherbert Bill).

[58] See, e.g., TNA, PC2/88, ff. 375, 394; TCD, King Papers, MS 2537, ff. 41–2, 55: King to Southwell, 21 Dec. 1723, 11 Jan. 1724 (Henry King Bill); TNA, PC2/90, ff. 258, 288–9, 292; PC1/4/70: petition of William Knox, 4 Apr. 1728 (Fleming Bill); PC2/93, ff. 326, 338, 369–70 (Campbell Bill); PC2/100, ff. 545, 571–3; PC1/6/8, f. 4: law officers' report, 12 Mar. 1748 (Ashe Bill); PC2/100, ff. 545, 600–12; PC1/6/8, ff. 4–5: law officers' report, 12 Mar. 1748 (Cusack Bill).

be deemed to 'break into the general rules of property', was usually reason enough to precipitate the rejection of a measure.[59]

The scrutiny to which private bills were subject at both the Irish and British council boards was a significant factor in ensuring that only two of the 169 bills which were returned to Ireland, having passed under the great seal, did not receive the royal assent between 1715 and 1782. It also contributed handsomely to the fact that 70% of all private bill initiatives (167 out of 240) were approved (Table 2). This was a striking improvement on the 44% success rate registered between 1692 and 1714 and is a convincing illustration of the fact that, though labyrinthine, the heads of bill process worked efficiently in the case of private law from 1715.

While it is reasonable to ascribe these impressive statistics to the effectiveness of the administrative and procedural arrangements put in place between 1692 and 1714, due acknowledgment must also be made to the refinements that were introduced thereafter. None was of the order of the establishment of the Irish bills committee at the British council, but even minor improvements contributed in other ways to the efficient processing of such legislation and, by implication, to the maintenance of administrative harmony at this crucial level of the Anglo-Irish nexus. One may certainly include in this category, improvements introduced in Ireland in the early 1720s that facilitated the Irish privy council to arrive at agreement when bills were disputed. This was identified as a significant issue by Archbishop William King in 1719, when he observed plaintively of a particular transmiss bearing private bills that it was 'with great difficulty that they are modelled to the consent of the parties'. Anxious that this should not reoccur, and that private bills were forwarded in an agreed state, councillors determined, four years later, that they would not decide on the fate of 'private bills without the presence and assistance of a judge or two and of the attorney and solicitor general', because such bills routinely required that they peruse 'deeds of settlement' and 'the consents of all who were judged necessary . . . or [had] a saving allowed for them'.[60] Councillors may have been encouraged to take this step by the decision of the house of commons in February 1723, in the case of the heads of a bill making provision for Martha, Viscountess Blessington, to require the submission of 'several deeds and writings recited in the bill', but it was evidence of their resolve to diminish the opportunity for error.[61] An agreed outcome could not always be guaranteed, of course, but because private measures were accompanied, increasingly, by petitions, affidavits, bills in chancery and other legal instruments, the practice of referring them to one or more, usually to two, judges for a report, was extended. The fact that this arrangement persisted is suggestive of its worth and it proved helpful to councillors when they were faced with the crucial decision of determining whether to approve, reject, or amend, individual bills.[62]

[59] TNA, PC2/90, ff. 258, 289–90, 292; PC1/4/71, ff. 21–22, 7–8: law officers' report, 3 Apr., Irish bills committee report, 3 Apr. 1728 (Fleming Bill – 1727–8); PC2/91, ff. 173, 205, 213; BL, Hardwicke Papers Add. MS 35872, ff. 28, 29, 31, 31: petition, 21 Feb. 1729, order in council, 21 Feb., Irish privy council letter 24 Jan. 1729 (Fleming Bill – 1729–30); PC2/93, ff. 326, 402 (Bolton Bill).

[60] TCD, King Papers, MS 750/5, f. 195; MS 2537, f. 43: King to Southwell, 18 Aug. 1719, 26 Dec. 1723.

[61] CJI, iii, 387.

[62] NAI, calendar of miscellaneous letters and papers prior to 1760, ff. 110, 153, 168, 182, 212, 218, 267, 269, 270, 282, 299, 305; calendar of miscellaneous letters and papers, 1760–89, f. 1; index of departmental letters and papers, 1760–89, ff. 51–3, 55, 56, 57, 58, 59, 60, 64, 65, 69, 70, 73, 74, 78, 79, 85.

Irish officials might have taken a further step at that moment and followed the British example, which required that individuals who intended to seek the leave of parliament to present a private bill advertise their intention, so that interested parties were aware of their intentions in advance. Indeed, Robert Maccarty, who pursued a vain claim to be the 5th earl of Clancarty, circulated such a notice in Ireland following the death of his father, abroad in October 1734, announcing his intention 'to apply to the parliament of Great Britain at the next ensuing sessions . . . for leave to bring in a [private] bill' to assist him recover his title and patrimony.[63] The absence of an equivalent procedure in Ireland meant that interested parties might not be aware that a private bill was in contemplation until a petition requesting leave to present was submitted to parliament, but peers took steps to put an end to this unsatisfactory state of affairs in 1739, when they pronounced that petitions for private bills would not be received unless a notice of intention was posted at the Four Courts or the Dublin Tholsel[64] two calendar months in advance of the commencement of the session and on the door of the house of lords eight days before it was presented. Subsequently, peers instituted a complex set of provisions requiring that both 'a petition for a private bill' and the heads of a private bill received from the Commons should be scrutinised by two judges, who were empowered to summon and to examine witnesses upon oath. Additional provisions for the printing and circulating of printed copies of private bills and for giving 'notice of . . . consent' in person, offered further protection against misrepresentation, malfeasance and fraud.[65]

A further procedural refinement that assisted with the expeditious and efficient processing of bills was the enhancement of the privy council letter that accompanied every bill transmitted from Ireland to the British council. This letter was of particular assistance to the crown's law officers in respect of private bills, as was made clear in 1719, when specific mention was made of 'the absence of any reference in the letters transmitted . . . from the Irish Council . . . that the facts alleged in those bills were proved to the satisfaction of the Council or that the proper parties were consenting thereto'.[66] Appropriate steps were taken thereafter to redress the problem by preparing fuller letters, but even this did not always prove sufficient. The failure in 1732 'to furnish . . . proper proofs' in respect of a private bill appertaining to the sale of an estate, prompted the law officers to decline to make a report.[67] Further additions were requested, and were made, and by the 1760s, the letters accompanying the heads of private measures commonly explained that 'the several facts and recitals therein contained have been fully approved', and that 'all partys concerned . . . have consented thereto', albeit after an intrinsically-formulaic fashion.[68]

[63] TNA, SP63/398, f. 94: 'advertisement', [1734].

[64] The Tholsel , formerly a merchants' assembly room, functioned in the 18th century as a city courthouse; it was located at the corner of St Nicholas Street and Christ Church place.

[65] Kelly, *Poynings' Law*, 170–1; *LJI*, iii, 458; *Rules and orders to be observed in the upper house of parliament of Ireland* (Dublin, 1784), 59–62.

[66] TNA, PC2/86, ff. 260–3, 332, 344; SP63/378: Webster to Delafaye, 15, 17 Oct. 1719, Bolton to lords justices, 17 Oct. 1719; SP67/10, f. 42: Carteret to Newcastle, 30 Apr. 1728.

[67] TNA, SP63/375: Newcastle to Dorset, 24 Feb. 1732.

[68] TNA, PC1/7/15; PC1/7/75/3, 5, 7; PC1/7/80/3, 5, 7; PC1/8/18, ff. 17–20; PC1/8/19, ff. 41, 47; PC1/82/3; PC1/9/15, f. 3; PC1/9/13, ff. 7–10, 15; PC1/9/14, f. 7; PC1/123/100, f. 7.

Another development that eased the path of private bills involved the use of agents. The employment of agents both to present and represent bills was not an innovation of the Hanoverian era. They were used with effect during the reign of Anne to represent public bills, and prompted by this, and by the realization that an advocate could make a difference, those *au fait* with the process came to perceive the value of the services of an individual who knew his way around Whitehall, both to represent a private bill and to respond to queries as they arose.[69] The usefulness of this was self-evident but it was not until 1724, when four sought-after public bills were respited, that Archbishop King commented to the effect that the use of agents to represent private bills meant that they were at an advantage compared with their public equivalents:

> our private bills have an easier and quieter passage than our public . . . because the private bills are commonly accompanied with a *particular agent*, who is acquainted with the circumstances of the case and prepared to answer the objections, and prosecute them with ready money from place to place and sollicite them in every office, whereas the publick go with a messenger that knoweth nothing of the matter, leaves them in the office and lets them shift for themselves.[70]

King almost certainly exaggerated the importance of agents, because of his unhappiness at the loss of a number of bills in which he had an especial interest, but he correctly identified not only how helpful it could be to the progress of a bill to have an individual available to speak on its behalf, but also to pay promptly the fees and charges that inevitably accrued.

The cost associated with securing the royal assent for a private bill was another consideration that weighed heavily, both with those who pursued the same and with those politicians who believed that fees should be kept in check. This matter was first addressed by the house of lords in 1695, when peers specified a schedule of payments to a variety of officials and functionaries amounting to some £30 for a bill of average length.[71] Saliently, these charges constituted only a minor part of the total costs that were incurred in securing a private bill. The trustees of the estate of Sir Thomas Hackett spent £410 5s. 3d in 1706–7 in securing approval for a bill to allow them to sell the estate and further costs associated with bringing the act into execution raised the total to £947 15s. 6d.[72] Expenses of this order were unusual, but they contributed to create the impression not only that the cost of securing a private bill was onerous, but also that they were appreciably higher at College Green than at Westminster. Eager to discourage Irish supplicants from looking across the Irish Sea, an attempt was made in 1709 to set Irish fees at 25% below the level obtaining in

[69] Kelly, *Poynings' Law*, 119–21, 136–7, 184–6; TNA, SP63/414, ff. 19–22: Devonshire to Fox, 17 Jan 1756; PRONI, Wilmot Papers, T3019/734: Potter to Wilmot, 1 Apr. 1746.

[70] TCD, King Papers, MS 2537, ff. 53–4: King to Southwell, 11 Jan. 1724; see also MS 2537, ff. 49, 52 74–5: King to Cork, 10 Jan., King to London, 10 Jan., King to Southwell, 8 Feb. 1724.

[71] *LJI*, i, 569–70. The house of commons also addressed the matter in 1695 and made its own order as to the fees to be paid the clerk of the house: *CJI*, ii, appendix, p. xx.

[72] Dublin Public Libraries, Gilbert Collection, Hackett Trustee Papers, MS 223, f. 81: the charges in passing and soliciting Sir Thomas Hackett's Bill, 28 Feb. 1706; Mark Tierney, *Murroe and Boher* (Dublin, 1966), 198 206–07; 4 Anne, c. 3 (private); 6 Anne, c. 7 (private).

England.[73] This was no more than a temporary solution, however. As a result, not only was it necessary periodically to revisit the matter,[74] it was determined also to designate certain categories of private bills, 'public' to 'avoid paying fees'.[75] This practice was singled out for criticism by the crown's law officers in the 1770s, but an agreed solution proved elusive, and the fact that the cost of private legislation continued to be debated into the 1790s indicated that this was a problem that defied resolution.[76]

The inability to establish clearly what constituted a private bill, and to agree a schedule of costs, contributed in no small way to the negative image that private legislation acquired in the course of the 18th century. This was implicit in the manner in which private legislation was addressed from the 1690s, but the insistence by a number of private bodies that sought the protection of statute that a private law was not sufficient, served to give expression to a prejudice that contributed over time to the marginalisation of such legislation. This was assisted in no small way by the categorisation of certain bills that ought to have been denominated private, as public. The largest category of bills to profit thereby was turnpike roads bills, which were designated public in 1729 and again in 1760 and, as such, permitted 'to pass . . . without fees'.[77] This did not secure turnpike bills against all costs, because the address seeking royal approval for their redesignation was not proceeded with, but it ensured that charges, which in two instances in the early 1760s amounted to £180 and £135, were kept within reasonable bounds.[78] However, it did reinforce the public perception that private bills related only to private family matters – settlements, wills, dowries, estates, divorce – and were, therefore, of lesser import, given the obvious public remit of parliament, than were public bills.[79] It was an ironic outcome, given the many administrative and procedural innovations that had taken place with respect to the manner in which this category of law was managed, and which, singly and cumulatively, contributed to ensure that the processing of private bills was as efficient and as stringent as it was in the case of public bills.

4. *Private Bills During the Era of Legislative Independence, 1782–1800*

The deprivation from the Irish and British privy councils of the power to amend and to respite Irish bills, as a result of the amendment in 1782 of Poynings' Law, signalled the

---

[73] *CJI*, ii, 599, 616, 621, 633–4, 669, 670.

[74] *CJI*, iii, 131; vi, 212; vii, 160; viii, 544; xiii, 184, 544.

[75] A good example is the measure 'for funding and regulating the hospital founded by Richard Stephens' (3 Geo. II, c. 33); see BL, Hardwicke Papers, Add. MS 36136, ff. 214–5: Southwell's remarks, [Feb. 1731]; for road bills, see *LJI*, iv, 183; *CJI*, v, 377; vi, 209, 212; x, 167; David Broderick, *The First Toll Roads: Ireland's Turnpike Roads, 1729–1858* (Cork, 2002), 50–1.

[76] Kelly, *Poynings' Law*, 188–9, 289–90; *CJI*, xi, 245; xii, 38; xiii, 199.

[77] *LJI*, iv, 183; *CJI*, v, 377; vi 209, 212; x, 167.

[78] PRONI, Wilmot Papers, T3019/4815–16: fees for turnpike bills, [Mar. 1764].

[79] National Library of Wales, Puleston Papers, MS 3580, f. 65: Spencer to Price, 5 July 1747; TNA, SP63/377–8: Conolly to [Delafaye], 20 Aug., Webster to [Delafaye], 27 Sept. 1719; TCD, King Papers, MS 750/8, f. 183: King to Annesley, 2 Mar. 1727.

end of the heads of bills process that was brought into being in the 1690s.[80] It was a change of sufficient magnitude to merit being denominated 'legislative independence' and, while this exaggerated the legislative reality, it mirrored the expectations of most of the Irish political nation. In so far as the making of law was concerned, the fact that the Irish parliament, which met annually from 1783, embarked on the most active phase in making law in its history, legislative independence made a palpable difference. The number of private acts also reached record levels. A total of 81 private acts were given the royal assent between the first meeting of 'Grattan's parliament' in October 1783 and its final assembly in August 1800, but since the enactment of public statutes proceeded at a still faster pace, private acts represented a shrinking percentage of the total. An imposing 92.3% of the statutes that received the royal assent in Ireland between 1783 and 1800 were public acts, the remaining 7.7% were private, which was half the percentage given the royal assent between 1715 and 1782, and a quarter of that approved during the reign of Anne. The sessional average was also below the 18th-century average; indeed, fewer private bills were approved per session than was the case at any time other than during the reign of George II (see Table 1).

As a consequence of the constitutional changes introduced in 1782, the pattern of law-making was transformed. Liberated from the requirement to present 'heads of bills', the most striking effect this had on the manner in which private law was made was that the house of lords replaced the house of commons as the forum in which most such bills took their rise. Since an overwhelming 89% of heads of private bills took their rise in the Commons in the decades prior to the achievement of legislative independence, the eclipse of the lower house of parliament was as unexpected as it was rapid. If it was not instantaneous, it was already firmly rooted by 1787, when all of the eight private bills that were offered that session took their rise in the Lords. In all, 76% of the 98 private bills initiated between 1783 and 1800 were presented in the house of lords. This mirrored the greater confidence of the upper House, consequent upon the restoration of the appellate jurisdiction in 1782, its improved public profile, and the presence on its benches (as a result of the augmentation of the Irish peerage) of a larger number of more independent voices.[81] It also had the advantage that it was a more efficient way of proceeding in an era of active law-making and the house of lords demonstrated that it could rise to the challenge by updating its rules and orders, revised editions of which were published in 1784 and in 1790.[82]

Imbued with a greater sense of purpose, peers not only processed the lion's share of private bills efficiently, they made it clear that bills had to be fair and accurately drafted by rejecting 20% of the bills submitted for their consideration. The proportion that fell in the Commons was 8% (Table 2). In all, 83% of private bills (22 from the Commons and 59 from the Lords) were forwarded to the Irish privy council, where they were examined by members of the judiciary, prior to their transmission in due form to the British council.[83] The bills were likewise subject to scrutiny by the law officers at the

[80] Kelly, *Poynings' Law*, 326–36; James Kelly, *Prelude to Union: Anglo-Irish Politics in the 1780s* (Cork, 1992), *passim*.

[81] *Proceedings of the Irish House of Lords, 1771–1800*, ed. James Kelly (3 vols, Dublin, 2008), *passim*.

[82] *Rules and orders to be observed in the upper house of parliament of Ireland* (Dublin, 1784). The first version of this text was published in 1778.

[83] NAI, index to departmental letters and official papers, 1760–89, ff. 93, 97.

British council, but since neither council possessed the authority any longer to amend or to respite the bills, this was largely a symbolic process. Yet because the attachment of the respective great seal by both boards was essential, if the bills were to receive the royal assent on their return to Ireland, both took their responsibilities seriously and the process was pursued with the scrupulousness that had ever characterised their activities. Inevitably, problems were identified with a handful of bills – six *in toto* – but, because the privy council could not intervene, the law officers could only flag the point of concern in the expectation that it would be drawn to the notice of the Irish executive and that appropriate steps would be taken. The Irish executive was disposed to take notice when they were advised that a private bill did not include an appropriate 'saving' clause or infringed the royal prerogative, but it was still more strongly disinclined to animate sensitive constitutional issues that would invite problems in the Irish parliament. As a result, they contrived successfully to minimise the potential for controversy by ensuring that all 81 private bills, which was the number forwarded from Ireland between 1783 and 1800, were given the royal assent on their return.[84]

5. *Conclusion*

Though the abolition of the Irish parliament did not signal the end of the making of private law with an Irish purpose and focus, as the publication of a notice in 1809 advising 'all persons' intending to seek such a measure of 'the previous steps required by the standing orders of the house of commons' of the United Kingdom of Great Britain and Ireland attests, it was a moment in the history of this category of law as significant as the inauguration of a regular parliament in the 1690s.[85] In the intervening period, some 485 private bills (or 7.6 per session) were presented as potential private acts and just short of two-thirds (313, or an average of 4.8 per session) received the royal assent.

The subphases into which the history of the making of private law can be assigned offer a revealing perspective on the 18th-century Irish legislature and how it quickly cast off the subordinate role to the Irish privy council it was afforded in advance of the brief 1692 session. The extended 1695–7 session was crucial in this respect, because it not only resulted in the enactment of the first private act but also set a pattern for the management of legislation that was to endure, with refinements, until the Anglo-Irish union. The formative phase, of which the 1695–7 session was a part, may be said to have lasted the duration of the reigns of William and Anne, for though further administrative refinements were introduced during the reign of George I in particular, the pattern of private law-making was firmly in place by the accession of the Hanoverians. This pattern persisted with minor alterations until 1782, for though the politi-cisation of Poynings' Law encouraged officials to assume a less-interventionist attitude prior to that date, legislative independence not only gave the Irish legislature unprec-edented influence over the private legislation that was approved, but also permitted the house of lords to assume primary responsibility for that category of legislation. The fact

---

[84] TNA, PC2/133, ff. 422, 425–9; PC2/134, ff. 14, 29–31, 36–9; PC1/18/A19: law officers' report, 17 Mar. 1789; HO122/3, ff. 9–10: Sydney to Buckingham, 19 Mar. 1789.

[85] *Freeman's Journal*, 6 Oct. 1809.

that this was the case supports the contemporary perspective, epitomised by the exclusion of the texts of private acts from the fullest editions of the statutes, that since private acts were by definition concerned with matters of a private character, they were inherently less consequential than public acts. This is impossible utterly to refute, but it must be acknowledged at the same time that private acts served a useful purpose, separate and additional to the law courts, in ensuring that property and financial rights, the right to modify family settlement, the entitlement to a divorce and other privileges, were within reach of the elite. These hardly equated with the big issues of money, war and religion; indeed, they were deemed less consequential than road bills in the legislative pecking order. However, like the estate acts approved at Westminster,[86] the fact that members of Ireland's *ancien regime* elite were entitled to appeal to parliament is a further illustration of the privileged place they were accorded in that society and another reason why private legislation ought not to be overlooked in any assessment of the legislative work of the Irish parliament.

[86] Michael McCahill, 'Estate Acts of Parliament, 1740–1800', in *Institutional Practice and Memory: Parliamentary People, Records and Histories: Essays in Honour of Sir John Sainty*, ed. Clyve Jones (Oxford, 2013), 148–68.

The Irish Parliament and Print, 1660–1782

TOBY BARNARD

The article considers the uses made of print by the Irish Parliament between 1660 and 1782. Proceedings were made more widely available, initially with printed *Votes* and then with fuller *Journals*. Just how widely is considered. The record of the house of commons and the house of lords is compared. Also the authorised publication of statutes is traced. Sizes of format and editions and costs are considered, concluding that these seriously limited access to the publications. In contrast, varieties of unofficial print, generated either by individual members and candidates or by partisans, are discussed. The effect of these productions was to increase awareness of politics and, arguably, to generate more intense controversies.

Keywords: Irish parliament; house of commons; house of lords; print; Irish lord lieutenant; laws; elections; parliamentary privilege; censorship

1

Ireland was slower than England and other continental countries in utilising the printing press. Nevertheless, as the 17th century progressed, the government and state Church of Ireland realized its utility. Until the 1690s, output from Dublin was dominated by what was authorised and needed by Church and state. Moreover, with few printers and presses, government surveillance was easy. By the 1690s, the situation was changing: more titles were published each year, and not just in Dublin but in a growing number of provincial towns. Moreover, official dominance and control weakened. The increase in printed matter originating in Ireland coincided with another notable development. From 1692, parliament became a regular event in Dublin. The assembly, convening every second year after 1703, generated print. Some was originated by one or other of the two Houses; more was directed, unsolicited, at the institution or its members.[1] A question, therefore, presents itself as to whether the two phenomena – more publications and more parliamentary business – were causally, as well as temporally, linked.

Initially, parliament was regarded as an adjunct to the permanent administration in Dublin Castle. Its functions were to pass laws and to vote taxes. However, the members quickly assumed the nebulous role claimed by its counterpart at Westminster: to represent 'the people', essentially the conformist protestants in

---

[1] T.C. Barnard, 'Print Culture, 1700–1800', in *The Oxford History of the Irish Book. III: The Irish Book in English* ed. R. Gillespie and A. Hadfield (3 vols so far, Oxford, 2006–11), 38–41; J. Kelly, 'Political Publishing, 1700–1800', in *Oxford History*, ed. Gillespie and Hadfield, 215–33.

Ireland.[2] The last function meant that parliament became a focus for complaint, advice and cajolery, some of it communicated through print. Members of the two Houses may sometimes have encouraged and abetted addresses and petitions, but many were spontaneous. This investigation concentrates on the print initiated by the two Houses. It suggests, but does not explore, a stark contrast between what was authorised and what was not. Each type of print, however, showed the degree to which printed material was being integrated into politics. A further question then arises: whether or not the dynamics and characteristics of politics were altered by print.

In 1692, a change occurred. The house of commons as a body decided to publish its own record as printed *Votes*.[3] These copied the *Votes* authorised by the Westminster parliament, some of which had been reprinted in Dublin during the agitated 1680s. The record had to be approved by the Speaker; it was checked by subordinate clerks.[4] The title *Votes* was misleading. Although the pages were not calculated to excite, they, nevertheless, provided a *résumé* of parliamentary proceedings (albeit terse), starting with the speech with which the lord lieutenant, or his deputy, had opened the session and ending with the viceroy's closing address. Issued daily while the House was sitting and varying from a double-sided sheet to several pages, the *Votes* circulated detail hitherto lacking to all except those seated in the assembly.[5] The publication, as much as the arrival of parliament itself as a permanent body, marked a decisive stage in the political maturation of Ireland.

If the Irish parliament now copied its counterpart at Westminster, hitherto it had lagged behind. This was true more generally in the production of print for routine and polemical purposes.[6] The earliest known Dublin news-sheets had coincided first with a convention which, in lieu of parliament, had assembled in 1660 and then, in 1663, with the concurrent sittings of the Court of Claims and parliament.[7] The later production, *Mercurius Hibernicus*, ran for at least 35 numbers.[8] However, its unsettling effects led the government to silence it.[9] Exposing 'to the world in print with inconsequent inferences'

---

[2] *The Irish Parliament in the Eighteenth-Century: The Long Apprenticeship*, ed. D.W. Hayton (Edinburgh, 2001); D.W. Hayton and James Kelly 'Introduction: The Irish Parliament in a European Context: A Representative Institution in a Composite State', in *The Eighteenth-Century Composite State: Representative Institutions in Ireland and Europe, 1689–1800*, ed. D.W. Hayton, James Kelly and John Bergin (Basingstoke, 2010), 3–16; D.W. Hayton, 'Patriots and Legislators: Irishmen and their Parliaments, c.1689–c.1740', in *Parliaments, Nations and Identities in Britain and Ireland, 1660–1850*, ed. Julian Hoppitt (Manchester, 2003), 103–23.

[3] *CJI*, ii, 13; D. Englefield, *The Printed Records of the Parliament of Ireland, 1613–1800* (1978), 42.

[4] *CJI*, iii, 121; *Votes*, nos 50, 51 (18, 19 Nov. 1695), pp. 189, 190, 194.

[5] Englefield, *Printed Records*, 5. A sample is illustrated in R. Munter, *The History of the Irish Newspaper 1685–1760* (Cambridge, 1967), plate 4.

[6] J. McElligott, *Royalism, Print and Censorship in Revolutionary England* (Woodbridge, 2007); J. Peacey, *Politicians and Pamphleteers: Propaganda during the English Civil Wars and Interregnum* (Aldershot, 2004); J. Raymond, *The Invention of the Newspaper: English Newsbooks, 1641–1649* (Oxford, 1996); J. Sutherland, *The Restoration Newspaper and its Development* (Cambridge, 1986).

[7] *An account of the chief occurrences of Ireland* (Dublin, 1659[60]); E. McClintock. Dix, *Catalogue of Early Dublin-Printed Books, 1601 to 1700* (Dublin, 1912), 106; cf. T.C. Barnard, *Cromwellian Ireland: English Government and Reform in Ireland, 1649–1660* (Oxford, 1975), 24 n. 38; A. Clarke, *Prelude to Restoration in Ireland: The End of the Commonwealth, 1659–1600* (Cambridge, 1999), 245, 252, 279.

[8] Two later issues among Sir William Petty's Papers (BL, Add. MS 72,879, ff. 76–83v) extend the run.

[9] T. Barnard, 'Conclusion: Restoration Ireland', in *Restoration Ireland*, ed. C. Dennehy (Aldershot, 2008), 182–3; Dix, *Catalogue of Early Dublin-Printed Books*, 120.

was not to be tolerated.[10] Government hostility alone did not explain the retardation of printed commentaries. Potential buyers were too few in Ireland to offset the financial and legal risks to publishers. Furthermore, Ireland's legal subjection to England, together with the lack of frequent parliaments in Dublin, had obliged political activists to conduct much of their business in London. One consequence was a craving for information about what was happening on the English side of the water. News-sheets, diurnals and pamphlets from London, as well as manuscript separates and letters, were eagerly sought.[11] Some *Votes* of the English parliament were reissued in Dublin.[12] After 1689, English events continued to fascinate so that the *Votes* and other political and topical print enjoyed brisk demand in Ireland.[13] In Irish politics, imported techniques and approaches were evident even when distinctive concerns asserted themselves.[14]

The decision to publish *Votes* was made by the house of commons, not the Castle administration. In itself, this indicated the swing of power towards College Green. Yet it was hardly the case that the members wished to throw open all their activities to the gaze of the vulgar. The information offered was severely factual and, for those unfamiliar with the mechanisms and personalities, opaque. The *Votes* were a prime example of print that required elucidation through the supplements of talk and privileged information communicated privately. Hugh Howard wrote plaintively from London in 1732 for detailed Dublin news, 'for we know little by your *Votes*'.[15] Yet, they were better than nothing.[16] In 1763, a London official was kept abreast of proceedings through the printed *Votes* sent by a Dublin colleague.[17] The *Votes* were acquired serially by Thomas Tilson, an officeholder, presumably as an essential work of reference.[18]

There is evidence that, especially when *Votes* were first published in the 1690s, they were valued for topical news. Through them, a lord deputy learned that one of his servants had been accused of dereliction and a clergyman in Ulster that he was commanded to attend the House. The *Votes* warned when individuals were protected by

[10] *CJI*, i, 640, 641.

[11] *CJI*, i, 394.

[12] *The votes and further proceedings of the Parliament of England, together with the king's speech* (Dublin, 1685); *Votes of the House of Commons, at Oxford* ([Dublin, 1681]); *Votes of the House of Commons, perused and signed to the printed according to the order of the House of Commons* ([Dublin], 1680[1]).

[13] National Library of Wales, Powis Castle MSS, no. 819: R. Birch to F. Herbert, Jan. 1715[16]; BL, Add. MS 38,157, f. 69: Sir R. Cox to E. Southwell, 19 Feb. 1713[14]; NLI PC 449/4, Vesey MSS, formerly J/2: T. Fitzgerald to Rev. T. Vesey, 10 Jan. 1688[9]; PC 449/4: W. Smythe to ?, 24 Jan. 1711[12]; Leicestershire RO, box 4950, bundle 22: E. Southwell to Lord Nottingham, 30 June 1698; BL, Add. MS 38,150, f. 127v: J. Waller to E. Southwell, 13 Dec. 1698; Add. MS 37,673, ff. 96, 131v–2: W. Wogan to E. Southwell, 4 July 1710, 30 June 1711.

[14] A. Aspinall, 'The Reporting and Publishing of the House of Commons Debates, 1771–1834', in *Essays Presented to Sir Lewis Namier*, ed. R. Pares and A.J.P. Taylor (1956), 227–57; S. Lambert, 'The Beginning of Printing for the House of Commons, 1640–42', *The Library*, 6th ser., iii (1981), 43–61; S. Lambert, *Printing for Parliament, 1641–1700* (1984); S. Lambert, 'Printing for the House of Commons in the Eighteenth Century', *The Library*, 5th ser., xxiii (1968), 25–46; P.D.G. Thomas, 'The Beginning of Parliamentary Reporting in Newspapers, 1768–1774', *English Historical Review*, lxxiv (1959), 623–36.

[15] NLI, MS 38,958/8: H. Howard to Bishop R. Howard, 12 or 13 Jan. 1731[2].

[16] BL, Add. MS 38,150, f. 107: J. Waller to Sir R. Southwell, 11 Oct. 1698.

[17] PRONI, T 3019/4760: R. Rigby to R. Wilmot, 24 Dec. 1763.

[18] Stormont copy. Tilson was registrar of chancery. Southampton University Library, BR 141/3: T. Tilson to H. Temple, 20 Feb. 1719[20].

parliamentary privilege.[19] Fear of publicity through inclusion in the *Votes* led one, named in the House as a common gamester, to plead – unsuccessfully – for this detail to be omitted from the published account.[20] In 1766, a group of merchants in New Ross, having read in the *Votes* of applications from trading corporations in Dublin and other cities, petitioned for similar statutory protection.[21] The utility of the *Votes* – a daily record published almost instantly – explained their survival even after the ponderous *Journals* had been introduced. Swift, contemptuous of the Commons, was unimpressed and (in *The Legion Club*) consigned its *Votes* to a more squalid, if useful, fate.[22]

Members of the upper House bought the *Votes* of the lower: in 1716, Archbishop King paid £1 10s. for two sets.[23] In 1737, the king's stationer and official printer to the house of commons, Samuel Fairbrother, supplied Sir John Vesey, an MP, with a collection for the sessions of 1737 at 9s. 2d.[24] This payment may have been for additional copies since, in the mid 18th century, the assumption is that each member was entitled to one free series.[25] Already, by the early 18th century, there are hints that the printed accounts were offering the basis for discussions among gentlemen in Waterford and Lismore. Coffee houses, as well as subscribing to a selection of newspapers wider than that which most families could afford, took the *Votes* of both the Westminster and Dublin parliaments.[26] In addition, members of both assemblies favoured acquaintances and clients with copies, as well as other topical prints.[27]

The right to print *Votes* belonged to the House itself, which delegated the choice of operative to the Speaker. The profitable perquisite was bestowed on successive holders of the patent of king's stationer in Ireland.[28] Through this system, the House strove to control reports. This proved an increasingly vain hope, as scurrilous and invented accounts appeared, frequently engineered by dissident or self-important members. In the early 1720s, printers were hauled before the house of lords for publishing without permission the lord lieutenant's speech at the opening of parliament. One plaintiff defended himself successfully by arguing that he took the text from the already published

[19] *CJI*, ii, 96, 100, 118, 277.

[20] *CJI*, ii, 281.

[21] *CJI*, viii, 89.

[22] 'The Legion Club', line 62, in *The Poems of Jonathan Swift*, ed. H. Williams (2nd edn, 3 vols, Oxford, 1958), iii, 831.

[23] TCD, MS 751/3, ff. 26v, 92: Archbishop W. King, account book, June 1716, Mar. 1718[19]. Cf. *Correspondence of Jonathan Swift*, ed. H. Williams (5 vols, Oxford, 1963–5), i, 247, 265.

[24] NLI, MS 38,897/2: S. Fairbrother, account with Sir J. Vesey, 25 May 1738; Edith Mary Johnston-Liik, *History of the Irish Parliament, 1692–1800* (6 vols, Belfast, 2002), vi, 472; BL, Add. MS 9713, f. 112: W. Lingen to E. Southwell, 9 Oct. 1735; Add. MS 47,008A, f. 63: W. Taylor to Lord Perceval, 23 Mar. 1741[2].

[25] *CJI*, viii, 41; ix, 362; x, 244.

[26] University College Cork, Boole Library, Villiers-Stuart MSS, B/1/22: A. Alcock to J. Mason, 12 Nov. 1737; duke of Devonshire, Chatsworth House, letter book of J. Waite, 1706–8: J. Waite to C. Musgrave, 25 Feb. 1706[7]. The author expresses his gratitude to the trustees, Chatsworth House Settlement (by permission of the duke of Devonshire) for permission to use and cite this material.

[27] NLI, MS 47,891/1: K. Chetwode to J. Ussher, 24 May, 19 July, 1 Aug. 1726; Chatsworth House, Waite letter book: J. Waite to C. Musgrave, 25 Feb. 1706[7]; *The Annals of Ballitore*, ed. M. Corrigan, M. Kavanagh and K. Kiely (Naas, 2009), 77; *CJI*, ii, 15.

[28] M. Pollard, *A Dictionary of the Members of the Dublin Book Trade, 1550–1800* (2000), 46–8, 195–6.

Votes.[29] The fact that printers were prepared to transgress, thereby risking fines and even imprisonment, indicated that they thought there was money (probably not much) to be earned from issuing illicitly the individual speeches.

While the House was sitting, curiosity about its doings was satisfied by the *Votes*. Once the session had ended, a fuller record was desired. In the 1750s, the Commons acted. Its journals, written up by clerks after each sitting, were to be printed. The decision, echoing that of the Westminster parliament, can be interpreted as a sign of greater confidence on the part of Irish members. Commons (and peers), veterans of resisting dictation from the nearby Castle and faraway London, had a high sense of their importance. More practically, because so many arguments and actions relied on precedents, an easier way to find them would be welcomed. The *Journals* appeared in a sequence of massive folios. The separate stages of the work were deputed to appropriate specialists (typefounders, papermakers and printers).[30] Not only were the volumes generous in size and eventually equipped with indices, but they were sumptuously bound. Also, they were printed on Irish-made paper, a choice which pushed up the price by one-third.[31] The magnificent productions proclaimed pride and self-importance, just as much as the parliament's modern buildings on College Green.[32]

Initially, 400 copies of the *Journals* were bespoken, primarily to be distributed to members.[33] One whose set survives is Bernard Ward, a County Down member of parliament.[34] By 1771, the print run had lengthened to 500. This left spares for favoured recipients outside parliament, but not many. Also, its bulk and cost ensured that the publication never circulated widely.[35] During the 1770s, a complete set cost £33 18s. 2d., equivalent to the annual income of a skilled craftsman or trader.[36]

The copy-text was provided by one of the clerks to the House.[37] Speeches and commentary were excluded. For juicier elements, those interested had to turn to unofficial (and sometimes illicit) publications. Those who tried to fill the gap were liable still to run into conflict with the House, touchy over its privileges and unconvinced of the right

---

[29] Cumbria County Library, Carlisle: Bishop W. Nicolson, diary, xxxvi, 19 Sept. 1722; *LJI*, ii, 689–90, 743; Pollard, *Dictionary*, 301.

[30] V. Kinane, 'A Fine Set of the Commons' *Journals*: A Study of its Production History', *Long Room*, xxx (1985), 11–28; Pollard, *Dictionary*, 47.

[31] *CJI*, viii, 196; A. Muir, 'Paper Manufacture in Ireland, *c*.1690–1825, with Particular Reference to the North of Ireland', Queen's University Belfast PhD, 2010, vol. 1, p. 177.

[32] M. Craig, 'The Irish Parliamentary Bindings', *Book Collector*, ii (1953), 24–36; D. Englefield, 'Printing the Journals of the Irish House of Commons, 1753–1802', in *Parliamentary History, Libraries and Records: Essays Presented to Maurice Bond*, ed. H.S. Cobb (1981), 33–43; Kinane, 'A Fine Set of the Commons' *Journals*', 11–28; J. McDonnell, 'Parliamentary Binder B Identified', *Bulletin of the Irish Georgian Society*, xxxv (1992–3), 52–6; Sir E. Sullivan, 'The Parliamentary Journals of Ireland, 1613–1800', *Country Life*, 5 Sept. 1908, pp. 313–16.

[33] *CJI*, vii, 82, 235, 356; viii, 431.

[34] M. Purcell, *The Big House Library in Ireland: Books in Ulster Country Houses* (Swindon, 2011), 31.

[35] T.C. Barnard, 'Marsh's Library and the Reading Public', in *The Making of Marsh's Library: Learning, Politics and Religion in Ireland, 1650–1750*, ed. M. McCarthy and A. Simmons (Dublin, 2004), 161–2; Pollard, *Dictionary*, 47.

[36] *CJI*, viii, 178, 196, 308, 320, 331, 431, 434; ix, 34, 37, 38, 204, 357, 363; x, 28.

[37] *CJI*, v, 145; ix, 38; x, 244, 383.

to know more of its activities.[38] In the absence of authorised versions, invention and misrepresentation flourished. Members themselves and partisans, embarking on populist campaigns and appealing for electors' support in defying the executive, were keen to involve more in the political process and knew that print could help. Supposedly authentic texts of speeches were released for unofficial publication. A prime offender in this regard, motivated by personal vanity, was Lord Mountmorres. He sent to favoured papers the text of his speech, interlarded with reports of cheering. The text was printed, but the debate had never occurred.[39] A harangue against the penal laws, delivered in 1774 by an articulate member, Robert Jephson, quickly appeared as a separate tract. Charles O'Conor, a leader of the campaign for catholic relief, had solicited the speech's publication and colluded with Jephson.[40] Already, unofficial lists of how named members had voted in contentious divisions had been printed in 1736, 1753 and 1763.[41]

Early in the 1760s, a gap in the market was spotted. Sir James Caldwell, flushed with recent success as an anonymous pamphleteer, professed a concern to rescue the drooping reputation of the Dublin parliament. He vowed to show how oratory and patriotism flourished in the lower House and, to this end, set about recording the debates of 1763 for publication.[42] Caldwell was not himself a member of the House – to his chagrin – and had, therefore, to sit in the gallery to note the speeches. Memory was fallible and Caldwell confessed: 'it is impossible but I must sometimes blend in the warmth of my imagination some of my thoughts with those of the speakers'.[43] His insistence on a disinterested wish to increase awareness of the eloquence and public spirit of the members may have been genuine, but he was also driven by self-promotion.

Published first in 1766, Caldwell's *Debates* failed to have the impact for which he had hoped.[44] Choosing to publish in London was in keeping with his aim of impressing ignorant English readers with the eloquence of Irish MPs. In London, too, were the potential patrons who might recommend his ennoblement. Critics felt that, in his zeal to make even the most taciturn member speak like Cicero or Demosthenes, he had devalued the few orators in the House. 'Who will believe you that such fine speeches

---

[38] J. Kelly, 'Regulating Print: The State and Control of Print in Eighteenth-Century Ireland', *Eighteenth Century Ireland*, xxiii (2008), 164–5; Pollard, *Dictionary*, 626.

[39] J. Barrington, *Personal Sketches and Recollections of His Own Time* (new edn, Dublin, 1997), 47; James Kelly, *Sir Edward Newenham MP, 1734–1814: Defender of the Protestant Constitution* (Dublin, 2004), 14–15, 39–40, 116, 124, 293–4.

[40] C. O'Conor, 'To the editor', in *The speech delivered by Robert Jephson, Esq: on the 11th of February 1774* (Dublin, 1774), pp. iii–vi; *Letters of Charles O'Conor of Belanagare*, ed. R.E. Ward, J.F. Wrynn and C.C. Ward (Washington, DC, 1988), 349, 355.

[41] *A list of such members as voted for and against the new demand of herbage in 1736* (Dublin, 1736); D.W. Hayton and S. Karian, 'Select Document: The Division in the Irish House of Commons on the "Tithe of Agistment", 18 Mar. 1736, and Swift's "Character . . . of the Legion Club" ', *Irish Historical Studies*, xxxviii (2012), 304–21; *Insula sacra et libera* (1753); *A list of the members of the Hon. House of Commons of Ireland, who voted on the question previous to the expulsion of Arthur Jones Nevill, esq.* ([?Dublin], 1753); *The H_ having agreed nem.con . . . the question being put, the black list voted for the government, the red list for the immediate enquiry . . .* ([Dublin, 1763]) (copy in TNA, SP63/422, 167); *Debates relative to the affairs of Ireland, in the year 1763 and 1764: Taken by a Military Officer* (2 vols, 1766), 674.

[42] *Debates relative to the affairs of Ireland, in the year 1763 and 1764.*

[43] John Rylands Library, University of Manchester [hereafter cited as JRL], B 3/10, Caldwell letter books, 2, pp. 167–70: Sir J. Caldwell to Lord Newtown, 10 Feb. 1761.

[44] *Debates relative to the affairs of Ireland, in the year 1763 and 1764.*

were made by Flood or Barry', he was asked, 'when they see pretty good ones given gratis to the dumb who know no more of language than Ay or No?'[45] Furthermore, in an effort to improve sluggish sales, Caldwell sought confrontation, hoping that the Speaker would haul him before the bar of the Commons for breaching the official's continuing monopoly over allowing reports.[46] However, members had no wish to pick a fight over an account, which, if often invented, was flattering to themselves.[47]

The need for more detailed reporting was recognized.[48] In the past, individual members had made notes of their own, but these were piecemeal and intended as private memoranda.[49] Only from 1777 did an English publisher switch his attention from the British to the Irish parliament, and then briefly. John Almon's *Narrative of Proceedings in the Parliament of Ireland* reported on the opening weeks of the 1775–6 session, but its partial character and publication a full year after the session was over was not well advised, and it was not until 1782 that a consortium of Irish publishers inaugurated a *Parliamentary Register*. Although full, the *Register* was not a verbatim report.[50] Meanwhile, newspapers were printing detailed reports of debates. Summaries were included in the columns of Belfast, Clonmel and Cork journals by the early 1770s.[51] Indeed, the house of lords' deliberations between 1771 and 1800 have been reconstructed principally from the press.[52] Questions of how the material was collected, the extent of editorial intervention and, indeed, the accuracy and bias of the selections that were published have yet to be answered. Also, the space allowed to Irish parliamentary affairs was dwarfed by the coverage of Europe, North America and Westminster.

The meetings of parliament provoked flurries of print. Lists of the members were published at the start of each parliament.[53] These were not authorised, but customarily

---

[45] JRL, B 3/17/74: P. Skelton to Sir J. Caldwell, 22 May 1771.

[46] *CJI*, viii, 11.

[47] JRL, B 3/15/83: Sir J. Caldwell to Lord Newtown, Oct. 1766; B 3/10, 4, pp. 767–8: same to E.S. Pery, 26 Oct. 1767; B 3/10, 4, pp. 755–62: same to J. Ponsonby, 10 Oct. 1767; B 3/16/16: G.E. Howard to Sir J. Caldwell, 23 Oct. 1767; B 3/21/7, p. 229: [Sir J. Caldwell], 'A letter to a noble lord on its being reported that a gentleman of the Irish parliament of great consequence and good abilities had taken amiss the publishing in the Irish Debates something that was said relative to him'; PRONI, D/1634/2/50: J. Hort to Lady Caldwell, 3 Nov. 1767.

[48] J. Kelly, 'Reporting the Irish Parliament: The *Parliamentary Register*', *Eighteenth Century Ireland*, xv (2000), 158–71; A.P.W. Malcomson and D.J. Jackson, 'Sir Henry Cavendish and the Proceedings of the Irish House of Commons, 1776–1800', in *The Irish Parliament in the Eighteenth Century*, ed. Hayton, 128–46.

[49] *Scholar Bishop: The Recollections and Diary of Narcissus Marsh, 1638–1696*, ed. R. Gillespie (Cork, 2003); D.W. Hayton, 'An Irish Parliamentary Diary from the Reign of Queen Anne', *Analecta Hibernica*, xxx (1982), 97–149; Malcomson and Jackson, 'Sir Henry Cavendish and the Proceedings of the Irish House of Commons', 128–46.

[50] Kelly, 'Reporting the Irish Parliament', 158–71; John Almon, *Narrative of proceedings in the parliament of Ireland* (1777). The first volume of the *Parliamentary Register* (Dublin, 1782), which reports the full 1781–2 session, was published by a consortium of Irish publishers: James Porter (Abbey St), Patrick Byrne (College Green) and William Porter (Skinner Row). The series eventually ran to 17 volumes.

[51] *Belfast Newsletter*, 29 Apr. 1760, 31 May 1768, 24–8 Dec. 1773, 25–8 Jan. 1774, 26–9 Dec. 1775; *The Clonmel Gazette; Hibernian Chronicle*, iii (1771), 822; U. Callaghan, 'Newspapers and Print Culture in Eighteenth-Century Limerick', University of Limerick PhD, 2010, vol. 1, pp. 111, 116, 118–19.

[52] *Proceedings of the Irish House of Lords, 1771–1800*, ed. James Kelly (3 vols, Dublin, 2008).

[53] *A true list of the lords spiritual and temporal together with the knights, citizens and burgesses of this present parliament* (Dublin, 1703).

© *The Parliamentary History Yearbook Trust 2014*

they were undertaken by the holder of the king's or queen's patent or the official printer
to the house of commons.[54] However, when the publisher of *The Gentleman's and
Citizen's Almanac* for 1742 presumed to include a list of peers, he was summoned before
the Lords for breaching privilege.[55] Compiling an accurate catalogue of current peers
involved Ulster king at arms in much labour on the Lords' behalf.[56] In 1762, a better-
established almanac-maker was accorded the privilege of printing annually the names of
'Lords of Parliament and peers of the realm'.[57] One sensitivity, addressed in the standing
orders of the Lords, was the assumption or attribution of suppositious titles. Any printer
or publisher guilty of such misuse was also guilty of 'a notorious breach' of the Lords'
privilege.[58] What may have been aimed at was the employment of titles conferred by
Stuart monarchs after 1689, or by peers who had been outlawed and legally degraded
from the peerage.

The Commons ordered an increasing variety of ancillary papers to be printed. Among
them were speeches delivered by the Speaker, usually at the bar of the house of lords
and summarizing achievements of Commons, Lords, and government in London and
Dublin. More innovative within the miscellany were accounts of how taxes were spent
and lists of pensions on the civil and military lists.[59] The award and payment of pensions
from Irish funds was a source of contention: between supporters and critics of the
administration and (in some instances) between defenders of Irish interests and their
British rulers. Manuscript lists were compiled for administrative purposes and, for a fee,
might be copied – as for Archbishop King in 1717.[60] A commercial initiative saw them
printed in *Hiberniae Notitia* in 1723. However, what was published there was out of
date.[61] Given the continuing rows over the issue, and the torrid relations between
sections of the Irish parliament and the executive throughout the 1750s, the Commons'
decision to authorise publication in 1763 was a bold one.[62] It coincided with a pamphlet
from one lawyer member of parliament which attacked the entire system of pensions.
This principled objection was provoked by a recent, dramatic increase in pensions and,
underlying that, an ominous increase in the influence of the crown as exercised by
ministers which, if left unchecked, would end 'Ireland's existence as a country of liberty
and property'.[63]

---

[54] *A true and compleat list of the Lords Spiritual and Temporal, together with the knights, citizens and burgesses, of
the present Parliament, summoned to meet the fifth of this instant October, 1692* (Dublin, 1692); *An alphabetical list
of the knights, citizens and burgesses of this present session of Parliament* (Dublin, 1731).

[55] *LJI*, iii, 508, 510; Pollard, *Dictionary*, 351–2.

[56] *LJI*, iii, 340–1.

[57] *LJI*, iv, 242.

[58] *LJI*, v, 433.

[59] *CJI*, viii, 200, 294; ix, 13, 362.

[60] TCD, MS 751/3, f. 61v: Archbishop W. King, account books, Dec. 1717.

[61] *Hiberniæ Notitia: or A list of the present officers in church and state, and of all payments to be made for civil an
military affairs for the kingdom of Ireland* (Dublin, 1723); A.P.W. Malcomson, *Nathaniel Clements: Government an
the Governing Elite in Ireland, 1725–75* (Dublin, 2005), 282.

[62] Malcomson, *Nathaniel Clements*, 246–88; E. Magennis, *The Irish Political System, 1740–1765* (Dublin,
2000), 117, 119, 175.

[63] *Debates relative to the affairs of Ireland, in the year 1763 and 1764*, pp. 182, 213, 216–17, 238–40, 322–4
475–6, 505–6, 510, 726; A. McAulay, *An inquiry into the legality of pensions on the Irish establishment* (Dublin
1763), 4.

With the Speaker's permission, a catalogue of the civil pensionaries soon appeared and was regularly updated; the military pensioners were slower to be catalogued in print.[64] As the opponents of wide disclosure feared, the 1766 list was soon included in the *Belfast Newsletter* and reissued in London.[65] Since many beneficiaries lived in Britain and not Ireland, the cross-channel interest was obvious.[66] But members of the Irish parliament had bowed to local pressures as well as venting their own resentments at the draining of money from their own kingdom. Just as it was suspected that the tactics of Wilkes and his supporters, including the use of print, were readily adopted by Irish *frondeurs*, evidence from Ireland assisted English campaigners.

By the 1740s, an increasing number of 'heads of bills' were printed.[67] Published versions reached those interested in legislation on the anvil. Merchants from Drogheda petitioned, on the basis of having read the printed heads, in support of a measure to improve the marketing of butter packed into casks.[68] It could be that promoters of bills prompted likely supporters outside parliament to express backing. The readier availability of the texts eased those wishing to comment, which, again, might be done through print, although not invariably.[69] Important measures during the 1750s, such as schemes to register catholic priests and for the regulation of Dublin corporation, were trailed through *Heads*, but so too were localised and limited bills.[70] The convenience to interested parties is clear. Printing suggested that parliament was responding to wider, albeit sectional, pressures; even that the enclosed chambers on College Green were being opened to observers throughout the island.

One task to be tackled in each session was the adjudication of disputed election results. A committee of elections and privileges managed this business. Objectors, usually defeated candidates, set out their cases; they might be answered by the victors. One of the earliest appeals to be printed and to have survived took up the cause of James Lennox, elected as member for County Londonderry in 1697. Only gradually did these printed petitions supplant the traditional manuscript

[64] *CJI*, vii, 188; viii, 301, 302, 418, 477; *A list of all the pensions now in being on the Civil Establishment* (Dublin, 1763); *A list of all pensions and incidents which have been placed on the Civil Establishment, from the 26th of August, 1763, to the 1st of November, 1765* (Dublin, 1765); *A list of pensions now in being on the Civil Establishment, granted for lives and years* (Dublin, 1769); *A list of the pensions on the military establishment, on the 18th of January, 1787* (Dublin, 1787).

[65] Malcomson, *Nathaniel Clements*, 284–5.

[66] McAulay, *An inquiry into the legality of pensions.*

[67] *CJI*, v, 67, 70, 321, 327, 330; vi, 43, 65, 66, 73, 77, 81, 158, 159, 160, 167, 169, 179, 180, 191, 197, 199; vii, 258, 259, 283, 284, 306.

[68] *CJI*, vii, 297.

[69] *An answer to a paper lately published, intituled, Reasons against the heads of a bill proposed for regulating the Six Clerks offices in the High Court of Chancery* ([Dublin, ?1737]); *Answers to some objections made to the heads of a bill now depending, for better regulating the city of Dublin* (Dublin, 1760); *Observations on the heads of a bill for a register of popish priests, proposed to be brought into a law* (Dublin, 1756); *Reasons humbly offered, why heads of a bill, For confirming and ascertaining the aids and contributions payable by the freemen and non-freemen of the several corporations in the city of Dublin . . . should not pass into a law* (Dublin, 1768).

[70] *Heads of a bill for a register of popish priests* (Dublin, 1756); *Heads of a bill for a general register of popish priests* (Dublin, 1757); *Heads of a bill, For better Regulating the elections of the Lord Mayor, Aldermen, Sheriffs, Commons, and other Officers of the City of Dublin* (Dublin, 1758, 1759).

submissions.[71] Intended primarily for the members of the parliamentary committee, the *Cases* never aimed at large readerships. However, the availability of multiple printed copies allowed the spread of the partisans' arguments into a bigger constituency. In time, the justifications would link up with the printed manifestoes and propaganda which had preceded and accompanied the elections themselves.

Other activities of the Houses and their committees generated print. In 1719, two gentlemen in County Down complained in a petition to the Commons about the grand jury. The latter responded with a printed defence.[72] For official bodies and the reasonably prosperous, spending money to print answers may have become routine. These rejoinders to actions initiated by parliament are distinct from printed petitions which the hopeful, the idealistic, the desperate and cranks directed at the Commons. Similarly, the printed statements about alleged electoral malpractices have to be distinguished from the manifestoes published by candidates or their partisans. It was the latter, rather than the measured official publications, that enlivened politics in 18th-century Ireland.

2

The house of lords was slower than the Commons to lift the veil on its deliberations. It was no less watchful over its, and its members', privileges.[73] In 1695, it demanded – and secured – an amendment to the *Votes*, the original version of which had misrepresented some peers.[74] The Lords' tardy adoption of print may tell of the smaller volume of business, especially of moment, that originated with it.[75] In addition, the members of the upper House had no constituents to humour. Not until 1778 did the house of lords arrange the publication of its proceedings. An obstacle was the need to transcribe from the manuscript journals: it was calculated that the task would occupy four clerks for a year and cost £400. More worrying were 'many chasms' in the records.[76] For an

---

[71] *The case of James Lennox, esq; in relation to an election of a knight of the shire in the County of Londonderry* ([Dublin, 1697]) [RIA, 3 B 53–56/317]. For a manuscript petition, TCD, MS 3821/285: John Blennerhasset to house of commons, [?1661]; M.A. Hickson, *Selections from Old Kerry Records* (1872), 170, 171. Later examples include: *The answer of Thomas Burdett, Esq. to the case of Jeffrey Paul, Esq.* ([Dublin, 1713]); *The case of Sir Richard Meade, Bart.* (?Dublin, [1725]); *The case of Anthony Stawell, Esq* (?Dublin, [1725]), the latter two both in University College, Cork, Boole Library, Kinsale Manorial Papers, 1698–1764, U 20; *The case of Stephen Moore, esq; in support of his petition* ([Dublin, 1733[4]); *The case of John Irwin, esq: referred to in his petition to the Hon. House of Commons* ([Dublin, 1737]); and the printed petitions of 1727 reported by A.P.W. Malcomson in the NLI calendar of the Headfort Papers, H/3/2–12; T.C. Barnard, 'Considering the Inconsiderable: Electors, Patrons and Irish Elections, 1659–1761', in *The Irish Parliament in the Eighteenth Century*, ed. Hayton, 107–27.

[72] *The case of the grand jury of the county of Down with relation to a petition exhibited against them in the House of Commons by Hugh Savage, esq. and Thomas Echlin, gent.* ([Dublin, 1719]); T.C. Barnard, 'What Became of Waring? The Making of an Ulster Squire', in T.C. Barnard, *Irish Protestant Ascents and Descents, 1641–1770* (Dublin, 2004), 243 n. 47.

[73] *LJI*, ii, 174; v, 436.

[74] *LJI*, i, 555.

[75] F.G. James, *Lords of the Ascendancy: The Irish House of Lords and its Members, 1600–1800* (Dublin, 1995), 160–1; *Proceedings*, ed. Kelly, i, p. xiv.

[76] *LJI*, v, 38–9.

estimate of costs, the Lords went neither to the king's printer nor the Commons' official printer, but to William Sleater.[77] Perhaps playing to the pride of members, Sleater planned to print in the same type used for the *Journals* of the British house of lords. The Lords approached the lord lieutenant to seek the necessary funds from the king.[78] There was not the conscious appeal to Irish patriotism which had characterised the arrangements for the *Commons Journals*. For the Lords, the print run was 210 for a three-volume set.[79] It would be supplied either in boards or, were something showier desired, in more expensive dress. Sumptuously-bound copies were given to successive lords lieutenant, and Dublin University was guaranteed its own set, albeit in more modest covers than the viceregal ones.[80]

Eight volumes of the *Journals of the House of Lords* memorialised the institution. Its production showed that print had become *de rigueur* for any organisation aspiring to attention and respect. Nevertheless, interest in the Lords' transactions is hard to assess. Published *Journals* catered – potentially at least – to a curiosity different from the antiquarian and legalistic inquisitiveness of a few members of each House, such as Bishop Dopping, Archbishop King, William Molyneux and Lord Mountmorres.[81] An ability to appeal to a collective sense of tradition and identity was evident in 1764. When the missing manuscript journal for the wartime 1640s reappeared, it was bought for £200 and then printed as an addendum – out of sequence – to the *Journals of the House of Commons*.[82]

3

Another official publication concerned parliament, but not exclusively. The statutes enacted in each session attested to the activism and (arguably) the public spirit of members. But they alone were not responsible, and this remained the case when it came to their printing. Legislation, even more than the proceedings day-by-day, was of undoubted public interest. Notionally, it governed and circumscribed the activities of all within Ireland. Unlike proclamations issued on the sole authority of the executive in Dublin Castle, the laws had hybrid origins. Understandably, the two Houses fretted

---

[77] Pollard, *Dictionary*, 527–8.

[78] *LJI*, v, 66.

[79] This contrasted with the 500 copies of the standing orders of the house of lords bespoken in 1778: *LJI*, v, 66.

[80] *LJI*, v, 463, 558.

[81] W. Domville, 'A Disquisition Touching that Great Question Whether an Act of Parliament Made in England shall Bind the Kingdom and People of Ireland', ed. P.H. Kelly, *Analecta Hibernica*, xl (2007), 17–70; [A. Dopping], *Modus tenendi parliamenta & consilia in Hibernia* (Dublin, 1692); M.E. Gilmore, 'Anthony Dopping and the Church of Ireland, 1685–1695', Queen's University Belfast MA, 1988; P.H. Kelly, 'Conquest *versus* Consent as the Basis to the English Title to Ireland in William Molyneux's *Case of Ireland* . . . Stated (1698)', in *British Interventions in Early Modern Ireland*, ed. C. Brady and J. Ohlmeyer (Cambridge, 2005), 334–56; P.H. Kelly, 'Recasting a Tradition: William Molyneux and the Sources of The Case of Ireland . . . Stated (1698)', in *Political Thought in Seventeenth-Century Ireland: Kingdom or Colony*, ed. J.H. Ohlmeyer (Cambridge, 2000), 83–106; J.I. McGuire, 'Dopping, Anthony', in *Dictionary of Irish Biography*, iii, p. 412; H. Morres, Viscount Mountmorres, *The history of the principal transactions of the Irish Parliament, from the year 1634 [t]o 1666* (2 vols, 1792).

[82] *CJI*, vii, 356; ix, 38.

© *The Parliamentary History Yearbook Trust 2014*

to ensure that the new enactments should be published. While parliaments remained occasional and short, the chore of updating the published collections was manageable. But the frequency of sessions after 1692, and the volume of additional statutes, overwhelmed the existing systems. The comprehensive edition of *Statutes at Large* was revised in 1678.[83] As early as 1695, members were complaining that the nominated printer had failed to issue 'the several acts'.[84] In the next parliament, the house of lords addressed the lords justice over the need to expedite the printing of new and the reprinting of old laws by the king's printer, Andrew Crooke.[85] Nearly 30 years later, the same operator was chided on the same grounds.[86] Critics underestimated the proliferation of new statutes in each successive session; also, the impediments to establishing accurate texts. Equally, Crooke had probably failed to appreciate how the complexity and scale of the task would expand.

It was a battle to keep pace as the trickle of new laws turned into a torrent. Collections were published for each session.[87] Routinely, single acts were printed. Of the 124 titles known to have been published in Dublin during 1709, at least 20% were separate acts of parliament.[88] But the lack of a complete collection, ideally indexed, was an obvious inconvenience, as Archbishop King of Dublin grumbled.[89] In order to mitigate the sense of confusion (although possibly adding to it), digests and abridgements were compiled.[90] So, too, were selections from specific genres: the administration of the

[83] *A collection of all the statutes now in use in the kingdom of Ireland* (Dublin, 1678).

[84] *Votes*, no. 50 (18 Nov. 1695), p. 191.

[85] *LJI*, i, 749–50, 751.

[86] *LJI*, ii, 854.

[87] *Acts and statutes made in a Parliament, begun at Dublin the fifth day of October, Anno Dom. 1692* (Dublin, 1692); *Acts and statutes, made in a Parliament, begun, at Dublin, the twenty-eighth day of November, anno dom. 1727* (Dublin, 1734); *Acts and statutes made in a Parliament, begun at Dublin the fifth day of October, anno Dom. 1692 . . . And continued by several adjournments* (Dublin, 1699); *Acts and Statutes made in a Parliament begun at Dublin, the fifth day of October, Anno Dom. 1692 . . . And continued . . . until the twenty seventh Day of August, Anno Dom. 1695. And further continued* (Dublin, 1713); *Acts and statutes made in a Parliament begun at Dublin, the twelfth day of November, Anno Dom. 1715* (Dublin, 1716); *Acts and statutes made in a Parliament begun at Dublin, the twenty eighth day of November, Anno Dom. 1727 . . . And continued . . . until the seventh day of October, 1735* (Dublin, 1736); *Acts and Statutes, made in a Parliament begun at Dublin, the twenty eighth day of November, Anno Dom. 1727 . . . And further continued . . . until the eleventh day of October, 1757* (Dublin, 1758); *Acts and statutes made in a Parliament begun at Dublin the twenty first day of September, Anno Dom. 1703 . . . and continued by several adjournments and prorogations . . . until the twelfth of July, 1711* (Dublin, 1711).

[88] *CJI*, viii, 222: 4 Feb. 1768; *Votes of the House of Commons, in the fourth session . . . the nineteenth day of May, 1761* (Dublin, 1767–8), 297–8.

[89] *Correspondence of Jonathan Swift*, ed. Williams, i, 50. In 1747, Robert French of Monivae bought (for 17*s* 4*d*.) the statutes for the two most recent sessions and then another; NLI, MS 4919, ff. 77, 79v: R. French accounts, 21 Feb. 1746[7], 9 July 1748.

[90] M. Bacon, *A new abridgment of the law* (5th edn, Dublin, 1786); E. Bullingbrooke and J. Belcher, *A abridgement of the statutes of Ireland, from the first session of parliament in the third year of the reign of King Edward the Second, to the end of the twenty fifth year of the reign of His Present Majesty King George the Second* (Dublin, 1754); E. Hunt, *An abridgment of all the statutes in Ireland, in the reign of King George the 1. in force and use* (Dublin, 1728); E. Lee, *The statute-law of Ireland common-placed* (Dublin, 1734); G. Meriton, *An exact abridgment of all the publick printed Irish statutes now in force, from the third year of the reign of King Edward the Second, to the end of the last session of Parliament, in the tenth year of his present Majesty's reign King William the Third* (Dublin, 1700); N. Robbins, *An exact abridgment of all the Irish statutes, from the first session Parliament in the third year of the reign of King Edward II. to the end of the seventh session of . . . King George II* (Dublin, 1736).

revenue; the laws governing the church and clergy; and relations between masters and servants or landlords and tenants.[91] In addition, magistrates and others enforcing the law were provided with printed guides.[92]

Eventually, but not until 1762, the Lords intervened over the backlog and confusion of published statutes.[93] The lord lieutenant having been addressed, it was agreed that a comprehensive edition should be undertaken. The right to print it was reserved to the holder of the patent as king's printer in Ireland. This functionary, now Hugh Boulter Grierson produced nine volumes which covered enactments to 1767.[94] Again, Irish-made paper was used.[95] One set for every member in both chambers was requisitioned. Perhaps 50 were left for outsiders. The edition was overseen by the lord chancellor and judges, and published by Grierson, but the real labourer was a lawyer: Francis Vesey, a cadet from a family well-represented in both Lords and Commons.[96] Vesey added an apparatus of marginal notes, tables of the titles of laws, references and (crucially) indices. It was agreed that Vesey had completed the task with 'care, skill and accuracy', and was rewarded with £1,000, which proved slow in payment.[97] No sooner was the project completed than supplementary volumes had to be added.[98]

After each member of Lords and Commons had received his copy, few were available for wider circulation. It may be that official recipients passed on their volumes as a favour to those who might make greater use of them.[99] As in the past, individuals and some organisations contented themselves with printed versions, issued separately, of individual laws that affected them directly.[100] In 1768, the Dublin Society decided to

[91] *An abridgement of all the English and Irish statutes now in force, or use, relating to the revenue of Ireland* (Dublin, 1769); *An abridgement of two Acts made in a Parliament . . . In the third year of the reign of King George II. for the better repairing of churches, and enabling the clergy to reside* (Dublin, 1730); E. Bullingbrooke, *Ecclesiastical law; or, the statutes, constitutions, canons, rubricks, and articles, of the Church of Ireland. Methodically digested under proper heads* (2 vols, Dublin, 1770); M. Dutton, *The law of landlords and tenants in Ireland* (Dublin, 1726); M. Dutton, *The law of masters and servants in Ireland* (Dublin, 1723); N. Robbins, *An exact abridgment of all the ecclesiastical statutes in force in Ireland* (Dublin, ?1740); J. Paul, *Every landlord or tenant his own lawyer* (Dublin, 1777).

[92] R. Bolton, *A justice of the peace for Ireland* (Dublin, 1683); M. Dutton, *The office and authority of a justice of peace for Ireland* (Dublin, 1718); M. Dutton, *The office and authority of sheriffs, Under-Sheriffs, Deputies, County-Clerks, and Coroners, in Ireland* (Dublin, 1721); 'M.S.', *Seasonable-advice: or an infallible guide to grand and petty juries . . . Collected from the common-law, statutes, &c* (4th edn, Dublin, 1725); *The office and duty of high and petty constables . . . in Ireland* (Dublin, 1720).

[93] *LJI*, iv, 252.

[94] J.W. Hammond, 'The King's Printers in Ireland, 1551–1919', *Dublin Historical Record*, xi (1950), 88–96; M. Pollard, 'Control of the Press in Ireland through the King's Printer's Patent, 1600–1800', *Irish Booklore*, iv (1978), 79–95; Pollard, *Dictionary*, 254–6.

[95] C. Benson and M. Pollard, 'The Rags of Ireland are by No Means the Same: Irish Paper Used in the *Statutes at Large*', *Long Room*, ii (1970), 20.

[96] E. Keane, P.B. Phair and T.U. Sadleir, *King's Inns Admissions Papers 1607–1867* (Dublin, 1982), 490.

[97] *LJI*, iv, 607, 622, 842.

[98] *LJI*, iv, 450; v, 156, 341, 668.

[99] *CJI*, viii, 308; *LJI*, iv, 252; *Votes . . . in the fourth session*, 297–8.

[100] Royal Society of Antiquaries of Ireland, masters' accounts of disbursements, 1702–3, 25 Apr. 1703; Weavers' Company accounts, 1691–1714; BL, Add. MS 47,008A, f. 24: W. Taylor to Lord Perceval, 2 July 738; St Michan's, Dublin, RCB, P 276/8/2, p. 43, account with R. Gunne, 1715, churchwardens' accounts, 723–61; University College, Cork, Boole Library, *A collection of all the statutes now in use in the kingdom of Ireland* (Dublin, 1678), copy from the Green Coat Hospital, Shandon; *The Council Book of the Corporation of Cork*, ed. R. Caulfield (Guildford, 1876), 477, 521; *Calendar of Kinsale Documents*, ed. M. Mulcahy (6 vols, Kinsale, 1988–98), vii, 12.

buy a collected volume of the parliamentary statutes since 1761. At the same time, it ordered 500 copies of an act felt to be particularly relevant to its concerns: this would then be distributed among its members.[101] The Incorporated Society derived much of its regular income from the sales of licences to peddlers and hawkers. When, in 1774, a new act was passed, the society had the statute printed as handbills. These were then sent to 'country printers', presumably as a template for further copies which were to be posted in conspicuous places.[102] Individual acts, printed in Dublin, were regularly advertised for sale in Belfast during the 1760s. They sold for as little as 3*d*. or 6*d*.[103]

A comprehensive collection of the Irish statutes might have been expected to obviate the earlier inconveniences which had obliged ingenious and entrepreneurial solutions. In some ways, the new volumes compounded the difficulties. The index and tables notwithstanding, it was a daunting task to locate, let alone understand, any selected law. So much is implied by a request of the Commons in 1785 to the lord lieutenant: that the king's printer prepare abridgements and abstracts of the statutes 'for the use of the several counties and towns of this kingdom'.[104] Lay understanding was not helped by the use of black letter or 'Old English', essentially Gothic, type. Guides and abridgements accordingly persisted. Moreover, the availability of the *Statutes* encouraged those, usually trained to the law, to produce handbooks on specific branches of litigation.[105] Printing – underwritten by government and parliament – brought the texts into the public realm. Even so, it is presently impossible to judge whether the publication illumined more than it obfuscated. The proliferation of legal treatises and expositors testified both to the obscurities and to the litigiousness of 18th-century Ireland. Again, it is debatable whether the more readily-accessible information improved the enforcement of, and obedience to, the laws.[106]

4

The tally of printing which can be traced directly to the Irish parliament is short, but weighty. Its purposes were overwhelmingly utilitarian, although institutional pride and patriotism played their parts. The impact and implications contrast with the flurries of print which enveloped elections, individuals, debates and decisions. These unofficial, and usually unauthorised, publications attest to a widening interest in parliamentary politics, although exactly how wide remains to be determined. An almost reflexive recourse to print in times of political excitability can first be detected, not unexpectedly, in Dublin Controversies over municipal elections in the city became entangled with the polarised

---

[101] Dublin Society, *Minutes*, 2 June 1768.

[102] TCD, MS 5225, pp. 350–1: Board Book, Incorporated Society, 1761–75, 13 May 1774.

[103] *Belfast Newsletter*, 4 July 1766, 16 Aug. 1768, 5–9 Aug. 1774.

[104] *CJI*, xi, 442.

[105] F. Butler, *An introduction to the law relative to trials at nisi prius* (Dublin, 1768); T. Cunningham, *The merchant's lawyer: or the law of trade in general* (3rd edn, 2 vols, Dublin, 1769); J. Sayer, *The law of costs* (Dublin 1768).

[106] T.C. Barnard, 'Local Courts in Later Seventeenth-Century and Eighteenth-Century Ireland', in *The Laws and Other Legalities of Ireland 1689–1850*, ed. M. Brown and S.P. Donlan (Farnham, 2011), 33–45; N Garnham, *The Courts, Crime and the Criminal Law in Ireland 1692–1760* (Dublin, 1996).

national and Britannic politics of whig and tory between 1710 and 1714. One consequence was to enlist print in the electoral battles of the capital. By 1727, when rival
candidates presented themselves to the voters, they had manifestoes printed in the Dublin
papers.[107] Concurrently, partisans directed printed squibs and satires at the electors. At
least 15 can be identified. Many were in verse. Furthermore, two (if not more) contributors to the 1727 Dublin hustings stole Swift's identity; a tribute to the way in which
the dean had energised politics through his writings earlier in the decade.[108]

Given the size of the Dublin electorate and the proximity of the presses, using print was
a natural development. Moreover, the practice was spreading into the countryside. In
October 1727, the *Dublin Journal* reported the state of the poll in County Kilkenny.[109]
Through the columns of newspapers, candidates tried to rebut calumnies spread by
political adversaries.[110] More useful, but still partisan, was the printed notice for freeholders living in the city about early-morning coaches laid on to take them to vote in County
Meath.[111] If print was eagerly annexed to the battery of political armaments, it did not
supersede the older weapons of manuscript, spectacle and talk. A by-election in Westmeath in 1723 inspired at least two lengthy sets of verses.[112] Similarly, during the 1740s, an
aggrieved opponent of two midlands members, Richard Edgeworth and Thomas
Pakenham, circulated scabrous and scatological doggerel in manuscript.[113] In County
Clare, too, versifiers focused on the personalities involved in electoral contests.[114] As late as
1783, the traditional medium of handwriting was used in a Galway election.[115]

Much of this material, allusive when not abusive, seems to have been aimed at those
in the know. In such restricted circles, manuscript sufficed, as it did for other ephemeral
interjections. But newspapers and print promised access to a larger readership. Accordingly, in 1741, when a by-election was held in Limerick, aspirants announced their
candidatures and appealed for votes through the papers.[116] By the time of the general
elections of 1761, 1768 and 1776, many inches of space were filled with rivals' requests
for votes.[117] In 1776, Richard Malone, hoping to succeed an uncle as member for
County Westmeath, sent a printed address (from Dublin) to the electors.[118] Yet voters,

[107] *Faulkner's Dublin Journal*, 25–9 Apr., 2–6 May, 30 May–3 June, 10–14 Oct. 1727.

[108] *Gulivers letter to the Tholsel, concerning the present election* ([Dublin, 1727]); *Seasonable reflections address'd to the citizens of Dublin, by Captain Gulliver* (Dublin, 1727).

[109] *Faulkner's Dublin Journal*, 10–14 Oct. 1727.

[110] *Faulkner's Dublin Journal*, 29 Aug.–2 Sept. 1727.

[111] *Faulkner's Dublin Journal*, 10–14 Oct. 1727.

[112] D.W. Hayton, 'Two Ballads on the County Westmeath By-Election of 1723', *Eighteenth-Century Ireland*, v (1989), 7–30.

[113] NAI, crown entry books, city of Dublin, 1746–7, 1 Dec. 1746, 14 Feb. 1746[7]; NLI, MS 1517: R. Edgeworth account book, 23 Nov. 1746.

[114] NLI, Inchiquin MSS, MS 45,356/5: 'A new ballad on an approaching election, to the tune of Fireaway Casey'; NLI, MS 45,375/3: 'A song on the election of 1768'.

[115] T. Bartlett, 'A Galway Election Squib of 1783', *Journal of the Galway Archaeological and Historical Society*, xxvii (1979–80), 85–9.

[116] Callaghan, 'Newspapers and Print Culture in Eighteenth-Century Limerick', vol. 1, p. 50; D.A. Fleming, *Politics and Provincial People: Sligo and Limerick, 1691–1761* (Manchester, 2010), 82–3.

[117] *Belfast Newsletter*, 2 June 1761, 14 Mar. 1766, 16 Oct., 13 Nov. 1767, 15, 18 Mar., 5 Apr., 13 Dec. 768, 14–17 Feb. 1775.

[118] NLI, MS 41,599/9: printed address of R. Malone, 11 May 1776.

deluged with round robins and printed appeals, could take offence at these impersonal approaches. As in other spheres, the growing ubiquity of print gave added weight to the handwritten. The receipt of the latter rather than the former flattered the recipient.[119]

Voters, for their part, used the press to address members or would-be members on issues in debate, such as Octennial and Septennial Bills. In 1773, the *Belfast Newsletter*, along with three Dublin diurnals, printed an address to the knights of the shire for Meath from freeholders gathered at Navan. It inveighed against the burden of pensions and the prospect of new taxes.[120] This emboldening of those who frequently dignified themselves as 'free and independent' electors raised a possibility of members being mandated by constituents and held to account.

Newspapers and printers were engaged in businesses, often precarious ones, which might easily fail. The inventive newspapers welcomed elections as a source of extra work. Early in George III's reign, an operative in Waterford received £2 5s. 6d. for providing ribbons, emblazoned presumably with the name of the favoured candidate. Indeed, it was a more lucrative job than printing 500 copies of *The Cobler's Letter* (a defence of Church of England principles against methodism)[121] and for 'printing and dispersing . . . the real Freeman's Letter'.[122] Newspaper columns were stuffed with advertisements, into which category fell much of what appeared to be objective political commentary. The committed were used to paying to promote their causes: print simply added to the bills. Supporters of one parliamentary candidate in County Louth used a newspaper to traduce an unfortunate innkeeper in Dundalk who had reneged on a promise to keep open house for them.[123]

Efforts to sustain the patriot cause during the 1750s through communicating the impression of a nationwide movement included the paid insertion of lists of the polemical toasts drunk at meetings.[124] In addition, the activities of the Patriot Club in County Armagh were publicised through print.[125] Planted items, and even titles, gave an illusion of a synchronised and national movement in which Monaghan, Ardbraccan, Ballyjamesduff, Kinsale and Bandon were united.[126] From England, an absentee Irish

---

[119] NLI, PC 445: J. Smythe to W. Smythe, [undated, ?1739/40].

[120] *Belfast Newsletter*, 16–19 Nov. 1773.

[121] *The cobler's letter to the Methodists, proving the necessity of good works, and the uselessness of faith without them* copy in RIA, where assigned to ?1750.

[122] *The Shapland Carew Papers*, ed. A.K. Longfield (Dublin, 1946), 135, 136; Johnston-Liik, *Irish Parliament* iii, 367–8.

[123] *Belfast Newsletter*, 15 Dec. 1767.

[124] PRONI, D 1556/16/14/21 and 22: Maxwell accounts, 30 Mar. 1755, 28 Jan. 1756. Cf. M. Powell 'Political Toasting in Eighteenth-Century Ireland', *History*, xci (2006), 508–29.

[125] *A layman's sermon, preached at the Patriot Club of the county of Armagh . . . the 3d of September, 175* (Dublin, 1755). Cf. D.A. Fleming, 'Politics and Patriots in Navan, 1753–55', *Irish Historical Studies*, xxxv (2009), 502–21; E. Magennis, 'Patriotism, Popery and Politics: The Armagh By-Election of 1753', in *Armagh History and Society*, ed. A.J. Hughes and W. Nolan (Dublin, 2001), 485–504.

[126] *The adventures and metamorphose of Queen Elizabeth's pocket-pistol, late of Charles-fort, near Kinsale* (Dublin 1756); *A few words of brotherly advice, to the free and independant electors of the town of Kinsale* (np, 1754), in University College, Cork, Boole Library, Kinsale Manorial Papers, 1698–1764, U 20; 'H.G.', *A just and true answer to scandalous pamphlet call'd a genuine letter* (Dublin, 1755); 'G.H.', *A genuine letter from a freeman of Bandon, to George Faulkner* (Dublin, 1755); *A letter from a burgess of Monaghan to the parish-clerk of Ardbraccan* (Dublin, 1754); *narrative of the dispute in the corporation of Kinsale, in a letter from a buff to his friend in Dublin* (Dublin, 1756).

peer commented on the 'political disputes and the long list of patriot bumpers, that are so well set forth in Mr Faulkner's paper, to be drunk by every Independent True Friend and Lover of [?liberty]'.[127] If there was illusionism thanks to the manipulation of the press, the identities, skills and motives of the *prestidigitateurs* have yet to be laid bare.[128] Orchestration coexisted with spontaneous provincial campaigns which drew on, and supplemented, what was happening in Dublin, as with Dean Massy's attack on municipal corruption in Limerick, which borrowed language and tactics from Charles Lucas.[129] Print attended electoral contests in Cork during the 1730s and Limerick in 1761. Cryptic, it had to be decoded, and did not obviously reach out to a readership larger than that for verses, satires and commentaries still being circulated in manuscript.[130] In the end, exactly how much the boisterousness of some electoral contests inside and outside Dublin owed to printed matter cannot yet be judged. The bawdy and abusive exchanges at election times occurred on the frontiers between song, balladry, speech, ritualised demonstrations, handwritten libels and crude prints.[131]

A contrast between the authorised and unofficial can be stressed. What Lords and Commons sanctioned, thanks to format and contents, enjoyed limited circulation and reading. This gulf between the voluminous and abstruse on the one hand, and the succinct and simplified on the other, marked the print relating to religion, medicine, technology, geography, history, and morality. Highly-trained adepts, like members of parliament, mistrusted popularisers. Nor did they welcome too close interest from amateurs. Parliament, through its impassive print, communicated its industry. It was left to outsiders to badger, scrutinise, congratulate and ridicule.

---

[127] TCD, MS 3821/228: Lord Darnley to ?W. Crosbie, 1 Apr. 1755; NLI, Talbot-Crosbie MSS, folder 63: same to same, 28 Dec. 1759.

[128] The essential guide is J. Hill, ' "Allegories, Fictions, and Feigned Representations": Decoding the Money Bill Dispute, 1752–6', *Eighteenth-Century Ireland*, xxi (2006), 66–88.

[129] Fleming, *Politics and Provincial People*, 89–96; C. Massy, *A collection of resolutions queries etc. wrote on occasion of the present disputes in the city of Limerick* (Limerick, 1749).

[130] T.C. Barnard, '*Strolabella* (1740) and the Varieties of Print in Provincial Ireland', *Irish University Review*, li (2011), 54–62; Fleming, *Politics and Provincial People*, 96; *Liberty and property or the downfall of arbitrary power: tragedy as it is now acting in the c[ity] of L[imerick]* (Limerick, 1761).

[131] Barnard, 'Considering the Inconsiderable', 107–27; P. Higgins, *A Nation of Politicians: Gender, Patriotism and Political Culture in Late Eighteenth-Century Ireland* (Madison, WI, 2010), 28–55.

© *The Parliamentary History Yearbook Trust 2014*

Censorship, Salvation and the Preaching of Francis Higgins: A Reconsideration of High Church Politics and Theology in the Early 18th Century*

ALEX W. BARBER

This article considers the exploitation of the pulpit by high churchmen between 1690 and 1710, focusing specifically on a series of sermons delivered by Francis Higgins. It is argued that high churchmen, motivated by disgust for the lax press policies pursued in the period, employed the pulpit to attack whig politicians and bishops and suggest that the Church was in danger. It is likewise argued that this strategy was accomplished through contending that the country was drenched in sin and that practices such as occasional conformity were endangering God's providential blessing. In the process of examining high church sermons, the article seeks to untangle the question of why Henry Sacheverell was prosecuted in 1710. Ultimately, the article argues that the events of 1710 were the culmination of a series of disputes between high churchmen and whig politicians and bishops over the power of the pulpit and the true nature of godly reformation.

Keywords: Francis Higgins; censorship; pulpit; Church in danger; high church; Henry Sacheverell; salvation

1

In 1710, shortly after the disastrous trial of Henry Sacheverell, Maurice Wheeler wrote to his confidant, Bishop Wake, commenting that: 'Passive obedience and resistance are the distinguishing notions' between whigs and tories.[1] Modern historians all agree with Wheeler that the impeachment of Henry Sacheverell was an attempt by the whig ministry of Sunderland and Godolphin to decide the legitimacy of the Glorious Revolution.[2] It is not an unduly difficult task, therefore, to marshal contemporary evidence which, by itself, creates an impression that the prosecution of a minor clergyman from Oxford was a political affair concerned with establishing the correct status of the constitution. Such an interpretation offers us one answer – albeit a starkly political one – to the problem of why government ministers embroiled themselves in a

* I am grateful to Mike Cressey, Stephen Taylor and Paul Wilkie for commenting on a draft of this article.

[1] Christ Church, Oxford, Wake MSS. Arch. W. Epist. 23, f. 207: 26 July 1710; cited in Geoffrey Holmes, *British Politics in the Age of Anne* (rev. edn, 1987), 52.

[2] Geoffrey Holmes, *The Trial of Doctor Sacheverell* (1973); G.M. Trevelyan, *England Under Queen Anne* (3 vols, 1930–4), iii, 48; Mark Goldie, 'Tory Political Thought, 1689–1714', University of Cambridge PhD, 1977. For the most recent interpretation of Sacheverell, see *The State Trial of Henry Sacheverell*, ed. Brian Cowan (2012).

public trial of such magnitude. But Maurice Wheeler, in common with other observers, was in no doubt that that there were other explanations for the trial. He regularly wrote to Wake, warning him that the whigs were losing the propaganda war in parliamentary constituencies outside of London. In his view, clergymen were persuading constituents to the high church position with rhetorically-skilful sermons that were seditious. High churchmen, Wheeler complained, railed from the pulpit that the Church was in danger and were able to warn receptive audiences that England was a country drenched in sin. Practices such as occasional conformity were endangering God's providential blessing and leaving England facing a future of ruin and damnation. High churchmen informed their flock that only the empowering of the anglican Church could hope to ensure God's grace through the power to coerce conformity.[3]

There was one other closely-related issue which contributed to the high church assertion that the country was in corporeal danger. Setting the correct limits of free expression was vital to the religious view of men such as Francis Atterbury, Henry Sacheverell and Francis Higgins. High churchmen, of course, lived in a world in which books were powerful. They believed that the press should be restrained consistently because reading and writing heretical and blasphemous books, or consuming them with indifference or without abhorrence, led the reader to partake of the sins contained within the book. High churchmen also articulated a relationship between the freedom of the press and social and political disorder. Impious books were texts that threatened the peace of Church and state and endangered the authority of bishop and magistrate. Such a vision, one that struck a chord with so many high churchmen, saw the lax press policy of the whig junto as a vital component of the Church in danger debate. 'No kingdom under heaven, professing the name of Christ', one high churchman thundered, has ever allowed the press to go 'unnoticed or unpunished'.[4] This is not to say that whig politicians of the early 18th century did not oppose the more excessive tendencies of the press. But their predisposition was primarily to inconsistent postpublication restraint, and not to see the reinstatement of prepublication censorship as a service to the coercive power of the Church and priesthood. The view, so beloved of high churchmen, that heretical and blasphemous publications blighted and corrupted the nation, was less of a conviction for whig bishops. No doubt men such as Tenison objected to the publication of *Christianity not Mysterious*, but they did not accept the intimate connection between the freedom of the press, the claim that the Church was in danger and the high church assertion that England was no longer a blessed nation.[5]

Given the very different premises from which most whigs and high churchmen approached the crucial issues of the power of the Church and the acceptable limits of free expression, it was hardly to be expected that the political ministries of William and

---

[3] For the best analysis of the Church in danger debate see Clyve Jones, 'Debates in the House of Lords on The Church in Danger'', 1705 and on Dr Sacheverell's Impeachment, 1710', *Historical Journal*, xix (1976), 59–71; Mary Ransome, 'Church and Dissent in the Election of 1710', *English Historical Review*, ccxxi (1941), 6–89.

[4] Francis Higgins, *A sermon preach'd at the Royal Chappel at White-Hall; on Ash-Wednesday, Feb 26, 1706/7* 1707), 8.

[5] For the reaction to the publication of *Christianity not Mysterious*, see Justin Champion, *Republican Learning: ohn Toland and the Crisis of Christian Culture, 1696–1722* (Manchester, 2003), 78–86. Both Wake and Gibson vere concerned with the laxity of the press: see Norman Sykes, *William Wake, Bishop of Lincoln 1705–1716, irchbishop of Canterbury, 1716–1737* (2 vols, Cambridge, 1957), ii, 170–1.

Alex W. Barber

Anne would be able to prevent the pulpit from being used as a forum for religious dissatisfaction. By the early 18th century, high churchmen were markedly keen to push the limits of acceptable expression in their sermons. Frustrated by their marginalisation from power and horrified by the offensive practice of occasional conformity, a loosely-co-ordinated band of skilled high church preachers attacked the whig junto of Sunderland, Godolphin and Marlborough, ceaselessly.[6] In turn, the sermons of the more extreme high churchmen forced members of the whig junto into a direct and, at times, public re-examination of the limits of acceptable preaching. Many whigs publicly agreed that high churchmen were going too far and urged Sunderland, their most natural ally, to condemn severely what they saw as the exploitation of the pulpit. Yet despite threatening gestures from Sunderland and Godolphin, the idea of legislating against the politicisation of the pulpit was unthinkable. Instead, various ministers warned, harried and occasionally prosecuted what whigs termed 'pulpit mongerers'.[7]

In the desire to emphasize the importance of Henry Sacheverell, the significance of other high church preachers and the long-term struggle between whigs and tories to set the limits of acceptable behaviour in the pulpit can be forgotten. By considering in greater depth the behaviour of other high churchmen besides Henry Sacheverell we can begin to understand the significant impact that the wider milieu of radical high church preaching had on religious politics before the trial of 1710. There can be no doubt that a high church programme of propaganda, including measures to exploit the pulpit, worried Sunderland and Harley. Thus the trial of Sacheverell was not just the culmination of more and more extreme sermons on constitutional issues. Instead, as this article reveals, the prosecution of Henry Sacheverell was the culmination of a series of disputes between whigs and tories: the restraint of the press, the power of the pulpit and the true nature of godly reformation, defined not just by providential claims but also a vibrant theological debate concerned with soteriological theory.

2

The more belligerent elements of high church preaching did not spring up fully fledged in the aftermath of the Glorious Revolution. However, as early as September 1688, the first protests against potential changes in the status of the Church can be discerned. 'I grows every day plainer to me', Bishop Turner wrote to Archbishop Sancroft, 'that many of our divines, men of name and note intend upon any overture for comprehension to

[6] Holmes, *Trial of Doctor Sacheverell*, 45; J.P. Kenyon, *Revolution Principles: The Politics of Party, 1689–1720* (Cambridge, 1977), 71–2.

[7] *Observator*, 13 Oct. 1711. This article serves to complement the developing literature on the early modern sermon. For the most impressive analysis see Arnold Hunt, *The Art of Hearing: English Preachers and their Audiences, 1590–1640* (Cambridge, 2010); David Appleby, *Black Bartholomew's Day* (Manchester, 2007). For this period, see Tony Claydon, 'The Sermon and the Public Sphere and the Political Culture of Late Seventeenth-Century England', and James Caudle, 'Preaching and Parliament: Patronage, Publicity, and Politics in Britain, 1701–1760', in *The English Sermon Revised*, ed. Lori Anne Ferrell and Peter McCullough (Manchester, 2000); Newton Key, 'The Political Culture and Political Rhetoric of Country Feasts and Feast Sermons, 1654–1714', *Journal of British Studies*, xxxiii (1994), 223–56; Mark Goldie, 'The Damning of King Monmouth: Pulpit Toryism in the Reign of James II', in *The Final Crisis of the Stuart Monarchy: The Revolution of 1688–91 in their British, Atlantic and European Contexts*, ed. Tim Harris and Stephen Taylor (Woodbridge, 2013).

offer all our ceremonies in sacrifice to the dissenters, kneeling at the sacrament and all'. Still convinced of the authority of the clergy of the established church, Turner urged his archbishop to 'increase as much as possible the number of those who, as true lovers of devotion and decency in it, may contend even for multitude and interest in the nation with those that would strip this poor church of all her ornaments'.[8] Turner's worst fears both did and did not come true: anglicans resisted the king's preferred reform of comprehension but were faced, instead, with the equally unsatisfactory compromise of limited toleration. One can scarcely overstress the contribution that hatred of toleration made to the development of high churchmen as a coherent and formidable political force. For many anglicans, the newly-established legal status of dissenters compromised their view of the Church of England as the guarantor of political stability and preserver of God's grace. And, of course, their distress was further enhanced by the suspension of bishops for refusing to take the oath of allegiance and the appointment in their stead of churchmen with latitudinarian tendencies; a sect of men who were, in the words of Henry Sacheverell, 'monsters and vipours in our bosom', and had been encouraged by the queen and the whig junto to 'threaten the ruin and downfall of our Church and State'.[9] Here, then, are the manifestations of the high church party that have been so ably identified by historians; the destruction of the hegemonic authority of the Church convinced men like Henry Sacheverell and his allies that the Church was in peril both from within and without.

There was, however, another major cause of high church disenchantment with government policy that is less well known. The seeming unhindered capacity of dissenters, latitudinarians, deists and atheists – in the language of high churchmen – to disseminate their views in the press, unhindered from consistent restraint and prosecution, enraged Francis Atterbury and others.[10] No doubt the concern at the distribution of unorthodox texts was heightened by the loss of licensing in 1695; it is quite clear, however, that such fears were already present in the early 1690s.[11] For high churchmen, the trinitarian disputes of post-revolutionary England were as much debates about the limits of free expression, the coercive power of the Church and the epistemological status of christianity, as they were concerned with the theological status of the son of God.[12] The burning of Arthur Bury's *Naked Gospel*, the most hated of the unorthodox books on the trinity in 1690, by the convocation of Oxford and supported by high church members, demonstrates the continued vitality of extirpating heretical and blasphemous books from earth.[13] Protests by the whig, James Parkinson, that Bury's book was an orthodox attempt to provide a 'Scheme of Christian Religion as is clear and plain

---

[8] E. Cardwell, *Conferences on the Book of Common Prayer* (1849), 404–5; cited in George Every, *The High Church Party, 1688–1718* (1956), 25.

[9] Henry Sacheverell, *The Perils of False Brethren* (1709), 15, 19; cited in Geoffrey Holmes, 'The Sacheverell Riots: The Crowd and the Church in Early Eighteenth-Century London', *Past & Present*, No. 72 (1976), 63.

[10] Mark Knights, *Representation and Misrepresentation in Later Stuart Britain: Partisanship and Political Culture* (Oxford, 2005), 267.

[11] Raymond Astbury, 'The Renewal of the Licensing Act in 1693 and its Lapse in 1695', *The Library*, 5th ser., xxxiii (1978), 296–322.

[12] Philip Dixon, *Nice and Hot Disputes: The Doctrine of the Trinity in the Seventeenth Century* (2003), 108–137; John Redwood, *Reason, Ridicule and Religion* (1986), 156–9; Every, *High Church Party*, 75–83.

[13] Arthur Bury, *The Naked Gospel* (1691).

to vulgar capacities', in order that men might find the 'true way of salvation', were dismissed by high churchmen.[14] On the contrary, James Harrington, a fellow of Oxford and devout anglican, maintained that Bury's book was 'infamous and heretical', and for the sake of good government it must be burnt and sent to hell where it deserved to reside.[15]

The high church view that doctrinal and theological orthodoxy should be enforced by the authority of the Church was unshakeable. The burning of books and the punishment of authors, whilst welcome, could never replace the licensing system. The taunting behaviour of William Freke, for example, who deliberately sent his work to both houses of parliament, in the hope that 'it might be burnt and so sell the better', enraged anglicans.[16] Freke's *Dialogue by way of question and answer* published in 1694, baited his opponents that trinitarianism was idolatrous, polytheistic, and antichristian. Even Sir Edward Harley, a politician of considerably more moderate views than many high churchmen, thought the book a 'vile and scurrilous blasphemy'.[17] The pathetic sight of Freke begging for his freedom at the court of king's bench did little to assuage high church anger.[18] The continued availability of his book and his personal freedom served only to demonstrate that William's ministries of the early 1690s were unable to contain the licentiousness of the press. Perhaps worse, the new king seemed not to understand the high church view that books must be restrained prepublication by the authority of the Church, so that unorthodox books could not infect the minds of the weak. Although William and his ministers, along with their latitudinarian allies, affected to believe that books should be restrained, they did not understand that the connection between reading bad books and damnation underpinned high church thinking. Or, put simply, many whigs failed to grasp that anger at the licentiousness of the press helped to form high church identity.[19]

The antipathy of high churchmen towards the press found its most eloquent expression in Francis Atterbury's *Letter to a convocation man*.[20] For most scholars, the real importance of Atterbury's intervention lies in his desire to demonstrate the historical evidence for the independence of the Church from the secular state.[21] But for all that Atterbury and his like desired a powerful, independent church, no threat to their existence was more tangible, more easily grasped by worried clergymen, than the free

---

[14] James Parkinson, *The Fire's Continued at Oxford: Or, The Decree of the Convocation for Burning the Naked Gospel, Considered* (1690).

[15] James Harrington, *Reasons for Reviving and Continuing the Act for the Regulation of Printing* (1693), 1; James Harrington, *A Defence of the Proceedings of the Right Reverend the Visitor and Fellows of Exeter College in Oxford* (1690), 46.

[16] William Freke, *A dialogue by way of question and answer concerning the deity of all the responses being taken out of the Scriptures* (1693).

[17] HMC, *Portland MSS*, iii, 548: Harley to Abigail Harley, 12 Dec. 1693.

[18] N. Luttrell, *A Brief Historical Relations of State Affairs from September 1678 to April 1714* (6 vols, 1857), ii, 268, 304, 313, 315.

[19] W.M. Spellman, *The Latitudinarians and the Church of England, 1660–1700* (Athens, GA, 1993), 148.

[20] Francis Atterbury, *A letter to a convocation man concerning the rights, powers, and priviledges of that body* (1697).

[21] Mark Goldie, 'The Nonjurors, Episcopacy and the Origins of the Convocation Controversy', in *Ideology and Conspiracy: Aspects of Jacobitism, 1689–1759*, ed. E. Cruickshanks (Edinburgh, 1982), 15–35; G.V. Bennett, *The Tory Crisis in Church and State 1688–1730* (Oxford, 1975), 48–62.

publication of deistic and atheistic points of view. Even in a publication concerned with arcane historical evidence, Atterbury took time to describe England as a debauched nation, overrun with heresy. 'You cannot imagine', he thundered, 'the mischievous effects, which these various Opinions and Heresies of late Published and Vindicated, have produced amongst the Laiety.' And like his fellow high churchmen, Atterbury emphasized that the salvation of his fellow men was at stake. You must command a declaration, he informed William, that 'there is a Religion enjoyned by Heaven; for otherwise you must expect, that the next Age will believe none; I am loath to be more particular, but the Cause and Effect are both plain'.[22] But what angered him no less was the weakening of the coercive power of the Church. 'It was a little too much to suppose Country Gentlemen, Merchants, or Lawyers, to be nicely skill'd in the Languages of the Bible', he noted. Rather, licensing must be reintroduced as only the clergymen of the Church of England possessed 'the Learning of the Fathers, or of the History of the Primitive Church', that was essential for those who would be 'Judges of Religious Doctrines and Opinion'.[23] The links made by Atterbury between restraining the press and the independence of the Church were far from tenuous. His pamphlet was written in the wake of John Toland's *Christianity not Mysterious*, a book that 'strutted in public' even after prosecution. One cannot doubt that the freedom of the press was a genuine concern among the lower clergy. To maintain the nation as godly, many thought, it was not sufficient even to restrain books piecemeal, rather, only the single coercive power of the Church could resist the spread of heresy and blasphemy.

To anyone reading Atterbury's book today, it is clear that the future bishop of Rochester was so angered at the spread of unorthodox doctrine that he believed the Church was in danger. However, it is also true that the potential seditious nature of his writing was disguised; he insisted that he was loyal to the king, who was no doubt a godly ruler. That said, it is also clear that, for disillusioned high churchmen, angered by the tolerance of dissenters, the weakening of the national Church, and furious at the laxity of censorship, only the accession of Queen Anne offered hope of change. Her initial insistence that: 'my own principles must always keep me entirely firm to the interests and religion of the Church of England, and will incline me to countenance those who have the truest zeal to support it' seemed to suggest that Anne's well-known natural sympathy for the high church position would actually effect ecclesiastical change.[24] Anne's proclamation, issued within months of taking the throne, that her new ministry would prevent the publication of blasphemous, heretical and irreligious books, added further succour to Atterbury's conviction that his political and religious agenda, outlined in a *Letter to a convocation man*, would now be enacted.[25] That Anne kept faith with the whig junto is a matter of historical record. Nevertheless, understanding how quickly high churchmen became dissatisfied with the new monarch's religious policy is crucial to understanding the emergence of the 'Church in danger' cry that was so important to high churchmen.

---

[22] Atterbury, *Letter to a convocation man*, 7.

[23] Atterbury, *Letter to a convocation man*, 15.

[24] Cited in Holmes, *British Politics in the Age of Anne*, 99.

[25] *A Proclamation for Restraining the Spreading of False News, and Printing and Publishing of Irreligious and Seditious Papers and Libels* (1702).

The first stirrings of dissent can be discerned in a series of separate, but ultimately connected, events. The fall of Nottingham, Seymour and Jersey in April 1704 and the promotion of the Harleyites effectively removed all high tories from office. The increasing prominence of Robert Harley, first as Speaker of the house of commons (1701–5) then as secretary of state for the north (1704–8), did little to assuage the anger of high churchmen as they appeared to lose any hope of political influence. Far from seeing him as a potential political ally, a man who could curry favour with the queen, high churchmen considered Harley the epitome of betrayal, a turncoat committed to a policy of religious moderation that favoured dissenters.[26] The hard truth also had to be admitted that high churchmen did not have the political votes in parliament to change policy. The simultaneous failure of two bills to outlaw occasional conformity, for example, heightened high church distress. Viewed by them as a 'pernicious and destructive principle that ever the Church of England suffer'd under, and the greatest cloak for spiritual hypocrisy', occasional conformity remained a central point of contention that poisoned relationships between anglicans and dissenters.[27] The attempt to tack an amendment to the Land Tax Bill simply reflected high church desperation as they realized that occasional conformity was supported by 'great patrons and advocates' and would remain a feature of daily life.[28]

But the reasons for the fissure between Anne and her natural religious allies must be sought primarily in the disastrous prosecution of a *Memorial of the Church of England*.[29] The anonymous pamphlet, published in 1705, suggested that the Church was in danger and queried Anne's displacement of high tory ministers. It was clear that such a vile accusation could not be allowed to stand and a lengthy investigation followed before the book was burnt in the autumn of 1705. The logic behind the prosecution was clear enough. To the whig members of Anne's ministry, a successful attempt to declare a *Memorial* illegal represented an opportunity to set the legal precedent that the high church cry of 'Church in danger' was seditious. There was, however, an undesirable consequence to the whig junto's pursuit of the pamphlet. Robert Harley spoke for most of his moderate tory allies when he cautioned his fellow ministers against extreme punishment for the author of a *Memorial*. He also warned Anne's courtiers that a stringent prosecution would confirm many high churchmen in the belief that the success of their cause could only be achieved outside of parliamentary politics. Indeed, Harley's natural scepticism at the value of a public prosecution was, in part, rewarded when James Drake, the supposed author, was saved from the public humiliation of the pillory and high churchmen were denied their chance to paint him as a martyr. Nevertheless, it was clear that the whig members of Anne's cabinet had got their way. In late 1705, Anne acceded to the demands of Sunderland and Godolphin and issued a proclamation

---

[26] Brilliantly constructed in J.A. Downie, *Robert Harley and the Press: Propaganda and Public Opinion in the Age of Swift and Defoe* (Cambridge, 1979).

[27] Henry Sacheverell, *The Character of Low-Church-Man* (Oxford, 1702), 6.

[28] Sacheverell, *Character of Low-Church-Man*, 6.

[29] Here I disagree with J.A. Downie's analysis of the affair. Taking a short-term view, Professor Downie believes that Harley got the better of the parties in print. The long-term view emphasized here suggests greater high church disillusionment even than Harley realized: Downie, *Harley and the Press*, 93. See also J.A. Downie, 'William Stephens and the *Letter to the Author of the Memorial of the State of England Reconsidered*', *Historical Research*, 1 (1977), 253–9.

declaring the cry of 'Church in danger' to be 'seditious and scandalous' and promising the harshest penalties for anyone found justifying the vile charge.[30]

Far from outlawing or controlling the cry of 'Church in danger', the prosecution of a *Memorial* only reinforced the belief among high churchmen that the press was being manipulated to political ends: righteous works such as a *Memorial* were liable to restraint, whilst deist, atheist and libertine texts strutted in public unrestrained. John Pakington's speech in the commons on 8 December 1705, for example, reveals that Atterbury's agenda, first set out in 1697, was being reinforced. A tory MP and one of Sacheverell's closest patrons, Pakington laced his speech on the Church in danger with complaints against the press. 'The writing and publishing pamphlets in a most spiteful and exposing manner against the church and clergy', Pakington protested, 'would not be tolerated in any Christian Government, Popish or Protestant, but ours.' The solution to the unbounded licentiousness of the press was obvious. 'This intolerable liberty is a most impudent use of their legal toleration, and perhaps it may become this House to let them understand that tis not to be endur'd.'[31]

The prosecution of a *Memorial*, then, was a crucial turning point in the history of high churchmen and, conceivably, party politics. It was at this point that the success of politically-split ministries receded. The tendency of William, Mary and Anne to appoint cabinets that possessed a spread of political viewpoints was less and less conceivable by 1706.[32] Indeed, Anne wrote to Godolphin asking him to appoint a moderate tory to the cabinet and was firmly rebuffed. And, as Harley had cautioned, high churchmen were confirmed in their alienation from parliamentary politics. Francis Atterbury, Henry Sacheverell and their fellow high church brethren were insistent that godly reform could not be achieved while Harley, Godolphin, Marlborough and Sunderland were trusted by Anne.

The high church solution to their alienation from power was to utilise the pulpit.[33] This is not to say that they did not continue to cultivate political connections, nor did high churchmen give up pamphleteering. However, as the first decade of the period progressed, it was clear that there was a co-ordinated propaganda campaign in which a ready-made collection of charismatic preachers inflamed national audiences and targeted electoral success by preaching in well-chosen parliamentary constituencies. Evidence for the existence of a co-ordinated group of high churchmen can be found in the dedication to the anonymous *Judgment of Whole Kingdoms*. Published in 1710, in the midst of the Sacheverell trial, an event it should be remembered that was concerned with the legality of preaching, the tract challenged a carefully-chosen collective of high churchmen to defend passive obedience.[34] George Hickes, the most erudite defender of the nonjuring position, Charles Leslie, the talented editor of the *Rehearsal* and Francis Atterbury,

---

[30] *A Complete Collection of State Trials*, ed. T.B. Howell (33 vols, 1811–26), xv, 44.

[31] Sir John Pakington's speech on 'the Church in danger', 8 Dec. 1705, printed as an appendix to An Anonymous Parliamentary Diary, 1705–6', ed. W.A. Speck (Camden Misc. xxiii, 4th ser., vii, 1969), 82–3.

[32] Holmes, *British Politics in the Age of Anne*, 46–7.

[33] For the continued importance of the pulpit in the 18th century, see Knights, *Representation and Misrepresentation*, 171.

[34] The authorship of the tract is discussed by Kenyon, *Revolution Principles: The Politics of Party*, 209–10.

future bishop of Rochester, were named by the author and are well known to historians. However, it is noticeable that most of the men are largely unknown to the scholarship. For the anonymous author, it was 'Dr. Welton, Mr. Milbourne, Mr. Higgins, Mr. Whaley and Mr. Tilly of Oxford', who represented the most powerful polemicists of the period.[35] These men gained their reputation from their abilities in the pulpit. Even Francis Atterbury, who, as we have seen was a skilled pamphleteer, was well known by contemporaries for his preaching style. He committed his sermons to memory and inflamed the emotion of his audience with his powerful delivery. His sermons, one contemporary noted, were constructed in such a way as to convince his 'hearers of the truth and importance of what he preached' and his delivery never 'failed to influence the wills of his auditors'.[36] It requires no deep analysis of the evidence to reveal the skill of high church preachers. William Bisset, the whig propagandist, often attended opposition sermons and was well aware that the delivery was as important as the message. Sacheverell, he noted, produced sermons of fierceness and rage that was reflected in a '*Fiery Red*' that overspread his face'.[37] White Kennett, an equally astute observer of sermons, thought Sacheverell an unoriginal theologian who should be ignored. Yet, the future bishop was forced to admit that Sacheverell had a winning humour in the pulpit that often convinced his listeners.[38]

All this evidence is a salutary reminder that, as well as being concerned with vital problems concerning politics, theology and ecclesiology, high churchmen were able to promote their message throughout the country and, by exploiting the pulpit, were circumventing the handicap of having few allies in the upper echelons of the Church.[39] John Oldmixon, a knowledgeable political commentator on the power of the press, commented in worried tones that tories could always find money to buy high church libellous sermons 'by the Dozen'. Even worse, high churchmen had penetrated official diocesan networks. Sacheverell's sermons, Oldmixon complained, were bundled up with '*Briefs* and *Fast-Prayers*', and distributed 'gratis to the poorest Vicars and Curates', before being further dispersed throughout the 'Country to Poyson the Minds of the People too easily impos'd by the plausible Pretence of a Concern for the Publick Interest'.[40] As the first decade of the 18th century progressed, whig churchmen became more alarmed at the persuasive power of high church sermons. Late in 1707, William Wake was informed that Sacheverell and his fellow high churchmen had persuaded the great mass of parish priests that voting tory was the only way to achieve godly reform and fortify the position of the anglican Church. Any attempt to oppose the high church faction in Buckinghamshire, Wake was informed, would 'stir a nest of hornets'.[41] As

---

[35] *The judgment of whole kingdoms and nations* (1710), frontispiece.

[36] *Epistolary correspondence of the Right Rev Francis Atterbury* (4 vols, 1783–7), ii, 443.

[37] William Bisset, *The Modern Fanatick* (1710), 1.

[38] G.V. Bennett, *White Kennett 1660–1728 Bishop of Peterborough: A Study in the Political and Ecclesiastical History of the Early Eighteenth Century* (1957), 104–5.

[39] J.O. Richards, *Party Propaganda under Queen Anne: The General Elections of 1702–13* (Athens, GA, 1972), 21.

[40] John Oldmixon, *Remarks on a False, Scandalous, and Seditious Libel* (1711), 28.

[41] Christ Church, Oxford, Wake MSS. Arch. W. Epist. 234 (unfoliated): John Grey to Bishop Wake, 2⁹ Dec. 1707.

early as 1707, then, Wake was confronted by evidence that the propaganda war in the constituencies was being lost to the tories and high churchmen.[42]

The ability of high churchmen to manipulate the pulpit worried whig and moderate tory politicians as much as it concerned their ecclesiastical allies. Both Harley and Sunderland, the ministers responsible for restraining the press in Anne's ministry, were told by informants that high churchmen were beginning to dominate the pulpit. As early as 1704, Sunderland was warned by his confidant, Edward Gould, that he should find a way to put a stop to the multiple 'seditious sermons lately Preach'd'.[43] Harley was also receiving similar reports. In 1705, Lord Poulet complained to him that the 'clergy preach nothing but the Church being now in their greatest danger, and the bishop himself is often named in their pulpits as an enemy to the church'.[44] And in autumn 1705, Godolphin wrote to Harley to complain of the power of high church political preaching. 'I have heard', he wrote, 'of several insolences of the clergy, which are really insufferable and next door to open rebellion.'[45] Never the most sophisticated analyst of the potential consequences of official restraint, as demonstrated by his role in the prosecution of a *Memorial*, Godolphin demanded that high churchmen should be 'punished; and whether the Parliament approve of all the noise that is fomented in the kingdom of the Church's danger, is in my humble opinion, the first thing that ought one way or other to be cleared upon their meeting'.[46]

The difficulty of making any worthwhile attempt to control high church preaching was underlined by Harley's response. He resisted Godolphin's suggestion and, instead, launched a propaganda campaign. In the autumn of 1705 and throughout 1706, Daniel Defoe turned his ire on preaching. Fed information by Harley, Defoe accused high churchmen of 'treason against the Queen' and 'treason against the Constitution and people of England'.[47] The pulpit, Defoe continued, must be used only for 'expounding the Scriptures and instructing the Hearers in the Christian Religion', not for the 'Railings, Exclamations and Revilings against the Constitution, and against the Queen'. Much like Oldmixon, Defoe worried that sermons were persuasive, for they would 'drive the hearers, and parishioners, from the service of God, tending to introduce Atheism, and bring the publick worship of God into contempt'. The potential dangers of publicly prosecuting high churchmen ensured that Harley's policy erred on the side of prescription rather than proscription. Accordingly, Defoe eschewed threats of censorship and simply warned men like Higgins, Milbourne and Tilly, that they were:

---

[42] Geoffrey Holmes's analysis of the 1705 Buckinghamshire poll reveals that, of 120 clergymen, 92 gave single votes for the tory candidate: G.S. Holmes, 'The Influence of the Peerage in English Parliamentary Elections, 1702–13', University of Oxford BLitt, 1952, pp. 103–4.

[43] BL, Add. MS 61546, ff. 162–3: Gould to Lord Sunderland, 19 Nov. 1705.

[44] Cited in Holmes, *Trial of Doctor Sacheverell*, 45–6.

[45] HMC, *Bath MSS*, i, 76: Godolphin to Robert Harley, 19 Sept. 1705.

[46] HMC, *Bath MSS*, i, 76: Godolphin to Robert Harley, 19 Sept. 1705.

[47] *Review*, 25 Oct. 1705. In fact, Defoe had attacked the distortion of the pulpit some months earlier. On 14 June he had commented: 'How is the Pulpit Daily Prophan'd with Invectives, Satyr, and Recriminations, instead of Sermons, and Expositions of the Sacred Text? How are you thundering out Curses and Exclamations, to stir up the Spirit of Strife in the People, the Daily Business of the Lord's Day, while the Good People, who come to Church, in order to Spiritual Ghostly Instruction, are frighted, and sent Home full of Apprehensions of their Innocent Neighbours.'

being scandalous to their profession, hateful to God and man; ungrateful to their patrons and benefactors, odious to their hearer; perverting the doctrine of the gospel, and work of the ministry; a disgrace to the Protestant religion, and destructive to the whole nation.[48]

Yet however much Harley may have warned high churchmen, not least because he had some sympathy with their predicament, there is no doubt that his policy of propaganda was a failure. Indeed, the ministry knew this very quickly. Within a month of the start of Defoe's campaign, one of Harley's lieutenants was informed by a paid press spy that Henry Sacheverell had preached a potentially-seditious sermon containing 'much viciousness and malice' that attacked the very existence of 'Quakers, Ranters and Mohometans'.[49] The preacher from Oxford had also excoriated dissenters and latitudinarians and 'desired the B[ishop]s to do their duty, to anathematize all their false brethren to send them to the Devil with whom they always discourse'.[50] As is obvious by the reported comment, Sacheverell's sermon was an early version of the infamous *Perils of False Brethren*, for which he was to be prosecuted some four years later.[51] Perhaps to avoid prosecution, Sacheverell had demurred from saying that the Church was in danger; nevertheless, he questioned the lack of tory ministers appointed by Anne. For the moment, however, Sacheverell was saved from Harley's wrath because his sermon remained unprinted. Nevertheless, it is clear that, as early as 1705, members of Anne's ministry were aware of illegal church preaching and were contemplating the best response. In fact, Harley's informant was clear that pre-emptive action should be taken. 'I believe the ministry will be remiss as not to prevent it', he commented, 'otherwise the world might be blessed with a piece of the most exquisite invective . . . he should be call'd upon by the Queen in Council to give some account of this sacred sermon.'[52] Not the least of the factors which influenced Harley's calculations was the conviction by high churchmen of the righteousness of their cause. As demands that they moderate their behaviour and language fell on deaf ears, it became all the more likely that whigs would eventually demand that high churchmen be stopped by a prosecution for seditious behaviour. However, it was far from clear whether this would be effective. Convinced of the righteousness of their campaign, could a high church preacher be intimidated by the threat of prison, fines or having their preaching licence removed?

3

The high church preachers named by opponents never formed a coherent group in the accepted sense of the word. Rather, they were a collection of individuals who had

---

[48] *Review*, 25 Oct. 1705.

[49] BL, Add. MS 61364, f. 88: 24 Dec. 1705.

[50] BL, Add. MS 61364, f. 88: 24 Dec. 1705.

[51] Thomas Hearne, *The Remarks of Thomas Hearne* (11 vols, Oxford, 1885–1921), i, 138–9.

[52] BL, Add. MS 61364, f. 88: 24 Dec. 1705.

certain beliefs in common. One of those men was Francis Higgins.[53] He was recognized by contemporaries as a skilled preacher and one of the more important high church clergymen. Born in Ireland in 1669 and presented to the rectory of Gowran in 1694, by the early 18th century he was notorious as the principal member of the Swan-Tripe Club.[54] Containing Dr Edward Worth, Archdeacon Perceval and two prominent lawyers, the Club was considered dangerous enough to be presented by the Dublin grand jury as a seditious and unlawful assembly 'with intent to create misunderstandings between Protestants ... and to instil dangerous principles into the youth of this Kingdom'.[55] By 1705, Higgins was in England and his reputation as an effective preacher and member of the Swan-Tripe Club preceded him. In one contemporary pamphlet, he was described as a typical high churchman who did not put enough care into his thoughts before he spoke for he 'thinks too little, but talks too much'. As early as 1705, then, Higgins was typical of the high-flying tribe. In the eyes of his opponents, he was an extreme high churchman who, nevertheless, had to be taken seriously, for he was an effective and charismatic preacher who could charm 'the listening throng'.[56]

One of his first sermons, delivered at Christ Church Cathedral, Dublin in 1705, but printed and distributed in London, bears analysis, for it reveals some of the preoccupations of high churchmen who have been excluded from the scholarly understanding of religious–politics in the early 18th century. Taking as his text Chronicles 16.34–6, Higgins argued that King David and his nation had been entirely dependent on God's grace for salvation. 'The daily and frequent struggles, skirmishes and battles he had with the *Philistines*', Higgins noted of the king, had been successfully resolved because of divine intervention. David had instructed his priests to entreat their deity, 'save us O God of our Salvation; and gather us together, and deliver us from the Heathen'.[57] This simple tale underpinned Higgins's view of how a godly society should operate. The story of a monarch saving his people from the ungodly by entreating his priests to pray for the nation was both an allegory designed to reinforce the power of the Church and priesthood but also served a wider discussion of justification and sanctification that was vital to high church thinking. Here, high churchmen were engaging in a debate that had been vital to English protestant identity since the Reformation. The initial 16th-century scholastic vision that justification (conferred freely by God and confirmed by faith) was separate from sanctification (the growth in grace through obedience and obeying correct doctrine), had been eroded by the theological disputes of the mid 17th century and Restoration.[58] By the early 18th century, high churchmen were committed to a theological vision that closely connected justification and sanctification for salvation to be achieved. Whilst they accepted that God's grace was awarded freely, high churchmen insisted that sanctification, demonstrated by a life of obedience, correct doctrine and

[53] D.W. Hayton, *Ruling Ireland, 1685–1742: Politics, Politicians and Parties* (Woodbridge, 2004), 135–7, 143; Jeffrey R. Wigelsworth, *Deism in Enlightenment England: Theology, Politics, and Newtonian Public Science* (Manchester, 2009), 55–6.

[54] *ODNB*.

[55] Cited in John Thomas Gilbert, *A History of the City of Dublin* (3 vols, Dublin, 1857–9), ii, 12.

[56] *The Swan Tripe Club: A Satyr on the High-Flyers* (1705), 6.

[57] Francis Higgins, *A sermon preach'd before their Excellencies the Lords Justices at Christ-Church, Dublin* (Dublin, 1705), 5.

[58] John Spurr, *The Restoration Church of England, 1646–1689* (1991), 296–311.

good works, was fundamental to salvation. The result of this interpretation, demonstrated by Higgins's 1705 sermon, was an essentially activist spiritual quest, in which individual members of society had to follow the doctrine of the Church of England and adhere to the authority of the anglican priesthood to achieve salvation.

It might be tempting to see in all this an irrelevant theological debate between religious sects. There are, however, problems with such a view. To begin with, Higgins's soteriological reasoning goes some way to explaining the high church detestation of the latitudinarians' position within the Church. Henry Sacheverell, William Tilly and Luke Milbourne, to name but three examples, regularly berated their audience with the message that living an exemplary moral life would not assuage temporal sins. Thus, the message from Benjamin Hoadly that virtue, morality and good living would ensure salvation was met with the charge from Henry Sacheverell that latitudinarians were a 'shuffling, treacherous' sect, who should be 'stigmatiz'd, and treated equally as dangerous enemies to the Government, as well as Church'.[59] Nor was high church soteriological reasoning confined to a debate between themselves and latitudinarians. On the contrary, the basic structure of Higgins's narrative alluded to the claim that the Church was in danger. Echoing Atterbury, Higgins maintained that England was a country endangering God's mercy, because it was awash with 'general irreligion, lewdness and prophaneness'.[60] 'Some sins', he commented, 'by long use and practice among us, seem to now to have lost all reproach, or offensive guilt.'[61] Once again, this was a vision of England as overrun by sin, endangering God's providence. The Act of Toleration, Higgins claimed, had embedded schism and sacrilege at the heart of political life. Worse, he continued, the lapse of licensing had unleashed 'the growing multitude of Atheists, Deists, Arians, Socinians, Libertines' who were multiplying because of their 'shallow prophane writings'.[62] In other words, there was in the minds of more radical high church preachers, a direct connection between the enactment of toleration and the loss of pre-publication censorship. Here, therefore, preached in 1705, were a number of concerns that were essential to high church preaching and came to dominate after the disastrous prosecution of a *Memorial* only months later. Society no longer worried enough about the consequences of sin and had, therefore, lost the fear of damnation; evidence for this assertion could be found not just in the Act of Toleration but in the spread of unorthodox thinking perpetuated by the loss of prepublication restraint. In practice, this meant that high church writing on soteriology had political consequences. The assertion that salvation could be achieved by leading a moral life was, in the view of many high churchmen, a practice shared by atheists, deists, latitudinarians and, conceivably, all dissenters. Linking such varying groups together was a beloved rhetorical tactic of high churchmen.

---

[59] Henry Sacheverell, *The Political Union. A discourse shewing the Dependence of Government on Religion in general* (Oxford, 1702), 49. For a debate between Hoadly and Atterbury on the nature of salvation, see B. Hoadly, *The Measures of Submission to the Civil Magistrate Consider'd* (1706); B. Hoadly, *A Letter to the Revered Dr. Francis Atterbury concerning Virtue and Vice* (1707); Francis Atterbury, *A sermon preached at the Cathedral Church of St. Paul; at the Funeral of Mr. Tho. Bennet* (1706).

[60] Higgins, *A sermon preach'd before their Excellencies*, 16.

[61] Higgins, *A sermon preach'd before their Excellencies*, 17.

[62] Higgins, *A sermon preach'd before their Excellencies*, 17.

Although, by summer 1705, Higgins was already professing himself alienated from ecclesiastical policy, he was still not so disillusioned that he was openly seditious. 'God Almighty', he proclaimed, has delivered to England a 'great protectress, and gracious Queen' and safeguarded the 'Protestant line'.[63] Thus, he continued to follow the position articulated by Atterbury eight years previously, that the monarch needed only to enact a different religious policy to confirm her godliness. However, clear distaste for the shape of religious policy ensured he tempered his professed loyalty to the monarch. 'Let all sincere, and true lovers of the Church, and Monarchy', he thundered, 'watch against the designs and practices and of such back friends.'[64] The back friends, as Higgins termed them, were promoters of moderation and followers of 1643. In other words, for all the impeccably-loyal credentials of his sermon, the preacher from Dublin was happy to point out that there were men embedded at the heart of the English political state that he did not trust. Moderation, the favoured policy of Robert Harley, was much detested by high churchmen, and was defined as a policy that saw the Church 'immoderately cheated, gull'd, abus'd and undone', whilst dissenters, many of whom had influence, were 'pernicious and publick enemies' to both Church and state.[65]

Yet, to appreciate the rapid disillusionment of high church preachers, one must consider Higgins's subsequent sermon, delivered on Ash Wednesday 1707. With Harley marginalised and Sunderland established as southern secretary, Anne's ministry offered little hope to high churchmen that a godly reformation could be enacted. In 1707, Higgins took as his text Revelation 3.2–3. He informed listener and reader that there was a direct comparison between contemporary England and the long-forgotten church of Sardis; a church which had lost both the power and form of godliness.[66] 'Its very Angels, Watchmen, or Bishops' had failed the Church by sinking into a state of 'listlessness, stupidity, or lethargy'. Only a voice from heaven could rouse the bishops from their stupor in order to return the Church to the 'care and diligence' it deserved.[67] Hardly subtle in its allegory, Higgins ensured that the reader and listener got the point of the sermon when he went on to suggest: 'from this account of the Church of Sardis, he that runs may read and observe in how many particulars, we agree with them in circumstances'. As with all high churchmen, Higgins warned his audience that they 'must expect the same Judgments and punishments from the Divine Justice, which the Scriptures threatened'.[68] It was this vision of the failing church of Sardis, combined with the human propensity to ignore the dangers of damnation, which provided the narrative thread for the rest of the sermon.

At the very root of Higgins's distaste for ecclesiastical policy, however, lay his understanding of free expression. The connection between the lapse of licensing and the immorality of the nation was made both by generalization and specific example. 'Fountains of Irreligion and Lewdness', Higgins claimed, had spread over the face of the

---

[63] Higgins, *A sermon preach'd before their Excellencies*, 2.

[64] Higgins, *A sermon preach'd before their Excellencies*, 21.

[65] Higgins, *A sermon preach'd before their Excellencies*, 21.

[66] Higgins, *A sermon preach'd at the Royal Chappel at White-Hall*, 3.

[67] Higgins, *A sermon preach'd at the Royal Chappel at White-Hall*, 3

[68] Higgins, *A sermon preach'd at the Royal Chappel at White-Hall*, 4.

land and caused a deluge of wickedness.[69] The abyss of impiety that the nation so obviously faced was attributed by the preacher directly to the 'unaccountable liberty that has of late been taken, not only in conversation, but in books publicly printed and sold about our streets'. Seen through the eyes of Higgins, the lapse of licensing was not a moment to celebrate; rather, it was disastrous political calculation that had unleashed 'the apostles of the devil, emissaries of the arch–rebel, and apostate Lucifer'. Of course, not everything was lost. The prosecution of three authors in Ireland, John Asgill, John Toland and Thomas Emlyn, provided examples of how the press could be restrained. All three men had been driven from Ireland to the everlasting honour of Church and parliament. The ostensible purpose of these examples was to emphasize the importance of exemplary punishment: all three men had their books burned, were taken into custody for heresy and blasphemy and had been expelled from their home country. The loss of licensing, Higgins contended, could be offset by warning authors of the consequences of their actions. Indeed, he went so far as to suggest that Toland's 'paws should feel the fire'.[70] These examples also served another purpose. The cases of Asgill, Toland and Emlyn were employed to shame the whig junto and their clerical allies. All three men were now living and publishing in England. Emlyn, it was claimed, 'has publickly set up, and preaches in this city to an assembly of divines', whilst Toland 'revives and publishes afresh'. These three examples were carefully chosen: one was a socinian (Asgill), one a deist (Toland) and one a dissenter (Emlyn). Combining the three men's cases returned Higgins to the high church contention that latitudinarian whigs were responsible for the spread of unorthodox thinking. The failure of both bishops and ministers to punish these three blasphemous men was a dereliction of duty. The loss of prepublication censorship, blow as it surely was, still left much power in the hands of clerics to 'brand authors and actors with ecclesiastical censures', whilst the secular arm must preserve the 'doctrines and orders, and ordinances of our holy religion from the visible and notorious attempts of such men, to undermine and destroy them'.[71] This, then, was a cause that rested on good government. There was no need for new legislation, only for the appointment of a high church administration that would elevate the power of the Church and restrain the press.

There can be no doubt, therefore, that the high church ideal found authentic expression after 1705 in the promotion of measures to restrict the press through the replacement of latitudinarian bishops. In some ways, the most interesting development of the high church party in the early 18th century was the steady politicisation of their theological reasoning. Returning to the example of the church of Sardis, for example, Higgins noted that only those who opposed heresy received assurance from their saviour and ascended to heaven. That God gave people grace to repent and thus be saved was an obvious point. However, the claim being advanced was that God required each person to confront heresy, blasphemy and licentiousness at every opportunity in order to receive grace. In other words, for Higgins and many of his fellow brethren, the licentiousness of the press transformed salvation into a political issue. 'How many of our angels and watchmen . . . are asleep', Higgins asked? Men of power, he noted, are 'set

[69] Higgins, *A sermon preach'd at the Royal Chappel at White-Hall*, 7.
[70] Higgins, *A sermon preach'd at the Royal Chappel at White-Hall*, 8.
[71] Higgins, *A sermon preach'd at the Royal Chappel at White-Hall*, 14.

apart and commission'd by God and the constitution to watch and ward against the practices' of blasphemers. Men of authority, both clergy and politicians, were obliged to 'cry aloud and spare not, to lift up their voices like trumpets, to shew the people their transgressions, and the house of Jacob their sins'.[72] The failure of bishops and ministers to restrain the press was compounded by the abandonment of those who had done their duty. 'Those who have sense of their duty', the preacher thundered, have been 'reproach'd, revil'd, and insulted, not only by the vile scribblers and pamphleteers against God, his church and his priests, but discountenanc'd, and brow-beaten by men of figure.'[73]

No contemporary material illustrates more vividly the connection between the freedom of the press and cry of 'Church in danger' than Higgins's Chapel Royal sermon. In a clear reference to the controversy created by the publication and prosecution of a *Memorial*, he rejected the claim made by queen, Lords and Commons that the Church was not in danger. Higgins also dismissed the concomitant case constructed by whigs that they were leading the nation to godliness and piety. The providential claims of politicians and bishops that successes both at home and abroad signified God's pleasure were irrelevant. Quite the contrary, Higgins claimed, the nation was being destroyed by impieties and abominations. The point, for Higgins of course, was to translate his central assertion that individuals, in neglecting to condemn, confront and censor books, compromised their own potential salvation, into the same claim but at a national level. Indeed, the providential signs of success claimed by whigs as signs of God's providence, victory at the battle of Ramillies for example, were simply the last overtures of mercy and favour before God visited on England his just wrath. The continual attacking of great and important men was an attempt to argue that those in charge of state and Church were neglecting their duty and were, therefore, endangering the collective soul of the nation. The accusation of national betrayal was a further development of the constant high church cry of 'Church in danger'. By 1707, the standard caveat that: 'God is pleas'd ... to Bless us with a Pious Queen at Home, (whose precious Life, God, in his Mercy to these Churches and Nations, long preserve) looked increasingly insincere.'[74] Rather, the exhortation by Higgins for his flock to pray for the preservation of people, Church and nation lest they be 'cursed bitterly' was a rallying call that resonated increasingly with many high churchmen.

4

Francis Higgins's sermon, given at the Chapel Royal on Ash Wednesday in 1707, was seditious. He assaulted the policies of Church government pursued by the whig junto, suggested that they encouraged unbelief and openly questioned the queen's commitment to true religion. However, this is only part of the story. The sermon also revealed the complete failure of whig attempts to deal with the pulpit. Warnings, threats, proclamations and the occasional prosecution had failed to moderate high church preaching.

---

[72] Higgins, *A sermon preach'd at the Royal Chappel at White-Hall*, 11

[73] Higgins, *A sermon preach'd at the Royal Chappel at White-Hall*, 12.

[74] Higgins, *A sermon preach'd at the Royal Chappel at White-Hall*, 12.

In this context, Higgins's sermon posed a variety of challenges to Anne's ministry. His behaviour confirmed the growing belief in the wider whig constituency that high church preaching was out of control. It was John Tutchin, author of the whig *Observator*, who reflected the mood, describing the pulpit as a political space in which the ecclesiastical drum was beaten with 'fist, instead of stick' and the queen was affronted 'into her face'.[75] The pressure on the ministry to prosecute Higgins was fostered by replies to his sermon.[76] Authors asserted that Higgins's association of the current Church with Sardis was synonymous with the cry of 'Church in danger'. One anonymous pamphleteer claimed that the interpretation of the gospel rendered Higgins a foolish man who had built his argument on a 'house of sand'.[77] From here it was but a short step to denouncing Higgins as seditious. 'The church', the author continued, was 'built upon a rock', and had a monarch who 'had nothing more in her heart than the peace and welfare of all her subjects'. Therefore, he continued, 'it is an unsupportable abuse to make the word of God the instrument of sedition and to move mens minds to follow the passions, party-piques, and private interests of the world'.[78] There was more at stake in the replies than a simple theological dispute about the future shape of the Church. For many, as one author explained, Higgins was 'infected with seditious principles' that were 'in opposition to the majority of men of all qualities and degrees in her Majesty's Dominions'.[79]

What is particularly evident is that the ministry faced a difficult challenge. Godolphin had to make a choice about whether Higgins should be prosecuted. His ability to instruct the public, through both pulpit and print, ensured that whigs worried that the high churchmen would lead others into sedition. It was obvious to observers that those in power, should they wish to do so, possessed the means to restrain Higgins and high church preaching. One author recounted with obvious relish all the antidotes that could be applied: both the upper and lower houses of convocation and parliament had issued resolutions that could be applied to Higgins.[80] Yet any prosecution posed a serious danger, for as Laurence Hanson has noted: 'particular industry was in truth necessary if libellers with popularity or backing behind them were to be prosecuted'.[81] Or, put simply, Higgins's extraordinarily-provocative sermon provided him with a public constituency. Assessing the size and commitment of public support for Higgins is almost impossible. It is clear, however, that he possessed patronage from the lower clergy. In early 1706, along with William Perceval, archdeacon of Cashel, Higgins presented a report to the lower house of convocation that stridently asserted the rights

[75] *Observator*, 1 Feb. 1707.

[76] *The prayer of the Reverend Mr. Higgins, before his text, and his case* (1707): *An answer to the sermon preach'd (by Francis Higgins, Prebendary of Christ-Church, Dublin)* (1707); *A word in season, in answer to the preface to Mr. Higgens's sermon* (1707); *The High-Church bully: or, the praises of Mr. Higgins* (1707); *Boanerges: Or, Mr. Higgins's history: with a reply to his infamous dialogue, in a letter to a friend* (1707); *The curtain-lecture: or, a dialogue between Mr. H-gg-ns and his l-dy* (1707).

[77] *A Word in Season in Answer to the Preface to Mr. Higgins's Sermon* (1707), 2.

[78] *A Word in Season in Answer to the Preface to Mr. Higgins's Sermon*, 4.

[79] *A Word in Season in Answer to the Preface to Mr. Higgins's Sermon*, 14.

[80] Richard Kingston, *The Church of England not in Danger* (1707), 14–16.

[81] Laurence Hanson, *Government and the Press, 1695–1763* (Oxford, 1936), 61.

of the lower House to act independently of the bishops.[82] It is unclear whether this indicates support or patronage, but the approbation received by Higgins seems to suggest that he was well regarded by the lower clergy. Clergymen also had a built-in advantage when faced with prosecution that required careful consideration. The most basic characteristic of high church clergy was that they claimed the apostolic right to preach freely from the pulpit. A bungled prosecution, far from being a single case of restraint, ran the risk of looking like persecution and an attempt to muzzle the right to preach.

One of the most remarkable features of Higgins's sermon, however, is that it is possible he was attempting to avoid prosecution. Richard Kingston, an astute observer of the press, noted that there was a legal requirement for a preacher 'to shew the Notes of his sermon' to a privy councillor if requested. In this case, the implication of Kingston's comment was clear. Higgins, it was being claimed, had preached a sermon that was even more radical than the one he printed. By supposedly refusing to show the original sermon notes to the ministry, he had demonstrated his seditious, underhand and unorthodox character and behaviour:

> He breaks in upon the constant Practice of all the Orthodox and Regular Clergy in her Majesty's Dominions, who if at any time accused or aspersed, for what they deliver'd from the Pulpit, always deliver their Notes to their Diocesan for their Justification, or in his Absence to some Principal Magistrate in the Neighbourhood.[83]

Another observer added credence to Kingston's claim. Impugning the credibility of Higgins and expressing his disgust at the preacher's potential escape, an anonymous author suggested that Higgins had, indeed, printed a different sermon from the one he preached. He claimed that he had a signed affidavit from a member of the audience that Higgins's spoken sermon was even more seditious than the printed version. Higgins had apparently contended: 'those that brought the Royal Martyr to the Scaffold and the Block, just as those are now Preferr'd to Places of the greatest Trust in the Kingdom', a clearly seditious assertion that went way beyond the claims of the printed version. In light of this new evidence, the anonymous author required:

> Mr. *Higgins* to subjoin and Publish the only Paragraph of that Sermon, Wherein any Mention is made of the *Royal Martyr The Scaffold or Block*; and to Appeal to the Multitudes, who from Time to Time heard him preach it . . . whether the following be a Faithful Relation of that Passage or not.[84]

Far from these accusations being a surprise, Higgins was well aware that he and his fellow high churchmen had to be careful when delivering sermons. The multitude, he complained, often attended sermons only to 'watch and spy, and lie upon the catch for the slips, or indiscretions of the preacher'.[85] Confronted by the possibility of prosecution,

---

[82] Lambeth Palace Library, MS 934/23, f. 34: *Report of two members of the Irish convocation to the lower house of the convocation of Canterbury*. One might also point out that he preached at the Chapel Royal.

[83] Kingston, *The Church of England not in Danger*, 11.

[84] *Isabella Foulks a very aged poor woman swears, that Mr. Higgins utter'd in his sermon at Whitehall on Ash-Wednesday last, these following words* (1707).

[85] Higgins, *A sermon preach'd at the Royal Chappel at White-Hall*, 13.

Higgins was aware that care should be taken, otherwise informants would 'furnish the hired paltry scribblers of the party with dirt to throw at us, and our Holy Profession, as soon as we come out of the pulpit and church'.[86]

In the event, the dangers of prosecution were ignored by Godolphin and Sunderland. Higgins's fate was almost certainly sealed by the marginalisation from power of Robert Harley and the end of mixed ministry. Charles Spencer, earl of Sunderland, was a politician of a very different temperament from Harley. Whilst not an unskilled observer of the press, Sunderland possessed none of the subtlety of Harley and was committed to the values of his party, effectively eschewing policies that smacked of moderation.[87] The Higgins case may have been the first time that Sunderland had attempted to restrain a clergyman but, as we have seen, he was not unaware of the power of the pulpit. Returning to the letter sent to Sunderland in 1705, Edward Gould had demanded both the specific restraint of Atterbury for preaching false doctrine and parliamentary legislation to:

> prevent the further Proceedings of such Ecclesiastical Disturbances, it would be necessary that a Law be made Penal against such as should Preach against State Affairs and seditiously disturb the nation, during her Majesties reign, or against any Protestant Dissenters whatsoever, and the Reformed Churches abroad, as is now practiced by a disaffected set of Jurant Preachers contrary to their oaths.[88]

Rather than enacting pre-emptive legislation, Sunderland appears to have contented himself with prosecuting single preachers. On 1 March 1707, only two days after the sermon had been preached, he ordered that Higgins be taken into custody. After a week in custody, Higgins wrote to the secretary to beg for relief. 'I am sorry to find myself necessitated to give your Lordships this enclosed trouble', the Irish preacher wrote, 'I no longer want to lay under the foul imputation of those foul crimes on which the warrant was grounded.' He had been debarred his liberty for a crime that my 'soul abhors' and he sought redress by being brought 'before your Lordship, or Her Majesty and Council to answer for my self'.[89]

Higgins's initial pleading had little effect. Sunderland, it seems, was determined to make an example of the errant preacher. On 24 April, the grand jury at Hicks Hall found a bill against Higgins for a sermon that asserted: 'those that brought the royal martyr to the scaffold and the block, such as those are now preferred in the greatest places of trust in the kingdom'.[90] However, on 29 May, six weeks after being taken into custody, the prosecution was brought to a halt; Narcissus Luttrell recorded in his journal that: 'yesterday the attorney general enter'd a *noli prosequi* to stop proceedings against Mr. Higgins, the Irish clergyman, for words in a sermon lately preach't at Whitehal'.[91]

---

[86] Higgins, *A sermon preach'd at the Royal Chappel at White-Hall*, 13.

[87] At this point, Harley's influence in the ministry was marginalised as the power struggle between the whig junto and the ministry reached its height: see Holmes, *British Politics in the Age of Anne*, 110–11.

[88] BL, Blenheim Papers, Add. MS 61546, ff. 162–3: Edward Gould to Lord Sunderland, London, 19 Nov. 1705.

[89] BL, Add. MS 61607, ff. 24–5; Higgins to Sunderland, 8 Mar. 1706/7.

[90] Luttrell, *Brief Historical Relations*, vi, 164.

[91] Luttrell, *Brief Historical Relations*, vi, 177.

As we have seen in the case of a *Memorial*, in the early 18th century, discontinuing cases was a well-known technique of politicians. Used properly, the technique was a crucial element of the arsenal of the prosecuting authorities. Once the protagonist had been sufficiently frightened by a spell in prison, the case could be discontinued to demonstrate both the power and mercy of authority. Such a policy also had the great advantage of denying publicity to censorship. Had the Higgins case ended at the entering of the *noli prosequi*, it would serve as an example of skilled political manœuvring in the new world of postpublication censorship. However, rather than being discontinued, Sunderland passed the case to the ecclesiastical authorities for resolution. Later that month, Higgins was called to Lambeth Palace, where Archbishop Tenison warned him to moderate his behaviour and language. Tenison's manuscript minute of the meeting reveals a largely convivial conversation in which the archbishop advised Higgins 'to keep such things to himselfe', and Higgins, in the face of clerical authority, acceded to the archbishop's request.[92]

Francis Higgins, like so many of his fellow high churchmen, believed in his apostolic calling, and in the righteousness of his own theological position.[93] Blessed with epistemological and soteriological certainty, and despite his private entreaty for relief and his penitence when face-to-face with Tenison, Higgins refused to self-censor. In the summer of 1707, with the help of Charles Leslie, Higgins released his own version of his conversation with the archbishop. Masquerading as a verbatim account, Higgins openly admitted that he believed the Church was in danger, and excoriated Tenison for his stewardship of the Church. It was his duty, he informed the archbishop, to oppose 'all Men, and Books, that attack or undermine the Christian Religion'.[94] Perhaps no one tract better demonstrates that much of the 'Church in danger' campaign was linked to frustration with religious and press policy in the period. As he detailed the policies and principles of restraint that represented, so Higgins claimed, a responsible press and righteous press policy, the reader was left in no doubt that high churchmen considered Tenison a weak and impotent puppet of the whig junto. Far from being the defender of the Church, Tenison was the leader of a whig policy that did not want to restrain an out-of-control and licentious press. This contemptuous treatment of the archbishop was augmented by an even more dangerous assertion. Higgins articulated publicly his apostolic right to preach and informed Tenison and the whig junto that neither he, nor his fellow high church preachers, would be censored:

I did not make the Sermon to keep it a secret, when I preach'd it, it was not a Whisper. I intend to preach it again in most of the Churches in Town; I'll preach it before your G[race] where you please to command me; you are concerned it, and I should be glad your G[race] would hear it from the Pulpit. For I have taken care

---

[92] HMC, *2nd Report*, 244: notes of Mr. Francis Higgins's conference with archbishop of Canterbury, 1707. For Tenison's attitude to censorship, see Hertfordshire Record Office, Cowper Papers (Nov. 1703–Jan. 1704), D/EP F136: 'An Act for the Better Regulating of Printing and Printing Presses'.

[93] Robert D. Cornwall, *Visible and Apostolic: The Constitution of the Church in High Church Anglican and Non-Juror Thought* (1993), 63–9.

[94] Charles Leslie and Francis Higgins, *A postscript to Mr. Higgins's sermon; very necessary for the better understanding it* (1707), 1.

to discharge my Duty to God in it, and to preserve my Duty to the Queen, and the Laws of the Land, which I shan't only study to conform my self to, but to perswade all others to do so too.[95]

Here, then, high churchmen were both responding to, and exploiting, the government's muddled response to the lapse of licensing. Embracing the publicity opportunities offered by the pulpit, and openly arguing that they believed the Church to be in danger, high churchmen gave notice that they would exploit any prosecution of their brethren. In other words, despite the presence of Harley, men such as Tenison, Sunderland and Godolphin largely lost the propaganda war to high churchmen. The archbishop never articulated a coherent response to the loss of prepublication censorship. Far too often, he stumbled when facing high church provocation. Tenison was never able to decide when books should be answered and when they should be restrained. The case of Francis Higgins demonstrates as much.

Tenison, perhaps understandably, was left outraged. In the face of Higgins's provocation he manœuvred for the house of lords to burn Higgins's version of the conversation and for the lower house of convocation to condemn it in print.[96] Tenison also attempted to combat Higgins in print. He authorised at least two replies to Higgins. Published by Benjamin Bragg, Harley and Defoe's favoured trade publisher, the anonymous pamphlet *Boanerges* roundly condemned Higgins. According to the author, Higgins represented everything that the whigs detested about high church exploitation of the pulpit. Higgins, he insisted, 'greedily affected popular applause' and sought 'noise and dust' rather than earnestness and passion.[97] The disrespectful behaviour of Higgins in the pulpit was equally manifested in the reply to the archbishop. The recently-published and false dialogue between Higgins and Tenison demonstrated insolence, ill manners and showed no respect to the archiepiscopal dignity.[98] In an attempt at damage control, the author also suggested that Higgins had reneged on the deal offered by Sunderland and Tenison. The Irish preacher had been taken into the 'custody of a messenger, by virtue of a Warrant from the principal Secretary of State', only to be released because of mediation from his friends and by his own promise of good behaviour.[99] While the monarch had been 'graciously pleased to forgive him and put a Stop to all further Proceedings', Higgins had impiously reneged on the deal. 'No sooner were his heels at liberty, and his neck secured from the danger of a wooden ruff, but out comes his seditious sermon in print.'[100]

The campaign against Higgins continued. Tenison instructed Richard Kingston, previously chaplain-in-ordinary to Charles II and a paid government spy, to inform the public that the errant preacher was an 'avowed enemy of the government' and had constructed 'imaginary dangers that were falling upon the church'.[101] Employing his

[95] Leslie and Higgins, *A postscript to Mr. Higgins's sermon*, 3.

[96] Luttrell, *Brief Historical Relations*, vi, 200.

[97] *Boanerges: Or, Mr. Higgins's History*, 2.

[98] *Boanerges: Or, Mr. Higgins's History*, 7.

[99] *Boanerges: Or, Mr. Higgins's History*, 5.

[100] *Boanerges: Or, Mr. Higgins's History*, 5.

[101] Kingston, *The Church of England not in Danger*; HMC, *Finch MSS*, iv, 515–16: Kingston to the earl of Nottingham, Nov. 1692.

tract as a lobby document, Kingston asserted that Higgins was a man 'notoriously *Disaffected* to her Majesty's Government' and his sermon sowed the seeds of 'scandal, Sedition and Discord'.[102] In an attempt to send a warning to future high church preachers, Kingston noted that Higgins's sermon had transgressed the 'express Words of Her Majesty's *Royal Proclamation*', and was an obvious continuation of 'Dr. *Drake*, the supposed Author of the *Memorial*'.[103]

5

Although the campaign waged by Francis Higgins traced in the previous sections – the protests against the licentiousness of the press, the heightening of 'Church in danger' rhetoric and the use of salvation as a political tool – tells us much about high churchmen in the early 18th century, it is more difficult to assess the exact connection between the Higgins case and the prosecution of Henry Sacheverell. It is clear, however, that the ability of leading whigs to contain high church preaching was put to the sternest test by both Higgins and Sacheverell. As we have seen, despite initially begging for relief, Higgins was a preacher who could not, and would not, be silenced or, indeed, moderated. He claimed the apostolic right to preach and insisted that the Church was in danger. The trial of Henry Sacheverell may never have occurred had Robert Harley remained in the ministry.[104] Despite the disaster of the prosecution of a *Memorial*, Harley had always urged his fellow ministers to resist making martyrs of high church polemicists by publicly prosecuting them. And, despite his unpopularity because of his policy of moderation, it is undeniable that he maintained links with many of the leading high churchmen. Indeed, there is some evidence that Harley was developing a policy that may have quietened some of their more extreme behaviour. In 1706, Harley received news that William Tilly, one of the high churchmen to be named in the *Judgment of Whole Kingdoms*, had preached a dangerous sermon. Clearly furious at another potentially-seditious publication, Harley raged at his placeman, William Stratford, that: 'the assize sermon is a composition of incoherencys, nonsense in English, and impertinence with Greek, with the very spirit of rage that one would think it was written by some furious Presbyterian Scot'.[105] Stratford was in an invidious position. He was the master of Christ Church, Oxford, one of the homes of high church preaching, and owed his position to the power of Harley.[106] One of the points of Stratford's appointment was to ensure that the secretary had an ally to place pressure on the more extreme elements of high church preaching. 'I shall be very glad therefore to hear from you the state of this matter, and your opinion of the best way to cover this', the angry politician

[102] Kingston, *The Church of England not in Danger*, 4.

[103] Kingston, *The Church of England not in Danger*, 5–7.

[104] This is not to argue that Harley engineered the trial of Sacheverell in order to bring down the Godolphin ministry. On the contrary, the evidence suggests that Harley was manœuvring only to remove the treasurer. For further explanation of this point, see D.W. Hayton with a postscript by W.A. Speck, 'In No One's Shadow: Geoffrey Holmes's *British Politics in the Age of Anne* and the Writing of the History of the House of Commons', *Parliamentary History*, xxviii (2009), 1–14.

[105] BL, Add. MS 61110, f. 31: Harley to William Stratford, 2 Sept. 1706.

[106] HMC, *Portland MSS*, iv, 203: Bromley to Robert Harley, 7 July 1705.

wrote, adding that Tilly's sermon was dangerous precisely because it would help in the 'disabling their friends, and arming their enemies'.[107] This policy of using private channels to contain high churchmen could occasionally work. On 22 April 1706, Stratford, for example, reported to Harley that a sermon had been preached at the college which 'I am afraid will be reported to our disadvantage'.[108] The sermon, by a preacher called Read, argued that the clergy were being persecuted, that the practice of occasional conformity was a betrayal of the Church and that God would surely find a way to place high churchmen in power.[109] In this case, Harley asked Tenison to caution the clergyman privately and to 'contradict any worse representation that without doubt will be made of it'. Harley's deployment of private restraint through Stratford and Tenison was successful; Read did not print the sermon and no further controversy ensued.[110] That Harley's policy could succeed is borne out by the behaviour of Francis Higgins during 1710. Hearing that the Irish preacher was to deliver a sermon in support of Sacheverell, Jonathan Trelawny, bishop of Winchester and a high churchman, dispatched his confidant, Thomas Horne, to warn at:

> his impudence in appointing such a preacher as Mr Higgins, whom his Lordship would not suffer to preach within his diocese; and if he did not take care to provide men of a better character to supply his lecture, the bishop himself would take that care.[111]

Higgins appears to have accepted Trelawny's benign intentions and stayed silent during Sacheverell's trial.

Harley's and Trelawny's approach is worth emphasizing, for it serves as a final comment on the problem of restraining high churchmen. As we have seen, many whigs believed that high churchmen were being allowed too much latitude. One more extreme pamphleteer maintained that the subordination of the clergy to the state should be written in 'Capital Letters, and plac'd in Churches directly over against the Pulpit, so that it may stare the Preachers in the face, when they are going to preach up their own Power in defiance of their Oaths'.[112] Neither Sunderland nor Godolphin would assent to such legislation, nor did either man possess the skills or the inclination to restrain high church preachers through private channels as Harley had done. Instead, they committed themselves to a policy of exemplary punishment.[113] The failure of the Higgins prosecution did not deter Sunderland from taking other churchmen to trial. Far from it: new evidence suggests that Sunderland was ever more committed to an ecclesiastical policy that emphasized public restraint rather than quiet admonishment. In a series of letters written in the autumn of 1708, a year before Sacheverell delivered his two incendiary sermons, Sunderland demanded that the lord advocate prosecute a number of clergymen

---

[107] BL, Add. MS 61110, f. 31: Harley to William Stratford, 2 Sept. 1706.

[108] HMC, *Portland MSS*, iv, 295: Stratford to Robert Harley, 22 Apr. 1706.

[109] HMC, *Portland MSS*, iv, 295: Stratford to Robert Harley, 22 Apr. 1706.

[110] HMC, *Portland MSS*, iv, 297: Stratford to Robert Harley, 22 Apr. 1706.

[111] BL, Lansdowne MS 1024, f. 201.

[112] Matthew Tindal, *A Defence of the Rights of the Christian Church* (1707), 21.

[113] The impeachment articles for Sacheverell called for exemplary punishment: see Holmes, *Trial of D* *Sacheverell*, 282.

for seditious behaviour. For Sunderland, it was intolerable that ministers, 'though deposed for disorderly behaviour', continued to preach and were endeavouring 'to seduce the people from their allegiance'. He was even more concerned by meetings of the 'disaffected Clergy' who, he demanded, should have an example made of them and be prosecuted in whatever court a case could 'properly be made'. To the lord advocate, he was quite frank about the reasons for his policy. He was quite resolved that an example be made of errant churchmen and that the proceedings of the trials be publicised for the reading public to consume.[114]

The substantial change which transformed the junto's press policy after the summer of 1708 was reflected in its greater willingness to confront high churchmen. That policy, when applied to Henry Sacheverell, was a disaster. Indeed, astute observers realized very quickly that was the case. Hearing the news that Henry Sacheverell was being prosecuted for his two sermons, William Stratford commented that this it would 'make the Doctor and his performance much more considerable than either of them could have been on any other account'.[115] On 25 March 1710, in the midst of the trial, Abigail Harley wrote to her brother Edward complaining of the debacle caused by the prosecution of the radical Oxford high church preacher. 'It is said abroad', she wrote, that we 'are all mad, may justly add fools too.' 'On Monday', she continued, 'the sermon is to be burnt.' Harley's uneasiness at the burning of Sacheverell's work was compounded by the extortionate cost of the trial, of £60 000 to the nation. In fact, she was anxious about the whole process of the trial and potential outcome of the prosecution, commenting to her brother that events had 'raised terrible animosities throughout the kingdom, of which I praise God avert the fatal consequences'.[116] Abigail Harley's caution was confirmed by her own experience. Twenty days earlier, from the window of her house, she had witnessed the militia racing to quell a rioting multitude that sacked dissenting meeting houses, attacked the Bank of England, and seemingly threatened the peace of the political state. Abigail Harley's letter to her nephew, then, reveals not just her despair at the events of March 1710, but also her own deep disquiet at the inability of the whig junto to quieten Henry Sacheverell successfully.

However, we should gravely misjudge the skill of high church preaching if we blame the debacle of the trial of Henry Sacheverell on the whig junto.[117] High churchmen, as we have seen, expressed undisguised distaste at the turn of events since 1688. As this article has demonstrated, too much emphasis has been put on the constitutional implications of Sacheverell's trial. It is only recently that a few historians of post-revolution England have begun to realize that the relative freedom of the press, owing to the lapse of licensing, may have caused bitter disillusionment rather than advancing England towards a modern nation.[118] In fact, the often ignored *Communication of Sin*, the first sermon of 1709 for which Sacheverell was to be prosecuted, fully articulated the high church position advanced by Higgins three years earlier, that all men must oppose

[114] BL, Add. MS 61652, f. 86: Sunderland to the lord advocate, 16 Sept. 1708; f. 101: Sunderland to the lord advocate, 18 Nov. 1708.

[115] Cited in Holmes, *Trial of Doctor Sacheverell*, 96.

[116] HMC, *Portland MSS*, iv, 539: Harley to Edward Harley, 25 Mar. 1710.

[117] Holmes, *Trial of Dr Sacheverell*, 78–9.

[118] For an understanding that many high churchmen did not welcome the press, see Knights, *Representation and Misrepresentation*, 266–71.

blasphemy lest they endanger their own salvation. There is not space here to trace fully the influence of Higgins on Sacheverell. Nevertheless, the importance to high church-men of the pernicious nature of the press can be found in the *Perils of False Brethren*. 'He is a false brother with relation to God, Religion or the Church in which he holds Communion', Sacheverell maintained, who also 'believes, maintains, or propagates any false, or heterodox tenet, or doctrine repugnant to the express declaration of scripture, and the decrees, or sense of the church, and antiquity thereupon'. Symptomatic to high churchmen's uneasy state of mind was the persistent inability of the Church to discipline the ungodly. Their vision of a christian community, represented by the Church of England alone, and able to enforce correct doctrine, had been swept away by the Act of Toleration and further eroded by the licentiousness of the press. It was all very well for Church whigs and latitudinarians to insist that they were godly men, seeking salvation through living a moral life, but high churchmen saw them as proponents of a 'Serious, and Deliberate Act of Treachery', who had undermined, 'our Church, as a sacred Body, and Fraternity, that ought to Preserve Inviolable Unity, professing One Faith, One Baptism, One God, and Saviour of Us All'.[119]

6

The issues that Francis Atterbury, Henry Sacheverell and Francis Higgins had been raising in the early 18th century did not vanish from the national agenda. In 1711, the lower house of convocation issued a *Representation* that defined the religious debate for the next four years. The lower clergy lamented the spread of blasphemy unleashed by the free press and, personally directed by the monarch, requested that an act might be obtained to restrain 'the present excessive and scandalous Liberty of Printing wicked books at home, or importing the like from abroad'.[120] Indeed, news of the campaign in convocation soon reached Scotland, where Robert Wodrow was informed that there was 'a fine representation of ye present state of ye Church wherein particular they Complain of yt liberty of ye press & playhouses'.[121] Nor did the concerns with the power of high church preaching disappear. In the country at large, individuals continued to complain of 'virulent seditious sermons' being preached.[122] Yet the tory victory in the 1710 general election and the promotion of Harley to chief minister did not deliver the high church agenda. Harley's moderation ensured that restraint of the press would never be placed in the hands of the Church, toleration remained a detested political reality, and the focus of government slowly turned to the Hanoverian succession.

It is not the intention of this article to offer a single explanation for the trial of Henry Sacheverell. Rather, it is to demonstrate that high churchmen were not committed to a backward agenda, defined by wanting to restore the country to the 'conditions of the

[119] Henry Sacheverell, *The Communication of Sin* (1709), 16.

[120] *A Representation of the Present State of Religion, with regard to the late Excessive Growth of Infidelity, Heresy and Profaneness* (1711), 4, 5, 6, 13, 21, 24.

[121] National Library of Scotland, Edinburgh, Wodrow Papers, Qu. v, f. 176v: John Crosse to Robert Wodrow, Glasgow 30 Mar. 1711.

[122] BL, Add. MS 61610, f. 30: Hereford, 12 Apr. 1710.

old establishment', as historians have claimed.[123] There was much more to high church politics in terms of theology and tactics. Hatred of the free press, to give the most prominent example, is only understandable within a soteriological framework. Recognition that high churchmen developed the Augustinian tradition helps us to explain why they detested latitudinarians and tells us a great deal about the prominence of the 'Church in danger' cry.[124] The theology of high churchmen only comes into focus when we realize how skilled they were at exploiting the pulpit and how much of a challenge their behaviour posed to whig politicians and bishops. In order to do so, it is necessary to recover the history of the intellectual content of high church sermons and analyse their delivery and reception. Above all, we must accept that to talk of sermons as representative of the public sphere is an over-simplification of the unique relationship between high church clergymen on the one hand and the whig junto on the other.[125]

[123] Bennett, *Tory Crisis in Church and State*, 20.

[124] Mark Goldie, 'The Theory of Religious Intolerance in Restoration England', in *From Persecution to Toleration: The Glorious Revolution and Religion in England*, ed. Ole Peter Grell, Jonathan I. Israel and Nicholas Tyacke (Oxford, 1991), 331–68; John Marshall, *John Locke, Toleration and Early Enlightenment Culture: Religious Intolerance and Arguments for Religious Toleration in Early Modern and 'Early Enlightenment' Europe* (Cambridge, 2006), 197–223.

[125] Claydon, 'The Sermon and the Public Sphere', 208–34.

Securing the Hanoverian Succession in Ireland: Jacobites, Money and Men, 1714–16

CHARLES IVAR McGRATH

This article examines the connection between issues of security, finance and the army in Ireland in the years 1714–16. The death of Queen Anne and succession of the first Hanoverian monarch, George I, in August 1714, offered renewed hope to the supporters of the jacobite cause in Ireland, Scotland, England and beyond. However, the threat of a Stuart restoration by force of arms served to galvanise the efforts of government in both England and Ireland in support of the Hanoverian succession, though the necessary military preparations and precautions resulted in increased public expenditure. In Ireland, the government's need to find new sources of revenue meant that parliament would have to be convened, which, in turn, necessitated compliance with a series of constitutional practices which had evolved since the 1690s in relation to Poynings' Law and supply legislation. Yet, despite a threatened jacobite invasion, factional political manœuvring, as ever, demanded compromise, though, ultimately, the wholly protestant Irish parliament took the necessary precautions to secure Ireland for the new Hanoverian regime by voting new taxes and facilitating the creation of a national debt in order to raise new regiments for the army. The coalescing of the issues of security, finance and the army thereby led to innovations in Irish parliamentary and financial practice which were to become key components of the constitutional framework in Ireland until legislative independence in 1782.

Keywords: money; national debt; Supply Bills; law; parliament; politics; army; protestant; catholic

1

As David Hayton has amply demonstrated in a series of groundbreaking publications since the 1970s, the Irish parliament embarked on a new and vibrant phase of its history in the aftermath of the Glorious Revolution. The advent of regular parliamentary sessions from 1692 onwards resulted in the Irish assembly becoming a much more vital institution of state than had previously been the case. Irish MPs thereby became more centrally involved in the running of the country, leading politicians found themselves having more day-to-day influence within government, and political, economic and other grievances could be more readily addressed at a national level. At the heart of such changes was a number of interconnected factors: security, finance, and the army – or jacobites, money and men.[1]

---

[1] For a selection of relevant publications, see D.W. Hayton, *Ruling Ireland, 1685–1742: Politics, Politicians and Parties* (Woodbridge, 2004); D.W. Hayton, 'Introduction: The Long Apprenticeship', *Parliamentary History*, xx (2001), 1–26; D.W. Hayton, 'Ideas of Union in Anglo-Irish Political Discourse, 1692–1720

In 1695, a political compromise was reached between government and parliament over the issue of financial supply legislation, which gave the Irish house of commons control over the raising of the majority of the additional income required by government to pay for a permanent and enlarged army in Ireland. The Commons ensured, thereafter, that parliamentary supplies were only voted for defined periods of time, thereby ensuring regular sessions throughout the 18th century. The acceptance of, and financial provision for, a permanent and enlarged army in Ireland was, at first, primarily motivated by security concerns: the Irish protestant ruling minority elite feared a renewed Irish Roman catholic rebellion and Franco-jacobite invasion and a large army offered security against that threat, whether real or perceived. But once England's war with France ended in 1697, Ireland began to serve a different purpose in a wider imperial strategy, as the location of the largest single part of Britain's peacetime standing army. The presence, however, of James II and, following his death in 1701, of the Stuart pretender on the Continent ensured that the threat of an attempted jacobite restoration continued to focus the minds of Irish protestants at key moments in the decades following the Glorious Revolution.[2]

At one time or another between 1692 and 1714, one or more of the three interconnected issues of security, finance and the army was the dominant factor when the Irish parliament met. However, the death of Queen Anne in August 1714 and the succession of the first Hanoverian monarch, George I, brought all three elements into play in relation to the Irish executive and legislature, as the governments in both Britain and Ireland looked to secure the new regime in the face of testing financial, security and military challenges. At the same time, even in dealing with those challenges, the Irish government and parliament demonstrated that the constitutional framework which had evolved since the 1690s had to be adhered to, though all were willing to allow necessity to be both the mother of innovation and of compromise.

2

Official news of the death of Queen Anne on 1 August 1714 and the succession of George I reached Ireland in just over a week. On 9 August, the under secretary, Joshua Dawson, recorded that an 'express' mail had 'brought us the melancholy account of her late majesty's death'. On receipt of the news, the Irish government 'immediately proclaimed the king and issued proclamations for proclaiming his majesty in all the cities and towns of Ireland'. They also took the precaution of issuing 'another proclamation

[1] (*continued*) Meaning and Use', in *Political Discourse in Seventeenth- and Eighteenth-Century Ireland*, ed. David George Boyce, Robert Eccleshall and Vincent Geoghegan (Basingstoke, 2001), 142–68; D.W. Hayton, 'A Debate in the Irish House of Commons in 1703: A Whiff of Tory Grapeshot', *Parliamentary History*, x (1991), 51–63; D.W. Hayton, 'Divisions in the Whig Junto in 1709: Some Irish Evidence', *Bulletin of the Institute of Historical Research*, lv (1982), 213–21; D.W. Hayton, 'An Irish Parliamentary Diary from the Reign of Queen Anne', *Analecta Hibernica*, xxx (1982), 97–149.

[2] See, in general, C.I. McGrath, *Ireland and Empire, 1692–1770* (2012), *passim*; C.I. McGrath, *The Making of the Eighteenth-Century Irish Constitution: Government, Parliament and the Revenue, 1692–1714* (Dublin, 2000), *passim*. For a recent account of Irish Protestant fears of the French in this period, see James Kelly, "Disappointing the Boundless Ambitions of France": Irish Protestants and the Fear of Invasion, 1661–1815', *Studia Hibernica*, xxxvii (2011), 39–46.

for seizing all the horses and [arms] of the papists, and we have no apprehensions of any disturbance or trouble in this country, and if there be any at all, it must arise I fancy in Scotland'.[3] The Irish government's decision to issue a proclamation for disarming Roman catholics, a policy which had been enshrined in law in 1695, was a manifestation of their anxiety lest there should be a jacobite attempt to overthrow the Hanoverian succession in favour of the Stuart pretender.

Events in both Ireland and England in the following months demonstrated the implications of the establishment of the Hanoverian succession. In mid-September, the sitting tory lords justices, Lord Chancellor Sir Constantine Phipps and Thomas Lindsey, archbishop of Armagh, were replaced by the more acceptably whiggish archbishop of Dublin, William King, and Robert Fitzgerald, earl of Kildare, which heralded the commencement of a policy of removing tories from government.[4] Coinciding with the change of lords justices was the appointment of a new lord lieutenant, in the person of Charles Spencer, earl of Sunderland.[5] The privy council was dissolved shortly afterwards and a new one formed in which the recently dominant tories were replaced with whigs.[6] The senior judicial offices were also given to whigs; Alan Brodrick became lord chancellor and William Whitshed, John Forster and Joseph Deane were made chief judges of the other three courts. Further changes to the puisne judges were made in the following months.[7]

Security concerns dominated the thinking of the new government in the early months of the Hanoverian succession. One of the first actions of the new lords justices was to respond to orders from London for half-pay officers from three recently-disbanded regiments to be transported from Ireland to Scotland in order to secure that region against an attempted Stuart restoration.[8] As for Ireland, even prior to the death of Queen Anne, the government's effort to combat the enlistment of Irishmen for the pretender's service had been intensifying,[9] while the first months of George I's reign witnessed the Irish commissioners of Oyer and Terminer finding 21 people guilty of that offence. In December, the lords justices advised that, if the king saw fit to pardon the lives of any of the 21, it would be of 'ill consequence to turn them loose to infest this country, in which there are so many in the Pretender's interest'. Better, therefore, that they should be 'transported to some of the foreign plantations' for 'examples sake and the common safety'. In early 1715, all 21 were sent to the West Indies, at which time a further 20 were awaiting trial for the same offence.[10]

In light of such events, it was not overly surprising that Archbishop King was much agitated by the perceived jacobite threat and the adherence of Irish catholics to the Stuart cause. At the end of December 1714, he advised Sunderland of the increased

---

[3] TNA, SP63/371/23: J[oshua] Dawson to [Sir Charles Delafaye], 9 Aug. 1714; S.J. Connolly, *Religion Law and Power: The Making of Protestant Ireland 1660–1760* (Oxford, 1992), 1.

[4] BL, Add. MS 61635, ff. 131–3. On the government changes in Ireland in general, see Patrick McNally *Parties, Patriots and Undertakers: Parliamentary Politics in Early Hanoverian Ireland* (Dublin, 1997), 67–78.

[5] TNA, PC2/85, 82–5; SP63/371/30.

[6] BL, Add. MS 61636, ff. 99–100, 101–2, 104.

[7] BL, Add. MS 61635, ff. 47, 81.

[8] BL, Add. MS 61635, ff. 33, 41; McGrath, *Ireland and Empire*, 155.

[9] TNA, SP63/370/30, 70, 240, 242–4.

[10] BL, Add. MS 61635, ff. 83, 109–10: lords justices to lord lieutenant, 5 Dec. 1714, 18 Jan. 1715; see also BL, Add. MS 61635, ff. 85–8.

lawlessness in the north of Ireland; he attributed this to 'the great encouragement the papists lately had . . . of the Pretender's coming', which had 'given them new spirit, and [their now] being disappointed they are madder and desperate, and venture on these extravagancies'.[11]

Yet in reality, the most pressing issue for government in both London and Dublin was the public finances. The political impasse that had arisen between the whigs and tories in the Irish parliament of 1713 had resulted in the essential additional parliamentary duties being voted for only three months to 25 March 1714. A twofold problem ensued when they lapsed: first, the Irish government's income decreased by about one-quarter per annum, resulting thereby in an increase in pay arrears, especially for the army; and second, the actual amount of lost income increased exponentially over the ensuing months, as merchants stockpiled goods while the hiatus in the imposition of the additional duties continued. In November 1714, the lords justices explained that merchants had imported 'a vast quantity of tobacco as soon as the additional duty on that commodity expired'. Although that importation had 'very much increased the revenue of this year', because of the augmented return from the permanent hereditary duty payable on tobacco, it meant inevitably that there would be a 'much greater drawback' the following year because, at a 'modest computation, . . . this kingdom is at present sufficiently stocked with tobacco for a year and a half'. Even when the additional duties were restored, the loss of revenue would continue, owing to the greatly-reduced need to import more tobacco until the stockpiles were used up.[12] While there seemed little chance that anything could be done to call parliament in Ireland before the pending crop of tobacco was imported to Ireland, Archbishop King entertained hopes that 'we may have one before the great quantity of wine from the last vintage be brought in, which will be in March or April [1715]'.[13]

But even with such pressing financial concerns, the process of convening parliament was long drawn out. The politics of party in Ireland, even with the tories in retreat, required management, while the interpretation of the 1695 compromise, and its ensuing evolution, required clarification on both sides of the Irish Sea.[14] The traditional desire to avoid having both the Westminster and Dublin parliaments sitting at the same time was also invoked as a reason for delaying the latter assembly.[15] The question of who would oversee parliament as chief governor would also become an issue at a later stage in the proceedings.

As had been the case in the lead-up to the election of new parliaments in Ireland in 1703 and 1711, much energy was expended on identifying potential candidates for Speaker of the Commons. The Speaker had significant influence with the lower House and so the candidates were a matter of great interest for the government and the political community at large. As early as October 1714, the matter was under active discussion. Lord Chancellor Brodrick, who had done much to make the speakership independent

[11] BL, Add. MS 61635, f. 153: Archbishop King to Sunderland, 31 Dec. 1714.

[12] BL, Add. MS 61635, f. 69: lords justices to lord lieutenant, 17 Nov. 1714.

[13] BL, Add. MS 61635, ff. 147–9: Archbishop King to [Sunderland], 21 Nov. 1714; see also Add. MS 61635, f. 188.

[14] McGrath, *Irish Constitution*, 118–290.

[15] BL, Add. MS 61635, f. 162.

of government when he held the position between 1703 and 1709, and again in 1713–14,[16] initially recommended George Gore, the incoming attorney general, but he declined on health grounds. Of the other mooted candidates, Brodrick was firmly opposed to Sir Richard Levinge, who had the dubious honour of being the successful government nominee in the 'sole right' parliament of 1692 and the unsuccessful government nominee in 1713 when Brodrick had prevailed on an opposition platform. Levinge's long-standing flirtations with the tory party also did not stand him in good stead. The best alternative was the assuredly whig, William Conolly, with whom Brodrick had been allied throughout Anne's reign. However, even then, Brodrick's conditional support for Conolly pointed to the future fallout between the two men – a fallout that anticipated the factionalism that characterised Irish whigs once they no longer felt the need to maintain a united front because the tory party had gone into irrevocable decline.[17]

The question of a parliamentary supply, and the origins and content of the Supply Bills, was central to the convening of parliament in Ireland. As was the norm since 1695, the government began preparing financial accounts in January 1715 to facilitate the Commons' assessment of the quantum of supply to be voted and the ways and means of raising that supply.[18] At the same time, discussions between London and Dublin turned to the delicate matter of the government's token Supply Bill which, in keeping with the 1695 compromise, was introduced at the beginning of a new parliament in keeping with Poynings' Law and the crown's prerogative right to initiate legislation. Sunderland transmitted to Ireland the opinion of the king and privy council in London that 'a bill for the additional duties should be one of those transmitted under the Great Seal at the opening of the parliament', which, Alan Brodrick mused, 'shows that to be a thing resolved on and determined, so that it no way becomes us to consider or debate that point'. Yet, true to form, he still tried to do so.[19]

The English government's aspiration to include a 'retrospect for charging stock in hand' in the government bill gave Brodrick his opportunity.[20] The leading whigs, Brodrick, Conolly, William Whitshed and Joseph Deane met on several occasions to discuss the matter and, having agreed an opinion, Brodrick was tasked with responding to London.[21] In a lengthy letter, he informed Sunderland that the proposed retrospect was a matter of 'great weight and difficulty'. Having enumerated the practical difficulties of trying to tax goods retrospectively, he counselled that it was the unanimous opinion of the leading whigs that 'if a money bill must be sent over, it should be the same bill as formerly for granting the additional duties for three or [four] months without any clause of retrospect'. Because of the 1695 compromise, the Commons 'had

[16] C.I. McGrath, 'Alan Brodrick and the Speakership of the Irish House of Commons, 1703–4', in *People Politics and Power: Essays on Irish History 1660–1850 in Honour of James I. McGuire*, ed. James Kelly, John McCafferty and C.I. McGrath (Dublin, 2009), 70–93.

[17] BL, Add. MS 61636, ff. 113–14, 115–16, 119–22: Brodrick to [Sunderland], [19], 26 Oct., 16 Nov., 2 Dec. 1714; Hayton, *Ruling Ireland*, 217–36; Patrick Walsh, *The Making of the Irish Protestant Ascendancy: The Life of William Conolly, 1662–1729* (Woodbridge, 2010), 101, 154–63, 168.

[18] BL, Add. MS 61636, ff. 203–4, 216–19.

[19] BL, Add. MS 61636, f. 125: Brodrick to [Sunderland], 7 Jan. 1715.

[20] BL, Add. MS 61636, f. 199: Conolly to [Sunderland], 4 Jan. 1715.

[21] BL, Add. MS 61636, ff. 123, 201–2.

the experience of that bill and, therefore, 'will not be surprised at it as a new thing'. However, the introduction of an innovation such as the retrospect, especially in a bill to be 'transmitted from England', could not 'be more distasteful to the House [of Commons]'. Moreover, there was 'no reason to doubt that good and effectual funds will be found out for raising such sums as the parliament shall see necessary to give: A deficient fund was never given here in the memory of any man living. Why then may not the manner be left to the House?' Saving his most obtuse argument for last, he concluded by suggesting that London should drop the idea of transmitting a token Supply Bill at all, on the convoluted grounds that the proposal for a retrospective clause had so muddied the waters that it was best to leave the raising of the whole supply to the Commons. However, this argument served mainly to demonstrate Brodrick's continuing commitment, more than 20 years after the 'sole right' crisis of 1692–3, to put an end to government Supply Bills by whatever means possible.[22]

The focus of attention upon a successful parliamentary supply and maximising the amount of income raised arose from the need to find more money for the pay of the army in Ireland. The end of the War of the Spanish Succession in 1713 had resulted in the demobilisation of most of the British army, with Ireland fulfilling its role as the location for the single largest part of the much-reduced army that remained. The increased public expenditure arose from both the pay of the returning soldiers, who brought the military establishment back up to its required peacetime level of 12,000 men, and the building of new barracks.[23] In January 1715, Conolly reassured Sunderland that 'it cannot be disagreeable to the parliament of Ireland to have the [military] establishment made up [to] 12,000 strong', but commented that it would be difficult to get a sufficient supply from parliament to cover the army's full pay, though, he observed reassuringly, this, too, 'will be done and I hope with satisfaction'. The removal of 'some of the unnecessary pensions on the establishment', which was a favourite grievance among Irish MPs, would help to pave the way, though a suggestion that the army in Ireland might be increased to 15,000 men was deemed a dangerous proposition, not least because there were already rumours of an impending land tax, 'which makes people uneasy'. Conolly counselled prudently that it would be unwise to add to that disquiet by increasing the size and cost of the army.[24]

For his part, Brodrick claimed that the 12,000 men would be supported financially only if 'they remain in Ireland while they are paid by it', thereby voicing the known concern of Irish MPs at the exportation of Irish money to pay soldiers serving overseas.[25] More disingenuously, he also warned that the opinions being offered from Ireland as to how parliament might act should not be made public because 'the persons advised with are branded with the name of undertakers'.[26] Brodrick's continuing fear that he should be perceived by his fellow MPs as managing parliament for the government, 20 years

---

[22] BL, Add. MS 61636, ff. 125–6: Brodrick to [Sunderland], 7 Jan. 1715; see also Add. MS 61636, ff. 127, 31–2.

[23] McGrath, *Ireland and Empire*, 69, 75–92, 107–9, 123–32.

[24] BL, Add. MS 61636, ff. 214–15: Conolly to [Sunderland], 25 Jan. 1715; see also Add. MS 61636, f. 216.

[25] BL, Add. MS 61636, ff. 131–2: Brodrick to [Sunderland], 25 Jan. 1715; McGrath, *Ireland and Empire*, 44–5, 151–5, 157–66.

[26] BL, Add. MS 61636, ff. 131–2: Brodrick to [Sunderland], 25 Jan. 1715.

after he had first been described as a parliamentary 'undertaker',[27] rang rather hollow, given that he had been a prime mover in the development of this 'undertaker system' over the preceding two decades.[28]

In terms of actual revenue raised, the government Supply Bill was merely a token offering which possessed more political and constitutional significance than financial reward. The key revenue measures were to be included in the heads of bills that took their rise in the Commons. On this point, Conolly made it clear that 'the parliament will be very unwilling to come into any other, than the additional duties formerly granted, for they [will] think it hard to go into new funds in time of peace, when the old ones answered in the time of war'.[29] He acknowledged that this would result in a reduced income in the first year, owing to the prior stockpiling of goods, but argued that any such 'arrear . . . will be cleared off in a year or two more, and at worst it will be but postponing some parts of the civil and military list, for the parliament here will not come into any clause for [borrowing] money, as is usual there [in England]'.[30] With less scruples on the matter of managing parliament than Brodrick feigned, Conolly assured Sunderland 'that care will be taken, that such funds as will be given will effectually answer and produce the sums for which they shall be given'.[31] To that end, he did not doubt but that 'the parliament will cheerfully and effectually supply the occasions of the government and pay the army they always desired'.[32] Brodrick also avowed there was 'no question but that the parliament will give supplies sufficient to defray the expense of his majesty's Establishment', but warned that 'nobody can foresee the manner of doing it'. He simply claimed that 'parliament here never yet gave a fund which did not answer more than it was given for', and that there was no reason to think the approaching parliament would not 'show as much loyalty to his majesty and readiness to support his Establishment'.[33]

In the early summer of 1715, the focus shifted from finance to security as fresh rumours circulated of an intended jacobite invasion and rebellion prompted by an outbreak of rioting in parts of England.[34] In Ireland, although the government was initially 'not . . . extremely apprehensive of an invasion', they still deemed it prudent to take appropriate precautions, including an assessment of the stores of weapons and the condition of the garrisons.[35] By late July, attitudes had changed somewhat, as the 'report of the Pretender's preparations [to invade], must sufficiently alarm a country in which besides non-jurors, Jacobites &c. there are at least six papists to one protestant'.[36] As a

---

[27] HMC, *Downshire MSS*, i, 492–3; C.I. McGrath, 'English Ministers, Irish Politicians and the Making of a Parliamentary Settlement in Ireland, 1692–5', *English Historical Review*, cxix (2004), 611.

[28] For the development of the 'Undertaker System', see D.W. Hayton, 'The Beginnings of the "Undertaker System"', in *Penal Era and Golden Age: Essays in Irish History, 1690–1800*, ed. Thomas Bartlett and D.W. Hayton (Belfast, 1979), 32–54; Hayton, *Ruling Ireland*, 106–30.

[29] BL, Add. MS 61636, f. 215: Conolly to [Sunderland], 25 Jan. 1715.

[30] BL, Add. MS 61636, f. 228: Conolly to [Sunderland], 15 Feb. 1715. In this latter respect, Conolly would be proved wrong, as the security situation changed dramatically for the worse as 1715 unfolded.

[31] BL, Add. MS 61636, ff. 230–1: Conolly to [Sunderland], 5 Mar. 1715.

[32] BL, Add. MS 61636, f. 232: Conolly to [Sunderland], 15 Mar. 1715; see also Add. MS 61636, ff. 235–6.

[33] BL, Add. MS 61636, ff. 143–4: Brodrick to [Sunderland], 19 Mar. 1714[/15].

[34] TNA, PC2/85, 250–7, 260–6.

[35] BL, Add. MS 61636, f. 189: Eustace Budgell to [Addison], 9 July 1715.

[36] BL, Add. MS 61636, f. 191: Budgell to Addison, 28 July 1715.

result, proclamations were issued requiring magistrates to ensure 'that the oaths be tendered to all papists and other suspected persons, [and] that they do search for and seize upon all such arms, armour, ammunition and serviceable horses as they shall find in the custody of, or belonging to, papists or non-jurors'. Accounts of all 'arms, ammunition and warlike stores' in the various localities were to be sent to the privy council, as were 'the names of all inmates, lodgers and strangers' in Dublin and elsewhere.[37] Reports were also transmitted to London dealing with individuals convicted of being 'the Pretender's men'.[38]

The need to establish the state of the stores of arms arose because orders were issued at the same time for the militia to array.[39] Unlike in England, the government was required to supply the militia with arms, hence their concern at the shortage of weapons in public storage.[40] By the end of July, the government had sent additional troops to the key locations of Galway, Limerick, Cork and Kinsale.[41] The coinciding receipt of instructions from London to send three regiments from Ireland to Scotland prompted the lords justices to request of Sunderland 'that[,] since the papists in this country are so vastly superior to the protestants and are at all times ready to rise upon us if an occasion offers, we may not be left naked and defenceless by the withdrawing any more of our troops'.[42] Despite such protests, a month later, a further three regiments were ordered to England.[43]

The evolving security crisis had a palpable effect on political thinking regarding parliament in Ireland. At the end of August, pursuant to a request that Sunderland send them as large a quantity of arms and ammunition as he could procure from the English Ordnance Office, the lords justices stated confidently that payment could be made from the Irish revenue at large because 'we can venture to assure your excellency that an Irish parliament, whenever it meets, will very readily make good any sum laid out for the defence of the nation at this time'.[44] Brodrick and Conolly's earlier arguments that it would be difficult to convince the Irish parliament to vote increased additional duties in peacetime carried little weight now that the country was in the grip of a security crisis.

At the same time, Sunderland's decision to stay in London as lord privy seal, rather than actually taking up his post as chief governor in Ireland, created a new degree of uncertainty in late summer 1715, which was exacerbated by the resulting decision in London to replace the lord lieutenants with a commission of lords justices.[45] Brodrick articulated genuine concern at the prospect of convening parliament under the governance of lords justices, on the grounds that a party already seemed to be emerging in Ireland that was 'dissatisfied at the present administration' and would aim to render 'the

---

[37] BL, Add. MS 61636, ff. 193: order in council, 28 July 1715; TNA, SP63/373/58–9.

[38] TNA, SP63/373/7–8: lords justices to Sunderland, 30 July 1715; see also SP63/373/21, 30–1, 32–3, 37–42.

[39] BL, Add. MS 61635, f. 123.

[40] TNA, SP63/373/90–1; Neal Garnham, *The Militia in Eighteenth-Century Ireland: In Defence of the Protestant Interest* (Woodbridge, 2012), 24–5.

[41] BL, Add. MS 61635, f. 125.

[42] BL, Add. MS 61635, f. 123: lords justices to lord lieutenant, 28 July 1715.

[43] BL, Add. MS 61635, f. 128.

[44] TNA, SP63/373/90–1: lords justices to Sunderland, 25 Aug. 1715.

[45] TNA, PC2/85, 283–4; McNally, *Parties, Patriots and Undertakers*, 47.

approaching session of parliament uneasy'.[46] Conolly was more circumspect when, in confiding his disappointment to Sunderland that he was not coming to Ireland, he stated that 'the great character' the outgoing lord lieutenant had given of Charles Fitzroy, duke of Grafton, one of the two incoming lords justices, would entitle Grafton 'to all the assistance your lordship's true friends can contribute to make his administration easy'. As for the second justice, Henri de Massue de Ruvigny, earl of Galway, Conolly acknowledged that 'he is well acquainted in this kingdom though things are much changed and upon another footing since he was in the government here'. This reservation notwithstanding, Conolly still hoped all would be carried on with success.[47]

In reality, Galway had been appointed because he had successfully overseen parliament in Ireland in 1697–9, when he had served as a lords justice with Charles Powlett, marquess of Winchester. Indeed, it had been the first occasion since 1661–2 that a commission of lords justices were given the responsibility, and it diminished the validity of Brodrick's claims in that respect. Galway had been appointed in 1697 as the senior figure in the commission responsible for educating and guiding the young Winchester in the art of the chief governor's office. In 1715, Galway was reappointed to do the same thing with the young Grafton. The usefulness of such an arrangement was seen in the fact that both Bolton (as Winchester had become) and Grafton went on to serve as lord lieutenants after 1716, though neither learned their lessons well from the more talented Galway, who could never hold the chief governor's office on his own because of his French nationality, despite his naturalisation as an English subject.[48]

The alterations in the chief governor's office coincided with the receipt in London of three proposed bills drafted by the Irish government as the first step in the process required by the terms of Poynings' Law to provide cause and consideration for convening parliament. The bills were for recognizing George I's title to the throne of Great Britain, France, and Ireland; for preventing Irish men from enlisting in foreign service; and the token government Supply Bill for granting, for six months, an additional duty on beer, ale, strong waters, tobacco, and other goods and merchandises.[49] On 14 September, the committee of the British privy council appointed to consider the bills judged that the prohibition on foreign service was unnecessary, 'there being an act passed in Great Britain' during Anne's reign 'in which Ireland is named: and therefore an exemplification of the said act under the great seal of Great Britain . . . will be sufficient' if sent to Ireland. That for recognizing the king's title to the throne was agreed without amendment, 'although their lordships do not think the same necessary; but only as it may be convenient there should be one bill for the House of Lords in Ireland to open the session with'. As for the Supply Bill, it was simply recommended that the start date be changed from 1 to 21 November. The committee also recommended that 'a commission to the lords justices now executing the said government' be

[46] BL, Add. MS 61636, ff. 154–5: Brodrick to [?], [Sept. 1715].

[47] TNA, SP63/373/142–3: Conolly to [Sunderland], 12 Sept. 1715.

[48] Hayton, *Ruling Ireland*, 63, 215; C.I. McGrath, 'Late Seventeenth- and Early Eighteenth-Century Governance and the Viceroyalty', in *The Irish Lord Lieutenancy, c. 1541–1922*, ed. Peter Gray and Olwen Purdue (Dublin, 2012), 52–5, 58–9; Marie Léoutre, 'Life of a Huguenot Exile: Henri de Ruvigny, Earl of Galway, 1648–1720', University College Dublin PhD, 2012, pp. 97–100, 282–5.

[49] TNA, PC2/85, 279–80; James Kelly, *Poynings' Law and the Making of Law in Ireland, 1660–1800* (Dublin, 2007), 190–1.

sent to Ireland 'to cause writs to be issued in the usual manner . . . as soon as may be convenient'.[50] The following day, the king and privy council agreed to all the recommendations and ordered the two bills back to Ireland with a commission for Galway and Grafton or, 'in their absence', given that both men were still in London, 'the persons now executing the office of lords justices', to convene parliament.[51]

The procedure followed in the first half of September in both Dublin and London was consistent with Poynings' Law and the 1695 compromise. The alteration to the start date of the Supply Bill was simply intended to allow more time for parliament to convene and go through the various preparatory stages of the supply process, as it had evolved since 1695, before the House actually turned its attention to the receipt of the token government bill. By 1713, the Commons had developed a procedure whereby the government bill was not presented to the House until after the Commons had taken the government's opening speech into consideration, passed a preliminary motion for a supply, convened the committee of the whole House on supply, agreed with that committee's resolution that a supply be granted, and appointed the all-important select committee of public accounts. In the 1713 parliament, it was actually argued that the process had evolved further since 1705 and that the Supply Bill should not be presented until after the public accounts committee had reported. It made sense that all Supply Bills would be better scrutinised when the Commons knew how much money the government needed, which was only made clear in the accounts committee report.[52]

It was therefore the case that sufficient time had to be made available for that parliamentary process to take place in advance of the presentation of the government Supply Bill. However, the actions of the British privy council created a twofold problem in that respect, which the Irish government raised after the two bills arrived back in Ireland on 30 September. The first issue was that, 'according to the forms of parliament here, it is necessary that the first sessions . . . should be opened by reading a bill, and no bill can be read that has not been remitted from England, [and] there must be a bill for each house'. Therefore, if the recognition bill was sent to the Commons, there would be no bill for the Lords, because Supply Bills could 'not begin there, nor can the Commons open their session with a money bill'. The solution lay in another transmission of three bills before parliament convened, but the time consumed in that process now meant that the earliest possible date for convening was 12 November. The delay created the second problem, which related to the start date of the Supply Bill. The Irish government, therefore, sent the bill back to London, in order to have the date changed to 1 December, on the grounds that allowing only nine days for the initial stages of the supply process was unwise because it would require MPs 'to break their rules' which might put them out of humour and disgust them'.[53] Galway added his weight to the argument while *en route* to Ireland, writing to London that 'you know we cannot in Ireland alter one syllable in that bill or any other after it returns from England' and that

[50] TNA, PC2/85, 282–3: privy council minutes, 14 Sept. 1715; Kelly, *Poynings' Law*, 191.

[51] TNA, PC2/85, 283–4: privy council minutes, 15 Sept. 1715.

[52] C.I. McGrath, 'Central Aspects of the Eighteenth-Century Constitutional Framework in Ireland: The Government Supply Bill and Biennial Parliamentary Sessions, 1715–82', *Eighteenth-Century Ireland*, xvi (2001), 3–15; McGrath, *Irish Constitution*, 118–290.

[53] TNA, SP63/373/148–9: [Archbishop King] to Stanhope, 7 Oct. 1715; Kelly, *Poynings' Law*, 191. On the second transmission of bills, see TNA, SP63/373/152, 154, 158.

'the people there would take it ill to be obliged to pass a money bill in a hurry'.[54] However, although the three bills were dealt with quickly in London, the start date for the Supply Bill was left unchanged.[55]

While the various Irish bills passed from one country to another, the long apprehended jacobite rebellion broke out in Scotland.[56] As a result, a further five regiments were ordered to Scotland and one more to England, bringing the total regimental contribution from Ireland to 12.[57] Ireland, however, remained 'in perfect peace[;] . . . the papists continue very quiet and seem not . . . to be in any disposition to give disturbance'. By the beginning of November, the government had issued commissions for a protestant militia of up to 30,000 men, though they had arms for only 15,000 men and an insufficiency of ammunition. Still, it was believed that, even with catholics outnumbering protestants by 'six to one', the remaining 'standing troops' and militia would be sufficient to prevent any unrest, unless the country was 'invaded from abroad'.[58] Such security considerations were to have a significant impact upon the proceedings of the Irish parliament when it finally convened.

By the beginning of November, Galway and Grafton were both in Dublin and the final preparations were in place for the assembly of parliament. The elections were deemed to have gone very favourably, with 'the Tories in most places giving up very [tamely]'.[59] The main point of concern for the new lords justices was the commencement date for the government Supply Bill.[60] Security questions also demanded their attention. The lack of arms and ammunition was exacerbated by the fact that, even 'though the country is hitherto quiet, . . . there appears a greater spirit among the papists and other disaffected persons'.[61] The fear that Irish catholics might rebel was heightened by the fact that the army was under strength. However, the lords justices were confident that the Irish parliament would provide for any expense necessary for securing the country, as long as they were not obliged to pay for troops stationed outside Ireland.[62]

Parliament assembled as planned on 12 November. In their opening speech, the lords justices emphasized the security question, noting that, despite the current calm in Ireland, it was still necessary 'to put yourselves in the best posture of defence'. To that end, they advised that the king had ordered arms for the militia and for 'an addition to be made to each [regular army] company' remaining in Ireland, until 'such time as he can replace those regiments which the necessity of his affairs has obliged him . . . to draw from hence, to suppress the rebels in Great Britain, wherein your safety is equally concerned with that of his other subjects'. They then turned their focus to money, adhering to the 1695 compromise by appealing directly to the Commons for supplies

---

[54] TNA, SP63/373/189–90: Galway to Stanhope, 21 Oct. 1715; see also TNA, SP63/373/183–4.

[55] TNA, PC2/85, 293–4.

[56] TNA, PC2/85, 288–90, 305–8.

[57] TNA, SP63/373/112, 144, 150, 193; McGrath, *Ireland and Empire*, 155.

[58] TNA, SP63/373/203–4: Archbishop King to Stanhope, 1 Nov. 1715.

[59] TNA, SP63/373/207: Delafaye to [Pringle], 3 Nov. 1715.

[60] TNA, SP63/373/205.

[61] TNA, SP63/373/236: Grafton and Galway to Stanhope, 8 Nov. 1715.

[62] TNA, SP63/373/242–3.

and promising delivery of a full state of the public accounts, while again emphasizing the need for parliament to provide sufficient funds 'to defray such expenses as you may think proper for your own security'.[63]

In the Commons, where Conolly was elected Speaker unopposed, the first order of business on the first full day of the session on 14 November was, as required, the reading of a government bill, which, as in 1713, was for preventing mischief by fire.[64] The House then moved immediately to commence the supply process by resolving to take the opening speech into consideration and by ordering addresses of thanks to the lords justices and of loyalty to the king, which, *inter alia*, was to promise that supplies would be granted 'as shall be necessary to enable his majesty to support his government with honour'.[65] On 15 November, the Commons addressed security concerns. Its first action was to order heads of bills for attainting the exiled former lord lieutenant, the tory, James Butler, duke of Ormond, of high treason, and for the further security of the king and government and the extinguishing of the hopes of the pretender and his 'open and secret abettors'. It then resolved that 'whoever advised the late queen to prorogue' the Irish parliament in 1714, 'at a time when a bill to attaint the Pretender was under consideration, . . . was an enemy to the succession in the illustrious house of Hanover, to the protestant interest in this kingdom, and a favourer of the Pretender and popery'. Having thus signalled their desire to seek retribution for the grievances suffered under the tory-led governments of 1711–14, the lower House turned to supply by taking the opening speech into consideration and passing the preliminary motion for supply.[66]

The first committee of the whole House on supply duly convened on 16 November and resolved that a supply be granted to the crown. Immediately thereafter, and well in advance of the Commons' own timetable for the initial stages of the supply process, the government Supply Bill was presented and read for the first time. The following day, it received a second reading and was referred to a committee of the whole House. In the interim, the public accounts were ordered for 18 November, the arrival of which prompted the appointment of the select committee of public accounts. The government Supply Bill then went through the committee of the whole House unhindered and, on 19 November, passed its final reading and was sent to the house of lords for its concurrence.[67] Despite the government's earlier fears, the bill did not encounter any resistance, even though its start date required the Commons to pass it in precipitate fashion. However, as soon as it had been passed, a tory lawyer, Edward Singleton, endeavoured to raise the 'sole right' question as a means of disrupting affairs, by moving 'a question that for the future the House should not receive any bills of the like kind that first did not take its rise in their House'. He was seconded by 'some young members', while 'several other questions relating to the same' were proposed. However, the debate was put to rest to the government's satisfaction when 'it was carried to

[63] *CJI*, iii, 9–10; TNA, SP63/373/242–3.

[64] *CJI*, iii, 9; TNA, SP63/373/242–3; McGrath, *Irish Constitution*, 272. The Lords commenced proceedings with the recognition bill.

[65] *CJI*, iii, 10, 11.

[66] *CJI*, iii, 12. For further evidence of the desire for retribution, see *CJI*, iii, 16, 20, 23–4, 28, 29–30, 32–3, 34–40, 42, 49–50, 60–4, 69–71, 83–5, 100–3, 105–6, 108–11.

[67] *CJI*, iii, 13–14, 16, 18–20, 22.

proceed on the order of the day by 117 against 57'.[68] The premature presentation of the government Supply Bill was not forgotten, however, as later in the session it was made a standing order of the Commons that, for the future, 'no money bill be read in this House until the report from the committee of accounts be first made'.[69]

With the government Supply Bill out of the way, attention shifted to raising the remainder of the necessary money. In accordance with established practice since 1695, the token government bill only provided for the imposition for six months of the main parliamentary additional duties.[70] The norm established over the preceding two decades was for parliamentary supplies of two years' duration; therefore, it remained for parliament to vote the existing duties for a further 18 months, and to consider whether the imposition of new duties for two years was required. In keeping with the procedures developed since 1695, the Commons carried out these tasks via their select committee of public accounts, the committees of the whole House on supply and ways and means, and the drafting committees for heads of Supply Bills.[71]

The first step in the process involved the committee of public accounts assessing all of the financial documentation laid before the Commons by the government. It was a complex undertaking, involving numerous subcommittees which sat on at least nine occasions before the report was delivered to the House on 10 December.[72] In the interval, attention in the Commons focused upon the continuing desire for retribution for events in 1711–14, on security legislation against a possible jacobite invasion or rebellion,[73] and in discussing whether or not wholly new additional duties should be voted. The government's main concern was that, since the cost of the establishment was higher than ever before, trying to force the issue on the additional duties might encourage MPs to focus on the reasons for that higher expenditure and, specifically, on the sensitive issue of the pensions paid to absentees.[74] However, despite opposition from 'some who have the highest obligations' to the king, the Irish chief secretary, Sir Charles Delafaye, did not doubt but that 'we shall carry what we propose, which [is] a duty of [£4] per ton upon all wine and 10*d.* per gallon on brandy'. The arguments against included:

> that when once they give a new fund it becomes perpetual; that if our treasury overflows you in England draw away the money by king's letters for bounty and pensions; that of those many are given to undeserving people, to persons that live out of this kingdom, so that the little money we can get, whom you deprive of all means of trading abroad, is drawn off to England.[75]

---

[68] TNA, SP63/373/256–7: Grafton and Galway to Stanhope, 23 Nov. 1715.

[69] *CJI*, iii, 91; McGrath, 'Central Aspects', 15.

[70] *The Statutes at Large Passed in the Parliaments Held in Ireland* (21 vols, Dublin, 1765–1804), iv, 315–17.

[71] C.I. McGrath, 'Parliamentary Additional Supply: The Development and Use of Regular Short-Term Taxation in the Irish Parliament, 1692–1716', *Parliamentary History*, xx (2001), 27–54.

[72] NAI, Frazer MSS 10 (unfoliated): minute book of the committee of public accounts, 21, 26, 29–30 Nov., 1–2, 4, 6, 8 Dec. 1715; *CJI*, iii, 44, Appendix, pp. xi–xxxii.

[73] *CJI*, iii, 23–4, 28, 29–30, 32–3, 34–40, 42.

[74] TNA, SP63/373/252–3, 256–7; McGrath, *Ireland and Empire*, 127–8.

[75] TNA, SP63/373/296: Delafaye to [Pringle], 6 Dec. 1715.

The main leverage available to the government was the ongoing security concerns. Alongside the heads of bills for the king's security and for attainting Ormond and the pretender, drafting commenced on a Militia Bill.[76] On 6 December, the Commons addressed the lords justices, requesting that the government apply to the king for an immediate supply of arms and ammunition for the militia. The government responded that the king had already ordered the sending from England of 10,000 muskets and ammunition. As for the cost, the Commons ordered that it be taken into consideration when the quantum of the supply was decided upon,[77] which, from the government's perspective, 'thereby secured' payment for the arms already requested.[78]

The committee of the whole House on supply sat on 12 December to consider the accounts committee report and resolved that the quantum be £187,587, 12s. 4d.[79] While discontent was expressed by a few MPs,[80] the lord justices felt that 'the justice of our demand supported by the good disposition of the Country gentlemen, has carried [the quantum] . . . for all that was desired . . . and . . . there is no room to doubt but the committee of ways and means will readily come into such new funds as together with the additional duties may be in some measure adequate'.[81] The ways and means committee, which sat twice on 15–16 December, resolved that the existing main additional duties be extended for a further 18 months from 21 May 1716 to 21 November 1717, and that a lapsed further additional duty from 1703 be reimposed upon wine, wholly new additional duties be imposed upon strong waters and spirits, a new tax on the salaries, fees, profits of employment and pensions of all absentee government officeholders be implemented, and the 6d. in the pound payable to the vice-treasurer on all the additional duties be appropriated to the public purse, all for 22 months from 1 February 1716 to 21 November 1717.[82] Drafting committees were then appointed for two heads of bills: for extending the main additional duties; and for imposing the new duties and taxes. In the latter case, the reason for the duration being two months less than two years was because of the House's desire that both bills would have the same end date in November 1717, while the earliest possible start date which would allow sufficient time for the bill to be drafted, transmitted and returned in accordance with Poynings' Law was deemed to be 1 February 1716. This bill was, therefore, the most urgent. With the Christmas recess pending, the draft heads were presented to the Commons on 20 December and, two days later, were ready to be sent to the lords justices for transmission to London in due form. Almost immediately thereafter, parliament was adjourned until 16 January 1716.[83]

In the lead up to the two-day sitting of the ways and means committee, concern had been expressed that 'some will endeavour to lay aside the funds that are understood

[76] *CJI*, iii, 12, 32; Garnham, *Militia*, 25–6.

[77] *CJI*, iii, 38, 41–2, 44.

[78] TNA, SP63/373/304: Grafton and Galway to Stanhope, 13 Dec. 1715.

[79] *CJI*, iii, 45–6.

[80] TNA, SP63/373/302.

[81] TNA, SP63/373/304–5: Grafton and Galway to Stanhope, 13 Dec. 1715.

[82] *CJI*, iii, 50–3.

[83] *CJI*, iii, 53–5, 59–60.

though not yet openly proposed'.[84] Much to the government's surprise, that opposition arose with the lord chancellor's son, St John Brodrick, who led the attack by focusing on pensions and by endeavouring to get the accounts committee report printed in order to make public the committee's criticisms of such expenditure. The government was able to defeat Brodrick's efforts by 154 votes to 51, which killed off any lingering attempt to oppose the actual supply. Obliged to refocus, 'Brodrick's party' proposed the tax on absentee officials and the appropriation of the vice-treasurer's fee, both of which it was known were unpopular in London, though the Irish government claimed that they 'were forced to accept' them.[85]

Overall, the government was happy with the outcome, though it had necessitated serious endeavour. Delafaye complained that the court party had been 'forced to meet every night with the chief of our friends to provide against the next day's battle', while the daytime 'was spent either in the House or in running about to solicit the members and keep our [forces] together whom Brodrick with as much diligence endeavoured to debauch, and had this work lasted but a week longer it would have killed us all'.[86] It was notable that, by his actions, St John Brodrick sought to make true his father's earlier prophecy of new party divisions emerging in Ireland.

By 24 December, the lords justices were ready to send the Supply Bill to London, at which time they requested that it 'should meet with the greatest dispatch'. They also took the opportunity to remind the British government 'of the danger there may be in making any alterations in this bill on your side, least the same should give a handle to dispute in the ... Commons here, and consequently risk the loss of the whole subsidy'.[87] In particular, they were concerned about the tax on absentee officials and the appropriation of the vice-treasurer's fees, both of which had been included 'in hopes that it will provoke you in England to alter this bill, and that will give them a pretense for throwing it out when it comes back'. It was a tactic that the Irish whigs under Alan Brodrick had employed in 1703 without success. Now the son was trying to succeed where the father had failed, but the government hoped that he, too, would be disappointed in his aims. Better that 'the pensioners ... lose part of their income ... than to have the whole bill lost, and consequently the government be unable to pay them anything'.[88]

Continuing rumours of possible alterations to the Supply Bill resulted in Delafaye reporting in early January that the government expected 'new battles' after the recess, 'for our opposers keep together and seem very active and industrious'.[89] However, the situation altered in the government's favour four days before parliament was due to reconvene, when news of the landing in Scotland of the pretender filtered through to Ireland.[90] The heightened threat to security that followed prompted a distinct alteration

---

[84] TNA, SP63/373/302: Maxwell to [Stanhope], 13 Dec. 1715.

[85] TNA, SP63/373/336–7: Delafaye to [Pringle], 17 Dec. 1715.

[86] TNA, SP63/373/336–7: Delafaye to [Pringle], 17 Dec. 1715.

[87] TNA, SP63/373/322–3: Grafton and Galway to Stanhope, 24 Dec. 1715.

[88] TNA, SP63/373/324: Delafaye to [Pringle], 24 Dec. 1715. For 1703, see McGrath, 'Alan Brodrick', 70–9; McGrath, *Ireland and Empire*, 84.

[89] TNA, SP63/374/18: Delafaye to [Pringle], 8 Jan. 1716.

[90] TNA, SP63/374/22, 26–7.

in the mind of MPs, whose wish to manifest their loyalty to the crown ensured greater compliance in providing for the increased financial demands of new and essential military precautions.

In the first instance, on 13 January, the lords justices requested permission from London to raise two extra companies per foot regiment in Ireland, in order to bring the military establishment back to full strength.[91] When parliament reconvened three days later, the readiness of MPs to do what was necessary to provide for the security of the kingdom was immediately evident with a series of unanimous resolutions: for an association to defend and support George I, his government 'and the protestant succession in his royal house, with their lives and fortunes, against the Pretender and all his adherents'; for an address for securing all catholics and others thought to be disaffected to the government; for magistrates to put the laws against catholic priests into execution; and, most importantly in practical terms, for an address that 'whatever forces his majesty shall think fit to raise, or whatever expense . . . [he] shall think necessary for the defence of this kingdom, this House shall enable his majesty to make good the same'.[92] The following day, the government issued printed instructions to local magistrates to muster the militia and to put the laws against catholics into execution.[93] At the same time, the association against the rebellion of 'papists and perjured traitors', which was to be subscribed to by all MPs, was agreed to. It professed that George I was the 'rightful and lawful' king of Great Britain, Ireland and France, and all dominions, and that the subscribers would support the king to the utmost of their power against the pretender and all his adherents.[94]

While the lords justices expressed their satisfaction with the resolutions of the Commons, it was the address desiring the king to take all necessary steps for the security of the kingdom that pleased them most.[95] Believing themselves 'in some measure warranted by the address of the . . . Commons to go into any necessary expense upon this occasion, though not within the rules prescribed by the Establishment', they put the half-pay officers and French pensioners on full pay, ordering some to assist with the militia in Dublin and around the country and others to serve with the army, while the dragoon and cavalry regiments were given augmented pay for cantonment at Athlone.[96] For good measure, Randal Mac Donnell, earl of Antrim, the leading catholic noble and perceived focal point for any rising in Ireland, was imprisoned, and permission was sought to arrest other catholic peers such as Richard, Viscount Dillon.[97]

In parliament, the main focus of attention for several days was upon subscribing to the association.[98] In a related matter, on 21 January the House resolved 85 to 46 that the vice-treasurer, Arthur Annesley, earl of Anglesey, who had been one of the principal advisers to Queen Anne on disbanding the army and proroguing the 1713–14 parliament when a bill to attaint the pretender had been under consideration, was therefore

---

[91] TNA, SP63/374/26–7.

[92] *CJI*, iii, 60–1.

[93] TNA, SP63/374/47; *CJI*, iii, 63.

[94] *CJI*, iii, 61.

[95] TNA, SP63/374/38; *CJI*, iii, 62, 64.

[96] TNA, SP63/374/42–3: Grafton and Galway to Stanhope, 20 Jan. 1716.

[97] TNA, SP63/374/53–4, 57–8.

[98] *CJI*, iii, 63.

an enemy of the king and kingdom and should be removed from office.[99] The pursuit of Anglesey was more immediately the result of the fact that he had evaded signing the association prior to his departure from Dublin and delegated the task to his proxy, James Hamilton, earl of Abercorn. The attack was led by St John Brodrick and his 'Cork squadron, to regain their credit by doing something popular and in which they were sure of a majority'. It was also noted that Archbishop Lindsey had delayed signing for three days and had done so with ill grace, placing his name at the very bottom 'from whence . . . [it] might be cut off in [time] convenient'.[100]

The Cork squadron's desire to win back popularity was bound up with the return in late January of the unaltered 22-month Supply Bill.[101] The bill passed through the Commons and Lords without any resistance, alongside the Bill for Attainting the Pretender.[102] The two bills received the royal assent on 28 January from the lords justices, who took the opportunity to notify both Houses that letters had arrived from London that morning informing them 'that there is reason to believe that this kingdom will be very suddenly invaded'. They recommended that parliament 'take such measures thereupon as may best conduce to the defence and security of your country'. Appealing directly to the Commons, they asked to be facilitated in doing 'what is further necessary to put the kingdom in a sufficient posture of defence, with the utmost expedition', promising that whatever 'expense shall be made at this time, will be so much laid out to preserve the whole'. By way of inducement, the king also sent word that the 12 regiments sent to Britain in 1715 would be paid on the British establishment from the time of their departure from Ireland.[103]

The response from the Commons was immediate and, as pointed out by the government, 'without precedent'.[104] The House first requested that the lords justices give immediate orders for raising a sufficient number of troops for bringing the establishment up to full strength, and to recruit 'as many more as they shall think necessary for the further security of the kingdom at this critical juncture'. The Commons also promised to 'make good whatever money shall be expended on this occasion', and then passed the all-important resolution that 'whatever sum or sums of money shall be advanced and paid into the treasury by any person or persons . . . for the defence of this kingdom, shall be made good by this House, with legal interest for the same, out of such aids as shall be granted to his majesty the next session of parliament'.[105] The resolution and ensuing address to that effect constituted the first ever 'vote of credit' by the Irish parliament, and formed the basis for the creation of the national debt.[106] By securing the loan to government upon future parliamentary taxation, the Commons had introduced to

---

[99] *CJI*, iii, 66, 67–8.

[100] TNA, SP63/374/57–8: Delafaye to [Pringle], 24 Jan. 1716.

[101] TNA, PC2/85, 329, 331–5; SP63/374/53–4, 57–8.

[102] *CJI*, iii, 66, 68, 70–3.

[103] *CJI*, iii, 73–4.

[104] TNA, SP63/374/63–5: Grafton and Galway to Stanhope, 30 Jan. 1716; see also SP63/374/59–60; C.I. McGrath, ' "The Public Wealth is the Sinew, the Life, of Every Public Measure": The Creation and Maintenance of a National Debt in Ireland, 1716–45', in *The Empire of Credit: The Financial Revolution in the British Atlantic World, 1700–1800*, ed. Daniel Carey and Christopher Finlay (Dublin, 2011), 174–5.

[105] *CJI*, iii, 73–5.

[106] TNA, SP63/374/59–60, 63–5; *CJI*, iii, 75–6.

Ireland the concept of an interest-bearing funded public debt, which brought into being a whole new level of interdependence between government, parliament and the wider community, in the guise of the public creditors, in a relationship that would serve to shape future political, economic and financial developments in 18th-century Ireland.[107]

It remained for the Commons to translate their resolution into a substantive financial instrument to facilitate public borrowing. In this respect, the earlier lack of urgency over the 18-month heads of a Supply Bill was now to prove opportune. The draft heads of that bill had finally been presented to the Commons on 27 January, the day before the vote of credit. Fortuitously, the bill could now be amended to include the necessary financial instrument. A committee of the whole House considered the heads on 1 and 3 February, when a clause was inserted 'for making effectual the vote of credit'. The heads were then sent to the lords justices for transmission to London. The need for MPs to return to their localities as part of the security precautions resulted in parliament adjourning several days later.[108]

The government used the borrowed money to raise 13 new regiments in Ireland. Unwilling to take advantage of the fact that the vote of credit was without limit, the lords justices borrowed only £50,000 for the purpose, which became the principal sum of the new national debt.[109] Recruitment of new soldiers commenced immediately, while the regiments cantoned in Athlone were moved to the centre of the Ormond heartland of Kilkenny because of a belief that the exiled duke would lead the rumoured jacobite invasion.[110] Prior to the February adjournment, the Commons had taken further steps to secure the country, including a request to the privy council to issue proclamations offering £10,000 for the seizure of Ormond if he landed in Ireland and for removing catholics from the army.[111]

Parliament remained in recess until early May, by which time the threat of invasion had receded.[112] In the interim, the government transmitted the Supply Bill to London, from whence it was returned without amendment.[113] When parliament reconvened, a small group of 'malcontents', numbering about 28, tried to 'insinuate with the people a jealousy of the government' by calling for an account 'of what had been done in pursuance of the former vote of credit'. Although the court party argued that 'it was pretty odd to call for that so soon',[114] an account of payments made out of the £50,000 was presented to the Commons on 10 May, followed by the Supply Bill. A week later, the bill had passed through all stages in the Commons without difficulty and was sent to the Lords for concurrence, which was forthcoming on 19 May when the bill also received the royal assent.[115] In his speech on the delivery of the bill to the lords justices, Speaker Conolly took the opportunity to emphasize once again the unique nature of the 'unlimited vote of credit', and the willingness of parliament to pass the Supply Bill

---

[107] McGrath, *Ireland and Empire*, 181–216; McGrath, 'Public Wealth', 171–207.

[108] *CJI*, iii, 78, 80, 83–5.

[109] McGrath, *Ireland and Empire*, 182–8; McGrath, 'Public Wealth', 174–9.

[110] TNA, SP63/374/63–5.

[111] *CJI*, iii, 74.

[112] TNA, SP63/374/103–4; *CJI*, iii, 86; McGrath, *Ireland and Empire*, 128–30.

[113] TNA, SP63/374/169–70, 175–6, 201–3, 205–6, 217–18, 221–2; PC2/85, 352–6, 359–72.

[114] TNA, SP63/374/219–20: Delafaye to [Pringle], 4 May 1716.

[115] *CJI*, iii, 86, 88–90, Appendix, p. xxxviii; TNA, SP63/374/240–1.

'before the other bills prepared by the Commons are ready for the royal assent'.[116] The growing awareness of the significance of what had occurred was also evident on 6 June, when the Commons took the opportunity, in an address to the king congratulating him on victory over the jacobite rebels, to point out that 'notwithstanding the poverty of this kingdom' they had entrusted the government 'with an unprecedented and unlimited vote of credit'.[117]

For the lords justices, the passage of the third and final Supply Bill of the session signalled the successful completion of the government's parliamentary business. They congratulated themselves on the fact that:

> Upon the whole considering that the Establishment we brought over, though exceeding any that had gone before it, was allowed without an open complaint, that the parliament have gone into ways and means never made use of before, that upon the first news of the Pretender's landing in Scotland they trusted us with an unlimited power to borrow money, and raise forces, promising to make good the expense, entering into a very hearty Association, and doing with a great deal of vigour and spirit everything that might show their zeal for his majesty and his government, we hope we shall not be thought to have made an ill sessions of it.[118]

Parliament continued to sit until 20 June in order to facilitate the passage of other returned bills. The problem of pensions dominated for a time, while the returned Militia Bill was a priority for the Commons. A short-lived flirtation with an idea, previously mooted in 1695 and 1703, of having heads of bills read in both Houses before sending them to the privy council, which originated on this occasion in the Commons, was dropped in the Lords following pressure from the government.[119] In no instance, however, did these activities detract from what had gone before. In their closing speech, the lords justices reiterated their own sense of what had been achieved. Informing the Commons that the king had sent his thanks for the supplies 'so cheerfully granted for his service, and your own defence', they went on 'thankfully [to] acknowledge the several marks of confidence you have placed in us, more particularly your seasonable and unprecedented vote of credit, which will remain a memorable proof of your unbounded zeal for his majesty's service'.[120]

While these sentiments might easily be dismissed as political hyperbole, the repeated emphasis placed upon the significance and unprecedented nature of the vote of credit suggested otherwise. The vote of credit was the central component of a series of important and successful steps taken by government and parliament in Ireland in the period 1714–16 to secure the new Hanoverian regime in the face of internal and external threats. The efforts in parliament to provide for the security of the kingdom in time of need included legislating for the attainder of the pretender, for capturing the exiled duke of Ormond, and for making the militia more useful, as well as the provision

[116] *CJI*, iii, 92–3.

[117] *CJI*, iii, 95, 98.

[118] TNA, SP63/374/225–6: Grafton and Galway to Stanhope, 17 May 1716.

[119] TNA, SP63/374/225–6, 229–30, 238–9, 242–3, 244–7, 252–3, 285–6; *CJI*, iii, 106–7, 111–12; Garnham, *Militia*, 24–6; Kelly, *Poynings' Law*, 200.

[120] *CJI*, iii, 112.

of funds to raise 13 new regiments. In the latter instance, the money was lent by public creditors whose capital investment and legal interest was secured on the credit of the nation – as represented by parliament – as a debt of the nation, by means of parliamentary legislation. The creation, thereby, of a national debt signalled the introduction into Ireland of a key aspect of the British financial revolution of the late 17th and early 18th centuries. It also demonstrated that financial necessity was the mother of fiscal innovation.[121] More specifically, it made clear that the coalescing of the three imperatives of security, finance, and the army – or jacobites, money and men – was a powerful combination when it came to focusing the minds of the ruling protestant elite in early-18th-century Ireland.

The creation of a national debt also provided a new dimension to the constitutional relationship between government and parliament which had been evolving since the 1690s. The dictates of that constitutional framework created in the 1690s had developed further during the 1715–16 parliamentary session, while scope for compromise in the face of immediate necessity had prevented unnecessary conflict. Thereafter, until legislative independence in 1782, that constitutional framework served as the basis for government-parliament relations in 18th-century Ireland.[122]

[121] C.I. McGrath, 'The Irish Experience of "Financial Revolution", 1660–1760', in *Money, Power and Print: Interdisciplinary Studies on the Financial Revolution in the British Isles*, ed. C.I. McGrath and Chris Fauske (Newark, NJ, 2008), 157–88.

[122] McGrath, *Ireland and Empire*, 167–216; McGrath, 'Central Aspects', 9–34; McGrath, 'Public Wealth', 171–207; C.I. McGrath, 'Money, Politics and Power: The Financial Legislation of the Irish Parliament', in *The Eighteenth-Century Composite State: Representative Institutions in Ireland and Europe, 1689–1800*, ed. D.W. Hayton, James Kelly and John Bergin (Basingstoke, 2010), 21–43.

The House of Lords and the Excise Crisis: The Storm and the Aftermath, 1733–5

CLYVE JONES

The excise crisis of 1733 was the first major parliamentary crisis Sir Robert Walpole's ministry faced in the house of commons. As a result of the huge public outcry, the proposal was dropped in the Commons, but the opposition to it in the house of lords was so great that the opposition lords switched their attack in 1734 to the accounts of the South Sea Company, and the ministry lost a crucial division in the Lords (the first such loss by any ministry for a generation). Walpole, with the king's approval, tried to discipline the members of the upper chamber by sacking some erstwhile supporters from their offices and the colonelcy of their regiments (the latter of which was considered by many to be an attack on property). This attempt to gain control alienated a further batch of lords who continued their opposition in the Lords well into 1735, particularly over the Scots' petition in that year against the ministry's conduct of the election of the Scottish representative peers in the summer of 1734. Some of the disciplined peers returned to the ministerial fold, but a number continued their opposition, some for the rest of the life of Walpole's ministry. The 1734–5 crisis in the Lords, which initially arose over the excise proposals, continued, largely fuelled by Walpole's treatment of some of the ministry's former supporters, and, in fact, can be considered a second separate crisis triggered by Walpole's treatment of the peerage.

Keywords: excise crisis 1733; Sir Robert Walpole; house of lords; opposition lords; South Sea Company accounts 1734; Scottish representative peers' election 1734; Scottish peers' petition 1735

1

The excise crisis of 1733, when Sir Robert Walpole tried to bring in new proposals for indirect taxation via the excise on tobacco[1] in order to reduce the direct land tax, and which were withdrawn while still before the house of commons, was the first major political crisis of his administration. It has also been seen by at least one historian as the possible beginning of the end of his ministry.[2] In 1742, upon Walpole's resignation, William Hay, MP and ministerial supporter, thought that:

---

[1] The opposition's claims that the excise scheme was to include wine 'were as untrue as they were incendiary': Andrew Thompson, *George II* (New Haven, 2010), 101.

[2] Reed Browning, *The Duke of Newcastle* (New Haven, 1975), 111.

there is no one Cause, to which the fall of the Minister is to be more ascribed, than to the hatred of the City of London. Which grew very inveterate after the Excise Scheme: by which particular Traders thought their Interests might be affected. And therefore endeavoured to render him Odious.[3]

Though the importance of this crisis has long been recognized, it was not until 40 years ago that the first full scholarly study was published, by Paul Langford.[4] Even so, possibly because the scheme was defeated in the Commons after an unprecedented public outcry against the excise, the role of the house of lords in the crisis and its aftermath has been all but ignored.[5] Paradoxically, while recognizing the influence of peers on many MPs in their opposition to the excise, and the crucial role of some lords at court which ended with 'a renewed and extended rebellion among the court peers', Langford concluded that: '[t]his phase was essentially a footnote to the major crisis'.[6] Yet Langford did recognize that if the excise had passed the Commons: 'the losses at court would have had a fatal effect elsewhere. Under Walpole, the house of lords was not the safe preserve of government that it was later to become.' Langford further went on to quote the evidence of the prime minister's brother, that as well as the loss of support in the Commons: 'another reason for giving up the Bill was the falling away of friends in the House of Lords'.[7]

Walpole's ploy to defuse the political situation by withdrawing the excise tax partly failed. The opposition, which had been engendered by the scheme and was so buoyed up by its success against the administration, decided that the centre of the attack upon the ministry should move to the Lords. Thus, in 1733, Walpole was to suffer the first two defeats of his premiership in the upper chamber on 3 and 24 May; indeed, the lost division of 24 May was the first significant defeat for a ministry in the Lords for a generation. Further, the troublesome upper House did not cease to be a problem after Walpole took revenge on several officeholding peers. Neither did the summer prorogation calm the situation. The 1734 session was to prove almost as disruptive for the ministry in the house of lords while, in 1735, problems continued for Walpole when some of the Scots' representative peers, who had lost their seats at the general election in 1734, petitioned the ministry over its handling of the election. Indeed, the 1733 and 1734 sessions were, arguably, the most successful for the opposition coalition in the

---

[3] *Tory and Whig: The Parliamentary Papers of Edward Harley, 3rd Earl of Oxford, and William Hay, MP for Seaford, 1716–1753*, ed. Stephen Taylor and Clyve Jones (Parliamentary History Record Series, 1, Woodbridge, 1998), 181.

[4] Paul Langford, *The Excise Crisis: Society and Politics in the Age of Walpole* (Oxford, 1975). The following year a thesis on the subject appeared: Peter C. Walters, 'Politics in the House of Lords in 1733', University of Leicester MPhil, 1976. Both Langford and Walters used a fairly limited number of manuscript sources compared with those now available and used for this study. Though there are similarities between Walters's interpretation and mine, there are also substantial differences.

[5] Langford gives this aspect of the crisis a few lines (*Excise Crisis*, 83–6, 99–100 *passim*), while J.H. Plumb, in his biography of Walpole, gives it more prominence but only devotes four pages: *Sir Robert Walpole* (2 vols, 1956–60), ii, 274–8. A.S. Turberville, *House of Lords in the XVIIIth Century* (Oxford, 1927), devotes seven pages to an outline of the Lords' proceedings in 1733 and only three to the equally disruptive session of 1734 (200–9).

[6] Langford, *Excise Crisis*, 69–70, 83–5, 99 (quotation).

[7] Langford, *Excise Crisis*, 85–6. Horace Walpole's evidence comes from HMC, *Egmont Diary*, i, 359.

Lords during the whole of Walpole's tenure of office, with the possible exception of the upper House's role in his fall in 1742.[8]

2

On the surface, the 1733 session did not start too well for the ministry in the house of lords. A significant number (32%) of those invited to the traditional pre-sessional meeting of members of the upper chamber on 15 January, to hear the contents of the king's speech and to choose a peer to move for an address in reply, did not turn up.[9] Of the 116 peers and bishops summoned, 37 almost certainly did not attend because they were either 'Not in Town', would be arriving only in time for the first day of sitting on the 16th, had left town before the meeting, or were ill. Of these 37, only nine, in fact, attended the first sitting of the Lords on 16 January, and a month later, only a further 11 had by then sat in the House.[10] If one compares attendance at the 1733 pre-sessional meeting with those in 1730 and 1732, a significant rise in non-attendance is revealed, with 15% 'no-shows' in 1730, 26% in 1732, and 32% in 1733.[11] This, however, may reveal nothing more than an increased lack of interest in proceedings in the Lords, a fact possibly confirmed by the low attendace figures for the early part of the 1733 session.[12]

However, while all but two (Townshend and Haddington)[13] of the 34 lords, who in the course of the 1733 session were to defect to the opposition (listed in Appendix 2), were summoned to the 1733 meeting and were presumably considered at the time as potential supporters by the ministry, 15 did not attend. Their previous record of largely untarnished support for the Walpole ministry might seem to indicate that many, if not all, of the 1733 deserters, had no major thoughts of dissatisfaction with the administration before the excise crisis.[14] In fact, most of them seem, on the surface at least, to have

[8] See Clyve Jones, 'The House of Lords and the Fall of Walpole', in *Hanoverian Britain and Empire: Essays in Memory of Philip Lawson*, ed. Stephen Taylor, Richard Conners and Clyve Jones (Woodbridge, 1998), 102–36. The defeat of Walpole in the Lords over the Quakers Tithes Bill can be considered as a special case, in which the inept religious policy of the ministry caused its staunchest supporters in the House – the bishops – to vote against it.

[9] See below, column 1 in Appendix 1.

[10] *LJ*, xxiv, 164–85 *passim*.

[11] See the lists of lords for the meetings in 1730 and 1732. The list for 1731 does not contain the necessary information: TNA, SP45/1.

[12] The attendance of the first day was 86, but it slumped thereafter and did not rise again to such a figure until mid-April. The average attendance for the first month was 47: *LJ*, xxiv, 164–85.

[13] While the absence of Townshend (who had broken with Walpole in 1730) is understandable, the absence of Haddington (who had consistently supported the government) is not, unless it was known by the ministry that he would be absent all session (his proxy is dated 20 January).

[14] Of the 15 'defectors' who did not show up for the meeting, one (Harborough) did not appear on any lists until 1733, seven (Bolton, Cobham, Cornwallis, Denbigh, Griffin, Stair and Bishop Reynolds of Lincoln) from the lists, appear to have had unblemished records of adherence to the ministry, while of the other seven (Bridgwater, Clinton, Fizwalter, Gainsborough, Greenwich [Argyll], St Albans and Westmorland) only Bridgwater, Gainsborough and Westmorland had more than the odd doubtfuls or contrary votes to their names. It must be remembered, however, that the above analysis is based on the 17 lists known between 1721 and 1732. Any of the lords on these lists may have voted against the ministry on any number of unlisted occasions.

remained loyal until mid-April, after the Excise Bill had been dropped, speaking and voting for the ministry.[15]

Despite a reported meeting of leaders of the opposition at the earl of Essex's country house in Hertfordshire in late December 1732, at which it was thought that 'the plan of opposition this session will be settled',[16] an inspection of the books in which the proxy votes of absent peers were recorded, reveals no flurry of pre-sessional organisation by either the ministry or the opposition. Only three proxies were registered before the first day of the session on 16 January 1733, one for each side (plus the earl of Warrington's, a whig independent who had, in the past, voted both for and against the government), while during the first month of parliament, only a further 23 proxies were registered: 12 for the ministry and 11 for the opposition. None of these were vacated until 19 February.[17]

The correspondence of some opposition peers also indicates that there appeared to be no hurry in arranging proxies.[18] It was thought improbable that proxies would be used, or if they were, then defeat would inevitably follow – 'I don't imagine numbers will ever come so near as to call for proxies', wrote Lord Berkeley, 'but in all events I always think my self safe in My Lord Strafford's hands tho I expect to be miserably defeated in the army [Mutiny] bill.'[19]

The record of divisions in the Lords for the beginning of the 1733 session also gives the impression to the historian of a lull before the storm. Though there were 12 divisions during the first month (an unusually large number this early in a session), these all related to two legal cases, and involved no more than 41 lords. It was not until the Pension Bill was defeated on its first reading on 23 February that a significant total voting figure of 121 was achieved (28 of which were proxy votes).[20]

The frequent appearances of a Place or Pension Bill and the annual Mutiny Bill were occasions which always caused the ministry concern, for they provided opportunities for the opposition, particularly the 'country' elements, to attack the ministry on traditional grounds – alleged corruption of members of parliament and opposition to a standing army. In 1733, the Pension Bill was voted on in the Lords on 23 February, and the Mutiny Bill on 6 March. Both occasions attracted a larger appearance in the House than had been experienced so far in the session – 95 and 114, respectively[21] – and in both

---

[15] Chesterfield, e.g., spoke for the ministry in the 6 March debate on the Mutiny Bill (Royal Archives, Windsor Castle, Stuart Papers [hereafter cited as RA, SP], 160/96: [Nathaniel Mist] to [Edgar], 2 Apr. 1733 ns. The Stuart Papers are used by the gracious permission of Her Majesty The Queen), while all but Bridgwater, Gainsborough and Bishop Reynolds of Lincoln voted for the ministry on 23 February and 6 March (the reconstructed list in Walters, 'House of Lords in 1733', 156–61).

[16] BL, Add. MS 27732, ff. 80–1: Henry Pelham to Essex, 1 Jan. 1732/3.

[17] Parliamentary Archives [hereafter cited as PA], HL/PO/JO/13/8. All information in this article on proxy registration for the 1733 session comes from this proxy book source.

[18] E.g., BL, Add. MS 31142, f. 57: Huntingdon to [Strafford], 13 Jan. 1732/3.

[19] BL, Add. MS 31142, f. 61: Berkeley to [Strafford], 3 Feb. 1732[/3]. Berkeley went on to write that: 'The noise made by the excises [*sic*] will I fear bring the load again upon the land. They talk as if the excise were a new thing, when almost every[thing] is soe already and noe care to prevent retailers raising the price at the same time.'

[20] All information on divisions in this article comes from *Divisions in the House of Lords: An Analytical List, 1685–1857*, comp. J.C. Sainty and D. Dewar (House of Lords Record Office Occasional Publications no. 2, 1976).

[21] *LJ*, xxiv, 194, 203.

votes the opposition was roundly defeated by 82 to 39 and 103 to 39. Similar bills regularly generated such levels of defeat for the opposition. The fact that only 14 opposition peers bothered to protest over the loss of the Pension Bill and that there was no protest at all over the vote on the Mutiny Bill on 6 March,[22] may indicate a sense of lethargy in the opposition. The proxy record, however, shows that some preparation may have been attempted by both the ministry and the opposition in the ten days before the vote on the Pension Bill: the government gained five proxies to the opposition's eight, and had three proxies vacated by attendance to the opposition's one. In the two weeks between the Pension Bill and the major vote on the Munity Bill,[23] the figures were five extra proxies for the ministry and only two for the opposition, with two and one vacated, respectively (significantly on the day of the vote itself). Though proxies were used on both occasions, they had no impact on the result. In the crucial vote on the South Sea Company on 24 May, however, proxies were to play a vital role (but less so in the succeeding vote on 1 June).

The proxy record also reveals a higher level of activity preceding the votes on 24 May and 1 June than before the votes on the Pension and Mutiny Bills. Lord Bathurst moved on 3 May that the South Sea Company accounts be placed before the House. Between that date and 24 May, the ministry organised 11 proxies to the opposition's 14, while four supporters for both sides vacated their proxies by attendance. From 25 May to 1 June, the ministry had a further seven proxies entered to none for the opposition, with four supporters vacating proxies to the opposition's two. Indeed, both sides were so keenly aware in these crucial days of the value of proxies, that several were entered for one day only when lords were temporarily unable to attend (one for the opposition, four for the ministry), an otherwise infrequent occurrence but a sign of tighter control of proxies. The proxies actually used in the crucial divisions of 24 May and 1 June, however, show that the opposition was more succesful in garnering such votes: on the two divisions of 23 February and 6 March, both sides had an equality of proxies on the first vote and 15 to 13 in favour of the ministry on the second, while on 24 May the ministry had 18 to the opposition's 27, and on 1 June the figures were 18 to 25.

This edge which the opposition had in gathering proxies tipped the balance in its favour in the vote of 24 May, when the figures were, for the ministry 57 present, plus 18 proxies; for the opposition, 48 present and 27 proxies: an equality of 75, with the ministry losing the vote 'according to the Rules or orders of the House; which preferr the Negatives, in all Equal Divisions'.[24] It is clear from these figures that while the government still had the majority of those attending on 24 May, as compared with the voting figures for 23 February and 6 March, there had been a dramatic shift from ministry to opposition. The administration's figures for those attending and voting had

---

[22] On the third reading of the Muntiny Bill on 8 March, when it was passed without a formal division, there was a protest by 13 lords: *LJ*, xxiv, 205–7.

[23] Both sides would have had forewarning of both bills and thus have had time to organise attendance or proxies. Though the vote on the Pension Bill on 23 February was on its first reading, its passing the Commons (it appeared in the lower House on 31 January and passed on 21 February) would have given ample warning, while the Mutiny Bill had given more warning for besides having its first and second readings in the Lords on 20 and 27 February, it had been ordered in the Commons on 6 February and had passed on the 19th: *CJ*, xxii, 15, 27, 46, 53.

[24] *The London Diaries of William Nicolson, Bishop of Carlisle, 1702–1718*, ed. Clyve Jones and Geoffrey Holmes (Oxford, 1985), 166.

risen from 68 to 88 between the two divisions of 23 February and 6 March, whereas the opposition's had only risen from 25 to 26. Two months later, however, warning bells must have gone off for the ministry on 3 May, the first vote on the South Sea Company accounts, for though the opposition's vote had only risen to 35, the ministry's own supporters present and voting had shrunk to 31, and it lost the division. This decline may be partly accounted for by the drop in attendance after the time of the Pension and Mutiny Bills in the comparatively tranquil month of March. The attendance in the Lords began to climb, however, in early April after the Easter recess.[25] Thus Bathurst sprang his motion on 3 May upon a reasonably well-attended House of 74.[26] By 24 May, it was clear to everyone that the ministry had a fight on its hands in the upper House, and the attendance of its supporters rose from 31 to 57, while the opposition rose from 35 to 48. By 1 June, the ministerial figure for supporters attending and voting remained the same as on 24 May, at 57, while the opposition's sank slightly to 45. The ministry's proxy votes remained constant at 18, while, again, the opposition's declined from 27 to 25; thus on 1 June, the opposition lost by five votes. Again, the switching of votes on 1 June from ministry to opposition was significant, but not as crucial as it had proved on 24 May. This time it was on a smaller scale, and this saved the ministry. Despite the report on 29 May that: 'the Tory [opposition] party had two more proxys, then before but . . . the Ministry seems well Content how to enter on it',[27] the vote on 1 June had been a close-run thing. The 'floating voters', who switched back and forth between the ministry and the opposition (see Appendix 2), are the key to the opposition's success in the 1733 session in the house of lords.

3

Though parliament had started at the normal time in mid-January, it was clear to some as early as late February 1733 that: 'we are likely to have a long Session, and a good deal of business'.[28] The trouble over the possible excise scheme had started as early as October 1732, when the *Craftsman* began a series of articles attacking the proposal.[29] Public agitation had risen considerably by the opening of parliament; so much so that the king's speech on 16 January stressed the need to 'avoid unreasonable heats and animosities'.[30] The opposition took little notice and embarked upon a campaign which was to last for the rest of the session. Though the bulk of the early attacks on the excise

[25] Following the passage of the Mutiny Bill on 8 March (an attendance of 79), the average attendance for the rest of that month was 56, while the average attendance for the period 3 April to 2 May was 65: *LJ*, xxiv, 203–54.

[26] An attendance of 74: *LJ*, xxiv, 234.

[27] National Library of Scotland [hereafter cited as NLS], Fletcher of Saltoun Papers, MS 16553, f. 134: Richard Graham to [Lord Milton], 29 May 1733. Graham, whose reports on the Lords in this session are so useful, attended the House frequently, partly in connection with his legal appeal, for which, see NLS, MS 16553, ff. 125–6: same to [same], 15 Mar. 1732/3.

[28] National Records of Scotland [hereafter cited as NRS], Montrose Papers, GD 220/5/883/8: [Montrose] to [Mungo Graham of Gorthie], 28 Feb. 1732/3. Up to 1724, nearly all sessions started before Christmas but, since 1726, January was the norm.

[29] Langford, *Excise Crisis*, 44.

[30] *LJ*, xxiv, 165.

came in the Commons, since that was where the excise, as a money bill, would be introduced, some of the opposition peers, while holding their fire in the Lords, were not idle. On 17 February, as a result of two tory MPs congratulating the lord mayor of London, on behalf of themselves 'and 29 other Lords and Gentlemen all Members of Parliament', on organising the common council to issue instructions to the City's members to oppose the excise, the lord mayor entertained all 31 to a dinner on 20 February.[31] This company contained some who would prove to be the most prominent members of the opposition's campaigns, both in the Commons and Lords. Eleven members of the upper House attended, a mixture of tories[32] and patriot whigs.[33]

Walpole's delay in not introducing the excise into the Commons until 14 March,[34] enabled the opposition in both houses to build up a considerable head of steam. Contrary to the ministry's hopes (they having comfortably won two divisions in the Commons on 14 and 16 March with majorities of around 60), the Easter recess at the end of March allowed the opposition to reorganise and to increase the pressure on the government. Following the recess, the Tobacco Bill (the first part of the excise scheme), had its first reading in the Commons on 4 April, and in various divisions the ministerial majority shrank to 36. Worse was to follow when, on 10 April, in a division on whether to accept the City of London's petition against the excise, the ministry won by only 17.[35] On the following day, the prime minister announced to the Commons that the project was to be postponed for two months, which meant, in effect, that it was being dropped.

Amongst the reasons that have been recounted for this change of policy was the crisis which the ministry faced at court in the period between the introduction of the excise into the Commons on 14 March and the vote on the City's petition on 10 April.[36] From the beginning of the scheme, rebellious courtiers had seized the opportunity to make trouble for the ministry; prominent amongst them the earls of Chesterfield and Stair (the latter a Scottish *Squadrone* representative peer) and the duke of Bolton. Stair, at an interview with the queen, attacked the Walpole administration as well as the excise. Furthermore, Lord Clinton and the earl of Scarbrough, two courtiers who had formerly been government supporters, took the opportunity to come out against the excise. Scarbrough was a courtier much respected by both the ministry and the opposition,

---

[31] RA, SP, 160/21: [Mist] to [Edgar], Boulogne, 13 Mar. 1733 ns. Langford, who cites this letter but does not note the significance of the dinner, dates the instructions of the corporation to the London MPs in January (*Excise Crisis*, 55). A date of 15 February is given in *The History of Parliament: The House of Commons, 1715–1754*, ed. Romney Sedgwick (2 vols, 1970) [hereafter cited as *HPC, 1715–54*], i, 281 (but no reference is given). Mist's letter makes it clear that the approach to the lord mayor by two tory MPs, which solicited the dinner invitation, took place on the Saturday (i.e., 20 February). These dates are more likely as Mist, despite being at Boulogne, was often quite up to date with the news he sent. Therefore, assuming that was the case here, and that the date 13 March is in new style, the dinner must have taken place in mid- to late-February.

[32] The earls of Winchilsea, Strafford, Lichfield, Northampton, Oxford and Scarsdale, and Lords Bathurst, Cravan and Gower.

[33] The marquess of Tweeddale (a Scottish *Squadrone* representative peer) and Lord Carteret. Two other lords are listed: Morpeth (heir to the earl of Carlisle) and Limerick; the first was a courtesy title and the second an Irish peerage and both men sat in the Commons.

[34] On 7 March, Walpole in his budget had outlined his plan: Langford, *Excise Crisis*, 63.

[35] Langford, *Excise Crisis*, 66, 78.

[36] Langford, *Excise Crisis*, 83–6.

whose future intermittent opposition to Walpole appears to have been based on principle and not on pique or the prospect of gain: later in 1734, while opposing the ministry over the duke of Marlborough's Army Bill,[37] he offered to resign all his employment to show that he was not acting from interested motives, and did, in fact, resign as master of the horse, and later refused the post of lord lieutenant of Ireland. In 1733, over the excise, he told Walpole:

> that he found the clamour so hot and so general, that it was his opinion the Administration ought to yield to it; that for his own part, how right soever he might think this scheme in an abstract light, yet, considering the turn it had taken, he was determined not to contribute to cram it down people's throats; and . . . if it should be forced through the House of Commons, and brought into the House of Lords, he would oppose it there.[38]

Scarbrough's opposition to the excise was considered a great coup for the parliamentary opposition and his departure from government an equally regrettable loss by the ministry.

When possible disciplinary action was muted by Walpole against these important court peers in 1733, a further rebellion took place, and the duke of Dorset (lord lieutenant of Ireland), the earl of Wilmington (lord president of the council), and Scarbrough (master of the horse) threatened to resign, the former two also being members of the cabinet. An attempted reconciliation between Walpole and all dissident court peers was engineered by the king, but Chesterfield, so incensed by the excise, refused to attend the meeting. However, for the time being, the threat of possible dismissal from office for the rebellious court peers was dropped. Chesterfield also refused to resign at this stage, in order to spite the prime minister who, apparently, wished him to go.

All this turmoil created a damaging picture of a ministry losing control of the court. Such control was as vital to the survival of any administration as was the control of parliament.[39] As a result of the rebellion, the king and queen had exerted pressure upon Walpole to end the crisis. Stair had made it very clear to the queen that the excise might be forced past a lower House by means of corruption and ministerial power, but as to the upper House: 'the defection there will be among the nobility on this point . . . [will] be such (for it is not conjecture) as will startle not only your minister when it breaks out, but even his master and yourself. I know it will be such as will make it impossible for this Bill to pass the Lords.'[40] There were even hints that the most stalwart of ministerial

---

[37] See Clyve Jones, 'The Duke of Marlborough's Army Bill of 1734: The Opposition's Reaction to Robert Walpole's Management of the House of Lords' (forthcoming).

[38] John, Lord Hervey, *Some Materials towards Memoirs of the Reign of George II*, ed. Romney Sedgwick (3 vols, 1931), i, 154.

[39] As John Drummond, MP for Perth Burghs, wrote in 1731 after the ministry had won a division on the address in the Lords, that the opposition toiled 'but all to little purpose The King having an entire confidence in his Ministers and belives them more able to carry on his bussiness than those who aim at their employment': NRS, Abercairny Papers, GD 24/1/484/57–8: to William Drummond, London, 23 Jan. 1730/1. I owe this reference to Dr Graham Townend.

[40] Hervey, *Memoirs*, ed. Sedgwick, i, 140–1.

supporters in the upper House, the bishops, were frightened at the scale of the public discontent against the excise and 'are like to vote against it, when it comes into their House'.[41]

Consequently, though the house of lords as an institution had no direct say in the collapse of the excise scheme, since the bill never reached the upper chamber, individual members of the Lords, as well as the increasingly coherent body of the opposition in the House, had an immense impact upon the outcome of the crisis. This was achieved through three interrelated spheres of influence: first, the influence of peers over individual MPs to oppose the scheme in the Commons, many of whom owed their seats to aristocratic interest; second, their influence upon the court; and third, not to be underestimated, their influence upon public opinion through print, newsmongering and gossip, particularly amongst the political and social elite, which created a climate inimical to the excise and to Walpole's administration.

The withdrawal of the excise on 11 April did not, however, end the political crisis. Two days later, the king, reversing his previous policy, dismissed Chesterfield and Clinton from their offices.[42] This was, no doubt, an act of revenge, but, more importantly, it was designed by Walpole as a warning to members of the Lords, particularly rebellious courtiers, to return to the ministerial fold. As such it failed, for the tory and patriot whig opposition in the Lords saw themselves riding a great wave of agitation directed against the prime minister and were determined to try, through actions in the upper House, to sweep Walpole away.[43]

Deprived of the excise, which had had an almost universal interest, the opposition in the Lords cast around for an issue on which the ministry was vulnerable and which might prove equally attractive to the public. They wisely chose the South Sea Company, the running of which since the 1720 bubble had been less than satisfactory, and the very name of which was forever linked to corruption, maladministation and financial disaster. Thus, on 3 May, Lord Bathurst moved:

> That the Directors of the South Sea Company may be required to lay before this House, an Account of what Sums of Money, South Sea Stock, and South Sea Annuities, have been received from the Trustees, for Sale of the Estates of the late Directors and others, in Pursuance of the Act of Parliament of the 13th year of His late Majesty.[44]

This move was almost certainly unforeseen by the ministry. On the vote at the end of the debate to adjourn until the following day, 66 lords voted out of the 74 recorded as attending and the ministry lost by 31 to 35. This result must have left the ministry in a state of shock for it was 'the first [question] that has been carried against the Court in

[41] HMC, *Egmont Diary*, i, 356.

[42] Chesterfield was dismissed as lord steward and Clinton as a gentleman of the bedchamber and lord lieutenant of Devon: see *The Letters of Phillip Dormer Stanhope, 4th Earl of Chesterfield*, ed. Bonamy Dobree (6 vols, 1932), ii, 266; and BL, Add. MS 32688, f. 3: Newcastle to Clinton, 13 Apr. 1733.

[43] But cf. Hervey, *Memoirs*, ed. Sedgwick, i, 177, where he claims that these 'demissions, saved the Ministry'. In the short run, they undoubtedly made the situation worse, but together with those of June and July, they may have brought some deserters to their senses.

[44] *LJ*, xxiv, 255.

that House these twenty Years'.[45] Furthermore, the manner of the defeat no doubt caused the government grave misgivings, for it was brought about by 'fifteen members who seldom or never before voted against the Court, [who had] opposed the ministry'.[46] In fact, the division list (for which see Appendix 1) shows that 16 erstwhile court supporters had defected to the opposition,[47] forming a remarkable 46% of the opposition vote. Though the opposition must have been elated, one member wisely urged a note of caution: 'Victory is soe new a thing to one side', wrote Lord Berkeley, 'that I wish they be not too much transported and behave with decency.'[48] Except for one private case, there were no more divisions until the crucial one on the South Sea Company on 24 May, so there was no occasion on which the two sides could test their voting strength.

Both the ministry and the opposition began to organise as many supporters as possible to attend or to register their proxies. According to Lord Hervey: 'many Lords were closeted, schooled, and tampered with by the ministers, some by the King and more by the Queen'.[49] The ministry was more successful than the opposition in increasing its attendance between 3 and 24 May (a rise of 84% as opposed to 37%), but the opposite was true as regards the registering of proxies (an opposition increase of 108% on the figure for 6 March, the last time proxies had been used, compared with 29% for the ministry).

Three case studies may help to put some flesh on these statistical bones. The earl of Dartmouth, an opposition peer, had registered a proxy on 6 March which had been vacated by his presence on 24 April. He sat again on the 27th, but after that he disappears from the attendance record in the *Lords Journals*.[50] Lord Bruce wrote to him shortly before the crucial vote on 24 May, asking him either to send his proxy or to attend: '[on] thursday . . . the Minister's Troops, I mean most of them, will leave him, by which, notwithstanding the Bench of Bishops, we do reckon to carry the South Sea points, and lay a foundation for somewhat better times'. Dartmouth failed to respond by either attending or registering a proxy. Perhaps he had left town and Bruce had not given him enough time to return. Why he did not register a proxy for the rest of the session and also failed to attend is a mystery. It may be that Bruce's sanguine prediction of victory had lulled Dartmouth into doing nothing.[51]

The earl of Sutherland, a Scottish representative peer, had had a very poor attendance record in 1733, having sat for only six days since the beginning of the session, the last being on 30 April. After Walpole wrote to him on 21 May, that '[t]here being business appointed in the House of Lords on Thursday next, I beg your Lordship will give your self the trouble to attend that day', Sutherland was in the house the next day and

[45] RA, SP, 162/81: [Mist] to [Edgar], 12 June 1733.

[46] NLS, MS 16553, f. 131: Richard Graham to [Lord Milton], 5 May 1733.

[47] Clinton was the peer missed out of Graham's list (see above, note 46).

[48] BL, Add. MS 31142, f. 73: Berkeley to [Strafford], 7 May 1733.

[49] Hervey, *Memoirs*, ed. Sedgwick, i, 190.

[50] PA, HL/PO/JO/13/8; *LJ*, xxiv, 243, 248.

[51] Staffordshire RO, Dartmouth Papers, D1778/V/795: Bruce to [Dartmouth], 'Tuesday evening' 22 May 1733]. The year is confirmed by the information that 'Lord Anglesey has sent me his proxy. Lord Burlington gave his to Lord Stair'; they were dated 21 and 23 May 1733, respectively: PA, HL/PO/ JO/13/8.

attended every sitting until 4 June except, ironically and unfortunately for the ministry, 24 May.[52]

With another peer, whose record of attendance was even worse than Sutherland's, the prime minister was more successful. On 23 May, Walpole wrote to the duke of Chandos urging him to attend. The duke had only once been at the house since the beginning of the session. Chandos replied (surely a little disingenuously):

> I assure you I have for some time, been so little inquisitive after publick affairs that I knew not, any business of moment was appointed for today in [the] House of Lords: by the letter I had the honour to receive from you last night, I guess it to be the South Sea Enquiry; and as this, in my opinion very sensibly and personally affects you in it's consequences . . . I am come to Town to contribute my Mite, towards putting a stop to it.[53]

Chandos did, indeed, attend on 24 May, but only did so thereafter on a further four occasions, though these did include the important division on 1 June, but not the one on the following day, when another vote on the South Sea Company took place.[54]

What is odd about Walpole's whipping of both Sutherland and Chandos (and also of Bruce's attempt on Dartmouth) is that it was done at the last minute; in Chandos's case it was only the day before, he being at his house at Canons in Middlesex when he received Walpole's letter. Both the ministry and the opposition knew on 3 May that the accounts would be laid before the House, so both sides had three weeks to prepare. Perhaps the slow rise in attendance rates between 3 and 24 May only convinced the ministry late in the day of impending trouble. But if Lord Bruce could produce such a highly-accurate estimate on 22 May of the opposition's likely strength – '[w]e reckon to muster present and by proxy between 70: and 80:',[55] in fact it was 75 – surely the ministerial leaders in the Lords could compute as well. However, it would seem that the prime minister did not realize that the opposition would become so substantial. While there had been overt opposition amongst erstwhile supporters in the rebellion at court over the excise crisis,[56] there had been no discernible rebellion amongst these peers in the Lords' chamber while the excise was before the Commons. The peers who had opposed the excise had used their influence over MPs to oppose it in the lower House. In effect they had been exercising proxy voting rights in the Commons.[57] However, by abandoning the excise, the ministry had quickly restored its authority in the lower House. By 22 April, it was being reported that the government's victory by 250 to 150:

---

[52] NLS, Sutherland Papers, Dep. 313/532/488a: Walpole to [Sutherland], 21 May 1733; *LJ*, xxiv, 169–296 *passim*. Sir Thomas Robinson (MP Morpeth), however, lists Sutherland as present but not voting on 24 May (HMC, *Carlisle MSS*, 118, 120: Robinson to [Carlisle], 26 May, 2 June 1733). See below, Appendix 3.

[53] Huntington Library, San Marino, CA, Stowe Papers, ST 57, vol. 41, pp. 346–7: Chandos to Walpole, London, 24 May 1733.

[54] *LJ*, xxiv, 231, 277–302 *passim*.

[55] Staffordshire RO, D1775/V/795: Bruce to [Dartmouth], [22 May 1733].

[56] Chesterfield admitted that he had openly opposed the Excise Bill, see *Letters of Chesterfield*, ed. Dobree ii, 265–6: to the king, 16 Apr. 1733.

[57] It was reported that, when the king heard that Chesterfield's brother, John, had voted against the excise in the Commons, the king wanted to remove both of them from their posts: HMC, *Egmont Diary*, i, 357. In fact, all three of Chesterfield's brothers who were MPs voted against the excise: see *HPC, 1715–54*, ii, 433–8

'plainly showed that, although numbers [of MPs] went off from the Court in the affair of the excising tobacco and wines, yet they had not deserted their party and become malcontents, as the minority flattered themselves'.[58] Even though this fact undoubtedly gave Walpole confidence, on the following day, at a large meeting of MPs at the Cockpit, he warned 'that the time was now come to look about them, it being evident from the persons resolved on by the other side that further things were designed than bare rectifying abuses in the Customs: that a push was made at the Administration, to throw the Government into confusion'.[59] Despite, or perhaps because of, this warning, the ministry's majority in the Commons continued to be consolidated. A division on 24 April was won by the government by a majority of 85 – '[t]his proved a terrible mortification to the malcontents who perceived so great a majority for the Ministry, although by a ballot they imagined numbers would have sided with them since they could do it without discovering themselves'.[60] Perhaps his success in the lower House deceived Walpole into agreeing with Hervey that this vote was 'the decisive and final stroke in the House of Commons this session, for the day after this ballot-struggle was over most of the members decamped into the country'.[61] After all, he had fired a warning shot across the bows of the upper chamber by getting the king to sack Chesterfield and Clinton. Walpole's confidence was also shared by Henry Pelham, paymaster general and brother to the duke of Newcastle, who, by mid-May, thought that the worst was over: 'by the steadiness of our Party . . . and the firmness of our master in the main point, we are now gott pretty firm in our seats again, and I doubt not in the least but we shall continue so'.[62]

Yet gradually, within the space of a month, the administation found itself with a major revolt in the upper House, nearly a third of its supporters being prepared to vote against it. Why? Clearly, the opposition's choice of the South Sea Company's accounts had been astute. Chandos, in his letter to Walpole of 24 May, hit the nail on the head when he opined that the debate on that day would 'personally affect' the prime minster, 'for those great Bodies as well as your other dependants, if once they find you are unable or unwilling to protect them, will soon, except such as are your personal friends be looking out for new Patrons'.[63] The opposition was, in effect, striking at the very heart of the Walpolian system of government – patronage. If the prime minister lost control of the Lords, his whole power base might collapse. This undoubtedly explains why his revenge on the peers when the crisis was over was very severe. But the first act of revenge, which had taken place on 13 April when the king dismissed Chesterfield and Clinton, might well be the clue to the whole post-excise crisis in the Lords. Could it be that Walpole *had* largely defused the original crisis, even in the Lords, when he dropped the Tobacco Bill, but that by taking revenge on two court peers for their part in the rebellion at court Walpole had unwittingly triggered off a second crisis, which

---

[58] HMC, *Egmont Diary*, i, 365.

[59] HMC, *Egmont Diary*, i, 365. For Hervey's version of the speech, see *Memoirs*, ed. Sedgwick, i, 179–84.

[60] HMC, *Egmont Diary*, i, 367.

[61] Hervey, *Memoirs*, ed. Sedgwick, i, 184.

[62] BL, Add. MS 27732, f. 170: Pelham to Essex, 17 May 1733, quoted in Paul Langford, *A Polite and Commercial People: England, 1727–1783* (Oxford, 1989), 31.

[63] Huntington Lib., ST 57, vol. 41, p. 347: Chandos to Walpole, 24 May 1733.

had at its root his treatment of the peerage? To many, it may have looked as though both he and the king had quickly reneged on their agreement that no court peer would be ejected from office.[64] The marquess of Tweeddale had, on 17 April, commented that 'the immediatt dismission of Chesterfield and Clinton is thought a surprising stroke of Politicks at this juncture'. The marquess went on to speculate that 'a little time must produce more alterations' and that 'I make no doubt but an end will be putt to this session of Parliament as soon as possible.'[65] A further alteration was not long in coming. On 30 April, the earl of Stair was dismissed from his post of vice admiral for Scotland for his impertinent treatment of the queen in his interview, when he had attacked Walpole and the excise.[66] As a result of this and the previous sackings, many in the upper House must have felt that the time had come to teach Walpole a lesson. With public opinion still in a state of anti-government agitation, there was no better time for those in the Lords who had had enough of the dismissive attitude of the ministry and the court to the peerage. The events of the next few weeks lends much credence to this hypothesis.

4

As we have seen, on 24 May the ministry lost the major division on the enquiry into the accounts of the South Sea Company. Admittedly it was defeated on a technicality, as the vote was a tie, but it had lost, none the less, and the result must have brought home to the government the seriousness of the crisis. After all, unlike the defeat on 3 May, which had occurred in a less-well-attended House on a surprise motion, the 24 May defeat was 'the first question that has been lost by the Court in the House of Lords during the last two reigns, and in a very full House, and upon a known debate, and great pains taken'.[67] Half the deserters from the ministry in the vote on the 24th were court peers currently holding pensions or offices (see Appendix 2). The impression it gave to the outside world was of an administration in disarray, not only in the house of lords but in that vital centre of power, the court. Lord Perceval noted in his diary: '[t]he Court being against this enquiry, 'tis much remarked that where they used to have a vast majority of sure votes, so many lords should appear for carrying the enquiry on'.[68] It is at this point that Walpole seems to have awakened to the disaster that had befallen the ministry and pulled out all the stops to retrieve the situation before the next major vote – which turned out to be only five days later.[69] Walpole must also have been

---

[64] Lord Perceval reported the decision not to sack Chesterfield on 9 April: HMC, *Egmont Diary*, i, 357.

[65] Hamilton Papers (the duke of Hamilton, Lennoxlove, Haddington), TD86/11/2, bundle 894/7 Tweeddale to Hamilton, 17 Apr. 1733. I am grateful to Stephen Taylor for allowing me to use his transcrip of this letter.

[66] HMC, *Egmont Diary*, i, 374–5. The famous meeting between Stair and the queen noted by Lord Herve (*Memoirs*, ed. Sedgwick, i, 135–43) was only one of many: see Richard Harding, 'Lord Cathcart, the Earl o Stair and the Scottish Opposition to Sir Robert Walpole', *Parliamentary History*, xi (1992), 198 n. 30.

[67] HMC, *Carlisle MSS*, 117: Robinson to [Carlisle], 26 May 1733.

[68] HMC, *Egmont Diary*, i, 380.

[69] The importance of the debate to the ministry was underlined by Walpole's attendance – he 'sat th whole day at the bar' – and his interventions at one stage via Lord Lynn to prevent Newcastle pressing fo a second division: HMC, *Carlisle MSS*, 117: Robinson to [Carlisle], 26 May 1733.

encouraged by the cracks that immediately appeared in the façade of the opposition on 24 May. Towards the end of the debate, after the defeat of the ministry, Bathurst:

> moved a very strong motion and severe question, which would have been the severest censure upon the whole body of the late S[outh] Sea Directors. [The] Duke [of] Argile and Lord Scarbro' both spoke extremely well against it (though they had voted against the Court in the other), . . . and that though they were for pushing this affair on with great zeal, yet they would avoid fury; and indeed the motion was so very severe that 'twas given up after a very short debate upon it.[70]

It is likely that Walpole hoped that these qualms of two of the deserters might be exploited to encourage a return to the court side.

On 25 May, on the question concerning the use of the sinking fund, without a division taking place, the opposition entered a protest signed by 18 peers. This may have been as much an attempt to rally support as to enter a dissent upon that specific issue, for the very long and well-argued protest is likely to have been the product of a sustained and planned campaign by the opposition. It does not bear the hallmarks of a document hurriedly cobbled together.[71]

Walpole's prospects for recovering control of the Lords were given a boost on 29 May, in a House almost as well attended as on the 24th (98 as opposed to 105), when, after a further examination of the accounts, it was ordered, without a division, that further consideration be put off until 1 June, 'and the Lords to be summond'. Later, on 29 May, a bill was introduced to convert part of the South Sea Company stock into annuities and, upon a division to adjourn the first reading until the following day, the ministry won by a majority of 11 votes (43 to 32). The odd thing about this result was that only 47 lords (27 to 20 in favour of the ministry) out of 98 recorded as attending that day voted in person, the rest being proxy votes. The answer may lie in the fact that the vote took place late in the day, and that many lords, weary of a long sitting, had left the chamber. Nevertheless, it was a win for the ministry, not on the South Sea enquiry as such, but on a related subject.

Meanwhile, not all the South Sea enquiry was adjourned until 1 June, and parts continued to concern the Lords on several sittings (25, 29, 30, 31 May), with the result that the average attendance on the last days of May was still high, particularly when the South Sea accounts were discussed (93, 98, 93, 88, respectively). Thus, on 1 June there was a record attendance for the session, of 106.[72] On the crucial division, 102 of those 106 cast their votes, together with 43 proxies, to give the ministry a majority of 5: 70 votes (including 25 proxies) for the opposition; 75 (including 18 proxies) for the government. A comparison of voting figures between this division and that on 24 May

---

[70] HMC, *Carlisle MSS*, 117: Robinson to [Carlisle], 26 May 1733. Scarbrough, on 30 May, again showed his independence from the opposition when he disagreed with Bathurst's motion on the sinking fund: *Cobbett's Parliamentary History of England* (36 vols, 1806–20), ix, cols 119–39.

[71] There is some evidence that the sustained campaign of the opposition in the following session in 1734 did include a long-term strategy for implementing protests, though this did come unstuck on at least one occasion: see Clyve Jones and Stephen Taylor, 'Viscount Bolingbroke and the Composition of an Opposition Protest in the House of Lords in 1734 on the Election of the Scottish Representative Peers', *Yale University Gazette*, lxxi (1996), 22–31.

[72] *LJ*, xxiv, 277–93.

shows that the ministry's was exactly the same – 57 present and 18 proxies – while the opposition's vote fell from 48 present and 27 proxies on 24 May to 45 present and 25 proxies on 1 June.

5

The rest of the session, which only lasted for another fortnight, was something of an anticlimax. On the following day, 2 June, with an attendance of 91, there were two divisions on the Stockjobbing and South Sea Stock Bills. The ministry won both comfortably with votes of 36 to 25 and 46 to 31. In between these bills, the question on whether to appoint 12 lords chosen by ballot to a committee to examine the South Sea accounts was defeated without a division. Twenty-two of the opposition protested, six of whom were defectors from the ministry.[73] On 4 June, with 85 attending, there were four divisions on the River Dee Navigation Bill, with voting totals ranging from 50 to 35. This bill's third reading on 8 June, when 93 lords sat, produced the fourth largest division of the session, when the question of whether a rider should be added to the bill was defeated. It is not clear how political this bill had become, but voting figures of 55 (including 21 proxies) to 69 (with 25 proxies), suggests that court/opposition rivalry might have played a part, for such high votes for a private bill were rare. The last division of the session on the same day, this time in the committee of the whole House, was on the South Sea Stock Bill, and produced a defeat for the opposition of 57 to 30. That the last three sittings of 9, 12 and 13 June, at a time when the dog days of the session would normally be poorly attended,[74] actually produced attendance figures of 74, 64 and 67, indicates that the tensions generated by the opposition's attack on the ministry in the Lords had not totally died away. The ministry, however, could not refrain from one last parting parliamentary shot at the opposition when, in his speech proroguing parliament, the king complained of 'the wicked Endeavours that have lately been made Use of, to inflame the Minds of the People, and, by the most unjust Misrepresentations, to raise Tumults and Disorders, that almost threatened the Peace of the Kingdom'.[75]

Walpole was, however, not quite done with the deserters in the house of lords. The day after parliament was prorogued, he purged the administration and the court of three recidivist peers.[76] Two days later, Lord Perceval recorded in his diary: 'I learned this day that my Lord Cobham's regiment is given to the Earl of Chomley [Walpole's son-in-law], and the Earl of Marchmont and Duke of Montrose are turned out. They were

[73] LJ, xxiv, 293–6. The protest was not entered until 5 June, though the House had sat on the 4th: NLS, MS 156554, f. 91: [Col. Middleton] to Lord Milton, 5 June [1733].

[74] A newsletter was speculating as early as 5 May that: ' 'Tis questioned whether the Lords will go through the above Enquiry the Session not on accou[unt] of the Session being pretty farr Advanced for their rising'. Huntington Lib., Hasting Papers, HA 13826: newsletter, 5 May 1733.

[75] LJ, xxiv, 302–11.

[76] Montrose wrote to Mungo Graham on 14 June upon the receipt of a letter from Newcastle, reporting his own dismissal along with Marchmont and Cobham: NRS, GD 220/5/884/9.

opposers of the Excise scheme and signers of the late protest.'[77] The duke of Montrose's reaction was defiant:

> Att no time were ever people under a Cloud more easie than those now in disgrace, having nothing to Reproach our selves with, nor any crime charge able upon us, unless it be one to give their opinion for the support of the King and the constitution in opposition to a measre evidently tending to hurt both. . . . we [the Scots] that are here [in London] are verie sensible and unanimouslie of opinion that nothing can concern us so much as easilie to have view to future Elections, both Peerrs and Commons, we apprehend, and sure with reason that if any spirit is left in our Countrie [Scotland], it ought to show it self upon this occasion, and I may tell you that we who have apeared together upon this occasion are detaermin'd one ane other for the interest of liberty which we haved been supporting, and which I may safely venture to affirm, we are approv'd off by the universall Cry of those of this syde of the Tweed.[78]

A month later, in mid-July, the duke of Bolton was also dismissed,[79] being deprived of his regiment and turned out of the lord lieutenancies of Hampshire and Dorset and his governorship of the Isle of Wight.[80] In all, Walpole purged seven members of the house of lords of their offices in April and June 1733. Most of them – Bolton, Chesterfield, Clinton, Cobham, Marchmont, Montrose and Stair – not surprisingly, became (with the exception of Clinton) long-term opponents of the ministry.[81]

These purges were no doubt designed by Walpole to have a dual function, to get rid of troublesome members in both the administration and the house of lords, and to send a warning '*pour encourager les autres*' to those who had deserted the government in the vote of 24 May, but had returned on 1 June, that they should remain loyal, and, perhaps, particularly to the two peers who had deserted for the first time on 1 June (Ancaster and Clarendon), to desist in their folly.[82] The message that Walpole was

[77] HMC, *Egmont Diary*, i, 387. Marchmont was turned out as lord clerk register for Scotland, and Montrose as keeper of the great seal for Scotland, both offices held since 1716.

[78] NRS, GD 220/5/884/10: to Mungo Graham, 6 June 1733.

[79] For the dating of Bolton's sacking, see Hervey, *Memoirs*, ed. Sedgwick, i, 205.

[80] Bolton seems to have had the most severe treatment of the English peers dismissed. One could speculate that this may have resulted from a possible deal between Walpole and Argyll. In exchange for Argyll's abstention in the 1 June vote and his leaving town on the 2nd to avoid any other divisions, Bolton, who had clashed with Argyll in debates over the army, on which both considered themselves experts, was to be punished in an exemplary fashion. The fact that Bolton returned to supporting the ministry in 1739, when Argyll made his final break with it, underscores this possiblity. Bolton's governorship of the Isle of Wight went to the duke of Montagu: 'who had been wavering between the Court ande the Opposition, and [he] took this opportunity to sell himself for full as muich as he was worth, by getting the income of this employment increased to £1,500 a year': Hervey, *Memoirs*, ed. Sedgwick, i, 205.

[81] The surviving parliamentary lists for 1734 to 1742 show that only Bolton returned to supporting the ministry (in 1739). The three purged Scottish representative peers, along with Buchan, Haddington, Rothes (all deserters in 1733) and Tweeddale, were all ditched by Walpole at the 1734 general election and failed to be re-elected.

[82] It is arguable that Clarendon's desertion was for longer than this vote. Unlike all the peers in column 1 of Appendix 2, below, Clarendon did not vote for the ministry over the duke of Marlborough's Army Bill on 13 Feb. 1734. He was absent, but had been considered doubtful in the ministry's forecast. Furthermore, Clarendon was the only one of the 1733 deserters not to be summoned to the 1736 pre-sessional meetings (see below, columns 9–10, Appendix 1).

regaining control of the Lords was underlined further on 11 June by the promotion from the Commons to the upper House, in his father's barony, of Lord Hervey.[83]

Though the dismissals were lamented in some government quarters for the high-handed loss of persons of alibity and merit – 'a great many people in the Ministry speake of the Alterations with great regrate'[84] – they were also seen as necessary. As Charles Delafaye, a senior civil servant in Secretary of State Newcastle's office wrote:

> but since the King was resolved to stand by his Minister [Walpole] (and to speak impartially, it is not easy to say how he could have been replaced, particularly with regard to the affairs of the Revenue) there was no doing it otherwise than with a high hand. The last protest of the Lords [on 2 June on the defeat of the proposal to ballot for a committee to investigate the South Sea accounts] seems to have been below the Dignity of the House; I have been told of one. who gave That as the reason for his not signing it, who otherwise is a thorough party Man. I believe there is no doubt of carrying matters thro' the next Session.[85]

Others also commented that the opposition's protest of 2 June – 'a most violent and personall one', 'a most flameing protest' – may have gone too far.[86] Sir Thomas Robinson reported on 'the most remarkable protest, signed by 21 Lords, that ever was entered upon the Journals; the last paragraph, No. 8, has many sharp stings in it'; while Delafaye further wrote that 'the very angry lords . . . made the most scandalous protest that I think ever was: I am sure had I been the greatest enemy Sir Robert Walpole ever had, I should not have been for such a paper's being in the journals for the sake of the dignity of the house'.[87] Lord Hervey wrote to Conyers Middleton to:

> let me know a little what People say of the King's Speech, Lord Cobham's Dismission, and the Lords protest; whether the political comentators have done talking of them already, or whether these Incidents and Heros still swell the dayly Tales of Coffee-House Romances.

[83] A newsletter of 5 May 1733 had reported that: 'Theres much talk of Several being Created peers of Great Britain and likewise of more removalls': Huntington Lib., HA 13826. In mid-June, at the time of the dismissals, there were further reports that: 'the Ministry are filling the house of Lords from the house of Commons, in place of the Noble Lords I have mentioned [Montrose, Bolton, Stair, Cobham and Rothes], who its probable will opposed the Ministry', and that: 'there will be nine new English [*sic.*: British] peers made in all. And some say nine of the Sixteen for Scotland will be changed, which the Minority says they will oppose with Out most [utmost] vigour' (NLS, MS 16553, ff. 137, 140: Richard Graham to [Milton], 14, 19 June 1733). Besides Hervey, Sir Philip Yorke and Charles Talbot were created Lords Hardwicke and Talbot respectively, in November and December 1733, and John Poulett, heir to Earl Poulett, was called up in his father's barony in January 1734. For Hervey's elevation, see *Memoirs*, ed. Sedgwick, i, 204.

[84] NLS, MS 16553, f. 137: Richard Graham to [Milton], 14 June 1733.

[85] BL, Add. MS 27732, f. 206: to Essex, 24 July 1733.

[86] NLS, MS 16553, f. 135: Richard Graham to [Milton], 7 June 1733 (who reported that the protest was written 'by Carteret, but others think its Bullenbrucke'); MS 16554, f. 91: [Col. Middleton] to Milton, 5 June 1733. Hervey thought Carteret was the author of the protest: *Memoirs*, ed. Sedgwick, i, 199.

[87] HMC, *Carlisle MSS*, 121: [to Carlisle], 7 June 1733; William Coxe, *The Memoirs of Sir Robert Walpole Administration* (3 vols, 1790), iii, 135: [Delafaye] to [Waldegrave], 18 June 1733. The protest was considered so 'violent and personal' because, in the eighth clause, it referred to: 'chalking out a safe method of committing the most flagitious frauds under the protection of some corrupt and all-screening minister' (*LJ*, xxiv, 293).

Middleton replied:

> whatever can be said on the policy of disgracing the great for dissenting from particular measures, yet none can Blame that of disarming those, who declare war so fiercely against the Court, as they have now openly done in the late extravagant Protest.[88]

If the opposition had, thus, lost the moral high ground with their protest, so much so that, as Delafaye reported, at least one of their number refused to sign, it was a temporary loss. The purges of mid-June caused deep misgivings amongst much of the political and social elite, particulary depriving Bolton and Cobham of their colonelcies, regarded by many as the equivalent of taking away their property. The removal of Bolton from his lord lieutenancies and governorship of the Isle of Wight was also disliked, because it deprived a major magnate of position, influence and patronage in his own locale, which for many peers was more important than national office.[89] These acts of vengeance by Walpole were to nurture the attack on the ministry in the 1734 session, first by those peers angered by the loss of commissions in the army,[90] while the removal of ministerial support from the bulk of the sitting Scottish representative peers in the 1734 general election, who thereby lost their seats in the Lords, caused those who had lost their seats to try to disrupt the ministry in 1735. Thus, while the purges had won Walpole a victory in the upper House, only time would tell how permanent it would prove and whether he had also made a rod for his own back.

6

The question remains as to why the ministry suffered such a large number of defections from its ranks in the 1733 session. The obvious answer would seem to be the great opposition to the excise scheme and, indeed, there is evidence to show that there were peers, other than those who did desert in the Lords. who were determined to prevent the new tax. So why, when the battle against the excise was, to all intents and purposes, won on 11 April, did the opposition in the Lords come out into the open? Why did those who had opposed the excise but had not expressed their opposition yet by voting against the ministry in the upper chamber begin to do so in May 1733? According to

[88] West Suffolk RO, Hervey (Ickworth) Papers, 941/47/7, p. 2: Hervey to Rev. Middleton, 20 June 1733; 941/47/8 (unpaginated): Middleton to Hervey, 24 June 1733. For Hervey's view on the 'severe invective' of the protest, which called the majority in the House: 'a pack of ignorant corrupt slaves to an ignorant corrupt minister', and the reason why a resolution to expunge it was not pressed by the ministry: see *Memoirs*, ed. Sedgwick, i, 198–9.

[89] Perhaps significantly, Cobham was allowed to retain his lord lieutenancy of Buckinghamshire. His governorship of Jersey was for life: Hervey, *Memoirs*, ed. Sedgwick, i, 200. Stair retained his regiment until 17 Apr. 1734, when it was taken away for his opposition in the Lords. See, Hervey, *Memoirs*, ed. Sedgwick, i, 200, for the reasons why Stair did not lose the regiment in 1733.

[90] The duke of Marlborough's bill to prevent dismissals of officers other than by a court martial or an address of parliament was presented to the Lords on 13 Feb. 1734. Three protests against its rejection by 100 votes to 62 (78 to 49 of those present) summarize the minority's concern over the politicisation of the deprivation of commissions: see *LJ*, xxiv, 345–7. The first protest was signed by 33 peers, the second by 36 and the third, significantly, only by Bolton and Cobham defending their record in the army.

Lord Hervey: 'almost all the great offices and employments were filled up by men who, though they did not directly vote against the present measures, yet took the liberty of talking very freely against them; and neither had, nor desired to be thought to have, any great cordiality towards Sir Robert'.[91] There is some evidence to support the speculation that it was the original sackings of Chesterfield and Clinton on 13 April, followed by Stair on the 30th, that acted as the final spur and pushed nearly one-third of the ministry's supporters in the Lords into voting in opposition at least once in May and June. Delafaye wrote that: 'I was surprised that the turning out of three lords for their activity in so unreasonable an opposition, could put matters upon such a foot in the house of peers, that upon a motion to call for the South-Sea accounts, (which had been made and *scarce heeded* in the other house) there should be an equality.'[92] Delafaye probably did not know that:

> a meeting of Many Lords was [held] on tuesday [8 May] at Lord Carterets, where it was Proposed they should all in one Body go to Court an[d] at once resighn [*sic.*] their places. This was opposed by Lord Willmingtoun, who said that was some thing like an affront done the King.

The report continued:

> but we are told they are not to Resighn, but to act in opposition to the great man, if Willmingtoun does oppose him, as its said, he will, and If Scarborough does the Same these two in Conjunction with the other Lords may work some change.[93]

This report, besides underlining the fact that it was the treatment of the three peers sacked in April that was at the bottom of the revolt in the Lords, reveals more of why the ministry was facing a major crisis in the Lords and at court. While Wilmington, unlike Scarbrough, did not in the end join the deserters and vote against the government,[94] the fact that the lord president of the council, a cabinet member and, perhaps most significant of all, a known favourite of the king,[95] was prepared to attend a meeting of dissident lords, could not but give a signal to the world that Walpole was in serious trouble.

Even the fact that 13 of those deserters of 24 May returned to support the ministry on 1 June indicates that either the pressure applied by Walpole was irresistible, or that

---

[91] See, Hervey, *Memoirs*, ed. Sedgwick, i, 173; see also 135–6. Hervey's observation that a contributory factor to the Lords agreeing to enquire into the South Sea accounts was 'the pride of the young Lords, who had heard their whole body so long treated as ciphers' (*Memoirs*, ed. Sedgwick, i, 187) does not survive an analysis of the ages of the 14 who defected on 3 May. Only three were in their 30s, while four were in their 60s.

[92] Coxe, *Walpole*, iii, 135 (emphasis added). The fact that the Commons made little of the South Sea accounts adds to the idea that, for the Lords, it was just a means to an end. As Delafaye put it: '[e]verybody knows that these oppositions are meant against a minister, let the question be what it will': Coxe, *Walpole*, iii, 135.

[93] NLS, MS 16553, ff. 132–3: Graham to [Milton], 10 May 1733.

[94] Wilmington was rewarded for his loyalty in voting by being granted the Garter on 11 June: Hervey *Memoirs*, ed. Sedgwick, i, 205.

[95] By this time, however, Hervey claims that the king disliked Wilmington: Hervey, *Memoirs*, ed. Sedgwick, i, 153.

their vote on the 24th was, in effect, a protest vote designed to warn the prime minister over his treatment of the peerage. Delafaye did consider that the opposition consisted of some out of pique, [as well as] some out of popularity, and some perhaps out of meer curiosity'.[96] The vote against the ministry by Ancaster and Clarendon on 1 June, having supported it on 24 May, again may be seen as another protest vote. Further, the continued opposition of 19 of the 1733 deserters into the 1734 session and, in some cases, beyond, together with the first-time defection of Weymouth in the 1734 session, adds weight to the proposition that it was Walpole's handling of the peerage that was the problem that prolonged the 1733 crisis in the Lords long after the excise had been settled. The duke of Montrose, dismissed as keeper of the great seal in Scotland on 16 June 1733, encapsulated the feelings of aggrieved peers when he wrote two days later that with a 'call to arms' to, in this case all Scots, but applicable to any peer who had lost a position: 'to joyn interest whenever we may be able to assist one [an]other for the interests of liberty which we have been supporting . . . I do in my conscience believe that its nixt [*sic.*] to impossible that those who are now att the helm can be so att the end of the next Session of Parl[iamen]t, but tho[ugh] that should happen things must be prepared'.[97] So, in effect, the 1733–4 sessions saw two separate, but interlinked, parliamentary crises – one concerning the excise in the Commons, and one concerning Walpole and the peerage in the Lords.

7

Much of the opposition in the Lords in the 1733 crisis came from the Scottish representative peers. Before 1733, only one such peer, Tweeddale, was in permanent opposition to the ministry. By the end of the session, he had been joined by five others – Buchan, Haddington, Marchmont, Montrose and Stair.[98] Four of these six were to

---

[96] Coxe, *Walpole*, iii, 135.

[97] NRS, GD 220/5/884/9, 10: [Montrose to Mungo Graham], 14, 16 June 1733 (quotation from the second letter). A little under a year later, Montrose wrote that: '[i]ts plane you see that the Minister [Walpole] has numbers in both Houses of Parl[iamen]t and yet he is under such weight both att home and abroad, that I must acknowledge I am not wise enough to see how it is possible for him to stand it, or to extricate himself out of the innumlerable [*sic.*] difficultys he is involv'd in. A little time must show what will happen notwithstanding his numbers he has a great party against him considerable for their weight and property in the nation, and so I believe he'l feel, for its certain his opposers stand firmly together, and he well knows that as corrupt as the age we live in is, many are above being tempted by him and dispyse the mean arguments by which he has gained too many': NRS, GD 220/5/889/5: [same to same], 16 Mar. 1733/4.

[98] The earl of Haddington was absent from the 1733 and the 1734 sessions. His proxy was held both times by Rothes. Haddington, who seems to have opposed the excise, wrote to Marchmont in mid-April 1733 that Rothes 'has for a great while been begging that I would send him orders how to vote for me. I had not done nor . . . did I ever in word or write give my opinion of the [Excise] Bill'. Despite this taciturnity, a rumour rose which came to the ear of Walpole, that Rothes had been instructed by Haddington, and Ilay advised Rothes to satisfy the prime minister that this was not the case: HMC, *Polwarth MSS*, v, 50–1: 18 Apr. 1733. We have no division list for the 1733 session, prior to the date of Haddington's letter, to know whether Rothes cast his vote and Haddington's proxy against the ministry on the Pension and Mutiny Bills. Nor do we know if Haddington sent Rothes instructions; the proxy, however, was used to oppose the ministry on 24 May and 1 June (see below, Appendix 1).

maintain their unwavering opposition into the 1734 session and would prove to be, t
some extent, the mainstay of the opposition's campaign.[99]

A good deal of this Scottish opposition to Walpole's administration had develope
since 1725, when the prime minister sacked the duke of Roxburghe as secretary of stat
for Scotland. Roxburghe was a leading member of the *Squadrone Volante*, one of the tw
contending whig factions in Scotland. Walpole now put the management of Scottis
affairs firmly in the hands of the *Squadrone*'s opponent, the earl of Ilay.[100] The resultin
rivalry between the two Scottish whig factions only added to the difficulty the Sco
after the union had always posed for an essentially English ministry. For example, it wa
almost an immutable law of politics, that the Scots in parliament in the early 18t
century acted on their own agenda, which often bore little relation to that of the
English counterparts. In 1733 in the Lords, however, the concerns of the Scots coin
cided, in part, with those of the English peers in opposition. Sir John Clerk of Penicuic
in London, on a tour of England, was visited on 7 May 1733 by Wilmington. '[O]u
discourse ran on publick affairs' noted Clerk in his diary, and Wilmington:

> regreted much the defection of some of the peers of Scotland from the Court Intere
> particularly the Duke of Montrose and the Earls of Stair and Marchmont. [T]hese
> seems were not so much angry at a project which had been carrying on for a lon
> time in the parliament about an Excise on Tobacco and wines as at the continuatio
> of the E[arl] of Illay and Sir Robert Walpole in the Kings Service.[101]

Thus it seems that the five *Squadrone* Scots' peers who had moved into opposition t
the ministry in 1733 had used the excise as both an excuse and an opportunity. Thei
reward for so doing was that three of them lost high-profile jobs in the Scottis
administration. Walpole regarded these peers as expendable, so long as he had th
support of the Argathelians (the other whig Scottish faction led by Argyll and Ilay). Ilay
sometimes known as 'the Scots Walpole',[102] remained studiously loyal to the prim
minister, while his brother Argyll, the greatest of the Scottish magnates and a force t
be reckoned with in Lords' debates, had, as we have seen, met Walpole half way b
abstaining on 1 June after his desertion on 24 May. The duke was to return to th
ministerial fold in 1734 and supported the administration until his final defection i
1739.

---

[99] Rothes (together with Haddington via his proxy) tempered his opposition to Walpole in 1734 b
supporting him over the duke of Marlborough's Army Bill on 13 February (see Appendix 1). It is clear fro
letters that Haddington wrote to Manchester in March, that Haddington supported his fellow *Squadrone* peer
campaign against the ministry. He claimed that: 'the letters I have write to him [Rothes] with my sentimen
of our affairs have been kept from him [by the government?] till a letter I sent up under a cover to the Duk
of Montrose with the express and upon getting that you se [Rothes] has changed his way with my vote
Haddington believed Rothes to be 'an honest upright man', whose current voting for the government 'come
from his thinking what he does right and that he scorns all influence from a minister': HMC, *Polwarth MS*
v, 84, 84–5: 4, 28 Mar. 1733. Rothes's temporary support for Walpole did not save him from being droppe
by the ministry at the 1734 general election.

[100] NRS, Clerk of Penicuick Papers, GD 18/2110, p. 18. I wish to thank Sir Robert Clerk bt, for allowin
me to use and quote from his family papers.

[101] See Harding, 'Lord Cathcart', 192–4.

[102] The name was given him by Walpole: NRS, Morton Papers, GD 124/15/1431: [Cleland] to [Grange
21 Mar. [1734].

When dealing with the Scottish deserters, Walpole also had in mind the forth-coming general election in the summer of 1734. He could ram home his warning to the opposition in the Lords with a few sackings of prominent Scots, mixed judiciously with a few English ones, and if the Scots persisted in opposition in 1734, which they did, remove them from the government's list of approved candidates for the 1734 election of representative peers. Delafaye confessed that Montrose and Marchmont, having lost office: 'have but one session more to oppose in, for very probably they will not be in the number of Scots peers returned upon the next election',[103] and this is what happened. However, Walpole's strategy did not work completely. Two of the replacement representative peers, Buccleuch and Bute (nephew of both Argyll and Islay, later to be George III's first prime minister, and not elected a representative peer until 1737 at a by-election), proved equally obstreperous in the next parliament and had to be got rid of at the 1741 general election. For most of the rest of Walpole's tenure of office, the Scots in the Lords were to prove something of a headache.

The first move by the opposition over the position of the Scottish representative peers was in the 1734 session, in the form of the introduction of a motion on 6 March: '[to] resolve, for the better securing the Freedom of the Election of a Peer, or Peers, to sit in the Parliament of Great Britain on the part of Scotland, that the Election shall be by way of [a] Ballot'.[104] The motion was immediately defeated by 96 to 63 (75 to 45 of those present). The resulting protest, which vigorously defended the position of inde-pendent Scottish representatives (an anathema to Walpole and Ilay) was signed by 34 peers, which included only two representative peers (Marchmont and Tweeddale) and Earl Ker (sitting by virtue of his British peerage).[105]

Later, in 1735, some of those Scottish representative peers who had failed to be re-elected at the 1734 general election (three of whom had also lost offices),[106] attempted at least to embarrass the ministry and hopefully, perhaps, cause some damage, by petitioning the Lords against the actions of the ministry during the election.[107] In February 1735, the petition accused the ministry of 'several undue Methods and illegal Practices [which] were used towards carrying on this Election'.[108] The petition was supported in the Lords by many in opposition to Walpole, including some of the former

---

[103] Coxe, *Walpole*, iii, 135.

[104] *LJ*, xxiv, 366: 6 Mar. 1734.

[105] *LJ*, xxiv, 367.

[106] Two, Hamilton and Queensbury, were barred from standing for election by a 1709 Lords' decision, and from sitting by virtue of their British peerages (Brandon and Dover, respectively) by the 1712 Lords' ruling.

[107] This petitioning was contrary to the expectations of some: Bishop Secker of Bristol thought that: 'It continues dobtfull whether any petition will be brought in against the Scotch peers'. Secker also wrote, significantly for such a petition, that: 'The Parliament hath done nothing yet besides giving each side an opportunity of shewing their numbers which are sufficiently in favour of the Court': BL, Add. MS 39311, f. 27: to [Bishop Berkely], 1 Feb. 1734/5.

[108] *LJ*, xxiv, 459. The petition was presented on 13 February and was finally dismissed after three crucial divisions, on 28 Feb. 1735. For full details of this campaign, see *LJ*, xxiv, 459, 465–7, 475–7; and Shin Matsuzono, ' "Attaque and Break Through a Phalanx of Corruption . . . the Court Party!" The Scottish Representative Peers' Election and the Opposition, 1733–5: Two New Division Lists of the House of Lords of 1735', *Parliamentary History*, xxxi (2012), 332–53.

'dissenters' from 1733 and 1734,[109] led, according to Lord Hervey, by the earl of Chesterfield, 'who had long been looked upon as Commander-in-Chief of this Scottish brigade'.[110]

Chesterfield's role with the disaffected Scottish peers can be seen in two of his letters to the earl of Marchmont in 1734. Basically, he realized the weakness of the opposition in the Lords, but thought a petition would give it a propaganda victory, even if it failed, while the opposition's plan should be to concentrate its attack in the Commons upon Walpole by impeaching his 'minister for Scotland', Lord Ilay. In June, Chesterfield wrote that he, Carteret and Pultney ('the only three of your friends now in town') had gone through the papers from Scotland concerning the election, and Carteret had sent a detailed answer, but Chesterfield was writing to give his support. The whig opposition's programme was, first, to 'get some of the lowest of your venal peers to come to our bar [of the house of lords] and confess the money they took to vote for the Court list'; second, to get a Scottish MP 'well armed with facts and proofs' to impeach Lord Ilay in the house of commons, which 'would be a capital stroke, and affect the master [Walpole] as well as the man [Ilay]'; third, present the Scottish petition on the first day of the session of the Lords and to be ready with all the material to conduct the case, though Chesterfield feared that the Scots 'must expect more justice from your appeals to the rest of mankind, than from your appeals to our House, where now our strength is so much diminished'; and last, that the petitioning lords do 'attend and solicit your petition in town at the opening of the Parliament, for solicitations *viva voce*, and of the persons themselves concerned, have much more weight than remote applications by letter, or the interventions of friends'.[111]

By the end of August 1734, Chesterfield, having consulted with the duke of Montrose and again with Poultney (both of whom would be writing separately), and who, he assured Marchmont, were in concurrance with Carteret ('though we did not see him'),[112] was reiterating the whig opposition's plan but with some caveats.[113] First, an objection to the election in the Lords without application from the petitioners would be impossible. Chesterfield reminded Marchmont of the House's enquiry into the South Sea, where the court's 'strong objection . . . was, that there was no application from any of the parties concerned, and therefore it was to be presumed that none of them were aggrieved'. Whereas with a petition concerning the election, even if it were rejected: 'at least in the course of our proceedings upon it, those infamous practices will be laid open to all mankind, and condemned by everybody but the House'. There would also be the benefit of fixing 'upon Isla crimes that will beget questions of censure, from which he can only be acquitted by the scandalous partiality of a majority as corrupt as himself' Thus co-operation with the Commons was essential, for though '[e]vidence you certainly have [it is] not sufficient to set aside votes enough to give you a majority; and our

[109] See below, Appendix 2. The voting in the two divisions of 20 and 28 Feb. 1735 can be seen in Appendix 1.

[110] Hervey, *Memoirs*, ed. Sedgwick, 410.

[111] *Letters of Chesterfield*, ed. Dobree, ii, 280–2: Chesterfield to Marchmont, 15 June 1734.

[112] This lack of personal contact at this stage may hint at a possible wavering by Carteret, whose position in 1735, as we shall see, was less firm, if Lord Hervey is to be believed, than it would appear from Chesterfield's comments in mid 1734.

[113] *Letters of Chesterfield*, ed. Dobree, ii, 287–90: Chesterfield to Marchmont, 27 Aug. 1734.

House is not at present of a complexion to vacate the election, because of some corrupt practices proved upon some of the electors'. The action by the ministry's opponents in the Commons, where 'we are much stronger than we were last Session',[114] was crucial for, he repeated, it would 'strike both the agent and his master'. Whereas '[I]n the House of Lords our strength is so much decreased, that we must wait for accidents and circumstances from without doors, before we can hope to do anything.'

By the end of August, the Scottish peers' reaction to this advice probably disappointed Chesterfield. Montrose wrote to Marchmont that: 'we have agreed upon the form of a Petition to be sign'd by us to the H[ouse] of L[ords] but the petition is in generall terms complaneing of undue practices, but not takeing it so high as our protests[115] and leaving it to the Lords to consider what is proper to be done in a matter that so highly concerns the dignity of the House [.] [W]e are sensible that our evidence is not sufficient to sett asyde the Court list but its thought there is foundation and prooff enough for fixing a Crime upon the agent [Ilay].'[116] (In fact, the petition was later weakened when some of 'the names of the Lords who sign'd the petition in Scotl[an]d can not be att this [i.e., could not attend at the House when the petition would be debated] the D[uke] of Roxburghe and M[arquess] of Tweeddale will not join with us. [T]he Petition therefor is sign'd only by 6 viz. D[uke of] Hamil[ton,] D[uke of] Queensb[erry,] E[arl of] Dundo[nal]d E[arl of] Marchm[on]t, E[arl of] Stair, and myself. [W]e did not think it proper that E[arl of] Rothes who has behav'd himself extrememly well, should sign it.')[117]

Chesterfield proved to be right: there was no success in the Commons, upon which Walpole had a tighter hold than the Lords, and while the opposition mustered a resonable vote, the ministry easily won the divisions concerning the Scots' petition, with, on 20 February, Lord Hardwicke picking apart the petition for its weakness in drafting.[118] This may be partially accounted for by the fact that not all former opponents of the ministry were enthusiastic in their support: Hervey noted that Lord Carteret (contrary to the impression given by Chesterfield) and the earl of Winchilsea, for example, 'refused positively to take any other part in pursuing this unfruitful affair or to give any other assistance, than their attendance and their votes'.[119] Carteret also had a personal grudge against Chesterfield (an instance of factions within the anti-Walpole forces).[120] Also, none of the new representative peers present in the House (15 out of 16)[121] for the three divisions voted with the opposition, despite the fact that the petitioners stated that it was not part of their campaign to unseat any of the representative peers elected in 1734. This should not be surprising, as the 16 Scots elected had been hand-picked by the ministry and, according to a document in the Marchmont

[114] Chesterfield went on: 'our numbers are a good two hundred and forty, which if well conducted, cannot, in my opinion, remain long a minority'.

[115] The protests of 1734 concerned elections of Scottish representative peers: *LJ*, xxiv, 366–7, 378.

[116] NRS, GD 220/5/889/7: [Montrose to Mungo Graham], 26 Aug. 1734.

[117] NRS, GD 220/5/891/8: [Montrose to Mungo Graham], 13 Feb. 1734[/5].

[118] HMC, *Egmont Diary*, ii, 152.

[119] In all three divisions, Carteret and Winchilsea did vote against the ministry; see below, Appendix 1.

[120] Hervey, *Memoirs*, ed. Sedgwick, i, 409–10.

[121] The absent one was the earl of Bute, later to be an opponent of Walpole's and dropped by him at the 1741 general election.

Papers, most had been 'bribed' to stand for election, while others were 'bribed' to vote for the king's list.[122] Such 'bribed' representative peers were unlikely to bite the hand that had fed them so early in their parliamentary careers, particularly in favour of petitioners who condemned the methods of their election.

However, two Scots in the Lords did support the opposition, Earl Graham (eldest surviving son of the duke of Montrose, one of the petitioners), and Earl Ker (eldest son of the duke of Roxburghe), both sitting by virtue of the British peerages granted in their father's lifetime (to Graham's elder, and since deceased, brother and to Ker, both of whom were not Scottish peers at the time of the creations and thus not covered by the 1711 ban on Scottish peers who were granted British peerages not being able to sit as British peers). The duke of Greenwich (Argyll) only voted (for the ministry) in the first division on 20 February, being absent from the other two.[123] Could this have been an early warning of his later conversion to his opposition against Walpole's ministry? Thus, it seems clear that the petition against the election procedures for the Scottish representative peers in 1735 was, at the time, a nuisance to Walpole, but little else. However, it may be seen as a possible augury of things to come.

8

That the 1734 session in the Lords was more contentious than that of 1733 can be seen by the number of divisions on major political issues in each: 23 in 1734 (plus one on a private bill) to ten in 1733 (plus 19 on private bills and causes). Of the 23 divisions in 1734, ten involved the use of proxies (an indication of increased political activity), as opposed to seven divisions with proxies in 1733. In the middle of April 1734, four days saw 12 divisions, six with the use of proxies; while one single topic, the procedures involved in the election of Scottish representative peers, also produced 12 divisions, five of which involved proxies. The 'Scottish problem', which had (on occasions) dominated proceedings in the Lords in the past, most notably in 1711, 1713 and 1719, was to do so again in 1734. Only two other subjects in the session – the duke of Marlborough's Officers' Commission Bill on 13 February and the Sinking Fund Bill on 11 and 15 April – were to provide similar levels of attendance and voting as did the question of the election of the Scottish peers in March and April 1734.

This upsurge in political activity by the opposition in 1734 had one crucial difference from that of the previous session; the ministry won every major division with majorities ranging from five to 43. As Haddington, writing from Scotland, put it: 'the damnd majority [for the ministry] was not near so great in either House last year as it is in this', concluding that he could 'never be brought to believe that we are able to put down a minister whose all was at stake and who was not only in great favour [with the king] but had such a command of money; for I am old enough to know how little gold is to

---

[122] HMC, *Polwarth MSS*, v, 111–12. Only two of the new 16 do not appear on this list: Dunmore and Morton. The 'bribery' took the form of pensions, offices, offices for relatives, regiments, money, acts of parliament in their favour, military promotion, while a couple were 'threatened'.

[123] NRS, Marchmont Papers, GD 158/1242/183, 212.

be resisted since virtue is so scarce'.[124] Equally, Tweeddale, despite his opinion that the duke of Bedford's motion on the Scottish peers, on 6 March, did 'with great spirit produced the best day I have seen in the House of Lords for this great while', recognized the inevitable:

> [though] greater things were expected of us this session of Parliament, The superiority of the Court party was not expected by some [that it] could have been so great this year ... we are still but a minority tho a considerable one, that [had] the superiority nott been so great, more would have been attempted and we must have prevailed, last year we succeeded in defeating the excise Scheme, butt we were on the defensive side, The same would have again happened had any such opportunitys happened ... [but] I am sorry to say we were nott able nor strong enough to attacque and break through a Phalanx of Corruption.[125]

Chesterfield, one of the opposition's most able politicians, had recognized as early as August 1733 that: '[i]n the House of Lords our strength is so much decreased, that we must wait for accidents and circumstances from without doors, before we can hope to do anything'.[126]

Though accident and circumstance would favour Walpole in 1734, his treatment of the dissident peers in 1733 may have delivered mixed blessings for the ministry in the Lords. In the short term, he had won back control of both the court and the upper House. In the long term, however, he had driven men of talent into the arms of the opposition, thus strengthening it in its future struggle with the ministry. He had also sown the seeds of disaffection within the body of the peerage, and the resultant growth blossomed in 1742 when many disgruntled lords absented themselves from the upper chamber, causing the ministry's majorities to fall steeply, and thus contributing to the great minister's own fall.[127] The year 1733 also saw the end of the period when Walpole could take the house of lords more or less for granted.[128] For the rest of his premiership, the upper chamber, taking a higher profile within the administration than previously, would demand greater vigilance by Walpole.

---

[124] HMC, *Polwarth MSS*, v, 83, 85: to Marchmont, 4, 28 Mar. 1734.

[125] Lennoxlove, Hamilton Papers, TD86/11/2, bundle 894/18: Tweeddale to [Hamilton], 20 Mar. 1733[/4].

[126] *Letters of Chesterfield*, ii, 289: to Marchmont, 27 Aug. 1733; see also 281: to same, 15 June 1733.

[127] See Jones, 'The House of Lords and the Fall of Walpole'.

[128] If one can judge the level of management from the chance survival of parliamentary lists, then the increasing number in both the public and private papers of Secretary of State Newcastle (see *British Parliamentary Lists, 1660–1800: A Register*, ed. G.M. Ditchfield, David Hayton and Clyve Jones (1995), 47–50; and Clyve Jones, 'New Parliamentary Lists', *Parliamentary History*, xxv (2006), 404–5) may indicate a change of attitude towards the Lords by the ministry. This possible change coincides with the resignation of Townshend from the ministry in 1730 (who, as secretary of state, was the unofficial 'leader' of the House) and his replacement by Harrington, who appears, from the little evidence we have, to have been somewhat reluctant as 'leader'. Newcastle, a compulsive manager, seems to have taken over much of the role of 'leader', thus the aftermath of the events of 1733 may merely have reinforced a fairly recent trend towards greater management of the Lords. However, this picture may be distorted by the fact that Newcastle's papers survive in abundance, whereas relatively few survive for Townshend and none for Harrington outside the official state papers. Virtually no work has been done on the management of the upper chamber for this period, but see Clyve Jones, 'The House of Lords and the Growth of Parliamentary Stability, 1701–1742', in *Britain in the First Age of Party, 1680–1750: Essays Presented to Geoffrey Holmes*, ed. Clyve Jones (1987), 85–110 *passim*.

Introduction to Appendices 1 and 2.

The dramatic shift of support from the ministry to opposition in 1733 can be easily demonstrated by an analysis of the parliamentary lists printed below in Appendix 1.[129] Of the members of the Lords listed who have been analysed,[130] three-quarters remained constant in their support of either the ministry or opposition throughout the two sessions of 1733 and 1734: for the ministry, 44 peers, six Scottish representative peers and 24 bishops, a total of 74; for the opposition, 40 peers, one Scottish representative peer and no bishops. Those who did not remain constant fall into three groups: the 15 who defected from the ministry to the opposition for the 1733 session only; the 19 who defected for both the 1733 and the 1734 sessions and, in some cases, for longer, and the one who defected only in 1734 (these groups are listed below in Appendix 2).[131] Based on these figures, the ministry started the 1733 session with a notional 109 supporters in the Lords (74 constant supporters plus the 35 future 'defectors'), while the opposition had a notional 41. These latter figures come fairly close to the two highest totals achieved in divisions in 1732, the session before the excise crisis: 95 to 40 on 17 February and 92 to 41 on 27 March. At times, in the 1733 session, the number of the ministry's supporters shrank to 75 (the core 74 plus the one 1734 defector), while the opposition rose to 75 (41 constant supporters plus the 1733 defectors). (This represented a shift to the opposition from the ministry of 31.2% of its initial supporters.) The division of 24 May, which saw the government defeated, did, indeed, produce an equality of votes of 75 to 75, with the following vote on 1 June giving figures of 75 to 70.[132] In the 1734 session, the ministry had 89 notional supporters and the opposition 61. (This represented a shift to the opposition from the ministry of 18.3% measured against the 109 supporters at the beginning of the 1733 session.) These figures can be compared with the largest divisions in the 1734 session (which included proxies): 100 to 62 (25 January), 96 to 63 (6 March), 99 to 60 (18 March) and 94 to 51 (11 April).[133]

---

[129] Not all of the lists analysed contain 'hard' information such as is recorded in division lists. Some record 'soft' information such as personal opinions in forecast lists. However, the analysis comes very close to reaching the same figures that were recorded in the division in which the ministry was defeated on 24 May 1733.

[130] Not all the lords listed in Appendix 1 figure in these calculations: e.g., some died and others succeeded during the period, while some were absent for the whole, or a large part, of the time.

[131] The previous record of support for either the ministry or the opposition prior to 1733 (based on the various lists available for analysis, but not presented here) has been used to determine a lord's position in 1733 and 1734 and beyond. For the lists available, see *British Parliamentary Lists*, ed. Ditchfield, Hayton and Jones, and Jones, 'New Parliamentary Lists', 401–9.

[132] Other divisions in 1733 show that the opposition did not build to its strongest until the excise crisis was over in the Commons in late April and, as with all such one issue opposition groupings, it is difficult, if not impossible, for it to sustain high levels of attendance and voting.

[133] Exact correlation cannot be expected between figures produced by this analysis and the voting figures produced by divisions in 1733 and 1734. This is largely for three reasons: first, to the 'soft' nature of some of the evidence alluded to above (note 129); second, to three groups of peers who do not appear in the 1733 section of Appendix 1 but do appear in 1734: Carlisle, Hatton and Portland, who tended to support the ministry; Arundel, Boyle, Dartmouth, Derby, Hereford, Leigh and Somerset, who supported the ministry; and Cleveland, Poulett, Stamford and Waldegrave, whose support was doubtful; and third, to the inconsistent attendance and voting records of individual lords. An example of inconsistency is Viscount Falmouth, who voted against the ministry on 3 and 24 May, but for on 1 June (see Appendix 3). According to Lord Hervey

APPENDIX 1: *Division, Forecast and Other Lists, 1733–5*

Key to the contents in cols 1–12 of the table.

1. *12/15 Jan. 1733*, list of lords summoned to the ministry's pre-sessional meeting: TNA, SP 45/1.

    p = those on the list.

    pa = known to be absent from meeting on 15 Jan.

    pa? = may have been absent.

2. *3 May 1733*, those voting for and against laying before the House the accounts of the South Sea Company: NLS, MS 16553, f. 131: Richard Graham to [Lord Milton], 5 May 1733; RA, SP, 162/81: Nathaniel Mist to James Edgar, 12 June 1733; *Cobbett's Parl. Hist.*, ix, 106.

    p = against (i.e., supporting the ministry).

    c = for.

3. *24 May 1733*, those voting for and against Newcastle's motion to examine a witness on the South Sea Company's affairs: BL, Egerton MS 2543, f. 410; RA, SP, Box 1/112 (marked with 33 of the 45 proxy votes cast); *Cobbett's Parl. Hist.*, ix, 115–6.

    p = for (i.e., against examining the witness).

    pp = proxy vote for.

    c = against.

    cp = proxy vote against.

    Note, proxy voting is calculated from comparing the lists with the lists of registered proxies in the PA, proxy book, HL/PO/JO/13/8.

4. *24 May–1 June 1733*, list of lords marked 'against' and 'absent', who were to be canvassed by the ministry prior to the division on 1 June: Cambridge University Library, Cholmondeley (Houghton) MSS, P 66/5, printed in Plumb, *Sir Robert Walpole*, ii, 277.

    cd = against (i.e., possible doubtful opponents of the ministry).

    a = absent.

5. *1 June 1733*, those voting for and against censuring the directors of the South Sea Company (incomplete): Cambridge UL, Cholmondeley (Houghton) MSS, Correspondence 1990: Newcastle to Walpole, 2 June 1733; RA, SP, Box 1/112 (list of those who voted on 24 May which marks 'deserters' to the court on 1 June).

    p = against (i.e., supporting the ministry).

    c = for.

    cp = proxy for (recorded on list).

    a = absent.

---

[133] *(continued)* Falmouth 'in the two most material questions . . . spoke on one side and voted on the other . . . Falmouth was determined to do the ministers all the hurt he could, for he spoke for them and voted against them': *Memoirs*, ed. Sedgwick, i, 188. Falmouth certainly spoke for the ministry on 2 June: RA, SP, Box 1/120.

6. *Early Jan. 1734*, a pre-sessional forecast: BL, Add. MS 33002, ff. 420–1.
   p = for the ministry.
   c = against.
   d = doubtful.
   ? = crossed out.

7. *Before 16 Jan. 1734*, list of lords summoned to the ministry's pre-sessional meeting: BL, Add. MS 33002, ff. 409–10; variant at Add. MS 32993, ff. 36–7; Add. MS 33002, f. 418, is a list of bishops classified as 'in and about London' and 'Absent', compiled before 14 January (information on the bishops in the full list of lords summoned has been amalgamated with the information on this list).
   p = those on the list.
   d = marked 'q' on list (i.e., doubtful supporter).
   a = recorded as absent from London and not summoned (bishops only).
   pa? = summoned but earlier recorded as absent from London (bishops only).
   paq = bishop listed as 'in and about London', marked 'qu[ery] if he staies', and not summoned.
   ? = listed as 'in and about London' but not summoned (bishops only).

8. *16 Jan. 1734*, list of lords who attended the ministry's pre-sessional meeting: BL, Add. MS 32993, f. 38.
   p = those on the list.

9. *Before 13 Feb. 1734*, forecast for the vote on the duke of Marlborough's Bill for the prevention of army officers being deprived of their commissions other than by court martial or an address of parliament: BL, Add. MS 33002, ff. 430–1.
   p = for.
   c = against.
   d = doubtful.
   q = query.
   a = absent.

10. *13 Feb. 1734*, those voting for and against the Duke of Marlborough's Bill: BL, Add. MS 33002, ff. 430–1 (annotated forecast): NRS, Montrose Papers, GD 220/5/8887/16.
    p = against (i.e., supporting the ministry).
    pp = proxy vote against.
    c = for.
    cp = proxy vote for (proxy voting recorded on the lists).
    ab = abstained.
    a = absent.

11. *20 Feb. 1735*, those voting for and against the petition by some Scottish peers over the conduct of the election of the 16 Scottish representative peers in 1734: NRS, GD 158/1242/183.[134]

[134] The divisions for 20 and 21 Feb. 1735 are recorded on the same sheet (f. 183); a note at the bottom states '21st Febry Leave out x', i.e., the three peers so marked were absent from the Lords: Greenwich, and Say and Sele, who voted for the ministry on 20 Feb., and Macclesfield, who voted for the opposition on 20 Feb. Otherwise the voting was the same as it had been on 20 Feb. 1735.

p = against (i.e., supporting the ministry).
c = for.
a = absent.

12. *28 Feb. 1735*, those voting for and against the petition by some Scottish peers over the conduct of the election of the 16 Scottish representative peers in 1734: NRS, GD 158/1242/212.
p = against (i.e., supporting the ministry).
c = for.
a = absent.

Note that the names given in brackets indicate the alternative title by which a peer was known or listed:

1. Irish titles by which the peer was better known (English titles were the ones by which they sat in the Lords): Boyle of Marston, Butler of Weston, Mountjoy and Tadcaster.
2. Scottish titles by which the peer was better known (English or British titles were the ones by which they sat in the Lords): Greenwich, Hay and Ker (the last one's Scottish title was a courtesy title as heir of the duke of Roxburghe).
3. Courtesy title by which the peer was better known (sat by virtue of being called up to the Lords in his father's barony): Percy (heir to the duke of Somerset).

Name	1733					1734					1735	
	1	2	3	4	5	6	7	8	9	10	11	12
Peers												
Abergavenny	p	p	p	–	–	p	p	–	p	p	p	p
Abingdon	–	–	cp	–	–	c	–	–	c	c	c	c
Albermarle	p	p	p	–	–	p	p	p	p	p	p	p
Ancaster	p	p	p	–	c	p	p	p	p	p	p	p
Anglesey	–	–	cp	–	–	c	–	–	c	c	c	c
Arundell of Terrice	–	–	–	–	–	c	–	–	c	a	–	–
Ashburnham	pa?	p	p	–	–	p	p	p	p	p	p	p
Aylesford	–	–	cp	–	–	c	–	–	c	cp	c	c
Barnard			cp	–	–	c	–	–	c	cp	–	–
Bathurst			cp	–	–	c	–	–	c	c	c	c
Beaufort	–	–	cp	–	–	c	–	–	c	cp	c	c
Bedford			c	–	–	c	d	–	c	c	c	c
Berkeley	–	–	cp	–	–	c	–	–	c	cp	–	–
Berkeley of Stratton	–	–	cp	–	–	c	–	–	c	cp	–	–
Berkshire	–	c	c	–	–	c	–	–	c	c	–	–
Bolton	pa	c	c	cd	c	c	–	–	c	c	–	–
Boyle of Marston (Orrery)	–	–	–	–	–	c	d	–	c	c	–	–
Bradford	p	–	–	–	–	d	p	–	d	ab	–	–
Bridgwater	pa	c	c	–	–	c	–	–	c	c	–	–
Bristol	–	–	cp	–	–	c	–	–	c	c	–	–
Bruce	–	c	c	–	–	c	–	–	c	c	–	–

Name	1733					1734					1735	
	1	2	3	4	5	6	7	8	9	10	11	12
Burlington	p	–	cp	cd	cp	c	–	–	c	c	c	c
Butler of Weston (Arran)	–	–	c	–	–	c	–	–	c	c	c	c
Byron	p	p	p	–	–	p	p	p	p	p	p	p
Cadogan	p	–	p	–	–	p	p	p		p	p	p
Cardigan						c	d	–	–	c		
Carlisle	–	–	–	–	–	p	–	–	p	pp	p	p
Carteret	–	c	c	–	–	c	–	–	c	c	c	c
Chandos	p	–	p	–	–	d	p	–	pq	p	a	a
Chesterfield	p	c	c	–	–	c	–	–	c	c	c	c
Cholmondeley	p	–	–	p	p	p	p	p	p	–	p	p
Clarendon	p	–	p	–	c	d	p	–	d	a	c	c
Cleveland	–	–	–	–	–	d	–	–	d	a		
Clinton	pa	c	c	–	p	c	–	–	c	c	–	–
Cobham	p	c	c	cd	c	c	–	–	c	c	c	c
Cornwallis	p	c	c	cd	p	p	p	p	p	pp	p	p
Coventry	–	c	c	–	–	c	–	–	c	cp	c	c
Cowper	p	p	p	–	–	p	p	–	p	p	p	p
Craven	–	–	c	–	–	c	–	–	c	c	c	c
Dartmouth	–	–	–	–	–	c	–	–	c	cp	–	–
Delawarr	p	p	p	–	–	p	p	p	p	p	p	–
Denbigh	pa	–	c	cd	c	d	p	–	d	c	c	–
Derby	–	–	–	–	–	c	–	–	c	a	–	–
Devonshire	p	p	p	–	–	p	p	p	p	pp	p	p
Dorset	p	–	p	–	–	p	–	–	p	pp	–	–
Ducie	pa	–	pp	–	–	p	p	p	p	p	p	p
Effingham	p	–	p	–	–	p	p	p	p	p	p	p
Essex	–	–	pp	–	–	p	–	–	p	pp	p	p
Exeter	–	–	cp	–	–	c	–	–	c	cp	c	–
Falmouth, 1v	p	c	c	cd	p	d	p	–	d	c		
Falmouth, 2v											c	c
Ferrers	–	–	–	–	–	–	d	–	d	a		
Fitzwalter	pa	c	c	cd	c	p	p	–	p	p	c	–
Foley	–	c	c	–	–	c	–	–	c	c	c	c
Gainsborough	pa	–	c	–	–	c	–	–	c	a	–	–
Godolphin	p	–	p	–	–	p	p	–	p	p	–	–
Gower	–	c	c	–	–	c	–	–	c	c	c	c
Grafton	p	–	p	–	–	p	p	p	p	p	p	p
Graham					–	c	–	–	c	c	c	c
Grantham	p	–	pp	–	–	p	p	p	p	p	p	p
Greenwich (Argyll)	pa	–	c	cd	a	p	p	p	p	p	c	a
Griffin	pa	–	–	–	–	d	p	–	d	c	–	–
Guilford	p	–	–	a/cd	–	d?	p	–	p	a	–	–
Halifax	pa?	p	p	–	–	p	p	p	p	p/a	p	p
Harborough	pa	–	c	cd	p	p	p	–	p	p	–	p
Hardwicke						p	p	p	p	p	p	–

Name	1733					1734					1735	
	1	2	3	4	5	6	7	8	9	10	11	12
Harrington	p	p	p	—	—	p	p	p?	p	p	p	p
Hatton	—	—	—	—	—	d	p	—	d	pp	—	—
Haversham	—	c	c	cd	cp	d?	p	—	p	c	c	c
Hay (Kinnoull)	—	—	—	—	—	d?	—	—	—	—	—	—
Herbert of Chirbury	pa	—	pp	—	—	p	p	—	p	p	p	p
Hereford	—	—	—	—	—	c	—	—	c	cp	—	—
Hervey						p	p	p	p	p	p	p
Hinton						p	p	p	p	p	p	p
Hobart	pa	p	pp	—	—	p	p	—	p	pp	p	p
Hunsdon	p	—	cp	cd	cp	p	p	p	p	p	p	p
Huntingdon	—	—	cp	—	—	c	—	—	c	cp	c	c
Jersey	p	p	p	—	—	d	p	p	p	a/p	p	p
Kent	p	c	c	cd	c	d	p	—	p	p	p	p
Ker (Bowmont)	—	c	c	—	—	c	—	—	c	c	c	c
King	p	—	p	—	—	p	p	—	p	pp	c	c
Kingston						d?	—	—	—	—		
Lansdown	—	—	pp	—	—	p	—	—	p	pp	p	p
Leicester	p	—	pp	—	—	p	p	—	p	pp	p	p
Leigh	—	—	—	—	—	c	—	—	c	a	—	—
Lichfield	—	—	c	—	—	c	—	—	c	c	c	c
Lonsdale	p	p	p	—	—	p	p	p	p	p	—	—
Lovel	pa	p	p	—	—	p	p	—	p	p	p	p
Lovelace	—	—	p	—	—	p	p	—	p	p	p	p
Lymington	pa	—	p	—	—	p	p	—	p	p	p	p
Lynn	p	p	p	—	—	p	p	p	p	p	p	p
Macclesfield	pa?	c	c	cd	c	p	d	—	d	a	c	c
Malton	pa	—	—	—	—	p	p	—	—	p	p	p
Manchester	pa	—	c	cd	p	p	p	p	p	p	p	p
Marlborough (Sunderland)	p	—	c	—	—	c	d	—	c	c	c	—
Masham	—	—	c	—	—	c	—	—	c	—	c	c
Maynard	—	—	cp	—	—	c	p	p	c	c	c	c
Middleton	—	—	cp	—	—	—	—	—	—	—	c	—
Monson	—	p	—	—	p	—	p	p	p	p	p	p
Montagu	p	—	p	—	—	p	p	—	p	p	p	p
Mountjoy (Windsor)	—	—	cp	—	—	c	—	—	c	c	c	c
Newcastle	p	p	p	—	—	p	—	p	p	p	p	p
Northampton	—	c	c	—	—	c	—	—	c	c	c	c
Onslow	p	—	—	a/cd	p	p	p	p	p	p	p	p
Oxford	—	—	c	—	—	c	—	—	c	c	c	c
Pembroke			p	—	—	p	p	p	p	p	p	p
Percy (Hertford)	p	—	—	a/cd	p	p	p	—	p	p	—	—
Peterborough	p	—	—	—	—	p	—	—	p	pp	—	—
Pomfret	p	c	c	cd	c	p	p	p	p	p	p	p
Portland	—	—	—	—	—	d	p	—	p	p	p	p
Poulett	—	—	—	—	—	d	—	—	d	a	—	—

Name	1733					1734					1735	
	1	2	3	4	5	6	7	8	9	10	11	12
Radnor	p	–	–	–	–	d	p	–	–	–	–	–
Richmond	p	–	pp	–	–	p	p	p	p	p	p	p
Rochford	p	–	cp	cd	cp	p	p	p	p	p	p	p
Romney						d	p	–	d	ab	–	–
Rutland	p	p	pp	–	–	p	p	–	p	p	–	–
St Albans	pa	c	c	cd	p	p	p	–	p	pp	–	–
St John	p	–	cp	cd	cp	d	p	–	d	pp	–	–
St John of Bletso	–	–	cp	–	–	c	–	–	c	cp	c	c
Say and Sele	p	–	–	a/cd	p	p	p	–	p	p	c	p
Scarbrough	p	c	c	cd	c	p	p	p	p	p	p	p
Scarsdale	–	–	cp	–	–	c	–	–	c	c	c	c
Shaftesbury	–	c	c	–	–	c	–	–	c	a	c	c
Somerset	–	–	–	–	–	c	–	–	c	a	c	c
Stamford	–	–	–	–	–	d?	–	–	–	–	–	–
Stawell	–	–	cp	–	–	c	–	–	c	a	–	–
Strafford	–	c	c	–	–	c	–	–	c	c	c	c
Suffolk, 9E	–	–	cp									
Suffolk, 10E						c	d	–	c	c	c	c
Sunderland, see Marlborough												
Tadcaster (Thomond)	–	c	c	–	–	c	–	–	c	c	c	c
Talbot						p	p	p	p	p	p	p
Tankerville	p	–	p	–	–	p	p	–	p	p	–	p
Thanet	–	c	c	–	–	c	–	–	c	c	c	c
Torrington	–	p	p	–	–	p	p	p	p	p	p	p
Townshend	–	–	cp	cd	cp	p	–	–	–	pp	–	
Trevor	–	–	cp	–	–	c	–	–	c	cp	–	–
Uxbridge	–	–	cp	cd	cp	c	–	–	c	a	–	–
Waldegrave	–	–	–	–	–	d?	–	–	–	–	–	–
Wales, prince of	–	–	–	–	–	–	–	–	–	–	p	p
Walpole	pa	p	p	–	–	p	p	–	p	p	p	p
Warrington	pa	c	cp	–	–	c	–	–	c	c	c	c
Warwick	pa	–	p	–	–	p	p	p	p	p	p	p
Westmorland	pa	–	cp	cd	cp	p	p	–	p	c	c	c
Weymouth	–	–	pp	–	–	c	d	–	c	c	c	c
Willoughby de Brooke	–	–	pp	–	–	p	p	p	p	c	p	–
Willoughby of Parham						p	–	–	p	p	p	p
Wilmington	p	p	–	–	–	p	p	p	p	p	–	–
Winchilsea	–	–	c			c	–	–	c	c	c	c
Scottish Representative Peers												
Atholl						p	p	p	p	p	p	p
Buchan	p	c	c	cd	c	c	p	p	c	c		
Crawford	pa	p	p	–	–	p	p	p	p	p		
Dunmore	p	p	p	–	–	p	p	p	p	a	p	p
Haddington	–	–	cp	cd	cp	d	–	–	d	pp		

| Name | 1733 | | | | | 1734 | | | | | 1735 | |
	1	2	3	4	5	6	7	8	9	10	11	12
Hopetoun	pa	–	–	–	–	d	p	–	d	a		
Ilay	p	p	p	–	–	p	p	p	p	p	p	p
Lothian	p	–	pp	–	–	p	p	p	p	p	p	p
Marchmont	p	c	c	cd	c	c	–	–	c	c		
Montrose	p	c	c	cd	c	c	–	–	c	c		
Morton	p	p	p	–	–	p	p	p	p	p	p	p
Orkney	p	–	p	–	–	p	p	p	p	p	p	p
Rothes	p	c	c	cd	c	d	p	–	d	p		
Selkirk	p	p	p	–	–	p	p	p	p	p	p	p
Stair	pa	c	c	–	–	c	–	–	c	c		
Sutherland 16E	pa?	–	–	a/cd	p							
Sutherland 17E											p	p
Tweeddale	–	c	c	–	–	c	–	–	c	c		
Bishops												
Blackburn (York)	p	–	pp	–	–	–	p	–	p	pp	–	–
Butts (Norwich)		p	–	–		–	p	p	p	p	p	p
Cecil (Bristol, Bangor)	p	–	–	–	p	–	p	p	p	p	p	p
Chandler (Durham)	p	–	p	–	–	–	p	p	p	p	p	p
Claggett (St David's)	p	–	p	–	–	–	p	p	p	p	p	p
Clavering (Peterborough)	p	–	pp	–	–	–	p	–	p	pp	p	p
Egerton (Hereford)	pa	–	pp	–	–	–	p	–	p	pp		
Gibson (London)	p	p	p	–	–	–	p	–	p	p	p	p
Greene (Ely)	p	–	p	–	–	–	p	–	p	p	p	p
Hare (Chichester)	pa?	–	p	–	–	–	p	–	p	p	p	p
Harris (Llandaff)	p	–	p	–	–	–	paq	p	p	p	p	p
Hoadly (Salisbury, Winchester)	p	–	p	–	–	–	p	–	p	p	p	p
Hough (Worcester)	pa	–	–	–	–	–	–	–	–	–		
Peploe (Chester)	pa	–	pp	–	–	–	p	–	p	p	p	p
Potter (Oxford)	–	p	–	–	–	–	p	–	p	p	p	p
Reynolds (Lincoln)	pa	c	c	cd	c	–	p	–	c	c		
Sherlock (Bangor, Salisbury)	p	–	p	–	–	–	p	p	p	p	p	p
Smalbroke (Coventry)	–	p	–	–	–	–	p	–	p	p	p	p
Sydall (Gloucester)	pa	–	pp									
Tanner (St Asaph)	p	–	p	–	–	–	p	–	p	p	p	p
Wake (Canterbury)	p	–	–	–	–	–	p	–	p	–		
Waugh (Carlisle)	p	–	pp	–	–	–	p	–	p	p	p	p
Weston (Exeter)	p	–	p	–	–	–	pa?	–	p	pp		
Wilcocks (Rochester)	p	–	p	–	–	–	p	p	p	p	p	p
Willis (Winchester)	p	–	p	–	–	–	p	–	p	p		
Wynne (Bath and Wells)	pa	–	p	–	–	–	pa?	–	p	pp		

APPENDIX 2: *Those Members of the Lords who Defected from the Ministry to the Opposition in 1733, 1734 and 1735*

1. Those who defected only in 1733	2. Those who defected in 1733 & 1734	3. Those who defected in 1733, 1734 & 1735	4. Those who defected in 1733 & 1735	5. Those who defected in 1734 & 1735	6. Those who defected only in 1735
Peers					
Ancaster	Clinton	Bolton	Clarendon	Weymouth	King
Cornwallis	Gainsborough	Bridgwater			Say and Sele
Greenwich (Argyll)	Griffin	Burlington			
Harborough		Chesterfield			
Hunsdon		Cobham			
Kent		Denbigh			
Manchester		Falmouth			
Pomfret		Fitzwalter[135]			
Rochford		Haversham			
St Albans		St John			
Scarbrough		Westmorland			
Townshend					
Scottish Representative Peers[136]					
	Buchan				
Haddington					
	Marchmont				
	Montrose				
Rothes					
	Stair				
Bishops[137]					
	Reynolds of Lincoln				

[135] Lord Egmont in his diary, records on 20 Feb. 1735 that: 'Lord Fitzwalter voted for the first time with the minority' (HMC, *Egmont Diary*, ii, 152). As this was the first division on the Scottish peers' petition over their 1734 repesentative peerage election, it must mean that this was Fitzwalter's first vote against the ministry. But this is untrue, as he had voted against the ministry over the 1731 Woollen Bill (HMC, *Egmont Diary*, i, 189), and he had also voted against the ministry three times during the South Sea enquiry in 1733 (*Cobbett's Parl. Hist.*, ix, 106, 115–6; Cambridge UL, Cholmondeley (Houghton) MSS, Correspondence 1990: Newcastle to [Walpole], 2 June 1733; RA, SP, Box 1/112). For the rest of Walpole's ministry (apart from his votes in 1735 over the Scottish peers' petition) he appears to have supported the ministry in divisions.

[136] All these Scottish representative peers were removed from the official 'king's list' of preferred candidates at the 1734 election of representative peers, and thus lost their seats in the Lords.

[137] Unlike the Scots, bishops could not be removed from their seats in the Lords, unless found guilty of a crime, such as Thomas Watson who was removed from St David's in 1699, having been suspended since 1694. The diocese remained vacant until 1705. The only sanction a ministry had was to block any preferment or promotion in the hierarchy. Reynolds was still bishop of Lincoln when he died in 1744.

Notes:

a) The peers in italics held office and/or had a pension at the time of their first desertion (or had recently held office, i.e., Chesterfield, Clinton and Stair, who had been dismissed on 13 and 30 Apr. 1733).

b) These lists give a total of 34 lords who deserted the ministry in 1733–4, 33 of whom were deserters in 1733. Peter C. Walters in his thesis ('Politics in the House of Lords in 1733', University of Leicester MPhil, 1976, pp. 144–51) reaches a figure of 31 for 1733. He does not include in his list the following: Bridgwater (whom he classifies as whig opposition), Gainsborough (tory opposition), Griffin (unclassified), and Bishop Reynolds of Lincoln (opposition). The record of these lords, as displayed in the 17 known parliamentary lists between 1721 and 1732, shows that they all voted consistently or frequently with the ministry, or were regarded as government supporters. Walters, in his list, includes one peer whom I have not: Macclesfield. His record in 1733 and 1734, given in Appendix 1, shows him to be largely con or doubtful, but as he did not succeed to the title until April 1732, he does not register in the lists until 1733, while his record as an MP 1722–7 was anti-Walpole, therefore he cannot be classified as a deserter.

c) The 'deserters' in 1735 come from the three division lists for 20, 21 and 28 Feb. 1735 (NRS, Marchmont Papers, GD 158/1242/183, 212), see Appendix 1.

APPENDIX 3: *Analysis of, and Sources for, the Divisions on 24 May and 1 June 1733 Showing Deserters from the Ministry*

There have been three previous attempts to analyse how the ministry turned round its disastrous position on 24 May 1733, and one has involved an attempt at a detailed reconstruction of the 1 June division for which no complete contemporary list is known to exist. All three attempts are in error in some way or another: first, because fewer lists than now exist were then known about; second, because the lists (for which see below) only give us the names of 33 lords whom it is claimed voted in person or by proxy, or were absent, out of a total of 102 lords who voted in person and 43 by proxy; and third, because some of the evidence we have may contain errors. J. Enoch Powell, in an article on proxy voting,[138] tried to narrow down the possibilities of those who voted by basing his analysis on the list of names sent to Lord Carlisle by Sir Thomas Robinson, MP for Morpeth (column 3 below). Peter Walters, in his thesis, claimed that Powell's analysis was flawed because Robinson's account was faulty.[139] Walters then went on to try and demonstrate where Robinson was at fault and then tried to reconstruct the division using the duke of Newcastle's letter to Walpole (column 5 below). Newcastle does, indeed, supply much more evidence for lords not mentioned by Robinson, but by comparing columns 3 and 5 below, it can be seen that the duke confirms in every particular what Robinson claimed about the eight peers in *his* list, plus, by implication, Bishop Reynolds of Lincoln.

Even with this new evidence provided by Newcastle, Walters's reconstructed opposition list for the division is still not final, as he has one too many lords voting in

---

[138] J. Enoch Powell, 'Proxy Voting in the House of Lords', *Parliamentary Affairs*, ix (1955–6), 203–14.
[139] Walters, 'House of Lords in 1733', 165–9.

person for the opposition. The answer to this problem may lie in the list provided by Andrew Cockburn (column 4 below), which neither Walters nor Powell used. This is a list of the division of 24 May, with six of the peers who then voted with the opposition marked with a 'D', meaning those who 'deserted' back (i.e., returned) to the ministry on 1 June. Five of these six also appear in the Robinson and Newcastle lists; Lord Clinton does not. It is possible that Clinton did support the ministry on 1 June, but several questions arise from this piece of evidence. First, Clinton is not recorded as so voting by Robinson and Newcastle, two eyewitnesses (which Cockburn was not), Newcastle being a careful chronicler of divisions (though, being human, also prone to mistakes), and both he and Robinson being particularly interested in the deserters of 24 May and their voting on 1 June. Second, Clinton was one of the three officeholders in the Lords to be dismissed in April and the other two who were sacked did not support the ministry; indeed, they remained constant opponents of Walpole for the rest of the prime minister's administration. Third, if one examines the parliamentary lists that have survived from 1733 to the fall of Walpole in 1742,[140] Clinton's own stance remained staunchly anti-Walpole except for this one possible vote. However, he may have supported the government because of the very nature of the question, or he may have given Walpole the benefit of the doubt, but if he did, the further purges which shortly followed the vote of 1 June probably drove him into permanent opposition.

Even if we allow that Clinton did vote with the ministry, this does not give us a final opposition list. Though Walters's figures are now correct, two other problems remain. Another piece of evidence, also not used by Walters or Powell, a letter of Andrew Cockburn, claims that: 'the Lord Sunderland was taken ill in the house and was obliged to reteer [retire] for self and proxy [of Lord Trevor] that he had'.[141] If this information is correct, then Walters's opposition list is now short by two votes. Cockburn's information was probably second hand, but a study of his many parliamentary letters in the Stuart Papers shows him to have been a well-informed reporter. However, in this same letter he also states that in the 1 June vote: 'the Duke of Argyll for himself and proxy went out'. While both Robinson and Newcastle agree that Argyll was either absent or left the House, the proxy book shows no record of Argyll holding a proxy in the 1733 session.[142] Finally, though Walters does not include Masham on his opposition list and, indeed, Masham is not recorded as attending on 1 June, Newcastle claimed that Uxbridge voted against the government by proxy and, according to the proxy book, Masham had held Uxbridge's proxy since 23 May.

Walters's reconstructed ministerial list also poses a problem in that he has two lords too many. He himself speculates that two on his list (one holding a proxy) left before the vote. Cornwallis, whom he lists as present and voting (as do all three lists below), is not recorded in the *Lords Journals* as attending. It is unlikely, however, that Newcastle, in the House at the time, would have made a mistake and recorded Cornwallis as voting if he had not.

---

[140] See Appendix 1 for those for 1734 and 1735.

[141] RA, SP, 162/23: Cockburn to Edgar, 4 June 1733.

[142] Recent work on proxy records in the later 17th century has shown that the proxy books are not always totally accurate.

Even with the evidence we now have available, it is still not possible to reconstruct an accurate division list for 1 June. There is too much inconsistency in the evidence and, even allowing for the fact that the attendance record compiled by the clerks of the House could sometimes be wrong,[143] we are still left with totals on both sides which do not match the voting figures.

The third historian to tackle the problem of the 1 June division was J.H. Plumb, in the second volume of his unfinished biography of Walpole. Plumb comes at the problem from a slightly different angle, concentrating first on the 24 May deserters whom Walpole and Newcastle successfully wooed back to vote for the ministry and, second, on the absent peers who were encouraged to attend or send proxies.[144] Plumb's account, based largely on Newcastle's letter, is correct (so far as one can tell) in stating that Argyll abstained; that Sutherland, Percy and Onslow attended and voted for the ministry having failed to do so on 24 May; that St Albans, Manchester, Harborough, Falmouth and Cornwallis returned to the ministerial fold; and that Ancaster and Clarendon voted against the government for the first time. However, Plumb is mistaken in stating that Say and Sele was persuaded to attend; Say and Sele is not recorded as present in the *Lords Journals* and his proxy had been registered with Lonsdale on 28 May. Clearly, in this case, Newcastle (Plumb's only source) made a minor mistake and failed to mark Say and Sele in his list of those 'For us' as voting by proxy.

Because we have a canvassing list used by the ministry between 24 May and 1 June (column 2 below), by concentrating on the 'deserters' who returned to the government, and on those who were absent on 24 May and who attended or sent proxies for 1 June, we can test how successful the government was in its management of the Lords in this crisis. The canvassing list contains the names of 33 lords, five marked as absent from the 24 May vote, and 28 as voting for the ministry. Of these 28, all but two (Macclesfield and Uxbridge) were 'deserters' who had first voted against the government on 24 May. Of the 33 names, 21 are ticked.[145] Plumb speculates that the ticks may mean those whom Walpole had been able to see himself, or those whom he hoped he had won over. The former suggestion cannot be wholly true as some, for example Haddington, Hunsdon, Rochford, Say and Sele and Westmorland, had been absent, some having registered proxies, for a large part, if not all, of the session. However, Walpole could have contacted those he did not see, by letter, This is the more likely explanation, for if he believed that he had won over those ticked, 'it betrays', in Plumb's words, 'a wild optimism'.[146] For, of the 21 ticked, only nine voted for the ministry, while one abstained and 11 voted against (a canvassing success rate for Walpole of 47.6%). Of the 33 on the full canvassing list, five lords changed their votes in favour of the ministry, one abstained, and four who were absent appeared or supplied a proxy (a total of ten who helped Walpole's position), while 22 did not change their anti-ministerial vote and one did not appear or supply a proxy (a success rate of 30.3%). We have no other comparable evidence with which to judge whether this particular canvass was any more

---

[143] See Clyve Jones, 'Seating Problems in the House of Lords in the Early Eighteenth Century: The Evidence of the Manuscript Minutes', *Bulletin of the Institute of Historical Research*, li (1978), 132–45.

[144] Plumb, *Walpole*, ii, 276–8. He misdates the debate and vote as 2 June.

[145] Plumb's printed version of this list has only 17 peers ticked: *Walpole*, ii, 277 n. 2.

[146] Plumb, *Walpole*, ii, 277 n. 2.

successful than others conducted by Walpole and Newcastle.[147] Thirteen of the peers who deserted only in 1733 are on this canvassing list. Perhaps without the pressure applied by Walpole, some may not have returned to the ministry so quickly and so permanently. However, there are also 13 lords who defected for the 1733 and the 1734 sessions (and in some cases permanently) who were on this list and who Walpole failed to persuade back to their former loyalties. However, as far as Walpole was concerned, he had achieved his immediate aim, and he won the 1 June division by five votes.

The Lists:

1. An incomplete list compiled by Sir Thomas Robinson (MP Morpeth) of those who voted against the court on 24 May (HMC, *Carlisle MSS*, 118: to [earl of Carlisle], 26 May).
   ab = on the list; recorded as present but not voting (abstaining).
   c = on the list and voted against the ministry.
   cpr = voted against the ministry by proxy.

2. List of lords 'against' and 'absent'; probably a canvassing list used by Walpole and Newcastle between 24 May and 1 June (Cambridge UL, Cholmondeley (Houghton) MSS, P 66/5; printed in Plumb, *Sir Robert Walpole*, ii, 277 n. 2).
   a = marked as absent.
   (a) = marked as absent and ticked.
   c = marked as against.
   (c) = marked as against and ticked.

3. Sir Thomas Robinson's list of those who voted with the court or abstained on 1 June, having deserted on 24 May (HMC, *Carlisle MSS*, 120: to [Carlisle], 2 June).
   ab = abstained.
   p = voted for the ministry having deserted on 24 May.

4. List of those who voted with the court on 1 June and had deserted on 24 May (RA, SP, Box 1/112).
   p = on the list.

5. An incomplete list of those voting for and against the ministry on 1 June sent by Newcastle to Walpole (Cambridge UL, Cholmondeley (Houghton) MSS, Correspondence 1990: Newcastle to [Walpole], 2 June 1733).
   ab = absent.
   c = against.
   cpr = against by proxy.
   p = for.

---

[147] The only other known Lords' lists for Walpole's premiership which may be associated with ministerial canvassing are two possible whipping lists for the Pension Bill in 1732 (see *British Parliamentary Lists*, ed. Ditchfield, Hayton and Jones, 48, lists 148–9). However, apart from the fact that these two lists cannot be identified with certainty (unlike Newcastle's 1733 lists), the political situation in 1733 was so radically different from that of 1732 that any comparison is fairly meaningless. There is one other personal lobbying or whipping list, compiled for the earl of Strafford in 1727 for use in a legal case: Jones, 'New Parliamentary Lists', 404, list 135A.

Name	24 May / 1 June				
	1	2	3	4	5
Peers					
Ancaster	—		—	—	c
Berkeley	c[148]		—	—	—
Bolton	c	c	—	—	c
Burlington	cpr[149]	c	—	—	—
Chesterfield	c		—	—	—
Clarendon			—	—	c
Clinton	—		—	p	—
Cobham	—	c	—	—	c
Cornwallis	c	(c)	p[150]	p	p
Denbigh	—	(c)	—	—	c
Falmouth	c	c	p	p	p
Fitzwalter	c	c	—	—	c
Greenwich (Argyll)	c	(c)	ab[151]	—	ab
Guilford	—	(a)	—	—	—
Harborough	(c)[152]	(c)	p	p	p
Haversham	—	(c)	—	—	cpr[153]
Hunsdon	—	(c)	—	—	cpr[154]
Kent	c	c	—	—	c
Macclesfield	c	(c)	—	—	c
Manchester	c	(c)	p	p	p
Onslow	ab[155]	(a)	p	—	p
Percy (Hertford)	—	(a)	—	—	p
Pomfret	c	(c)	—	—	c
Rochford	—	(c)	—	—	cpr[156]
St Albans	c	(c)	p	p	p

[148] The earl of Berkeley was not recorded as present on 24 May: *LJ*, xxiv, 277–8. Strafford, who was present and voted, had held his proxy since 6 February: PA, HL/PO/JO/13/8.

[149] Proxy held by Stair since 23 May. Stair was present and voted on the 24th.

[150] Not recorded as attending on 1 June: *LJ*, xxiv, 291.

[151] Robinson recorded in his letter of 2 June that: '[t]he Duke of Argile went away half an hour before the Division' (HMC, *Carlisle MMS*, 120); while, according to Newcastle, he was 'absent' at the vote (Cambridge UL, Cholmondeley (Houghton) MSS, Correspondence 1990). Andrew Cockburn recorded that: 'the D[uke] of Argyll for himself and his proxy went out (RA, SP, 162/23: to Edgar, 4 June 1733), but there is no record of a proxy being registered with Argyll in the 1733 session. The duke is reported as having left London on 2 June, leaving his proxy with Ilay (NLS, MS 16553, f. 135: Richard Graham to [Milton], 7 June 1733); the registering of Argyll's proxy is confirmed by the proxy book, PA HL/PO/JO/13/8.

[152] Harborough was not included by Robinson in his 24 May list (HMC, *Carlisle MSS*, 118), but his 1 June list implies that Harborough did vote against the court on 24 May (HMC, *Carlisle MSS*, 120).

[153] A proxy had been registered with Westmorland between 26 February and 12 March, but none had been registered later, since Haversham is recorded as attending.

[154] Held by Kent since 1 May. Kent was present and voted.

[155] Robinson claimed that Onslow had spoken for the opposition in the debate on 24 May, but had not voted, and this he confirmed in his 2 June letter (HMC, *Carlisle MSS*, 118, 120). However, Onslow is not recorded as attending and he is described as absent in column 2.

[156] Proxy held by Kent since 30 April. Rochford is not recorded as attending on 24 May.

Name	24 May / 1 June				
	1	2	3	4	5
St John	–	c	–	–	cpr[157]
Say and Sele	–	(a)	–	–	p[158]
Scarbrough	c	(c)	–	–	c
Somerset	c		–	–	–
Strafford	c		–	–	–
Townshend	cpr[159]	c	–	–	cpr
Uxbridge	–	c	–	–	cpr[160]
Westmorland	–	(c)	–	–	cpr[161]
Scottish Representative Peers					
Buchan	–	(c)	–	–	c
Haddington	cpr[162]	(c)	–	–	cpr
Marchmont	c	c	–	–	c
Montrose	c	c	–	–	c
Rothes	c	(c)	–	–	c
Stair	c		–	–	–
Sutherland, 16E	ab[163]	(a)	p	–	p
Tweeddale	c		–	–	–
Bishops					
Reynolds of Lincoln	c	c	–	–	c

[157] Proxy held by Scarbrough since 22 May. Scarbrough was present and voted.

[158] Not recorded as attending. Say and Sele's proxy was registered with Lonsdale on 28 May. Lonsdale was present and voted.

[159] Proxy held by Scarbrough since 13 Dec. 1732.

[160] Proxy registered with Masham on 23 May. Masham was present and voted on 24 May but is not recorded as attending on 1 June.

[161] Proxy held by Haversham since 11 April. Haversham was recorded as present on both 24 May and 1 June.

[162] Proxy held by Rothes since 20 January. Rothes was present and voted on 24 May and was present on 1 June.

[163] He was officially recorded as present, but Robinson lists him as present but not voting (HMC, *Carlisle MSS*, 118). His absence is confirmed in column 2.

The Attack of the Creolian Powers:
West Indians at the Parliamentary Elections of
Mid-Georgian Britain, 1754–74★

This article seeks to build upon recent work on the impact of empire in mid-18th-century Britain by study of the electoral experience of parliamentary candidates who had lived in the West Indies and could boast a direct familiarity with the Caribbean. By 1750, a significant number of rich planters had relocated to Britain, and, in common with the Indian nabobs, their efforts to enter parliament aroused much adverse commentary at the elections of 1754–74. While these attacks were damaging to their interest, and occasioned the most thorough review of Caribbean society to date, the West Indians were able to respond by adapting their political campaigns to assuage metropolitan sensibilities, thereby ensuring that they were not bracketed with the nabobs or rebellious North Americans as imperial sources of domestic upheaval. Their success highlights the possibilities for successful imperial integration in mid-Georgian Britain, although the West Indians could not rely on the same strategies to combat the abolitionist movement after 1787.

Keywords: parliamentary elections; West Indies; absentees; empire; William Beckford; London; Bristol; Liverpool

1

This article seeks to pay tribute to David Hayton's enormous contribution to the field of parliamentary history by examining the interplay of Britain and its empire through the electoral politics of mid-Georgian Britain. There has been great historiographical interest in the impact of the 18th-century empire, especially in the field of politics, led by scholars such as David Armitage and Kathleen Wilson, who have outlined significant ideological exchanges between the mother country and its dependencies. With particular regard to elections, scholars have shown great interest in the Indian nabobs, the 'execrable banditti', whose borough mongering incurred increasing domestic censure, most obviously in the 1784 contest. This article looks to build on this work by studying the electoral experience of parliamentary candidates who had lived in the West Indies and could boast a direct familiarity with the Caribbean. Important research has been completed on the wider West India interest, led by the formidable Namier, and we now have a much better sense of their impact at Westminster across the long 18th century, thanks to the scholarship of Nuala Zahedieh, Andrew O'Shaughnessy, and

★ I would like to thank Yale University Press for permission to use material from my book, *William Beckford: First Prime Minister of the London Empire* (New Haven, 2013).

Christopher Brown.[1] Surprisingly little has been written on the experiences of the West Indians at the electoral hustings, however, or on the challenges they faced when establishing a parliamentary interest. Their strategies not only reveal much about the colonists' views of Britain and its responses to empire, but also about the domestic political world.[2]

The time period chosen here will enable a review of West Indian electoral experiences during the first crisis of the empire, ahead of the full-scale abolitionist campaign. Although West Indian planters had begun to sit in the House in the later 17th century, it was not until the 1750s that metropolitan observers began to take notice of their parliamentary presence, as a significant increase in absentees aroused broader social commentary.[3] By the 1760s, the attacks on West Indians increased in both number and vigour, and their electoral pretensions received opprobrium similar to that encountered by the East Indian nabobs. As Lawson and Phillips observed, at the 1761 general election, the 'West Indians' were first in the list of contemptible species castigated by Horace Walpole for contesting constituencies across the nation.[4] However, while the West Indians suffered from comparison with the East Indians and other corruptors of the parliamentary system, this article will argue that the nature and incidence of these attacks was very much conditioned by their particular strategies, and by the audiences they wished to target. Censure of Caribbean influences was also specific to the perceived deficiencies of West Indian society. Although these attacks were damaging, their specificity enabled the absentee planters to respond to their critics by careful political management. Thus, although it is tempting to see these critiques as generic, as the fruits of a political generation adapting to significant domestic and imperial change, closer inspection suggests a more disciplined and informed dialogue. Namier and Brooke

---

[1] D. Armitage, *The Ideological Origins of the British Empire* (Cambridge, 2000); K. Wilson, *The Sense of the People* (Cambridge, 1995); P. Lawson and J. Phillips, ' "Our Execrable Banditti": Perceptions of Nabobs in Mid-Eighteenth Century Britain', *Albion*, xvi (1984), 225–41; C. McCreery, 'Satiric Images of Fox, Pitt and George III: The East India Bill Crisis, 1783–4', *Word and Image*, ix (1993), 163–85. See also T. Nechtman, *Nabobs: Empire and Identity in Eighteenth-Century Britain* (Cambridge, 2010). For the earliest accounts of the impact of the West Indians in domestic politics, see L. Namier, *England in the Age of the American Revolution* (1930), 234–41; L. Penson, 'The London West India Interest in the Eighteenth Century', *English Historical Review*, xxx (1921), 373–92; L. Penson, *The Colonial Agents of the British West Indies* (1924).

[2] A.J. O'Shaughnessy, 'The Formation of a Commercial Lobby: The West India Interest, British Colonial Policy and the American Revolution', *Historical Journal*, xl (1997), 71–95; C. Brown, 'The Politics of Slavery', in *The British Atlantic World, 1500–1800*, ed. D. Armitage and M. Braddick (Basingstoke, 2002), 214–32; B. Higman, 'The West India Interest in Parliament, 1807–1833', *Historical Studies*, xiii (1967), 1–19; N. Zahedieh, *The Capital and the Colonies* (Cambridge, 2010), 113–27. Much of the pre-1787 work on the politics of the West Indians has focused on activity at Westminster, reserving wider political studies for the abolitionist era. However, as C.L. Brown has argued, more stable political times can be just as revealing as the stormier periods: C.L. Brown, 'The British Government and the Slave Trade: Early Parliamentary Enquiries, 1713–83', in *The British Slave Trade: Abolition, Parliament and the People*, ed. S. Farrell, M. Unwin and J. Walvin (Edinburgh, 2007), 27–41.

[3] For a list of Augustan MPs with transatlantic interests, see David Hayton's definitive introduction in *The History of Parliament: The House of Commons 1690–1715*, ed. E. Cruickshanks, S. Handley and D.W. Hayton (5 vols, Cambridge, 2002), i, 734–5. Significantly, in the History of Parliament series, the first separate commentary on members with colonial backgrounds comes with the 1754–90 volumes.

[4] Lawson and Phillips, ' "Our Execrable Banditti" ', 225. The other miscreants identified by Walpole as dangerous electoral forces were 'conquerors, nabobs and admirals': *The Yale Edition of Horace Walpole's Correspondence*, ed. W.S. Lewis (48 vols, 1937–83), xxi, 484.

established long ago that the West Indians took greater care than the nabobs to avoid provocative campaigns in venal boroughs, and a wider review of their electoral experience provides further evidence of their sensitive reading of metropolitan politics, helping to explain why they were largely spared the public vilification which greeted the East Indians during the elections of the American war. In common with other studies of absentee politics, this perspective highlights the resourcefulness of the West Indians in adapting to the British political climate, both in terms of ideology and practical political strategies. Furthermore, it also suggests that, for all of the rancour the empire inspired, the metropolitan political world could accommodate novel imperial influences.[5]

The article will analyse responses to the West Indians at the four general elections of the 1754–74 period. Significantly, the most striking domestic responses were sparked by the candidacy of West Indians who had lived in the Caribbean for some time, and this concentration on 'real' West Indians focuses attention on the most direct exchanges – whether real or imagined – between Britain and the Caribbean.[6] Scholars have rightly highlighted the broader impact of the West India interest, which stretched well beyond the absentee planters, but critiques of Caribbean influence at the polls were largely reserved for more genuinely transatlantic figures. Pre-eminent among them was William Beckford (1709–70), whose politicking after his return to Britain in 1745 played a key role in promoting Anglo-Caribbean exchanges. The 1754 election saw the West Indians' presence in the Commons nearly double, and this success sparked opposition in larger constituencies with links to the Caribbean. These public attacks are suggestive of the growing metropolitan significance of the empire, but it is important to note that attacks on the West Indians at both this and the 1761 election can be directly linked to sectional politics, for at their heart lay longer-term criticism over monopolies and the favouritism shown to the sugar planters. The 1768 election, coming in the wake of the Stamp Act and other imperial controversies, saw a much greater congruence between domestic and colonial politics, and ideological concerns featured much more strongly amid the most thorough review of Caribbean society and culture to date. At this stage, the West Indians were just as vilified as the East Indian nabobs, and it was only the conscious efforts of the absentees to temper their political strategies which ensured that they were not bracketed with the nabobs or the rebellious North Americans.[7] This success brought them only a brief respite, before the all-out attacks launched by the abolitionist campaigns after 1787, but their adaptation to mid-century electoral politics

---

[5] *The History of Parliament: The House of Commons 1754–90*, ed. Sir Lewis Namier and John Brooke (3 vols, 1964) [hereafter cited as *HPC, 1754–90*], i, 156–62. This survey also pointed out that the West Indians lacked coherence as a political interest (especially when compared with the East India Company), and this may have helped to temper their public impact. Due to differences between the islands, they formed a much more heterogeneous body, whose collectiveness was often promoted by family ties rather than by common interest.

[6] In their assessment of West Indian influences, the History of Parliament volumes helpfully concentrate on members who had been born, or spent a significant period of time, in the Caribbean. This is not to ignore the impact of members with West Indian interests, whose numbers may have been as high as 40 to 50 MPs at any one time: O'Shaughnessy, 'The West India Interest', esp. 72–4.

[7] For the best overview of the electoral success of candidates with direct familiarity with the West Indies, see *HPC, 1754–90*, i, 156–62. The sensitivity of West Indian families to such attacks has been highlighted by Paul Langford, who quoted John Pinney's resolve in 1778 to 'avoid even the name of a West-Indian': Paul Langford, *Public Life and the Propertied Englishman, 1689–1798* (Oxford, 1991), 294–5.

illuminates the possibilities for successful imperial integration during the first great crisis of empire.[8]

2

Until the 1740s, there were few MPs who could boast a direct familiarity with the West Indian colonies. The West Indian interest developed into a formidable political lobby by the reign of George II, taking advantage of every metropolitan channel at its disposal. Whether linked to the Caribbean by commercial interest, landed stake, or political office, British-based politicians were marshalled to advance West Indian views, most obviously in the promotion of the dominant sugar industry. In more spectacular terms, the campaign for the Spanish war in 1739, and the lionisation of Admiral Edward Vernon at the general election of 1741, bore testimony to the political reach of the Caribbean. None the less, there was still only one MP returned in 1741 who had lived in the West Indies for any significant period.[9] At the 1747 election, however, their number rose to six (with another returned soon afterwards at a by-election), reflecting the growing metropolitan imprint of the absentee planter. The economic success of the sugar industry was critical to this development, enabling politically-ambitious planters to contemplate a seat in the House as a more achievable goal. The rise of the super-planter, especially in Jamaica, saw many of the most prosperous West Indians return to Great Britain in steady numbers from the 1730s, and by the third quarter of the century there may have been as many as 150 absentee Jamaican proprietors alone, many with London homes. Although successful at the polls, they elicited little political comment, largely because they were unexceptional in their electioneering, either working with established local patrons, or buying estates near their constituency. It was not until the 1754 election, when their number doubled, that a metropolitan audience began to take notice.[10]

A critical differential in 1754 was the leadership supplied by William Beckford, who, in the wake of his establishment of a Wiltshire country seat in 1745, became the

[8] As Lawson and Phillips argued, beyond questions of 'actual power', there are 'valuable lessons' to be learnt from study of contemporary fears about new political influences: Lawson and Philips, ' "Our Execrable Banditti" ', 226. For the great public campaigns against the slave trade after 1787, see R. Anstey, *The Atlantic Slave Trade and British Abolition, 1760–1810* (1975); J.R. Oldfield, *Popular Politics and British Anti-Slavery: The Mobilisation of Public Opinion against the Slave Trade, 1787–1807* (Manchester, 1995).

[9] Penson, 'The London West India Interest', 377–81; Brown, 'Politics of Slavery', 225–7; P. Gauci, 'Learning the Ropes of Sand: The West India Lobby, 1714–60', in *Regulating the British Economy, 1660–1850*, ed. Perry Gauci (Farnham, 2011), 107–21; Wilson, *The Sense of the People*, ch. 3. In 1741, Thomas Foster, a Jamaican plantation owner, was brought in by the prince of Wales's interest at the Cornish borough of Bossiney. For a list of MPs with significant West Indian connections in the 1715–54 period, see *The History of Parliament: The House of Commons, 1715–1754*, ed. Romney Sedgwick (2 vols, 1970) [hereafter cited as *HPC, 1715–54*], i, 153. Twenty-seven MPs are recorded there, two-thirds of whom were either born in the West Indies, or had lived there for some time.

[10] T. Burnard, 'Passengers Only: The Extent and Significance of Absenteeism in Eighteenth-Century Jamaica', *Atlantic Studies*, i (2004), 178–95. He estimates that Jamaicans may have made up about half of the total West Indian absentees. In 1747, the only West Indian to have secured success in a large constituency was Slingsby Bethel in London, and he did face significant opposition for his lack of service in the City corporation. His supporters responded by emphasizing his status as an established City merchant, and his familial link to his namesake (the whig martyr and London sheriff), but there was no censure of his colonial links: *General Advertiser*, 27, 29 June, 1, 7 July 1747. He was keen to strengthen his position during the 1747 parliament, becoming an alderman and an active promoter of several City projects.

undoubted leader of the West India interest in Britain. In the late 1730s and early 1740s, he had backed the successful political campaigns of the West India interest, but his return to Britain revealed a much greater political ambition. Henry Pelham had been warned by the Jamaican governor, Edward Trelawny, of Beckford's plans as early as 1749. Trelawny even suggested that there was 'a scheme . . . among the West Indians to make themselves formidable: as many as can are to get into the House and keep together', which might have dire consequences for the stability of metropolitan politics. No further evidence of a co-ordinated campaign among the West Indians has survived, but there can be no doubt that Beckford regarded a Caribbean presence in the Commons as key to the future of the West Indies.[11] In his eagerness to gain a seat in 1747, Beckford had made several blunders when trying to secure a parliamentary interest, unwisely leaving his associates to manage his campaign in the Cornish borough of Penryn. In the wake of this rebuff, he then turned his attention to Shaftesbury, where he sought to curry an interest from his new estate at Fonthill. Although successful, this campaign taught Beckford important lessons, and the mismanagement of his allies cost him £1,000. Beckford subsequently spared no pains in trying to cultivate a more certain political interest via a number of channels. His successful campaign to become a London alderman (by 1752) was a notable coup ahead of the 1754 election, and he also undertook the courtship of regional grandees to establish himself more securely in Wiltshire. Early electoral experiences had evidently inculcated patience in the political newcomer, and Beckford could have been in no doubt that increased public visibility could rebound on the absentees.[12]

Metropolitan debates on the Caribbean over the past decade suggested that the most likely sources of concerted opposition to the West Indians were the interest groups with a direct stake in Atlantic commerce. Since 1740, the centrality of the empire to the national interest had been confidently asserted by leading politicians, if only to expose the Hanoverian bias of government foreign policy, but these pronouncements had not garnered a widespread familiarity (or antipathy) with the colonies at electoral ground level.[13] As the most high-profile West Indian, Beckford had been singled out on several occasions in colonial debates, but the most direct attacks clearly emanated from rival sectional interests. A tract of 1753 calling for the increased production of sugar actually recalled the testimony of 'a worthy planter of Jamaica' at the bar of the House in 1739,

---

[11] National Library of Jamaica, Kingston, MS 306: Edward Trelawny to Henry Pelham, 14 Apr. 1749. His strategies within the 1747–54 parliament had demonstrated how imperial spokesmen had to adapt their appeals to a parliamentary audience. All his pronouncements suggest that he had to acknowledge domestic models of argument and interest if he wanted to gain his point, even if he was convinced that the Caribbean was sufficiently important to fix the attention of the metropolitan parliament. His readiness to align himself with oppositional leaders threatened to jeopardise these endeavours, but it is important to note that even his rivals did not think that he had undermined his colonial political interest by backing the opposition to the Pelhams.

[12] HMC, *Fortescue MSS*, 119; *HPC, 1715–54*, i, 452. 'A great blunder-headed fellow from Mr. Bickford, the West Indian' was blamed for the failure to reach an electoral settlement at Penryn in 1747.

[13] For a question mark against the direct familiarity and interest of the British in their empire, see J.M. Price, 'Who Cared about the Colonies?: The Impact of the Thirteen Colonies on British Society and Politics, c. 1714–75', in *Strangers within the Realm*, ed. B. Bailyn and P. Morgan (Chapel Hill, NC, 1991), 395–436. Although regarding the Seven Years War as an important watershed, M. Peters has also cautioned against exaggerating or pre-dating British imperial interest, identifying Britain's status as a European power as 'the end to which "empire" was a means': M. Peters, 'Early Hanoverian Consciousness: Empire or Europe?', *English Historical Review*, cxxii (2007), 632–68.

when Beckford had boasted that Jamaica alone could supply all Britain's needs if thoroughly cultivated. More combatively still, in that same year, a friend to the grocers and sugar refiners of London attacked the self-interest of the planters for under-production, and thought that their extravagant profits would encourage 'still more of them to quit their plantations for the pleasures of the capital', identifying Jamaica as especially vulnerable in this regard. This censure alluded to the changing political character of the West India interest in Britain, and hinted at the much more contro-versial figure the West Indians would make at the general election of 1754.[14]

The increased scrutiny to which the West Indians were subjected can be largely attributed to Beckford's decision to go onto the political offensive, and his readiness to contest much larger constituencies than Caribbean candidates had usually fought. In significant contrast to the six West Indians returned in 1747, who all managed to retain their seats in 1754, on the basis of solid electoral interests, Beckford was thinking much bigger, and thereby left himself and his allies much more open to attack. With some experience of British politics now behind him, and a more certain domestic political profile as an anti-Court spokesman, Beckford sought seats for family members at no less than four boroughs – London and the Hampshire borough of Petersfield for himself (with the reversion of Petersfield for brother, Francis); the nation's second port, Bristol, for brother, Richard; and the Wiltshire borough of Salisbury for brother, Julines. Although Governor Trelawny's dire warnings of a creole parliament proved illusory, William gained a seat at all four constituencies, although eventually yielding Petersfield to his ally, Sir John Phillips. He was also successful in securing the return of James Dawkins at Hindon, the parliamentary borough closest to Fonthill, thus accounting for four of the 13 West Indians returned at this election.[15] These successes represented a great personal triumph, especially the success in the capital, for the London election was always deemed a true test of any politician, widely regarded as a weathervane of popular opinion by dint of its large electorate, its proud traditions of independence, and its central importance to the national economy. On the other hand, his extensive elec-tioneering promised to give the relative newcomer the most thorough review of his political character, in which his claims, and those of the interests he represented, would be minutely scrutinised. He had worked tirelessly to secure connections in the years since his return to Britain, but his appearance at the City hustings would reveal the real political progress he had made.[16]

---

[14] *An Enquiry into the Causes of the Present High Price of Muscovada Sugars* (1753), esp. 21; *An Account of the Late Application to Parliament from the Sugar Refiners, Grocers, etc of the Cities of London and Westminster* (1753), esp. 45–6.

[15] More particularly, in 1754 Beckford gave direct support to four of the seven West Indians who had not been returned at the general election in 1747. The other three were: Charles Barrow, who had been successful at a Gloucester by-election in 1751 and was re-elected in 1754 (his interest supported by his marriage into a local family, and his attention to borough affairs); Samuel Dicker, who reportedly had government support for his return at Plymouth (although his family had Devon links); and John Gibbons, a wealthy Barbadian and the only obviously venal candidate, who was returned at Stockbridge.

[16] *HPC, 1754–90*, i, 156–7. Beckford was clearly planning a multiple assault in the summer of 1753, and continued to discuss electoral matters with the duke of Bedford from that time: *Correspondence of John, Fourth Duke of Bedford* (3 vols, 1842), ii, 128, 145–6, 150. Their connection can explain the erroneous report in the press in September 1753, that Beckford had been elected a freeman of the town of Bedford after treating the corporation to a large turtle: *London Evening Post*, 6 Sept. 1753. Beckford later sought a seat for Francis Beckford from the duke, at which time he intimated that his only non-fraternal campaign (i.e., for Dawkins) had resulted in the return of 'a good friend and patriot': *Bedford Correspondence*, ii, 145.

As with all London elections of this era, there was extensive newspaper coverage of the campaign, especially from the announcement of the candidates on Valentine's day, some ten weeks ahead of the poll. Beckford prudently and predictably styled himself as the City patriot, determined to oppose 'every measure that may affect either the religion or liberties of this kingdom in general or the rights and privileges of the City in particular'. He also aligned himself with patriots of a more established pedigree, such as Sir John Barnard. The importance of having such backing is reflected in the very first published image of him, *The City Up-and-Down*, which pictured him alongside Barnard and Slingsby Bethel, a former Antiguan plantation manager who had a much more established interest within City mercantile circles. Beckford was depicted as saying: 'it becomes a man of character to keep good company', a satire on the novelty of his candidacy, and on his relative lack of a natural power base in London. He knew that the City had always favoured candidates with long civic careers behind them, and he had to work hard to compensate for such missing credentials. He certainly worked his constituency hard, and redoubled his efforts to exploit his recently-acquired associational connections. He duly appeared as one of the stewards for the anniversary feast of the London Hospital at Merchant Taylors' Hall, and took a prominent part in debate at the Society of the Free British Fishery alongside Lord Shaftesbury. Graphic artists were actively broadcasting the benefits of the Society, especially through depictions of its current president and Beckford's running mate, Bethel, who was often shown with herring barrels. It was also no mere coincidence that a report of Beckford's mercy to a petty criminal managed to make its way into the papers.[17]

As poll day drew closer, the first major attacks appeared against him, his enemies deliberately targeting his *nouveau* status as his vulnerable flank before the livery. On 12 April, a broadside discussed the ideal character of the London MP, and concluded that long-serving officers were best suited, who by their efforts had earned themselves the repute of being 'a good citizen in London'. Later that week, Beckford acted as steward for another City feast (this time on behalf of the London Lying-In Hospital for poor married women), but the pressure on him only mounted. Attacks on his political principles were common, and he was accused of enlisting whig support for his brother's candidacy at Bristol, while acting himself as 'a nominal tory' at London. The only conclusion to be drawn from this was that he was a 'person of interested principles', whose values 'appear to be thus conveniently suited to the interest of different places', a charge to which the colonial broker was naturally susceptible.[18] Recent enemies in colonial debates also surfaced to question his patriotism, with one tract roundly censuring him as 'the Great Jamaica Planter' who had worked tirelessly in his own interest to defeat reform of the island economy. His supporters quickly hit back, declaring his speeches as a member to have shown that 'his abilities, his public spirit, his importance as a merchant well versed in the commercial strengths of England are so thoroughly known'. The emphasis on England's benefit was clearly deliberate here, for as the poll

---

[17] I. Doolittle, *City of London Politics from Shaftesbury to Wilkes: Another Viewpoint* (Haslemere, 2010), esp. 5–6; *Catalogue of the Prints and Drawings in the British Museum*, ed. F.G. Stephens and M. Dorothy George (11 vols, 1870–1954), iii, 909–10, 913, 915; all newspaper references are from the *Public Advertiser*, 14 Feb.–25 May 1754.

[18] For contemporary perceptions of Beckford's alliance with City high tories, see Bob Harris, *Politics and the Nation: Britain in the Mid-Eighteenth Century* (Oxford, 2002), 53.

began, his rivals renewed their endeavours to portray him as a self-interested outsider, going to the lengths of publishing his attendance record as alderman, an underwhelming 24% in 54 courts.[19]

Beckford had done enough, however, and came home in fourth place, clinching a seat ahead of two fellow aldermen of longer-standing. He thanked his supporters for doing him 'the greatest honour', and, while admitting that they had only known him a 'short time', he rejected fiercely 'the prejudices that have been injuriously raised against me'. Significantly, his supporters had not sought to raise his colonial character to boost his campaign in any printed works or cartoons, which suggests that neither they nor Beckford thought it a vote winner. In fact, there is evidence that Beckford had to mollify an individual who sought to expose failures to encourage white settlement on the island by publishing 'an account of the miseries, wants, insults, disappointments and deaths'. Instead, Beckford's supporters concentrated on issues which resonated strongly with the constituency, such as jewish naturalisation and the building of Blackfriars Bridge, for the electoral appeal of the empire was, as yet, unclear. Broad appeals to the defence of commerce were sufficient to appease City opinion, without drawing him into distracting battles between rival sectional interests. It is, perhaps, more surprising that only one of his rivals sought to exploit his imperial background as evidence of his non-Londoner status, especially given later attacks. His detractors probably thought it sufficient to provide evidence of 'outsider' characteristics, especially his lack of civic commitment and his provincial political interests, without developing specific critiques of colonial interference. All that would come later, when he became a leading critic of imperial policy, and the ally of Pitt the Elder.[20]

The sensitive, almost evasive, manner in which Beckford's supporters tackled questions of empire before a metropolitan audience was vindicated by the family's electoral experience at Bristol. With its own political traditions and strong partisan interests, the nation's leading provincial port was always going to present a mighty challenge for its would-be MP, Richard Beckford. These difficulties were multiplied by his absence from the country, and the lack of any familial interest in the City corporation. Moreover, in significant contrast to London, where the sheer multiplicity of sectional interests ensured that debate on particular economic sectors rarely had a decisive electoral impact, the predominance of the West India trade in Bristol saw Beckford's rivals eagerly seize opportunities to demonstrate how the Jamaicans might undermine the values and interests of the borough. Attacks on Richard, in fact, suggested a close familiarity among Bristolians with developments in Jamaica, and an awareness of how they might influence domestic English affairs. In this way, the Bristol election anticipated many of the future

---

[19] *A Short Account of the Interest and Conduct of the Jamaica Planters* (1754), esp. 3, 12, 15. He was also attacked for his borough mongering in other constituencies.

[20] East Sussex RO, SAS-RF 20/5: case of Edward Wilson, [c.1757]. The previous year, Beckford had argued strongly against jewish naturalisation: *HPC, 1715–54*, i, 651–2. He also became strongly identified as a supporter of Blackfriars Bridge, and it would later appear in one of his civic portraits of 1769–70 (now at Parham House, Sussex): S. O'Connell, *London 1753* (2003), 125. The first reference to him as Alderman Sugarcane, the despotic and mercenary slave-owner, comes in 1757: *The City Farce*, a modern edition of which can be found in *The New Foundling Hospital for Wit*, ed. D.W. Nichol (3 vols, 2006), i, 231–8. Andrew O'Shaughnessy notes growing metropolitan familiarity with West Indian stereotypes by the 1760s: A. O'Shaughnessy, *An Empire Divided: The American Revolution and the British Caribbean* (Philadelphia, 2000), 12–14.

difficulties which the Beckfords and their fellow West Indians would face as they strove to create a more effective transatlantic interest.[21]

William's political skills and reputation were closely tested at Bristol due to his prominent role as Richard's electoral agent. The first overt sign of their familial ambitions had come in March 1754, when the town's Tory Steadfast Society admitted Richard as a member and recommended him as the town's MP alongside Beckford's ally, Sir John Phillips. Within a few weeks, William, Julines and Francis Beckford had also become members of the society, and on 9 April the alderman made an election tour of Bristol, making 'a handsome speech' to the corporation. He then impressed the citizens with an oration at the Exchange in which he demonstrated his 'spirit of liberty' by his opposition to monopolies and his support for their trade. In the wake of this visit, opponents of the Beckford-Phillips ticket were much more ready than their metropolitan counterparts to besmirch the West Indian by reference to his actions in the Caribbean, reflecting the familiarity of Bristolians with West Indian life and culture. In an all-out attack on 12 April, a whig writer likened a pro-Beckford journalist to a master 'tyrannically dictating to his negro slaves in Jamaica'. William himself was likened to a West Indian hog – 'large and tall (tho' not very fat)' – whose departure from Bristol had robbed local tories of the chance to hold an election-day entertainment 'peculiar to the Jamaican taste call'd Barbequed Pig'. Within a week, the attacks broadened into a broader censure of the family's insidious influence within Bristol's Atlantic hinterland, with stories circulating of their economic coercion of Jamaican merchants, and their opposition to the removal of the island capital from Spanish Town to Kingston. The family was held to be a 'mighty Leviathan' whose influence could crush Bristol's traders, and opposition was encouraged against all four brothers to stop the 'arbitrary deeds of this overgrown arbitrary family'. These colonial themes were grafted onto pre-existing religious and political divisions within the Bristol citizenry, highlighting how imperial expansion had influenced the political culture of communities directly tied to the Atlantic by the 1750s.[22]

This bitter contention ensured a hard-fought poll, and all William's efforts could not prevent Richard from trailing for most of the week of voting, although a late rally saw him pip his running mate, Phillips, to the second seat. Newspapers speculated that it was only the detestation of whig supporters for Phillips that ensured Beckford's success, and there could be no doubt that the new member still would have to win over his new constituency when he arrived back in England in late June. The ferocity of the attacks on his family provoked him to publish an open letter ahead of his personal appearance, in which he promised to support 'the public good and the trade and interest of the City

---

[21] For Bristol's role within the Atlantic, and resultant influences on its society, see K. Morgan, *Bristol and the Atlantic World* (Cambridge, 1993); M. Dresser, *Slavery Obscured: The Social History of the Slave Trade in an English Port* (2001). For a survey of its 18th-century politics, see Nicholas Rogers, *Whigs and Cities: Popular Politics in the Age of Walpole and Pitt* (Oxford, 1989), esp. ch. 8.

[22] Bristol RO, SMV/8/2/2/1, 67–70; *Felix Farley's Bristol Journal*, 6–13 Apr. 1754; *The Bristol contest: being a collection of all the papers published by both parties on the election of 1754* (Bristol, 1754), 37–9, 64–6. The proposal for the removal of the island's government from Spanish Town to Kingston had been mooted for some time, but gained momentum with the arrival of the controversial governor, Admiral Knowles. Richard Beckford had arranged an anti-Kingston petition before he sailed for Britain: G. Metcalf, *Royal Government and Political Conflict in Jamaica, 1729–83* (1965), 118–26; J. Robertson, *Gone is the Ancient Glory: Spanish Town, Jamaica, 1534–2000* (Kingston, 2005), ch. 3.

of Bristol', but his presence did little to curb factious exchanges in the local press. More senior political observers were just as censorious of the family, with the duke of Newcastle preferring the 'broken jacobite', Phillips, over the 'wild West Indian', Beckford, a view shared by the king himself. In the wake of the family's electoral success, the verdict on William was also still out, with one of the Duke's contacts reporting:

> people are so divided in their opinions of him that very few think so well of him as he seems to value himself, and that in reality lessens him in the breasts of many who thought better of him before. He mimicked the man of importance, and his very advocate can deck him with nothing higher than that he is rich in fortune and will be as troublesome to the court as he can.

Thus, for all their advancement, questions remained concerning the true political interest of the Beckfords in Britain, and their familial success only placed their transatlantic networks under closer scrutiny.[23] Beckford had proved himself endlessly resourceful in taking advantage of every possible avenue for political advancement, and had exploited both his island interests and his metropolitan networks in order to strengthen his transatlantic powerbase. He had achieved much by 1754 but, as he clambered the slippery pole of political favour, it only exposed his family and his island to closer critical review. The candidacy of his brother, Richard, at Bristol had highlighted this fact of transatlantic political life most explicitly, where the rumblings of discontent over issues such as the fate of Spanish Town had reverberated across the Atlantic, and would pose ever-growing challenges for imperial brokers on both sides of the ocean. Equally, the importance of such issues would counsel the Jamaicans to continue to strengthen their metropolitan presence, convinced as they were of the importance of British power for the future of the island. The 1754 elections had, thus, highlighted the political strengths *and* weaknesses of the West Indians, and their successes only highlighted their need for sensitive management of their parliamentary interests.[24]

The increased number of West Indians in the House did not go unnoticed, and in a Commons debate of November 1754, Beckford was goaded by Horace Walpole with the observation that 'political geniuses' were the 'new commodity' imported from the American colonies. Such disparagement was not unusual in the experience of newcomers to elite metropolitan circles, but as yet there was little indication that

---

[23] *Felix Farley's Bristol Journal*, 15–22, 22–9 June 1754; BL, Add. MS 32735, ff. 48–50, 228: duke of Newcastle to the king, 6 Apr. 1754, J. Gordon to the duke of Newcastle, 24 May 1754. Gordon also reported that Beckford had bought the seat at Petersfield for £2,200.

[24] Beckford's ability to adapt to metropolitan political practice was best illustrated by his words of reassurance to a humble Bristol voter: 'I had much rather shew all the respect and regard in my power to a lover of liberty and his country (although poor) than to the first nobleman in the kingdom who had barter'd away the freedoms of the people and his own independency; for the sake of empty titles or the lucre of place, pension or employment . . . I am perfectly convinced from my own experience that the middling sort of people are the most uncorrupt and consequently the most to be depended on in case of danger either from our enemies abroad or from our own intestine commotions': Yale University, Beinecke Library, General MS 102, b. 4, folder 81: William Beckford to John Kirke, 25 May 1754. His embrace of the language of independence placed him firmly in the ranks of opposition, while his respect for the virtue of the middling classes echoed a brand of patriotism which aimed to rid the country of the corruption of government contractors, libertines and Francophiles.

Westminster opinion was unusually perturbed by the arrival of a significant cohort of West Indians in their midst.[25] Mild distaste, however, would turn to greater opprobrium when the Seven Years War catapulted the Caribbean to the centre of national concerns amid an all-out global competition with the French. This heightened importance was personified by Beckford's close political alliance, from late 1756, with William Pitt. This relationship took several years to mature, and was strained at several key points, as the war tested their imperial visions as never before. None the less, their common commitment to the destruction of France as an imperial force cemented their friendship, and concentrated the attention of both allies and enemies on the West Indies as a critical player in the nation's fortunes. Both Beckford and Pitt have been seen to be principal agents in popularising the empire as a force within metropolitan politics and society, especially within London itself, thereby helping, in turn, to promote the colonies as integral to British interests and values. As a tide of British colonial victories stirred popular opinion from 1758 onwards, the two politicians were keen to garner widespread support, and did their very best to ensure that the empire reached a new peak of interest in the press. West Indian politicians could take heart that the merits of possible peace settlements, or an expansion of the war effort, were earnestly debated from 1760 onwards, but they also recognized that they faced a significant political test of their metropolitan interest.[26]

3

The parliamentary elections of the spring of 1761 came at a most uncertain time for the West Indians. The great victories of the war may have cheered many commercial interests, but Pitt's bellicose stance towards Spain was a much more controversial move, presaging enduring conflict, and an even greater change to the political *status quo* in the Atlantic. The accession of George III also added further uncertainties to domestic politics, and his favouritism for Bute had already unnerved supporters of the Newcastle-Pitt administration. These uncertainties did not dissuade West Indians from standing at this election, and four new members were returned who could boast close familiarity with the Caribbean. They helped to make up for the shortfall caused by the deaths of five West Indian members since the last election, and, in general, showed the same commitment to establishing permanent interests through estate purchase or the courtship of local politicians. These campaigns helped to ensure a complement of 11 West Indian

---

[25] Warwickshire RO, L6/1336: John Dobson to George Lucy, 16 [Nov.] 1754. For instructive comparison, see David Hayton's account of the impact of the Scots at Westminster in the immediate aftermath of the union: David Hayton, 'Adjustment and Integration: The Scottish Representation in the British House of Commons, 1707–14', *Parliamentary History*, xxvii (2008), 410–35.

[26] Wilson, *The Sense of the People*, esp. ch. 3; M. Peters, *Pitt and Popularity: The Patriot Minister and London Opinion during the Seven Years War* (Oxford, 1980); E. Gould, *The Persistence of Empire* (Chapel Hill, NC, 2000); Harris, *Politics and the Nation*; Peters, 'Early Hanoverian Consciousness: Empire or Europe?', 632–68. For a question mark against the coherence of 'middling' views on the empire, see B. Harris, 'American Idols: Empire, War and the Middling Ranks in Mid-Eighteenth Century Britain', *Past & Present*, No. 150 (1996), 111–41. For the broader impact of the war on society, see S. Conway, *War, State and Society in Mid-Eighteenth Century Britain and Ireland* (Oxford, 2006). Brendan Simms also offers an important reminder of the centrality of European affairs during this age of imperial expansion: Brendan Simms, *Three Victories and a Defeat: the Rise and Fall of the British Empire, 1714–83* (2007).

MPs in all. However, this general success could not mask the increasing pressure on the West Indians, most obviously voiced by the acerbic Horace Walpole on the eve of the election, which, in turn, sparked an ever-greater scrutiny of their patriotic credentials.[27]

Inevitably, the most searching commentary centred on Beckford, due to his proximity to Pitt, and by his decision to contest the City. Significantly, he did not seek to back any candidate at Bristol, but he calculated that his great personal investment in London politics over many years could overcome war-induced concerns. At a meeting of the livery to choose candidates, some six weeks before the poll, he began most defensively, attempting to clear himself from charges that he had neglected his aldermanic duties. While admitting that these charges were 'just', he pointed to the superior importance of his role as an MP, and then launched into his most explicit attack on the representativeness of parliament to date. By his calculations, 'this great City' paid one-sixteenth of the land tax and one-eighth of taxes in general, but only elected four of the 558 MPs. He thus regarded his parliamentary duties as a 'more essential' service. Warming to this theme, he then defied anyone to contest that he had not done his utmost 'where the trade, liberty and franchises of the City were concerned', taking particular pride in his role as a militia captain, where he had 'done his duty as an officer and a soldier'. His protestation evidently struck a chord with the electorate, for he finished third in the poll, nearly 500 votes above fifth place. His victory speech, again, suggested his sensitivity to his critics, who had labelled him as either despotic or arbitrary in his principles. He remained defiant, however, insisting that his independence mirrored that of the City itself, and that he remained loyal to a patriot minister and a patriot king.[28]

Although confirmed in his London constituency, Beckford revealed that the pressures on his position were steadily growing, and that his partnership with Pitt had not been an unalloyed boon to his interests. In particular, once the election results had been digested, there were renewed attacks on the pervasive influence of the planting interest, sparked by continuing debate on the likely territorial settlement with France, and the prospect of a war with Spain. The most notable of these assaults came in a September issue of the *London Chronicle*, in which a provincial correspondent argued for the retention of Guadeloupe as a means to lower sugar prices and defeat the schemes of monopolising 'overgrown sugar-planters'. The article not only dwelt on economic arguments, but attacked the absentees for their influence in Britain, suggesting that the current sugar market 'served only to mount several planters in gilded coaches'. These riches permitted them to flit between Britain and the Caribbean as their extravagance dictated, only to 'appear again in Old England as comets or blazing stars'. If Beckford had any doubts about the target of such abuse, the author concluded that high sugar prices could only be attributed to 'the cunning management of our rich planters, the

---

[27] Lawson and Phillips, ' "Our Execrable Banditti" ', 225; *HPC, 1754–90*, i, 156–7. In terms of open corruption, only two of the 11 West Indians used their wealth to secure venal seats: John Gibbons (for a second election running, on this occasion Wallingford); and William Matthew Burt (to enter parliament for the first time in 1761 at Great Marlow).

[28] *London Chronicle*, 3–5 Mar. 1761; *Gentleman's Magazine*, xxxi (Apr. 1761), 158–9. In his acceptance speech, Beckford insisted that he had not solicited votes either in 1754 or on this occasion, evidently to justify his stance on parliamentary reform. John Brewer has argued that Beckford's stance on the issue in 1761 was 'highly uncharacteristic, if not unique': John Brewer, *Party Ideology and Popular Politics at the Accession of George III* (Cambridge, 1976), 215.

Jamaican planters in particular'. With attacks on the number of absentee West Indians returned at the general election, these pressures were likely to grow while key questions regarding the fate of the American empire remained unresolved.[29]

While assailed for his Caribbean interests, Beckford faced growing political uncertainty on account of his alliance with Pitt.[30] The political storm finally broke in October 1761, with Pitt's resignation from office, ostensibly over his failure to secure backing for a pre-emptive strike against Spain. Given their close political relationship over the past four years, it was inevitable that this event would be seen as a devastating blow for Beckford, and the press response can be read as a summary of the successes and failures of the alderman and the West India interest to date. Although not all opponents of the Spanish war were censorious of Beckford, or saw his actions as determined by his political interests, his most bitter enemies delighted in his political confusion, and sought to expose the self-interestedness of the absentee planters. Philip Francis was the most cutting critic, spuriously attempting to preserve the public pronouncements of Pitt and Beckford for posterity, lest they be 'lost to remembrance, or be sent, in their newspapers, perhaps to Jamaica to exercise the criticism of sugar planters, Negroes, and Creolians?' In some of the most direct personal attacks on Beckford to date, he sought to expose the unpatriotic nature of Beckford's position, even to the extent of highlighting the otherness of the alderman's skin-colour:

> Then should creolian B------d, like himself,
> Start from the Canvas in his Native Hues,
> The bronze tartarean, and Jamaica Tint,
> Sun-burnt and deep enamell'd.

These personal reflections were a natural product of Beckford's political prominence at a time of intense factionalism. Although they did not deflect him from his current political path, these attacks did serve as a signal warning that there were political costs to the advancement of the West India interest. It certainly put them on the defensive, and there were even fears that the prominence of leaders such as Beckford might harm the cause of the Caribbean colonies. As the Antiguan, Samuel Martin, vented to his son, the re-elected member for Camelford, Beckford's friendship with Pitt 'seems to have been the foundation of the little regard paid to the extension of our sugar colonies'. Thus, even though the 1761 election results were nearly as satisfying for the West Indians as those of 1754, and attested to their general adoption of prudent political strategies to gain seats, their public profile threatened to harm their longer-term electoral prospects.[31]

---

[29] *London Chronicle*, 5–8 Sept. 1761.

[30] Bute's hostility towards Beckford in August 1761 is suggested by his comment to Lord Devonshire that Pitt had ceased to insist on the retention of Guadeloupe to humour the alderman: 'The Devonshire Diary', ed. P. Brown and K. Schweizer (Camden, 4th ser., xxvii, 1982), 109.

[31] *A Letter to the Right Honourable W----- P----, by a Citizen* (1761); BL, Add. MS 41347, f. 131: Samuel Martin sr to Samuel Martin jr, 20 Mar. 1762. Beckford's cause was not helped by the public letter of self-exculpation which Pitt issued within weeks of his resignation: *A Letter from a Right Honourable Person to ------- in the City* (1761), in which he offered the alderman 'sincere acknowledgements for all your kind friendship'.

While acknowledging the increasingly-testy relationship between the West Indians and the London press and politicians, it is important to recognize that not all Caribbean interests were faced by the invective directed at Beckford. At the Liverpool election, for instance, a very different set of West Indian influences were at work. The port had a great stake in the colonies, particularly on account of the slave trade, and one of the leading London merchants in the Africa and West Indian trade, Charles Pole, stood for re-election at Liverpool in 1761. In a bitterly-contested poll, no imagery of Caribbean society surfaced, even though Pole was thrown on the defensive on account of the politics of the West India interest. Instead, opponents tried to undermine him by suggestions that he had previously backed the interest of the London-based Royal African Company. His supporters were quick to scotch these rumours, promoting him as 'a zealous and indefatigable promoter of the free and open traffic to Africa', who had argued vehemently against moves to support a London-based joint-stock company. More generally, they emphatically denied that he might prioritise London over Liverpool, asserting that 'the interest of these great trading ports are generally the same', and that his London residence would be an aid to the general interest of the port. Amid a plethora of squibs, songs and broadsides, there was little concern to embrace any rhetoric of empire to assert the superior credentials of any of the candidates, and the key battle was to be portrayed as the true servant of the town's interests. Pole lost the election, but metropolitan attacks on the growing influence of the planters cannot be held responsible for his defeat. Rather, Pole's experiences highlight the organic character of local political culture, shaped by the town's traditions and interests, as well as by the identity of the candidates. West Indians, and those allied to their interests, could not afford to dismiss the caustic barbs of the likes of Walpole too lightly, but it is important not to exaggerate their potential resonance at the polls.[32]

The West Indians could take little comfort from these enduring electoral realities, for the 1768 general election saw the strongest attacks on their interests at the polls to date. In the autumn of 1767, John Almon's *Political Register* issued a general warning to voters not to return 'the vain West Indian', hinting that the planter wished to be relieved of his debts by 'the sale of his conscience'. Within a few months, this censure had broadened into a scathing censure of the likely influence of the colonists, with particular venom reserved for the monopolists of 'our Southern American colonies'. The 'increasing riches and power' of the colonists was seen as a major threat to the constitution, and the attack ended with an impassioned plea: 'let Americans . . . be kept in their proper sphere, and no interest but a genuine British one be ever suffered to prevail in a British House of

[32] *An Entire and Impartial Collection of all the Papers, etc, published on both sides, concerning the late Election at Liverpool* (Liverpool, 1761), 14, 18; *HPC, 1754–90*, i, 317–8. Pole served on the executive committee for both Liverpool and London in the Company of Merchants Trading to Africa, established in 1752 to replace the London-based Royal African Company. There is no evidence to suggest that he had lived in the West Indies, or boasted any close familial connection with any of the major planters there. For the politicking surrounding the Company for Africa, see Brown, 'The British Government and the Slave Trade', esp 31–40. For the continuing mistrust of Liverpool merchants towards the capital in the abolitionist era, see J Civin, 'Slaves, Sati and Sugar: Constructing Imperial Identity through Liverpool Petition Struggles', in *Parliaments, Nations and Identities in Britain and Ireland, 1660–1850*, ed. J. Hoppit (Manchester, 2003) 187–205.

Commons'.[33] This increasing rancour echoed the stormy debates over the empire since the last election, most obviously the Stamp Act and the other imperial reforms of the post-1763 period. Even though the Caribbean was much more submissive in its response to imperial regulation, prominent London-based politicians such as Beckford and Rose Fuller openly opposed the notorious stamp duties, thereby risking metropolitan censure. More generally, Beckford's high profile was, again, a mixed blessing, and his continuing alliance with the mercurial Pitt was not calculated to win public favour for either himself or his Caribbean allies. It also did not help the colonists' cause that India also became a major cause for metropolitan concern in the wake of the East India Company's establishment as a territorial power. With a significant increase in the number of East Indian directors competing for seats, domestic commentators were likely to redouble their critiques of imperial influences. The resultant volley of criticism clearly discomforted the West Indians, but it was the ideological character of these attacks which caused them most alarm, for their critics were now prepared to make a much stronger connection between metropolitan and imperial issues. Self-interest was still one of the most bitter charges levelled at the colonists, but they were now represented as a more general challenge to British values, especially in the ways in which plantation slavery might offer a direct threat to cherished notions of liberty. The metropolitan battles centred on the figures of Bute, Wilkes and the king were clearly important influences behind these depictions, and it was vital for the West Indians that they did not allow these forms of transatlantic political discourse to gain any momentum.[34]

Given the political turmoil of the previous seven years, with no less than five administrations since the previous election, it was inevitable that feverish electioneering greeted the issue of writs in 1768. In Beckford's case, his candidacy in the City would be watched with particular interest, following his recent prominence as a spokesman for the Chatham ministry. His recent stance on parliamentary reform would also attract the attention of more disenchanted politicians, who could look to the alderman as one of the few politicians of any standing ready to contemplate serious reform. As yet, there was no co-ordinated radical movement or leadership to channel the discontents raised by a decade of war, economic distress and imperial dysfunction. At the eleventh hour, John Wilkes would return from his French exile and stand as a candidate at London, but the outspoken opposition of the alderman to general warrants and the Stamp Act rendered him one of the most consistent voices of reform in the 1760s. His enemies clearly relished the opportunity to label him as a dangerous demagogue alongside Wilkes, as the darling of the mob, who would undermine the constitution to gain the popular vote.

---

[33] *Political Register*, i (Sept. 1767), 307–8; ii (Jan. 1768), 42–3. The writer did attack colonies more generally for their 'eye to independence', but the prime target was the West Indians, who were identified as unsuitable candidates, alongside lawyers, placemen, merchants (especially with government links), and spendthrifts. Less specific attacks might censure those (beyond the East Indian nabobs) who, 'to the disgrace of human nature in calamitous times, have amassed vast over-grown fortunes': 'Lover of His King and Country', *An Address to the Electors of Great Britain* (1768), 25.

[34] For the response of the West Indians to the imperial reforms of the 1760s, see O'Shaughnessy, *An Empire Divided*, ch. 4. He describes the British-based West Indians as divided, and argues that 'their inactivity and prevarication contributed to the isolation of the North American lobby in London'. Lawson and Philips saw the 1768 election as the moment when 'hostility to returned East Indians went beyond simply envy or resentment of newcomers', noting that five of the 19 elected nabobs were returned for venal boroughs: Lawson and Philips, ' "Our Execrable Banditti" ', 232–3.

For his own part, Beckford saw the poll as an opportunity to clarify his views, and to alert the electorate to the dangers which the country now faced. Thanks, in part, to Beckford's recent campaigns, however, the battle developed into a heated debate on the intertwined challenges to liberty faced by Britain and its colonies.[35]

Beckford formally announced his candidacy in the press in mid-March, declaring that he had 'served my country and my constituents . . . faithfully and honestly'. He faced six rivals, the most significant of whom was undoubtedly Wilkes, whose quest for publicity promoted his candidacy in the City's high-profile parliamentary poll. While Wilkes attracted most of the headlines, the candidacy of the American merchant, Barlow Trecothick, also elicited much discussion, and prompted debate of the colonial sympathies of Beckford too. Although they shared similar political views, and Trecothick held significant Jamaican lands, at no point did either suggest that they were standing in the same interest. Beckford's supporters appeared careful not to align the two creole politicians together, suggesting the continuing reticence of the West Indians to establish a common platform with the northern colonists. Early attacks on Trecothick suggested the wisdom of this tactic, with the *Public Advertiser* dismissing him as 'a Bostonian . . . [who] has upon all occasions shown himself a true friend to the trade and interests of ----- America'. By contrast, in the very same issue, Beckford was heralded as 'an orator, a man of sense, spirit and independency, and one who has always loved to put himself forward in the service of his country'. Despite these precautions, in a bitterly-fought contest it was impossible to prevent damaging attacks on the alderman's colonial links. In a more conventional vein, the scurrilous *City Races* satirised Beckford as Chatham's 'brown horse PREROGATIVE'. His ancestry, however, was linked to 'Noll's [Oliver Cromwell's] Old Trumpeter', highlighting Jamaica's status as a Cromwellian conquest to emphasize his radical character. His promiscuity 'as a stallion to the African Fillies' was another mark of dishonour, while his 'very numerous' offspring attested to his ill-discipline. Having been the butt of remarkable anti-colonial attacks in the wake of the last general election, Beckford could not risk the poll being turned into a personal plebiscite on imperial policy, but his allies struggled to protect him.[36]

---

[35] Lucy Sutherland argued, in part by reference to Beckford's recent activity, that there would have been a renewed alliance between the City and parliamentary opposition groups even without the appearance of Wilkes: L. Sutherland, *Politics and Finance in the Eighteenth Century*, ed. A Newman (1984), 124–6. For Wilkes's candidacy in the City election, see Arthur Cash, *John Wilkes: The Scandalous Father of Civil Liberty* (New Haven, 2006), 204–8.

[36] *Public Advertiser*, 11, 14 Mar. 1768; *Political Register*, ii (Jan. 1768), 42–3; *Now or Never, Old England for Ever* (1768); *City Races* (1768). *Now or Never* backed Beckford and the three other sitting MPs as in the interest of Old England, while Trecothick was listed as on his own as representative of New England. Mid-poll advertisements suggested that Beckford's supporters were working in tandem with those of mayor, Thomas Harley, and father of the City, Sir Robert Ladbroke: *To the Worthy Liverymen of the City of London* (1768). In order to circumvent accusations that his American loyalties were inimical to the national interest, pro-Trecothick supporters stressed his positive qualities as a merchant, who must be supported 'if his fortune be ample, his mind enlarged and his soul independent'. His rivals duly asked how could any merchants 'under the influence of a few North American houses' support 'a gentleman educated, apprenticed, married, and many years resident in Boston with his family, and [with] commercial connections in that town?' It was also reported that the City election was being closely watched in the colonies: *Public Advertiser*, 16, 18, 21 Mar. 1768. Within weeks of the election, Trecothick's name appeared alongside that of Beckford's as fellow petitioners in favour of the Jamaican Counties Act of 1758, which was seen to protect Spanish Town interests: TNA, CO137/34, no. 139–41. Across the Atlantic, there was delight at the return of 'Beckford, a Jamaica-man, and Trecothick, a Bostonian . . . and the wisdom of that choice has since conspicuously manifested itself by the actions of those worthy patriots': *The Defence of Injured Merit Unmasked* (1771), 1.

Beckford's appreciation of the controversy surrounding the colonies was most pow-
erfully displayed on the hustings on election day itself, 16 March. He gave a defiant
performance, insisting that he had been misrepresented: 'not only in common conversation, but in the public papers, and in hand bills dispersed in coffee-houses and other
places'. He then confronted more specific charges against him, defending his support for
the use of the dispensing power in the grain emergency of 1766 on grounds that it was
subject to subsequent parliamentary review. He also sought to justify his actions towards
the East India Company in the 1767 session, characterising monopolies as 'against the
spirit of the constitution' and as 'injurious to the trade and manufacture of this
kingdom'. His final flourish reminded those present of his core principles: 'I prefer the
character of an honest, free and independent citizen of London to the greatest title in
the power of the Crown to confer'. He did not refer directly to American affairs,
however, an omission which was pounced upon by his adversaries. His supposed
disregard for the East India Company's charter was held forth as a symbol of his
self-interested inconsistency, for 'had Jamaica been a charter government like the City
of London, he probably would have not been such a volunteer' in leading this assault
on the Company. His denial of parliament's right to tax the colonists was also dismissed
as 'his creolian creed', while another castigated him as 'a Negro man, a mere sugar sop
and a rum man into the bargain'. These attacks helped his enemies to characterise the
speech as 'wild, desultory, and better calculated to catch a mob than to collect the
deliberate suffrages of a thinking, independent and free people'. Their vehemence only
increased as the votes were counted in the following week, when Beckford was forced
to issue a published form of the speech in order to refute rival claims. He insisted that
he had spoken 'without taking a single note', but dutifully collected his thoughts in
print, thereby acknowledging the intense scrutiny to which his public performances
were subjected at this time.[37]

Amid 'prodigious' noise, with the crowds roaring 'Wilkes and Liberty' and other
political slogans, on 23 March Beckford was returned in third place with 3,402 votes,
some 450 votes ahead of the fourth-placed Trecothick. Although their opponents had
sought to exploit recent colonial tensions, the pair had managed to preserve their
credentials as loyal servants of the City. The most significant loser on this occasion was
Wilkes himself, who finished last of the seven with only 1,247 votes. His belated
candidacy clearly contributed to this failure, but the reticence of any candidate to align
themselves too closely with his cause was a significant blow. Unlike Beckford in 1754,
who had associated with City heavyweights such as Barnard, and appealed to a familial
London heritage, Wilkes could not play the loyal citizen. In subsequent months, he
would seek to rectify this by building a stronger base with the liverymen, who, as the
election squibs had indicated, prized their independence as a mark of distinction from

---

[37] *Public Advertiser*, 19, 22, 23 Mar. 1768; [William Beckford], *To the Worthy Liverymen of London* (1768).
He also defended his vote for land tax cuts to support the poor, observing that probably 'few private men'
would pay more than him. Significantly, his failure to mount a defence of being pro-colonist was noted by
a critic on 23 March, who also called upon the 'hundreds of the members who have sat in Parliament with
him' to testify to his mob-friendly speeches. Critics went on to suggest that he was anti-London, rather than
anti-monopoly, in opposing the East India Company, identifying him as the member who had urged the
House to look to the 'rising sun' for heavy taxes.

mobbish elements in the capital. The election result proved that Beckford, for all his recent tribulations, could still count upon their support, and that they regarded him as a credible spokesman for their interests. His critics, such as Horace Walpole, still wished to bracket him (and Trecothick) with Wilkes, by suggesting that the two colonials had shown 'much civility' to the latter, but the London electorate demonstrated greater discrimination.[38]

Other West Indians also found themselves on the defensive on account of their Caribbean links, and their experiences bore testimony to a more general antipathy towards carpet-bagging candidates in uncertain political times. For instance, Crisp Molineux, who had chosen to settle in England in 1754 in preference to his birthplace of St Kitts, encountered significant opposition when he unsuccessfully contested King's Lynn. He had bought a Norfolk estate, thus allowing him to be styled a gentlemen 'of considerable property in the county', but even his supporters had to admit that he was 'a stranger to the town'. As a strident defender of domestic liberties against government policy, Molineux could have expected partisan attacks too, but his enemies went beyond the standard fare of general warrants and courtly corruption, branding his allies as 'creoles', or as 'bl[a]cks' who showed obsequious deference to their leaders. This outlook was even shared by political heavyweight, Lord Rockingham, who may possibly have had Molineux in mind when discussing a borough 'which was attacked by Creolian Powers', only to be later saved by a rally of neighbouring gentlemen who had 'beat the Creole'.[39] Henry Dawkins did not face such inflammatory language when he sought a seat at Salisbury, but found that even the tried-and-tested formula of purchasing a local estate could not prevent condemnation at the pretensions of the 'outsider':

> Is it possible that a man can think himself entitled to represent a city by buying an estate and living a few years near it? A man whose very name is new in Wiltshire and whose person was entirely unknown in Salisbury when I left?

Dawkins managed a creditable joint second at the poll, but did not choose to pursue a petition, and opted for the quieter route to enter the Commons via a by-election the

---

[38] *Boswell in Search of a Wife 1766–9*, ed. F. Brady and F.A. Pottle (New Haven, 1957), 152; *Horace Walpole: Memoirs of the Reign of King George III*, ed. D. Le Marchant and G.F.R. Barker (4 vols, 1894), iii, 126–7. Boswell regarded the poll as a 'really grand' event, with the candidates on a raised platform all demonstrating 'true London countenances'. One account suggested that a candidate was saved from 'the resentment of the mob' by Wilkes's departure and by the fact that he 'sheltered himself by Mr. Beckford's presence': *Political Register*, ii (May 1768), 328. Several tracts attacked Beckford for self-interest, and predicted that he would desert the Londoners to back Pitt and Bute in hopes of a peerage. The election also saw a reprint of the *City Farce* of 1757: *The New Foundling Hospital for Wit*, ed. Nichol, i, 94–104, 113–17, 231–8.

[39] *The Lynn Magazine* (1768), 29, 50; Nottinghamshire Archives, Foljambe of Osberton MSS, DD/F3/11/1/7/97: Lord Rockingham to Sir George Savile, 24 Mar. 1768; *HPC, 1754–90*, i, 341. The political conduct of Rockingham and his allies gained the approval of at least one observer at King's Lynn: *Lynn Magazine*, 62–3. Molineux's defeat owed much to the electoral tactics of his pro-government rival, and he went on to secure a lasting interest in the borough, even though the term 'creole' continued to be heard: *The Consultation*, [?1774].

following year. Overall, only seven West Indians made it to Westminster, returning their parliamentary complement to the level of 1747.[40]

These experiences counselled caution amongst the West Indians, as they sought to maintain influence within British politics. Beckford could be in no doubt of the growing disquiet with planter politicking, when he received a letter from Granville Sharp only weeks after the election. Embarking on a 40-year crusade against the evils of slavery, Sharp implored the champion of liberty to recognize the hypocrisy of his enslavement of sugar workers, thereby highlighting the ways in which domestic and imperial discourses could be linked to significant effect. Beckford remained tight-lipped, not wishing this kind of exchange to develop into a public debate on the stark contrasts offered by Britain and its empire. In opposition to the apparent tyrannies of the Grafton ministry, he would offer more unequivocal support to the American patriots and domestic reformers in subsequent debates, but he studiously avoided any reference to Caribbean slavery. Thus, although his death in 1770 was clearly a blow to the West Indians, it helped to pre-empt accusations that they shared common cause with the increasingly-truculent Northern patriots, and removed the most tempting of targets for the anti-slavers. For certain, many of the absentee planters had profound concerns with the metropolitan authorities, but, as Andrew O'Shaughnessy has shown, they were willing to tuck in their horns to preserve their longer-term interests. Rather than adopt a pan-imperial vision of imperial dysfunction, the West Indians refused to take up the North American cause, and did not plead special interest or knowledge to advance prescriptions for the resolution of the Atlantic crisis.[41]

Without the more hot-headed leadership of Beckford, the 1774 elections were a much quieter affair for the West Indians, and they largely escaped censure, despite wider anxieties over the American conflict. Their number increased to eight, and a further six were returned in subsequent by-elections during this parliament. Their political stance was closely monitored at this election, nevertheless, and, on the eve of the contest, the *Gentleman's Magazine* warned voters not to back West Indians 'who publicly deny the legislative power of Great Britain over the American colonies'. By this stage, however, few British-based planters were willing to back the North American cause so openly, and even critics of the Coercive Acts, most notably Rose Fuller, began to temper their support.[42] The nearest to a damaging public controversy came at Hindon, one of the

---

[40] *HPC, 1754–90*, i, 419–20. Among the sitting West Indians defeated in 1768 were John Gibbons at Wallingford, Sir Alex Grant at Inverness Burghs and William Matthew Burt at Great Marlow. Anti-colonialism was not explicitly raised at these elections, and Grant's loss was, in fact, to the benefit of the nabob, Hector Munro. None the less, the absence of overt controversy should not obscure the ways in which elections helped to deepen the 'social and commercial connections' between Britain and its empire, which, in turn, encouraged greater censure of slavery in the 1750s and 1760s: Brown, 'Politics of Slavery', 227.

[41] O'Shaughnessy, *An Empire Divided*, ch. 5. Note, in particular, the generally passive response of the West Indians to the Coercive Acts of 1774. They were stirred into a brief flurry of agitation in late 1774 and early 1775, voicing their concern over the economic impact of the impending war in petitions and in testimony before the Commons, but they did not engage in the key issues of imperial sovereignty: O'Shaughnessy, *An Empire Divided*, ch. 6.

[42] *Gentleman's Magazine*, xliv (Sept. 1774), 404–5; S. Foote, *The Nabob* (1772), esp. 42–7. John Sainsbury argued that 'organized support for the colonists was largely confined to London', at the 1774 elections, with little but apathy or hostility to colonial aspirations elsewhere. He linked the stance of the *Gentleman's Magazine* to the pro-American leanings of Richard Oliver and Samuel Estwick, although without acknowledging the wider critique of the West Indians at recent elections: John Sainsbury, *Disaffected Patriots* (Montreal, 1987), 62–9, 76–8.

handful of boroughs which had returned a number of West Indians in recent elections, largely on account of the patronage of the Beckford family. With William's heir still a minor, a number of rival interests contested a flagrantly-corrupt election. Most notably, an illegitimate son of William's, Richard Beckford, stood, but faced stiff competition from Richard Smith, the archetypal East Indian nabob. So open was the bribery that the Commons prosecuted all four candidates, and the borough itself was threatened with disfranchisement. The scandal even inspired a biting satire on the venality of the West Indians, who were accused of seeking the services of a 'borough broker' to secure the Hindon seat. This attack showed that the West Indians were still vulnerable to criticism, however careful their political strategies. Yet, the savagery of the satire was much tamer than Samuel Foote's famed *Nabob* of 1772, whose fictional embodiment, Sir Mathew Mite, threatened to subvert all Britain's cultural values. A loathsome character with no redeeming features, Mite focused his political ambitions on the borough of Bribe'em, whose corrupted voters were even indifferent to the candidacy of a black slave. The more conventional Hindon satire suggested that the West Indians could not afford any electoral complacency, but it did not prevent a member of the Dawkins family from eventually prevailing in the borough, a success aided by the social and political invest-ment of the Beckfords over the past 20 years.[43]

4

The electoral fortunes of the West Indians reveal important perspectives on the devel-opment of both domestic and imperial politics at a key juncture. During a period when metropolitan commentators expressed continual concerns about the speed and character of contemporary societal change, the absentee planters were prime candidates for satire and invective. Closer study has suggested that these attacks can be linked to very specific contexts, and that the West Indians could adapt their political strategies to combat them. In common with the planters themselves, we should be wary of detecting too much novelty or alarmism in these critiques of imperial influence. The evidence of the polls suggests that the most crucial priority for the West Indians was to prevent their critics from establishing causative links between their metropolitan impact and domestic politi-cal discourses. Such was the growing congruence of debates in Britain and its empire in the 1760s that the West Indians were obvious targets, and their influence on British morals and political principles received much greater attention. While graphic and far-reaching in character, however, these assaults were not the vanguard of an incipient abolitionist movement, and were more concerned to find convenient scapegoats for domestic upheavals. In fact, as Christopher Brown has argued: 'the British public knew

---

[43] *The Borough-Broker; Or a Nobleman Trick'd* (1774), 12–13, 37; *HPC, 1754–90*, i, 415–6; Lawson and Phillips, ' "Our Execrable Banditti" ', 229, 235. Hindon did not share the fate of New Shoreham in 1771, which was disfranchised after open electoral bribery: Langford, *Public Life and the Propertied Englishman*, 320–2. Significantly, in the 1774 attack, the West Indians were portrayed as only having 'the ostensible character of having large fortunes, when they are at the same time under the greatest strictures and embarrassments'; an informed insight into the perennial pressures of the absentee planter. Dawkins himself appears to have learnt the lessons of 1774 by subsequently establishing a stronger propertied interest at Chippenham, and successfully passed the seat to his son in 1784.

surprisingly little about the character of Caribbean society' in the mid 1780s. The depth of this ignorance should be partially attributed to the careful political manœuvring of the West Indians themselves. The profound national uncertainties following defeat in America would be a much more secure foundation for the abolitionists, permitting a more direct and wide-ranging debate on the moral and political inconsistencies between metropolitan and colonial societies. The West Indians had always dreaded this scenario, and the organisational vigour and mass petitioning of their opponents gave them little hope of successfully controlling the controversy over Caribbean slavery itself.[44]

In common with other political interests, the West Indians had always struggled to influence their public image, but their mid-century electoral experience suggested that they had learnt to play the political system to tolerable effect. When they were patient, and built electoral interests by strategic propertied purchases and the courtship of established aristocratic families, they could win and retain seats. Popular constituencies were more risky and volatile, but were not beyond the grasp of their leaders. Their general antipathy towards the North Americans, and their willingness to play a different political game from the troublesome patriots, worked to their interest, even if these political positions could not cure them of 'outsider' status in the eyes of a metropolitan audience still adjusting to imperial change. Spokesmen such as the Beckfords or the Fullers could also alert Britons to the Caribbean's massive contribution to the national treasury, and planters could seek to model themselves as industrious patriots. In fact, as the nabobs would readily acknowledge, the biggest challenges faced by the colonists were responses to their success, and the widespread attacks of the 1760s were simply commensurate with the growth of empire.[45] These exchanges did not ultimately help the West Indians, but their patient attention to building bridges within metropolitan society worked to preserve their longer-term political interest. British familiarity with the Caribbean did breed contempt (on both sides) and the development of lurid stereotypes, but it must also be recognized that the West Indian call for mutual understanding and common interest was heeded, especially if Caribbean excess was

---

[44] C.L. Brown, *Moral Capital: Foundations of British Abolitionism* (Chapel Hill, NC, 2006), esp. 367–70. At this juncture, Caribbean-based politicians did seek to correct metropolitan views of the West Indies, most notably Edward Long's three-volume *History of Jamaica* (1774). Brown also links this metropolitan ignorance of the Caribbean to the subsequent abolitionist campaign to bombard British audiences with written and visual images of slavery. However, it is significant that abolitionists did not seek to play up the electoral interests of the absentee planters in the same way as critics of the East India Company. In part, this can simply be credited to the relative paucity of Caribbean members in the House, for the disparity between East and West Indians became more pronounced across the general elections of 1774–84, with 22 nabobs and eight West Indians returned in 1774; 27 nabobs and 13 West Indians in 1780; and 33 nabobs and eight West Indians in 1784. Nabob numbers would continue to rise, peaking at 46 in 1802, but Caribbean-born MPs were still there to attack, with at least 17 elected in the 1790–1820 period: *HPC, 1754–90*, i, 152, 157; *The History of Parliament: The House of Commons 1790–1820*, ed. R.G. Thorne (5 vols, 1986), i, 325–6. Recent work has also shown that, in the last phase of the campaign against the slave trade, there was active canvassing before contests in the 1806 general election, and this constituency pressure was important in producing a House amenable to abolition. This electioneering, in turn, sparked retaliation by pro-slaving sectional interests in subsequent contests: S. Farrell, 'Contrary to the Principles of Justice, Humanity and Sound Policy: The Slave Trade, Parliamentary Politics and the Abolition Act, 1807', and S. Drescher, 'Public Opinion and Parliament in the Abolition of the British Slave Trade', in *The British Slave Trade*, ed. Farrell, Unwin and Walvin, esp. 61–3, 160–5.

[45] For the self-fashioning of Caribbean planters as industrious, loyal subjects, see C. Petley, 'Home and This Country: Britishness and Creole Identity in the Letters of a Transatlantic Slaveholder', *Atlantic Studies*, vi (2009), 43–61.

muted. Indeed, the lessons which the West Indians learnt in the cut and thrust of electoral politics would prepare them for the more decisive battles after 1787. The planters had already developed strategies to head off arguments arising from questions of power, liberty and slavery, and would continue to develop their organisational strength in Britain, while remaining sensitive to metropolitan political norms. As a result, the abolitionists would have a hard battle on their hands, even as they forced Britons to confront the structural inhumanities of their empire.[46]

[46] In his recent comparative study of abolitionism across several countries, Seymour Drescher identified the public sphere as a key differential in helping British reformers to gain political momentum, but he adds the significant caveat that British experiences also highlight the difficulties 'in converting public pressure into law and policy': Seymour Drescher, *Abolition: A History of Slavery and Antislavery* (Cambridge, 2009), esp. ch. 8. Ian Barrett has also highlighted the ways in which pro-slavers strove to influence public inquiries into the trade, revealing the continuing adaptation of the West Indians to metropolitan politics, albeit in a losing cause: Ian Barrett, 'Investigation as a Prelude to Regulation: Information, Investigation and the Abolition of the Slave Trade', in *Regulating the British Economy*, ed. Gauci, 161–76.

Loyal Opposition? Prince Frederick and Parliament (1729–51)*

ROBIN EAGLES

History of Parliament

This article seeks to reappraise the role of Prince Frederick as a parliamentarian and also to reconsider the size and significance of his association in both Lords and Commons. Previous studies of Prince Frederick and of the so-called Leicester House grouping have tended to emphasize the prince's limitations as a political figure of real weight, to play down the extent of his activities as a parliamentary figure in his own right and have also paid scant attention to the role of the house of lords in Leicester House's schemes. By reconsidering some of the major political dramas of the 1730s and 1740s, this article aims to redress the balance, arguing that Prince Frederick was an active member of the Lords and that his association, though fluid, was more coherent and significant than is usually acknowledged.

Keywords: house of lords; house of commons; parliament; Prince Frederick; Sir Robert Walpole; excise crisis; jacobitism

1

On 10 May 1751, the house of lords debated a bill providing for the establishment of a regency in the event that the ailing King George II died before his grandson and heir apparent, the newly-created George, prince of Wales,[1] came of age. The bill was passed by an overwhelming majority. Two divisions held in a committee of the whole House accepted the inclusion of amended clauses within the bill, the first being carried by 98 votes to 12 and the second by an even larger margin: 106 to 12.[2] Of the peers who voted against the amendments, one, Earl Stanhope (who also acted as one of the tellers

* This article was originally given at a conference marking the 300th anniversary of the prince's birth held at the History of Parliament, on Saturday 14 Apr. 2007. I am grateful to Her Majesty The Queen for granting permission to quote from the Royal Archives at Windsor, to The Bodleian Library, University of Oxford, the Board of the British Library, and to Sir Edward Dashwood bt for granting permission to publish their manuscripts. I would also like to thank Stuart Handley for providing numerous references for this piece and to all of those who participated in the conference for their comments.

[1] The prince, who had inherited the dukedom of Edinburgh from his father, was created prince of Wales and earl of Chester on 20 Apr. 1751: *Peerage Creations: Chronological Lists of Creations in the Peerages of England and Great Britain 1649–1800 and of Ireland 1603–1898*, comp. J.C. Sainty (Parliamentary History: Texts & Studies, 1, Oxford, 2008), 41.

[2] *Divisions in the House of Lords: An Analytical List 1685 to 1857*, comp. J.C. Sainty and D. Dewar (House of Lords Record Office Occasional Publications no. 2, 1976); Horace Walpole, *The Memoirs of King George II*, ed. J. Brooke (3 vols, New Haven, 1985), i, 78–9; George Bubb Dodington gave the figures for the division by which the bill passed as 92 to 12.

on the second vote) was dismissed by Horace Walpole as an old republican, but several of the remaining minority peers[3] were distinguished by their association with the party of the former prince of Wales (Frederick), whose death earlier in the year had necessitated the composition of the bill. Historians have studied Prince Frederick's party, the so-called 'reversionary interest', sporadically over the years,[4] but such studies have tended to concentrate on the prince's household and his party in the Commons to the detriment of the prince's own role as a parliamentarian and that of the house of lords. They have also tended to emphasize the unwieldy nature of the fragile alliance forged with the tories after 1747, the prince's notorious unreliability[5] and of the apparent disintegration of the party in the aftermath of Frederick's death, helping thereby to perpetuate the view propounded by contemporary commentators such as Lord Hervey and by historians, such as Linda Colley, that as a political figure, Prince Frederick, to say the very least, lacked weight.[6] This article will seek to redress this balance in two ways: first by considering Prince Frederick himself as an active member of parliament in his own right; and second by reconsidering the actions and extent of his parliamentary association both in the Commons and in the house of lords. The Lords has tended to be rather overlooked by parliamentary historians of the mid 18th century, convinced by the opinions of contemporary observers like Dodington and Chesterfield, and by influential historians such as Sir Lewis Namier, that by the accession of George II (if not before) the House had lost much of its authority and independence. Such a view is not without evidence. One of those peers frequently associated with the prince, the earl of Bath, apparently echoing such an assessment, responded to a request to attend the House conveyed to him at Bath by one of the prince's household, Sir Thomas Bootle:

> Pray present my most humble duty to your master, and let him know that I am ready to come to town at an hour's warning, whenever he apprehends I may be of the least service to him, but as the House of Lords have seldom much to do, during the whole sessions, and never anything at the beginning of it, I think I may as well stay here a fortnight longer.[7]

But Bath's lethargic rejection of the importance of the upper chamber should not be taken at face value. The work of Michael McCahill has gone some way towards revising this dismissive interpretation,[8] which is also supported by the correspondence of Sarah, duchess of Marlborough with her husband's former comrade-in-arms, John Dalrymple, 2nd earl of Stair, in the later 1730s and early 1740s. Although the duchess was

---

[3] The earls of Thanet, Shaftesbury, Oxford, Lichfield, Viscounts Hereford and Townshend, and Barons Ward, Maynard, Foley, Romney and Talbot.

[4] *A Leicester House Political Diary, 1742–3*, ed. R. Harris (Camden misc. xxxi, 4th ser. xliv, 1992), 376–83; Linda Colley, *In Defiance of Oligarchy: The Tory Party 1714–60* (Cambridge, 1982), 221–2, 239–41, 253–60.

[5] 'The diary provides ample evidence of the cause of the prince's vacillation: his susceptibility to manipulation by stronger political personalities and intelligences': *Leicester House Political Diary*, ed. Harris, 380.

[6] Colley, *In Defiance of Oligarchy*, 222.

[7] Royal Archives, Windsor Castle [hereafter cited as RA], GEO/54099–100.

[8] 'The House of Lords did not invariably subordinate itself to the Crown, nor were its members naturally servile': M. McCahill, 'The House of Lords in the 1760s', in *A Pillar of the Constitution: The House of Lords in British Politics, 1640–1784*, ed. C. Jones (1989), 166; see also M. McCahill, *The House of Lords in the Age of George III (1760–1811)* (Parliamentary History: Texts & Studies, 3, Oxford, 2009).

undoubtedly decidedly cynical about the membership of much of the House, commenting on one occasion dismissively that: 'I really think that they might pass an Act there, if they pleased, to take away Magna Charta',[9] another letter revealed the extent to which, although the duchess herself remained unconvinced on this occasion, contemporaries retained a sense that the Lords at this time remained an active and dynamic part of parliament: 'Some people seem to think that some good must still happen from what is done in the House of Lords concerning the Spanish affair.'[10] Indeed, the duchess's correspondence as a whole with Stair emphasizes the continuing influence of members of the upper chamber both through the employment of their interest with members of the Commons and their direct interventions as parliamentarians in their own right. The career of Prince Frederick also seems to indicate that consideration of the House in the period prior to the accession of George III is deserving of further study.

2

Given the various confusions that surround other parts of his career, it seems not inappropriate that a degree of confusion surrounded the process by which Prince Frederick was first promoted to the peerage. From the time of his grandfather's accession to the throne until his arrival in England, Prince Frederick was the beneficiary of a number of honours as befitted his role in the line of succession, beginning with his admission to the order of the Garter in 1717.[11] The prince's evident pleasure in the accoutrements of this particular distinction was remarked upon wryly by the earl of Harold (heir to the dukedom of Kent) who visited Hanover at this time and noted that: 'Our young prince . . . proposes to himself a great deal of pleasure upon his installation and putting on of the Garter, and often looks upon the robes and ornaments of the order which have been brought him by Mr Le Neve the King at Arms.'[12] Between January and October 1718 there were six new peerage creations (all of them advancements),[13] but according to the *London Gazette* of 11 January, there ought to have been a seventh, as it was announced there that a warrant for Prince Frederick's creation as duke of Gloucester had been drawn up. Indeed Prince Frederick seems to have been styled duke of Gloucester from his grandfather's accession in 1714.[14] Yet, no mention was made of this title at the time of his installation as a knight of the Garter on 30 April

---

[9] Yale University, Beinecke Library, Osborn Papers, OSB MS 24, Box 1, folder 6, no. 3: duchess of Marlborough to earl of Stair, 3 Mar. 1736/7.

[10] Beinecke Library, OSB MS 24, Box 1, folder 8, no. 28: duchess of Marlborough to earl of Stair, 27 May 1738.

[11] The prince was invested at Hanover on 24 Dec. 1717 and installed by proxy the following year: W.A. Shaw, *The Knights of England: A Complete Record from the Earliest Time to the Present Day of the Knights of all the Orders of Chivalry in England, Scotland, and of Knights Bachelors* (2 vols, 1906), i, 41.

[12] Bedfordshire and Luton Archives and Records Service, Lucas MSS, L30/8/33/22: earl of Harold to duke of Kent, 3 Nov. 1716.

[13] Wharton, Cowper, Stanhope, Cadogan, Cobham, Sherard.

[14] Ragnhild Hatton believed that he was so styled from the age of 11 years (in 1718): see Ragnhild Hatton, *George I* (Yale, 2001), 156.

1718,[15] and when, in 1726, he was finally, incontrovertibly, raised to the peerage as duke of Edinburgh, no reference was made to the apparent former creation then either.[16] Even this award was muddled in its presentation. On 15 July, George Tilson wrote to the prince to congratulate him, stating that: 'tho' prince Frederic wants no addition to make him more valued and beloved; yet this new mark of the king's affection, with titles known among us will endear your highness more to the nation'.[17] But a month later, Tilson was forced to write again explaining that the original grant had had to be altered following a challenge from Viscount Windsor concerning one of the prince's supplementary titles. Thus:

> instead of Marquis of the Isle of Wight, it is now of the Isle of Ely. Lord Viscount Windsor, who has the title of Lord Mountjoy of the Isle of Wight, laid claim to the title of that island, which tho' wrong founded; yet it was thought better to leave out a title which had the least dispute, and put in another, which being proper for the Royal family, was not at all litigated.[18]

Such confusions and alterations of honours were far from uncommon. When Sir Henry Bennet was raised to the peerage during the reign of Charles II, he initially favoured taking the title of Cheney, but was then forced to rethink when members of the Cheney family objected to his selection. He eventually settled for the title of Arlington after a village where his brother was lord of the manor.[19] Another example of a peer being forced to change his mind about his preferred title was John, Lord Robartes, who, when promoted in the peerage to an earldom, seems originally to have selected the title 'earl of Falmouth'[20] but, following interjection from his countess that she did not wish to be associated with a town so notorious for corruption, Robartes changed his mind and selected the title of 'Radnor' instead.[21] At almost exactly the same time, Charles Gerard, Lord Gerard of Brandon, was also forced to alter his original preference to be advanced earl of Newbury and had to settle for the style of earl of Macclesfield.[22] When Frederick's father was still electoral prince of Hanover, the earl of Oxford made mention of a 'snivelling project' to make him duke of Clarence rather than of Cambridge, but that this, too, was laid aside.[23] Honoured with a further dukedom, that of Cornwall, in 1727, on 8 January 1729, Frederick added prince of Wales and earl of Chester to his fast-growing portfolio of titles[24] and on 21 January, he took his seat in the house of lords

---

[15] Shaw, *Knights of England*, i, 41.

[16] G.E. Cokayne, *The Complete Peerage of England Scotland Ireland Great Britain and the United Kingdom* (13 vols, 1910–59), vol. v, ed. Vicary Gibbs and H.A. Doubleday, 6–7; the prince's full honours were duke of Edinburgh, marquess of Ely, earl of Eltham, Viscount Launceston and Baron Snowdon: see below, note 24 and Sainty, *Peerage Creations*, 35.

[17] RA, GEO/Add. 1/5.

[18] RA, GEO/Add. 1/7.

[19] *CSP Dom., 1664–5*, pp. 232–54.

[20] *CSP Dom., 1679–80*, p. 196.

[21] *Magna Britannica*, iii (1814), 99–112.

[22] HMC, *Le Fleming MSS*, 161; TNA, C231/8, p. 12.

[23] HMC, *Portland MSS*, ii, 196.

[24] Frederick Lewis, baron of Snowdon, Viscount Launceston, earl of Eltham and Chester, marquess of Ely, duke of Edinburgh and Cornwall, prince of Wales.

for the first time, paying a fee of £30 to black rod for his introduction.[25] The prince, resident in Hanover until the winter of 1728, had been entitled to sit for almost a whole year prior to his creation as prince of Wales and, according to Hervey, the king had finally been compelled to summon his despised, eldest son from Germany against his better inclinations, eventually capitulating to political pressure 'as children take physic', and only allowing 'himself to swallow this bitter draught for fear of having it poured down his throat'.[26] Even then, questions were raised about his promotion as prince of Wales, Lord Egmont querying whether parliament should ratify the creation.[27]

Despite this none-too-auspicious beginning, relations between father and son proved to be noticeably cordial at first and Frederick's attendance at parliament appears initially to have been closely related to the king's own appearances. Of the ten occasions on which Frederick sat in his first session as a member of the House, four were on days when the king was also in attendance.[28] Yet he soon established a separate career of his own and after he resumed his seat for the third session of the 1727 parliament on 13 January 1730, he proceeded to attend on a further 21 occasions, only three of which were attended by the king.[29] The following session revealed a similar pattern, with Frederick present on 30 days, of which the king attended on just four.[30] In all, Frederick sat on 273 occasions, an average of just under 12 attendances per session. When the king had been prince of Wales he had attended rather more frequently, being present on 304 occasions before his accession, an average of 23 sittings per session. But while Frederick's attendance at the House was hardly diligent, and towards the end of his life his attendance did, indeed, decline to the extent that he did little more than mirror the king's occasional appearances (about five per session), it seems clear that at times his participation in the business of parliament went beyond the merely ceremonial.[31] He was, for instance, present in the House in March 1744, to witness the speech given by his former bugbear, Orford (Robert Walpole) and the motion for an address to the king, following which he was noted to have sat by the lord chancellor to look over the document while it was being drafted.[32]

Quite how active Prince Frederick truly was in the House itself is difficult to determine precisely. One study of the opposition in the period drew attention to at least two of the problems facing the historian attempting to establish Frederick's role as more than a merely ephemeral figure in the life of parliament, noting that: 'he seems never to have addressed the peers or cast a vote. He sought rather to inspire the opposition and bring over waverers by canvassing and applause.'[33] Yet it seems clear that early on,

---

[25] *A new and correct list of the Lords spiritual and temporal: with a double list of the Commons, chosen to serve in the present Parliament* (1742).

[26] *Lord Hervey's Memoirs*, ed. Romney Sedgwick (1952), 50.

[27] HMC, *Egmont Diary*, i, 9.

[28] *LJ*, xxiii, 297, 323, 372, 435.

[29] *LJ*, xxiii, 484, 520, 576.

[30] *LJ*, xxiii, 590, 646, 666, 705.

[31] See Clyve Jones, 'The House of Lords and the Fall of Walpole', in *Hanoverian Britain and Empire*, ed. Stephen Taylor, Richard Connors and Clyve Jones (Woodbridge, 1998), 118–9.

[32] *Correspondence of John Campbell*, ed. John E. Davis (Parliamentary History: Texts & Studies, 8, Oxford, 2013): John Campbell to Pryse Campbell, 1 Mar. 1743/4.

[33] A.S. Foord, *His Majesty's Opposition, 1714–1830* (Oxford, 1964), 167 n.

Prince Frederick was more active as a member of the House than this assessment suggests. On 5 May 1731, Viscount Perceval (later one of Frederick's principal men of business as earl of Egmont) recorded his own vigorous canvassing among the Lords for the passing of the Wool Bill. Although debate was put off to another occasion, he noted seeing the prince in the House and being 'told by one of his retinue that he came down to vote for the bill'. Encouraged by this, Percival called on Prince Frederick the following day, in advance of the postponed debate, in the hopes of securing his support for the measure. In the event, the bill was voted down by 38 to 35 and the prince did not turn out, perhaps having come under pressure not to lend his support to the bill, but it is indicative of the fact that the prince was perceived to be an active member of the House willing to exercise his vote.[34] Two years later, the prince was to the fore in exercising his interest on a rather more controversial measure than the Wool Bill. Commenting on his attitude to the Excise Bill[35] in his inaugural lecture to the University of Leicester, Aubrey Newman noted how:

> Fritz had expressed no opinion about the Excise Bill in public, but his private actions betrayed that he, like Lord Stair, took his politics from Bolingbroke . . . In flaunting his friendship for the 'Rump Steak' lords,[36] Fritz sailed near mutiny himself.[37]

Newman's interpretation follows closely Lord Hervey's analysis of the crisis, who described how:

> In all this excise affair the Prince in public acted a silent, quiet part, and Dodington, as his first minister, followed an example which in all probability was set him by his own dictates. However, by Dodington's never speaking in the House for the excise, and by Mr Townshend . . . voting against it, and by the distinctions the Prince showed on all occasions to Lord Cobham, Lord Stair, Lord Chesterfield, and all that were the most violent against this scheme, it was not difficult to guess what His Royal Highness's opinion of it was, or which way his wishes pointed.[38]

A few years later, another divisive measure also found the prince flexing his political muscles, as John Selwyn reported to Stephen Poyntz following the debate in the Commons on 17 March 1739 on the Spanish convention. The convention was Walpole's, ultimately unsuccessful, effort to keep Britain and Spain from descending into conflict following such alarming events as the appearance in parliament of Captain Robert Jenkins bearing a jar containing his ear, which had been severed by a Spanish coastguard. Selwyn described how:

---

[34] HMC, *Egmont Diary*, i, 188–90.

[35] For the excise crisis, see W.A. Speck, *Stability and Strife: England 1714–1760* (1977), 158, 213–16, 218–19; Paul Langford, *The Excise Crisis* (Oxford, 1975); Geoffrey Holmes and Daniel Szechi, *The Age of Oligarchy: Pre-Industrial Britain 1722–1783* (1993), 76–7, 82–4; and Clyve Jones, 'The House of Lords and the Excise Crisis', above, pp. 160–200.

[36] Presumably a reference to the Rump Steak or Liberty Club (also known as the Patriots Club), one of a number of associations of men in opposition to Walpole that was in existence between 1733 and 1734.

[37] A.N. Newman, *The World Turned Inside Out: New Views on George II. An Inaugural Lecture Delivered in the University of Leicester 10 October 1987* (Leicester, 1988).

[38] *Hervey's Memoirs*, ed. Sedgwick, 176.

The Prince's behaviour has not been only imprudent with regard to himself, but improper with regard to the parliament. He was the whole time in the House, applauding all abuse and canvassing the members. Mr Whitmore[39] he got within the last hour, and he kissed Mr Pitt in the House for his speech, which was very pretty and more scurrilous.[40]

Frederick's activities during this affair overturn Foord's conclusion that the prince never cast a vote, for he certainly did so on this occasion.[41] After the motion to pass the address was carried by 95 to 74, a list of the lords who had voted for and against the convention was printed with the list of those in opposition, headed prominently by the prince of Wales.[42] Prince Frederick's actions here precipitated some critical comment, as Duchess Sarah noted to Lord Stair that: 'I hear some People find fault with the Prince's having Voted in the House of Lords with the Minority; but I can see no Reason for that. For, surely He was as much at Liberty to do it, as any other Peer. And I can't Comprehend why he should not give his Vote in any thing that so manifestly was for the Good of England.'[43] Of the remaining 73 peers and bishops who joined Prince Frederick on this occasion only one, Lord North, was noted particularly as being a member of the prince's household and in receipt of an annual pension of £600, but a further seven can be closely identified with the prince's opposition grouping,[44] at least one more voted by proxy[45] and five others were to become closely associated with the prince and later went on to oppose the amendments to the 1751 Regency Bill.[46] It seems hard to deny that this was an example of Frederick actively participating in parliament and, perhaps, even emerging as the head of an interest. It is also clear that this was no isolated incident. Two years later, in April 1741, he held his nose and voted with the ministry in supporting the award of a subsidy to Austria.[47] A stray reference in Dudley Ryder's diary, citing evidence provided by the earl of Jersey of the prince's character, related that the prince had also intended to speak in the House on the subject of the army reductions, but that 'his servants with great difficulty prevented him'.[48] By 1745, the prince's association and those areas in which he was particularly interested had evolved further, underlined by his presence in the House to hear the committee report into the

[39] Thomas Whitmore, member for Bridgnorth.

[40] *Memoirs of the Life and Administration of Sir Robert Walpole*, ed. William Coxe (3 vols, 1798), iii, 607–9.

[41] Colley, *In Defiance of Oligarchy*, 225.

[42] *An exact list of the lords, spiritual and temporal; who voted for and against the late Convention* (1739); Clyve Jones and Frances Harris, ' "A Question . . . Carried by Bishops, Pensioners, Place-men, Idiots": Sarah, Duchess of Marlborough and the Lords' Division over the Spanish Convention, 1 March 1739', *Parliamentary History*, xi (1992), 270.

[43] Beinecke Library, OSB MS 24, Box 1, folder 8, no. 4: duchess of Marlborough to earl of Stair, 3 Apr. 1739.

[44] Argyll, Bathurst, Carteret, Clinton, Cobham, Scarbrough, Talbot.

[45] Bute.

[46] Foley, Lichfield, Shaftesbury, Thanet, Townshend.

[47] Clyve Jones, 'Further Evidence of the Splits in the Anti-Walpole Opposition in the House of Lords: A List for the Division of 9 April 1741 on the Subsidy for Austria', *Parliamentary History*, xxiv (2005), 373.

[48] Harrowby MSS Trust, earl of Harrowby, Sandon Hall, Staffordshire, vol. 430, Dudley Ryder diaries, document 27 pt. 1b.

Northwest Passage Bill.[49] Yet although he was undoubtedly more active than Foord implied, as a parliamentarian, Prince Frederick undoubtedly remains a somewhat mercurial figure. Forecasts and division lists for some of the great causes that emerged during his time as a member of the House are relatively insubstantial and, even on the issue of the removal of Walpole, something for which the prince laboured long and hard, he remained officially neutral.[50]

While Frederick may not have spoken himself, or cast his own vote frequently, he undoubtedly influenced others who did, and actively made use of parliament to further his own designs. For instance, when Lord Archibald Hamilton voted against the motion proposed by Lord Baltimore[51] in the house of commons, for the establishment of a committee to enquire into the navy debt, the prince turned him out from his place as cofferer of the household, though he did offer him a pension of £1,200 in compensation,[52] and in March 1745, Frederick turned out another of his servants, Edward Bayntun Rolt, for refusing to countenance opposition to the scheme for raising supply of £3 million.[53] It is, thus, to the prince's association within the Commons and Lords and his activities as the holder of one of the most substantial electoral interests in the country, that one should turn to establish more clearly the extent of the prince's significance as a peer of parliament.

3

While the prince's employment of his interest against the excise seems to have been his first foray into concerted opposition to the ministry, the question of his allowance soon offered him a further opportunity to develop his relations with a number of opposition politicians. In March 1734, the prospect of proposing an increase to his allowance of £50,000 was widely believed to be one of the major subjects to be debated in parliament in the new session and Egmont recorded how: 'the angry gentlemen design among other things to bring into Parliament the £100,000 pa which they say the king ought to allow the Prince'. (£100,000 had been the allowance paid to George II while prince of Wales.)[54] The affair threatened to place members of the court in uncomfortable positions, Egmont noting how he had:

> heard from others that my Lord Cholmondeley, Master of the Horse to the Prince, and son in law to Sir Robert Walpole, had refused to move for an address of thanks to the King's speech, on account of his near alliance to Sir Robert, and his being the

---

[49] Marie Peters, 'State, Parliament and Empire in the Mid 18th Century: Hudson's Bay and the Parliamentary Enquiry of 1749', *Parliamentary History*, xxix (2010), 182.

[50] BL, Add. MS 47000, f. 112.

[51] Charles Calvert, 5th Baron Baltimore [I], a gentleman of the bedchamber to the prince from 1731–47 and cofferer of the prince's household from 1747 until the prince's death.

[52] *The History of Parliament: The House of Commons, 1715–1754*, ed. Romney Sedgwick (2 vols, 1970) [hereafter cited as *HPC, 1715–54*], ii, 99. Hamilton was also significant as the husband of Prince Frederick's long-term mistress.

[53] HMC, *Egmont Diary*, iii, 315.

[54] Hatton, *George I*, 145.

Prince's servant, which he thought rendered him unfit to make such motion, and would come better from a country lord.[55]

Although Prince Frederick was able to garner a significant level of support, having 'personally approached every influential acquaintance who might help to bring his cause to victory in parliament',[56] according to Hervey, he soon squandered the goodwill of those he had been courting:

> The Prince's affair was often talked of in private, but never mentioned in either House. He contrived to irritate the Court by alarming them with caballing, and to disoblige those with whom he caballed by stopping there, and not giving his consent to have it prosecuted in Parliament. The Tories and discontented Whigs were so dissatisfied with his conduct that they abused him more than they did his father and said that he had only drawn them in to make the offer of standing by him that he might make a merit to his father of rejecting that offer and betraying them. On the other hand his father and mother, though they were frightened out of their senses if they thought their son's name was near being mentioned in Parliament, whenever these fears abated treated him in the most provoking manner and spoke of him in the most contemptuous terms.[57]

The question of the prince's allowance refused to go away and three years later, a further concerted effort was made to secure Frederick what many considered his due. According to Romney Sedgwick: 'in 1737 the only question on which Walpole was seriously pressed was Pulteney's motion for an increase of the prince's allowance'.[58] This certainly appears to have been the impression made on the duchess of Marlborough, who reported to Stair how:

> Since my last there has been a great Bustle in the Houses of Parliament concerning the Revenue which the Publick pays to the King to support the Prince of Wales. The Court carry'd it by a majority of thirty, not without the Expense of a great deal of Mony, & a most shameful Proceeding to threaten & fetch sick men out of their Beds to vote for fear of losing their Bread. But notwithstanding this, the Minority for the Prince was 204, And a great many other members who would have been in it, if they had been in Town . . . I am confident that tho the Prince lost the Question, the Ministers are mightily frighted & not without reason: For it is a heavy weight, 204, who were certainly on the right side of the Question.[59]

The prince's own canvassing was said to have gained his cause 27 friends, while Egmont noted that Mr Herbert, 'though a great friend of Sir Robert Walpole', had engaged three more and that there was a real prospect of the motion being carried. When Walpole proposed a compromise, the prince refused it, claiming that: 'the Affair was

[55] HMC, *Egmont Diary*, ii, 7.

[56] John Walters, *The Royal Griffin: Frederick Prince of Wales 1707–1751* (1972), 133.

[57] *Hervey's Memoirs*, ed. Sedgwick, 255.

[58] *HPC, 1715–54*, i, 43–4.

[59] Beinecke Library, OSB MS 24, Box 1, folder 6, no. 3: duchess of Marlborough to earl of Stair, 3 Mar. 1736/7.

now out of his Hands, and therefore he could give no answer to it'.[60] Despite these efforts and the fact that 35 government supporters rebelled on the issue, in February the motion to compel the king to increase Frederick's allowance was defeated in the Commons by 234 to 204 and in the Lords by 103 to 40, where the lead had been taken on the prince's part by Lord Carteret and the earl of Westmorland, while the earls of Strafford and Oxford, all the bishops and all the Scottish peers held firm for the ministry.[61] Following the defeat, 14 peers in Frederick's interest protested (three of them – Bathurst, Cobham and Carteret – being peers who had previously featured in divisions in which the prince had been interested): Winchelsea, Berkshire, Cobham, Chesterfield, Cardigan, Marlborough, Carteret, Bridgwater, Bedford, Weymouth, Bathurst, Coventry, Ker and Suffolk.[62] And although the government had undoubtedly experienced a very close shave in the lower House, defeat of the measure appears to have put the matter to rest for the time being. It was not, of course, the end of the prince's association with opposition. Walpole's grip on power was weakened after the defeat of the Excise Bill and further undermined by the death of Queen Caroline, but it was ultimately as the result of parliamentary pressure brought by an alliance of opposition groups, among them those associated with the prince, that he was finally brought down. One of the things that made this possible was the effective marshalling of the prince's interest in the 1741 election, which resulted in seven gains in Cornwall and ten in Scotland (through the interest of the duke of Argyll), and which contributed to the reduction of Walpole's majority in the Commons from 42 to 19.[63] More important still, was the successful election of Frederick's close associate, Dr George Lee, as chairman of the Commons' elections committee.[64] Walpole's fall enabled the king and prince to forge a reconciliation[65] and the vexed question of the prince's allowance was finally resolved when the Commons voted the prince his desired income of £100,000 a year in May 1742. It is perhaps worth noting Pulteney's response to the situation created by Walpole's removal. Refusing office himself, he declared that 'he had pulled down the ministry but he would not pull down the king', and Hardwicke's belief that Prince Frederick, by now eager to be reconciled as well, suggests that his position was not so very different.[66] Peace between the king and Prince Frederick, strengthened by the general threat to dynasty posed by the jacobite rebellion in 1745, was maintained until 1746, after which Frederick once more espoused opposition. Dudley Ryder noted in January 1746, that: 'the Prince showed in the House by Lord Baltimore's motion that he intended a perpetual opposition',[67] and two months later he reported a conversation with Henry Pelham in which Pelham had confided that: 'the Prince had

[60] *Gentleman's Magazine*, vii, 483, quoted in *ODNB*.

[61] HMC, *Egmont Diary*, ii, 360.

[62] *History and Proceedings of the House of Lords from the Restoration in 1660, to the Present Time*, ed. Ebernezer Timberland (7 vols, 1742), v, 161.

[63] *HPC, 1715–54*, i, 46. Speck notes that when Prince Frederick went into opposition following his quarrel with the king in 1737, he took with him '8 dependent members': Speck, *Stability and Strife*, 236.

[64] *HPC, 1715–54*, i, 47–8.

[65] *HPC, 1715–54*, i, 52.

[66] *HPC, 1715–54*, i, 52.

[67] Harrowby MSS Trust, Dudley Ryder notes, document 21: 22 Jan. 1746.

told some of the Ministers that there was no way for the Prince of Wales to make a figure here but in war or by opposition. He, being precluded the former, would use the latter.'[68]

The defeat of the jacobite rebellion and the prospects of peace in Europe and America were the occasion of the prince's return to opposition, taking the lead at the head of those who considered the prospective peace being negotiated by Sandwich at Aix-la-Chapelle as dishonourable and precipitant.[69] The Leicester House declaration of June 1747, which has been discussed elsewhere,[70] attempted to lay out in more concrete terms than previously, the way in which an alliance between dissident whigs and tories might be made to work, but it was viewed with distrust by many and Frederick's hopes of possessing a genuinely commanding interest in the Commons were quashed by the snap general election held the following month.[71] Not that the prince's interest was taken particularly by surprise, as it was commented on in October 1746 that he had already started making preparations for elections then believed to be two years distant[72] and in November that he 'closets many persons on that head'.[73] The death of John Hylton at Carlisle in the autumn of 1746 encouraged Prince Frederick to approach the earl of Carlisle in the hopes of gaining his support for one of the prince's candidates,[74] though in the event, Carlisle backed one of his own associates, John Stanwix, and in the subsequent general election of July 1747, the prince failed to garner the support for which he had hoped. In Cornwall, whereas in 1741, 29 opposition members had been returned, in 1747, they could muster only 19, and in Scotland, opposition members were reduced to ten. A concerted effort by the Pelhams against the duke of Somerset's interest at Midhurst provoked a particularly aggrieved response from Frederick, who complained to Sir Thomas Bootle:

I can't help being vex'd to see these fellows insolence strike at somebody so respectable, and so staunch a friend to my family, in the worst of times too, as the duke is, where will they stop? and what must mankind expect in generall, when the first subject, in rank, dignity, and worth, is not to be spar'd.[75]

Despite these reversals, the prince remained confident and his initial forecast as confided to Bootle was that his association should win 225 seats in England alone.[76] Writing to his west country ally, Lord Clinton, he was forced to revise this buoyant estimate, but still seemed satisfied with the state of affairs:

---

[68] Harrowby MSS Trust, Dudley Ryder notes, document 21: 10 Mar. 1746.

[69] Speck notes that: 'The only serious threat the Pelhams had to face after 1746 came from Frederick, the Prince of Wales, who wanted "to have the influence due to his rank" ': Speck, *Stability and Strife*, 251.

[70] *Leicester House Politics, 1750–60, from the Papers of John, 2nd Earl of Egmont*, ed. A.N. Newman (Camden misc. xxiii, 4th ser., vii, 1969), 89–91.

[71] Speck, *Stability and Strife*, 252.

[72] *HPC, 1715–54*, i, 56.

[73] *HPC, 1715–54*, i, 56.

[74] RA, GEO/54051: Prince Frederick to Lord Carlisle, 1 Oct. 1746.

[75] RA, GEO/54055—6: Prince Frederick to Sir Thomas Bootle, 8 June 1747.

[76] RA, GEO/54057: prince of Wales to Sir Thomas Bootle, [1747].

The Pelhams allow us 205, without Scotland, where I know of 10. The confusion amongst 'em is great, as every body says, and several changes are spoken off, which with the miseries of Flanders, will destroy 'em, but I'm afraid so late, that this country will perish with 'em.[77]

Henry Rolle's promotion to the peerage following this election provided the prince with a further opportunity to add to his grouping in the Commons, and his correspondence with Clinton in preparation for the by-election at Barnstaple demonstrates clearly how active the prince was as an electoral manager in his own right. Still confident that 'things appear in a very good way', Frederick recommended that Clinton's: 'brother-in-law might stop the officers of the Revenue of flying in your face, but if his Christianity, morality, or servile obedience to Pelham or to the recanting Pay Master should hinder him of it, the Free-men will set all right'.[78]

In the event, despite Prince Frederick's undertaking to provide £1,800 towards the expenses of the election, Clinton and his Fortescue kinsmen withdrew, leaving the ministry's candidate, Sir Bourchier Wrey, to carry the seat unchallenged.[79] The example of Barnstaple proved to be ominous. Writing in October, Thomas Birch noted how he had seen a list of the new parliament: 'which reckons the Tories to be 136, the Prince's Party 53, and the Whimsicals 14'.[80] On the face of it, a coalition of 203 (just two short of the figure that the Pelhams had anticipated) was an impressive body and had the prince's association held firm as he hoped, a grouping that remained in excess of 200 would have proved a formidable interest within parliament, but the reality was that the coalition was anything but secure and belied the confident predictions of February 1748 that fracturing within the ministry would shortly result in the prince securing a majority in the house of commons.[81] Not surprisingly, like Hervey, Ryder viewed the prince's motives with more than a hint of cynicism and in advance of the new parliamentary session of 1748, he noted again that: 'The general end proposed by the Prince is to make a figure in the world as a man of consequence. Since he cannot have the actual government, he may be able to govern by the ministry he would impose on the king.'[82] But as the session progressed, Frederick's association in the Commons dwindled steadily such that by the time of his death it was reckoned at between just 40 and 60 strong[83] with his core support fragmented between the squabbling heads of several factions.[84]

The situation in the Lords is slightly more difficult to assess. To begin with, peers untrammelled by the vicissitudes of elections for their places in parliament were more free to fluctuate in their allegiances and during the 23 years between the prince's arrival in England and his death, there were, unsurprisingly, a number of changes in allegiance

[77] Devon RO, Fortescue of Castle Hill MSS, 1262M/O/EP/4: Prince Frederick to Lord Clinton, 5 [ ] 1747.

[78] Devon RO, Fortescue of Castle Hill MSS, 1262M/0/EP/4: Prince Frederick to Lord Clinton, Saturday evening [between July 1747 and Jan. 1748].

[79] *HPC, 1715–54*, i, 225.

[80] BL, Add. MS 35397, ff. 84–5. I am grateful to Clyve Jones for providing me with this reference.

[81] Harrowby MSS Trust, Dudley Ryder notes, document 21: 6 Feb. 1748.

[82] Harrowby MSS Trust, vol. 432, Dudley Ryder notes, document 35 (1): 26 Nov. 1748.

[83] Foord, *His Majesty's Opposition*, 267.

[84] *HPC, 1715–54*, i, 59.

as well as alterations brought about by the succession of new members to the peerage. Some, like Lord Chesterfield, who had been associated with the prince in the 1730s, had returned to government in the late 1740s, while Falmouth's decision to support the ministry in the 1747 election proved crucial in eroding the prince's interest in Cornwall.[85] Carteret, at one time closely associated with the prince, had also gone his own way and since the death of the 2nd duke of Argyll, the prince's principal managers seem to have been concentrated in the Commons: Baltimore, Lee, Egmont and Dodington. Another prominent member of the Leicester House set, Frederick's master of the horse, the earl of Middlesex, though the heir to a dukedom, was also in the Commons. Indeed in 1741, the prince had just two placemen in the house of lords.[86] This modest figure doubled the following year with the appointments of the earls of Halifax and Darnley (Baron Clifton in the English peerage) as gentlemen of the bedchamber (though both of these two had ceased to act as such by 1745).[87] In 1744, the marquess of Carnarvon, the prince's groom of the stole, succeeded to the dukedom of Chandos, thereby adding one more. But there were clearly other members of the Lords who were identified with the prince's party. When the motion to remove Sir Robert Walpole in February 1741 was defeated by 108 to 59,[88] although the prince himself was noted as neutral on the issue, almost a third of those either supporting, or expected to support, Walpole's removal, were closely associated with Frederick[89] and of the 26 lords who signed the protest at the failure to pass the measure, again, several members of the prince's entourage were prominent among the signatories: Lichfield, Westmorland, Falmouth, Talbot, Bathurst, Clinton, St John of Bletso and Carlisle.[90] Following Walpole's fall, the prince insisted on several of these being offered places by the king, among them Bathurst, Gower, Carlisle, Westmorland and Cobham.[91] Two sources that seem not to have been much utilised provide further insight into those members of the Lords on whom Frederick and his managers believed they were able to rely in the latter stages of his career. The first is a list in the Dashwood Papers, probably drawn up following the 1747 election providing a list of opposition members in both Houses of which 24 were members of the house of lords. Of these, a number were tories and not necessarily particular friends of the prince, but about a third were closely associated with Leicester House.[92] The second source is one of a series of lists of likely officeholders to be appointed to the government in the event of the king's death, which was drawn up by Prince Frederick and Egmont

---

[85] *HPC, 1715–54*, i, 220.

[86] Francis, Lord North (gentleman of the bedchamber 1730–51) and Thomas, 3rd earl of Scarbrough (treasurer and receiver general 1738–51).

[87] Jones, 'The House of Lords and the Fall of Walpole', 118.

[88] In his letter to Henry Etough describing the division, John Orlebar failed to take account of the proxies that were added to the tally and gave the margin as 89 to 47 votes, see *Memoirs of the Life and Administration of Sir Robert Walpole*, ed. Coxe (3 vols, 1798), iii, 563–4.

[89] *Divisions in the House of Lords*, comp. Sainty and Dewar; BL, Add. MS 47000, f. 112; Add. MS 33034, ff. 1–3, 21–4.

[90] *History and Proceedings of the House of Lords*, ed. Timberland, vii, 728.

[91] Frances Vivian, *A Life of Frederick, Prince of Wales, 1707–1751: A Connoisseur of the Arts*, ed. Roger White (2006), 340.

[92] Bodl., MS D.D. Dashwood, D1/3/13: list of Lords and Commons in opposition, undated; see Appendix A.

in about 1750. Here, too, members of the Lords feature prominently, with some 34 listed as potential officeholders in an administration appointed by the prince.[93] Between these two lists there is, as one might expect, a degree of overlap with three members of the upper House featuring in both: the earls of Lichfield and Westmorland and Lord Talbot. While the prince's following in the house of lords was clearly more limited than that in the Commons, where for much of the late 1730s and 1740s he could expect a degree of loyalty from about 200 members, it is clear that a significant rump of the upper House was consistent in its support for the prince's measures. It is also clear that the prince recognized the importance of the upper chamber. In an undated letter of 1748, the prince related to his electoral manager, George Lee, how the Lords had become his principal point of focus:

> Th'affair of Bucks being o'er in the House of Commons, the House of Lords has been my great attention this week, and I can tell you with great pleasure, that matters are there in a great forwardness. Lord Granville, Chesterfield, Bath, the old opposing lords and several of the courtiers will fight it. I dare say things will come nearer there than can be imagined. The court will have but the two secretaries of state and the Chancellor to support the Bill, and how even he will dare do it against all West-minster Hall, I can't conceive.[94]

Maintaining a loyal group in the upper chamber was, clearly, of the utmost importance and among the various lists devised with Egmont is one (previously printed by Aubrey Newman in *Leicester House Politics*) outlining which Scottish representative peers should be brought in following his accession to help bolster his support in the Lords.[95]

4

Just how effective was Prince Frederick's 'loyal opposition' to the governments he faced and what did he hope to achieve from abandoning the court for opposition? Certainly, the king was in no doubt of the essentially inimical nature of Frederick's associates. During the crisis precipitated by the prince's flight from court in the summer of 1737, letters between Prince Frederick and his father reveal only too clearly where the king laid the blame for his son's actions. Unwilling to countenance the prince's fulsome apologies, the king spelled out the only way by which he might be restored to his improved opinion:

> The professions you have lately made me in your letters of your particular regard to me are so contradictory to all your actions that I cannot suffer myself to be imposed on by 'em . . . This extravagant and undutiful behaviour in so essential a point as the birth of an heir to my crown, is such a contempt of my authority and of the natural right belonging to your parents as cannot be excused by the pretended innocence of intentions or palliated or disguised by specious words only . . . Until you withdraw

[93] BL, Add. MS 47012A, ff. 72–3; see Appendix B.
[94] RA, GEO/73977: Prince Frederick to Dr Lee, [16–22 Mar. 1748].
[95] *Leicester House Politics*, ed. Newman, 171.

your regard and confidence from those by whose instigation or advice you are directed or encouraged in your unwarrantable behaviour to me and the queen and until you return to your duty you shall not reside in my palace, which I will not suffer to be a resort of 'em who under the appearance of an attachment to you foment the division which you have made in my family and thereby weakened the common interest of the whole.[96]

Foord also echoes this depiction of a man out to make trouble quite as much as anything else. In summarizing Prince Frederick's character, he suggested that:

Whatever his personal weaknesses, the inescapable consequences of his situation as heir to the throne do more to account for his failures. A royal personage without functions, he had nothing to do but dabble in politics … To this conventional motive Frederick added only a desire for revenge upon his parents.[97]

Disloyal to his family, at times, Prince Frederick may have been. But to concede that, is not to suggest that his political campaigns were ineffective or without purpose, nor to explain why his reputation as a parliamentary figure has been so sorely neglected. Henry Fielding's *True Patriot*, while concurring, in part, with Foord's analysis, differs with him on several salient points, contesting in the spring of 1746 that:

His Royal Highness hath never yet had a single opportunity of carrying any great political or martial quality into act; and I am justified in saying it is owing to the want of such an opportunity only that the world do not see the most shining examples of both, when I speak first from the testimony of those who have the honour to be near his person, and to be admitted to his conversation; and secondly, from his exemplary conduct in his own family.[98]

Moreover, if the prince's own loyalty might remain in question, his personal charisma and ability to inspire loyalty in others should not. One equerry noted how the manner in which the prince conferred the office on him, 'very much enhances its value'[99] while Dodington's account of his interview with the prince in July 1749 to discuss plans for a government-in-waiting, although no doubt bearing some of Dodington's personal gloss, reveals the prince as an earnest and enthusiastic character, eager to employ his interest.[100] Writing to Egmont in February 1749, the ailing rake, Thomas Potter, 'completely knocked up' by his exertions in the House the previous day and warned by his physicians that his life would be in danger if he returned to the Commons again that session, assured Egmont that: 'my obligations to his Royal Highness and my attachments to him are such that if his interests were at stake (which as yet I hope they are not very deeply) I should willingly spend my last breath in his service'.[101]

---

[96] Bodl., MS film 2022 (Shelburne Papers), Box 116, ff. 143–4.

[97] Foord, *His Majesty's Opposition*, 167.

[98] Henry Fielding, *The True Patriot and Related Writings*, ed. W.B. Coley (Oxford, 1987), 281.

[99] Hannah Smith, *Georgian Monarchy: Politics and Culture, 1714–1760* (Cambridge, 2006), 214.

[100] *The Eighteenth Century Constitution 1688–1815: Documents and Commentary*, ed. E.N. Williams (1960), 203–4.

[101] BL, Add. MS 47012 B, f. 165.

As far as the prince's own motivations were concerned, clearly, there was an extent to which he was not so very different from other princes of Wales of this, or any other, period floundering in search of a role while real authority was denied them. Carswell and Dralle, the editors of Dodington's journal, detected 'in Frederick a yearning for continuity with the old dynasty',[102] while Frederick himself, viewed his opposition as essentially loyal to his family, assuring Bootle at the time of the 1747 election that:

> My upright intentions are known to you, my duty towards my father calls for it, one must redeem him out of those hands that have sullied the Crown, and are very near to ruin all. I'll endeavour it, and I hope with my friends' assistance to rescue a second time this nation, out of wicked hands.[103]

Whether Prince Frederick's programmes were, indeed, based on ideology or on opportunism, it seems clear that as an active peer of parliament and the head of an influential association within both the Commons and the Lords, he is a figure that should no longer be neglected.

APPENDIX A: *List of Lords and Commons in Opposition*

(The Bodleian Library, MS D.D. Dashwood, D1/3/13)

Duke of Beaufort
Lds Abingdon
Aylesford
Denbigh
Litchfield
Oxford
Orrery
Shaftesbury
Thanet
Westmorland
Stanhope
Northampton
Suffolk
Folkestone
Craven
Foley
Windsor
St John [John St John,
    2nd Viscount St John]
St John [John St John,
    11th Baron St John of Bletso]

---

[102] *The Political Journal of George Bubb Dodington*, ed. J. Carswell and L.A. Dralle (Oxford, 1965), p. xix.
[103] RA, GEO/54059: Prince Frederick to Sir Thomas Bootle, [June 1747].

Talbott
Masham
Maynard
Wentworth
Ward

Sr Robt Abdy
Sr John Astley
John Affleck
Sr John St Aubin
Sr Walter Baggott
Sr Ricd Bampfylde
Honble Ricd Barry
Benj: Bathurst
Norborne Berkeley
Norris Bertie
Thos Best
Walter Blacket
George Bowes
Ld Bulkeley
John Butler
Thomas Bury
Honble Wm Boverie
John Browne
Mr Coventry Carew
Thos Cartwright
Geo Chaffin
Thos Chester
Ricd Clayton
John Conyers
Sr Jno H. Cotton
Velters Cornwall
Sr Wm Courtenay
Wm Craven
John Crew
Sr Nat: Curzon
Wm Curzon
Saml Child
Cha: Cholmondeley
Ld Cornbury
Honble Geo: Compton
Sr Fra: Dashwood
Sr James Dashwood
Wm Drake
Wm Dowdeswell
Sr Thos Egerton

Nick. Fazakerly
John Fenwick
Sr Cord: Firebrace
Thos Foley
Hen: Furnese
Coulson Fellows
Chas Gray
Fulk Greville
Sr Robt Grosvenor
Wm Gore
Fra: Gwyn
Ld Harley
Sr Hen: Harpur
Wm Hervey
Thos Hawkins
Robt Henley
Philip Herbert
Ld Hillsborough
Robt Hoblyn
Paul Humfrey
Sr Edmd Isham
Edwd Kynaston
Peter Legh
Thos Lyster
Ricd Lyster
Sr Robt Long
Ricd Lowndes
J. Robinson Lytton
Herbert Mackworth
Sr Henry Marshall
Thos Master
Paul Methuen
Sr John Molesworth
Sr Chas Mordaunt
Sr Wm Morice
Wrighton Mundy
Sr Thos Mostyn
John Morton
James Noel
Wm Northey
Per: Palmer
Sr John Peachy
James Peachy
John Fredk Pinney
George Pitt
Edwd Popham

Penyston Powney
Thos Prowse
Henry Pye
Edmd Pytts
Jonthn Rashleigh
Mat Robinson
Thos Rowney
Ricd Shuttleworth
Jas Shuttleworth
Edwd Smith
Edwd Southwell
Sr Miles Stapleton
Ld Strange
Ant. Langley Swymmer
Humphrey Sydenham
Sr Chas. Sedley
Seawallis Shirley
Coningsby Sibthorpe
Sr Henry Slingsby
John Symmonds
Chas. Taylor
Sr Edwd. Turner
Sr Roger Twysden
Sr Charles Tynte
John Talbot
John Tempest
Edwd Vernon
Robt Vyner
Philip Warburton
James Wigley
Randle Wilbraham
Kyffin Williams
Thos Whichcott
Thos Wyndford
Armine Woodhouse
George Wright
Sr Wat. Williams Wynne

APPENDIX B: *Prince Frederick and Lord Egmont's Proposals for Peers to be Included in a New Ministry c.1750*

(BL, Add. MS 47012A, f. 72: © British Library Board)

Lord Bath – President Council
Lord Oxford or Lord Northampton – Privy Seal

duke of Rutland – Ld Chamberlain
duke of Marlborough – Ld Steward
duke of Chandos – groom of the stole
earl of Harrington – Secretary of State
marquess of Tweeddale – ditto for Scotland
duke of Argyll – as he is
earl of Halifax – first commissioner for trade
Lord Chesterfield – ld lt of Ireland
earl of Carlisle – 1 Commr Treasury
Earl of Westmorland – master of the ordnance
Lord Dodington – master of the wardrobe
Lord Talbot – master of the jewel office
Lord Lichfield – lord chief justice Trent north
Lord Romney – treasurer to the queen
earl of Scarbrough – cabinet & £3,000 p.a.
Earl Granville – ranger of the parks, cabinet counsellor & £3,000 p.a.
Lord Berkeley – ambassador to Spain
earl of Winchelsea – warden of the cinque ports and constable of Dover Castle
duke of Kingston – master of the horse to the queen
duke of Ancaster – master of the buckhounds
Lord North – governor to the Prince
earl of Northumberland (or H. Furnese) – treasurer to the Prince or lord chief justice
Trent north
Lord Ravensworth
Lord Bathurst – cabinet & £3,000 p.a.
duke of St Albans – as he is
Lord Cornwallis – as he is
Lord Falmouth – as he is is
Lord Cholmondeley – as he is, vice treasurer
Lord Edgecumbe
Lord Delawarr

Peel's Other Repeal:
The Test and Corporation Acts, 1828[*]

RICHARD A. GAUNT

This article considers Robert Peel's role in the repeal of the Test and Corporation Acts in 1828. Traditionally overshadowed by the larger campaign to secure catholic emancipation in 1829, the repeal legislation assumes importance in Peel's political career for three reasons. It was Peel's first major challenge as leader of the house of commons in Wellington's ministry; his handling of the issue revealed all his strengths and weaknesses in the role. Peel's insistence on the active participation of the anglican Church hierarchy in passing repeal with appropriate safeguards (through a declaration to be taken by the majority of officeholders) foreshadowed his later tactics in settling contentious Church issues by negotiation with the Church's leaders (leading to the formation of the Ecclesiastical Commission in 1835). The success of Russell's original repeal motion challenged the expectation (shared by Peel) that repeal would follow, rather than precede, emancipation. The necessity of confronting repeal head-on formed a backdrop to that 'ripening' of Peel's views which commentators and historians have detected during this period.

Keywords: Robert Peel; Test Acts; Corporation Act; catholic emancipation; dissenters; toryism; Anglicanism

1

The repeal of the Test and Corporation Acts in May 1828 does not normally rank high in the list of Robert Peel's achievements. The relative speed and unexpectedness of those acts' passing may be one explanation for their comparative neglect in the historiography of Peel's career. The speedy reassertion of catholic emancipation as the principal issue of British domestic politics, following the election of Daniel O'Connell for County Clare in July 1828, has also overshadowed, to some extent, their historical importance.[1] Historians will look in vain, in Peel's parliamentary speeches on repeal, for any evidence of that telling, if rather egotistical, tendency to make an identification between himself and his subject as the agent of reform. Anyone looking for such evidence will find it more easily upon numerous other occasions: in Peel's 1819 speech announcing his conversion to bullionist theory, which divided him from his father's

[*] This article began life as a paper to the Modern British History and Politics seminar at St John's College, Oxford, in March 2011. I am grateful to Simon Skinner, Robert Saunders and all those who subsequently commented on the paper for me.

[1] The standard account is Norman Gash, *Mr Secretary Peel* (2nd edn, Harlow, 1985), 461–5. Also, see Fergus O'Ferrall, *Catholic Emancipation: Daniel O'Connell and the Birth of Irish Democracy, 1820–1830* (Dublin, 1985), 181–2.

views on the subject; in Peel's highly personal association with criminal law reform in 1826; and, most famously, in the peroration to Peel's resignation speech following the repeal of the corn laws in 1846.[2] The nearest Peel came to this style of argument was in winding up his speech opposing Lord John Russell's repeal motion, on 26 February 1828: 'If the motion of the noble lord opposite shall be defeated, any sentiment of triumph which I may experience from the success of my own policy or opinions will be greatly abated by the fact, that such a result must be attended with disappointment to a class of persons for whom I have the highest respect.'[3] In one respect, Peel's self-restraint was understandable. Whereas, on the other three occasions, Peel was clearly an important agent of reform – an identification he was at pains to stress – in the case of the Test and Corporation Acts, his initial response to Russell's repeal measure was hostile and he would have been happier if the issue had never been raised. Thereafter, Peel's principal role was in steering a compromise settlement through the house of commons in such a way as, he hoped, would shore up the protestant constitution.

Yet there are good reasons to treat Peel's role in the other major repeal of his political career with some importance. It was his first major test, as leader of the house of commons, in the government formed by the duke of Wellington in January 1828; his handling of the issue revealed all his strengths and weaknesses in the role. It also came at something of a personal crossroads for Peel, who turned 40 years at the beginning of the month in which the repeal motion was brought forward. Gladstone in the late 19th century and Boyd Hilton in the late 20th each, in their own ways, identified the period after 1829 as the moment at which Peel's political conduct 'ripened' as he matured out of his unabashed youthful toryism and truly came of age.[4] By contrast, events in 1828 seemed to exemplify the confused responses of a man oscillating between his former and evolving selves. As the *Leicester Chronicle* observed at the time: 'Mr Peel . . . is a tory; but he is very different from the Tories of the last generation; the Mr Peel of 1828 is a very different man from the Mr Peel of 1808, or 1798.'[5]

In later life, Peel consciously decided to include what might otherwise be seen as a 37-page diversion, in the first volume of his posthumously published *Memoirs* (1856), to discuss the passage of the repeal legislation. Peel argued that: 'As the subject is of considerable importance, as the repeal of the Test and Corporation Acts was not without its influence on the removal of Roman Catholic disabilities . . . I shall probably be pardoned for giving such parts of [my] correspondence as are likely to have any public interest.'[6] Seeing the repeal of the Test and Corporation Acts as a prelude to catholic emancipation was entirely justifiable, in terms of developing a narrative – the first stage

[2] For a recent interpretation which makes much of Peel's egotistical tendencies, see R.A. Gaunt, *Sir Robert Peel: The Life and Legacy* (2010). For Peel's 'self-congratulatory speech' to the house of commons during the Reform Bill debates (12 Dec. 1831), see *The History of Parliament: The House of Commons, 1820–1832*, ed. David Fisher (7 vols, Cambridge, 2009) [hereafter cited as *HPC, 1820–32*], i, 362.

[3] *Speeches Delivered in the House of Commons by the Late Rt. Hon. Sir Robert Peel* (4 vols, New York, 1972), i, 551–6.

[4] *Prime Ministers Papers: W. E. Gladstone*, ed. John Brooke and Mary Sorensen (4 vols, 1971–81), iii, 77; Boyd Hilton, 'The Ripening of Robert Peel', in *Public and Private Doctrine: Essays in British History Presented to Maurice Cowling*, ed. Michael Bentley (Cambridge, 1993), 63–84.

[5] *Leicester Chronicle*, 12 Apr. 1828.

[6] *Memoirs of Sir Robert Peel*, ed. Lord Mahon and E. Cardwell (2 vols, New York, 1969), i, 64.

in the 'Constitutional Revolution' of 1828–32.[7] However, it had the unfortunate consequence of eliding Peel's responses on both issues, rather than considering the two issues (however intimately related) within their own context. In 1828, having figured amongst the minority of 193 MPs who opposed Russell's repeal motion, Peel subsequently took a decisive lead in providing for that measure to pass the house of commons with safeguards or securities. In particular, he introduced the requirement for all holders of corporate office, and a large number of those employed by the crown in the local government of England and Wales, regardless of religious affiliation, to make a declaration against using the 'power, authority or influence' of their office to undermine the 'rights and privileges' of the Church of England.[8] Substituting an affirmation for an oath was pregnant with all sorts of symbolic significance of the changing relationship between state and Church, yet it was one which largely passed unnoticed in contemporary debates. Only recently, in the wake of Jonathan Clark's argument that repeal inaugurated the collapse of the 'Confessional State' in Britain, has the significance of the measure begun to be debated in the historical literature.[9]

Equally significant was the fact that, in developing the repeal legislation, Peel placed a good deal of responsibility for devising the terms of settlement on the anglican Church itself. This, in embryo, was the tactic which Peel would bring to fruition with the foundation of the Ecclesiastical Commission in 1835.[10] Peel's strategy over repeal also raises interesting comparisons with his tactics a year later when piloting the Catholic Relief Bill through the house of commons, stripped of all manner of 'wings' or provisions, such as a royal veto on catholic bishops, concordat with the papacy or state-salaried priesthood.[11]

2

Under the Test and Corporation Acts of 1661 and 1673, all holders of civic, military and corporate offices in England and Wales were required to meet a sacramental test, by proving that they had 'received the sacrament of the Lord's Supper according to the rites of the Church of England'.[12] Whatever the original intentions of the framers of this legislation, it increasingly served as a barrier to the various dissenting denominations in providing access to such offices, especially in the corporations. The periodic declarations of monarchs such as Charles II, William III and George I to rectify this situation came to nothing. Whilst a series of Indemnity Acts, from the late 1720s, served to indemnify those dissenters who conformed occasionally, by taking the sacrament in order to meet the letter of the legislation, this indemnity was predicated upon the assumption that the

---

[7] G.F.A. Best, 'The Constitutional Revolution, 1828–32', *Theology*, lxii (1959), 226–34; Norman Gash, *Aristocracy and People: Britain 1815–1865* (1979), ch. 5.

[8] For the repeal legislation, *English Historical Documents, VIII 1783–1832*, ed. Arthur Aspinall and E.A. Smith (1959), 674–5.

[9] J.C.D. Clark, *English Society 1660–1832* (2nd edn, Cambridge, 2000), 440, 527–47; Richard W. Davis, 'The Politics of the Confessional State', *Parliamentary History*, ix (1990), 38–49.

[10] Richard W. Davis, 'Toryism to Tamworth: The Triumph of Reform', *Albion*, xii (1980), 132–46.

[11] Boyd Hilton, *A Mad, Bad, & Dangerous People? England, 1783–1846* (Oxford, 2006), 379–84.

[12] *Statutes of the Realm*, v, 321–3, 894–6.

person so indemnified had 'failed to take the Test for ignorance, absence or unavoidable accident' and not as a matter of conscience.[13] As the *Liverpool Mercury* observed, in March 1828, the Indemnity Acts could 'be withheld at pleasure, and the provisions . . . defeated by private pique, mistaken zeal, or party hostility'. As such, they may be said to have offered an 'illusory protection'.[14] Occasional conformers ran the risk of ostracism and exclusion by their brethren, who did not view the sacrifice of religious conscience for public office lightly. The Indemnity Acts did nothing for the conscientious objector and were principally useful in allowing an extended period of grace in which to comply with the terms of the Corporation Act, which required the sacrament to have been taken in the year prior to assuming office rather than, as in the Test Act, within three months of admission to office.

Defenders of the Test and Corporation Acts habitually referred to the Indemnity Acts as proof that the original legislation was not acting against dissenters' ambitions. Corporations such as Bristol, Nottingham and London had a dissenting complexion whilst, in the decade before repeal, three mayors of London (Matthew Wood, Robert Waithman and Anthony Brown) were dissenters. The Corporation Act did not extend to Ireland and the Test Act was suspended there in 1780.[15] The acts only affected Scotland to the extent that members of the presbyterian church were subject to the test on appointment to offices in England as well as posts in the army and navy, where they were treated as equivalent to other dissenting bodies. Nor were dissenters excluded from parliament, *en masse*, because many were willing to take the oaths of allegiance and supremacy and the declaration against the doctrine of transubstantiation – which formed an important part of the legislative securities of the Test Acts of 1673 and 1678 – as well as the oath of abjuration after 1702. Retaining the Test and Corporation Acts was thus regarded as a useful symbol, rather than a practical and effectual barrier, and their retention seen as necessary in case those admitted to office should attempt to perpetrate what the duke of Wellington described as 'mischief'.[16] As Lord Eldon argued, in 1828, the Indemnity Acts constituted a continuing declaration by parliament that the Test and Corporation Acts 'ought not to be repealed'.[17] This was the principal reason why the last three attempts to repeal the acts, before 1828, had failed. During the years 1787–90, Pitt the Younger was gradually converted from favouring to opposing repeal. Advised by his former Cambridge tutor, Dr Pretyman (who had been elevated, under Pitt's recommendation, to become bishop of Lincoln), Pitt was persuaded, using Bishop Sherlock's

---

[13] Robert Hole, *Pulpits, Politics and Public Order in England* (Cambridge, 1989), 239. For early-18th-century attempts at repeal, see N. Hunt, *Two Early Political Associations* (Oxford, 1961).

[14] *Liverpool Mercury*, 7 Mar. 1828; K.R.M. Short, 'The English Indemnity Acts 1726–1867', *Church History*, xlii (1973), 372.

[15] D.W. Hayton, 'Exclusion, Conformity, and Parliamentary Representation: The Impact of the Sacramental Test on Irish Dissenting Politics', in his *Ruling Ireland, 1685–1742: Politics, Politicians and Parties* (Woodbridge, 2004), 188; D.W. Hayton, 'Parliament and the Established Church: Reform and Reaction', in *The Eighteenth-Century Composite State: Representative Institutions in Ireland and Europe, 1689–1800*, ed. D.W. Hayton, James Kelly and John Bergin (Basingstoke, 2010), 78–106.

[16] *Political Diary of Edward Law, Lord Ellenborough, 1828–30*, ed. Lord Colchester (2 vols, 1881), i, 39. For the growth of organised dissent from the late 18th century, see Ursula Henriques, *Religious Toleration in England, 1787–1833* (1961); B.L. Manning, *The Protestant Dissenting Deputies* (Cambridge, 1952); R.W. Davis, *Dissent in Politics, 1780–1830: The Political Life of William Smith MP* (1971).

[17] *The Public and Private Life of Lord Chancellor Eldon, with Selections from his Correspondence*, ed. H. Twiss (3 vols, 1844), ii, 200–1.

argument of 1718, that the sacramental test 'was not the qualification [for office] but the evidence [and the proof it incidentally affords] of it'.[18]

Thirty-eight years later, Dr Charles Lloyd, Peel's former Oxford tutor, recently elevated under Peel's recommendation as bishop of Oxford, failed to perform a similar service. In advance of Russell's repeal motion, Lloyd immersed himself in volumes of scholarly and theological disputation upon the acts before fastening upon Sherlock's distinction for the benefit of his ex-pupil. Peel regarded the distinction as 'too refined' for the house of commons, where (in his view) hungry bellies and slow intellects ruled over nice points of debate and arguments had to be formulated with a view to their prospects of success.[19] Peel's opposition to the repeal motion was, thus, predicated upon the 'low' ground of political pragmatism rather than the 'high ground' of anglican Church supremacy, to the disappointment of many observers. As Peel informed his cabinet colleague, Lord Ellenborough, some days before the debate, the dissenters suffered no 'practical grievance, and . . . he had rather continue this sort of quiet and rest to the church than open a new state of things which might not be accompanied with the same degree of tranquillity'. Peel thought it would prejudice consideration of the catholic question and, if he were a supporter of catholic relief, he would vote against repeal on that basis alone – a sentiment which seems to have weighed heavily with Ellenborough, Huskisson and Palmerston in directing their line of conduct in the subsequent parliamentary debate.[20]

In taking this approach, Peel was being entirely consistent with his existing parliamentary declarations on the subject. If Peel's views on the Test and Corporation Acts before 1828 were not aired with the regularity, or celebrity, of those on catholic relief, they were, none the less, clear. In 1821, Peel 'had maintained that it was not the right of every subject to enjoy access to every office . . . There was a "clear distinction" . . . between penal laws and laws which only excluded from civil office':[21]

If a permanent right of this kind were acknowledged in the one body [by which he meant the catholics], one equally permanent and co-extensive must be recognised in the other. This being taken as granted, what would be the inevitable consequence? Why, it would be necessary to repeal the Test and Corporation Acts – not to modify, but to destroy their operation by a total and unequivocal repeal.[22]

However, the same logic did not work in reverse – that is to say, the granting of repeal first would not inevitably lead to the concession of emancipation – for many dissenters who favoured repeal (not least those represented, after 1811, in the Protestant Society for the Protection of Religious Liberty) were known to have an anti-catholic bias. Conceding repeal might thus serve to shore up the protestant line of defence the better

---

[18] Clark, *English Society*, 414–17, 530–2; Peel, *Memoirs*, ed. Mahon and Cardwell, i, 66. On the earlier parliamentary repeal campaign, see G.M. Ditchfield, 'The Parliamentary Struggle over the Repeal of the Test and Corporation Acts, 1787–90', *English Historical Review*, lxxxix (1974), 551–7.

[19] Peel, *Memoirs*, ed. Mahon and Cardwell, i, 77.

[20] Ellenborough, *Political Diary*, ed. Colchester, i, 39.

[21] O'Ferrall, *Catholic Emancipation*, 181.

[22] Peel, *Speeches*, i, 149.

to resist catholic relief. That is why some 20 opponents of catholic relief in the house of commons voted for repeal of the Test and Corporation Acts in February 1828.[23]

Peel was not above using the strategic dilemma amongst the supporters of repeal and emancipation to 'divide and rule' in parliament as the occasion demanded. In May 1827, on the formation of Canning's administration from a mixture of whigs and pro-catholic tories, Peel specifically challenged the prime minister on his attitude towards the Test and Corporation Acts, in the face of Russell's impending motion for their repeal. In response to Peel's clear statement of intent on the issue – 'I give him notice that I intend to oppose him, and that I will always do so, whether in or out of power'[24] – Canning responded that he would not consider repeal before emancipation and would oppose the motion. This sentiment accorded with the arrangements previously settled between Canning and those whigs, under Lord Lansdowne, who consented to join the government.[25] However, its public declaration cut the parliamentary ground from under the dissenters' feet. In the face of this reverse, the 'United Committee' – which had been formed from all the major representative bodies of English dissent (other than the Protestant Society) to co-ordinate extra-parliamentary support for Russell's motion – decided to make a tactical retreat. Russell's motion was withdrawn for the session, on the clear understanding that it would be reintroduced the following year.[26]

In the interim, a campaign of petitioning and propaganda was pursued by the dissenters which, as Wendy Hinde observed, 'a modern lobbyist would find hard to beat'.[27] Robert Aspland founded the *Test Act Reporter* to place the repeal campaign in its historical context and report upon its contemporary continuance. Some 20,000 copies of Edgar Taylor's *Statement of the Case of the Protestant Dissenters under the Corporation and Test Acts* (first composed in 1824) were distributed – many of them stitched into copies of the *Quarterly* and *Edinburgh* reviews – and a circular letter was distributed to all dissenting ministers containing a 'model petition' and advice on generating new support. This bore fruit in the healthy number of petitions favouring repeal; some 1,200 in 1827 and 1,300 in 1828.[28] Peel was, throughout, suspicious of regarding these as representative of 'the real sense of public opinion' and observed that he 'should be disposed to pay much more attention to them' if he had been convinced that they had not been 'set in motion by any external influence'.[29]

By the time that Russell's motion was reintroduced, in February 1828, the situation had been dramatically transformed by Canning's death and Goderich's distress, as well as a key strategic coup in disentangling the public presentation of the repeal issue from the campaign for catholic emancipation. In January 1828, the Catholic Association, which

[23] G.I.T. Machin, 'Resistance to Repeal of the Test and Corporation Acts, 1828', *Historical Journal*, xxii (1979), 124; Peter Jupp, *British Politics on the Eve of Reform: The Duke of Wellington's Administration, 1828–30* (Basingstoke, 1998), 278.

[24] Peel, *Speeches*, i, 512.

[25] Arthur Aspinall, *The Formation of Canning's Ministry February to August 1827* (Camden Soc., 3rd ser., lix, 1937), 124, 158, 190.

[26] *Committees for Repeal of the Test and Corporation Acts, Minutes 1786–90 and 1827–8*, ed. T.W. Davis (London Record Soc., xiv, 1978).

[27] Wendy Hinde, *Catholic Emancipation: 'A Shake to Men's Minds'* (Oxford, 1992), 31.

[28] Machin, 'Resistance', 119.

[29] William A. Hay, *The Whig Revival 1808–1830* (Basingstoke, 2005), 155; Peel, *Speeches*, i, 551–6.

had been campaigning for catholic relief since 1823, proposed a union with the dissenters for the purposes of achieving complete civil and religious liberty for them all. The association subsequently published an *Address . . . to the Protestant Dissenters of England* and returned 100,000 signatures in favour of repeal. However, Russell strongly advised against such a union and the United Committee, in conformity to his view, publicly followed suit. However intimately the issues of repeal and emancipation were connected in the public mind, it was important (on purely strategic grounds) that the individual character-istics of the two measures should be stressed. The polite rebuff afforded the Catholic Association helped to defuse the suspicions of the Protestant Society as to the underlying motivations behind the repeal campaign and allowed them to send representatives to the United Committee. This resulted in the first united front, on the part of all the representa-tive bodies of dissent, in the history of the repeal campaign.[30]

Meanwhile, the government (as well as Peel) were deciding their course. Wellington's new cabinet was balanced no less delicately than Canning's and Goderich's had been, in that it comprised members of the Canningite group (Grant, Dudley, Huskisson and Palmerston) who were generally favourable to repeal in principle but doubtful of the wisdom of conceding it before emancipation, alongside representatives of the protestant interest such as Wellington, Bathurst and Peel. The extreme (or ultra) protestant position represented by the likes of Eldon and Westmorland had deliberately been excluded from the cabinet; a move which was not without significance for the subse-quent passage of the repeal bill through the house of lords.[31] It was finally decided to oppose the motion as a government question, for much the same reasons as Peel had communicated to Ellenborough previously.[32] However, the subsequent parliamentary presentation of the case by the government's speakers (Huskisson, Peel and Palmerston) turned out to be anything but effective. Huskisson was howled down for supporting repeal in the abstract whilst declining to vote for it in the present, whilst Palmerston put a similar case no better in stating that he did not wish to show 'partiality' by 'relieving the dissenter from that which is merely nominal, while the catholic labours under real and substantial difficulties'.[33] For his part, Peel dwelt upon the 'system of kindly feeling' which had subsisted between Church and dissent, for the duration of the acts, and the 'practical enjoyment of rights' which dissenters enjoyed within a framework which recognized the 'predominance of the Established church'. As such, the dissenters had no 'practical grievance' of which to complain – a fact borne out by nearly 40 years of inaction on the subject. More significantly, Peel directed a salvo at the higher claims made for the Acts' retention: 'I am not prepared, I confess, to argue this question as if the continuance of the Test and Corporation Acts was so essentially interwoven with the protection of the constitution, or the security of the protestant Establishment, that one or both must fall by the concession which the Dissenters require.'[34] A month later, in correspondence with Lloyd, Peel significantly extended his position: 'I do not think

---

[30] O'Ferrall, *Catholic Emancipation*, 181–2; *Committees*, ed. Davis, 62–106.

[31] Richard W. Davis, *A Political History of the House of Lords 1811–1846: From the Regency to Corn Law Repeal* (Stanford, CA, 2008), 143–5.

[32] Ellenborough, *Political Diary*, ed. Colchester, i, 35–6, 39.

[33] G.H. Francis, *Opinions and Policy of the Right Honourable Viscount Palmerston as Minister, Diplomatist, and Statesman during more than Forty Years of Public Life* (1852), 53–7.

[34] *The Monthly Repository and Review of Theology and General Literature*, ii (1828), 274.

that it is . . . possible to contend from the abstract position that the true test . . . of an Established church – is the superior privilege as to civil rights of its members.'[35] This was diametrically opposed to Eldon's view that the sacramental test 'was well calculated to maintain' the connection between Church and state.[36] Peel's unwillingness to defend the principle of anglican supremacy raised consternation amongst peers and bishops, including Lloyd himself and the ultra-tory duke of Newcastle. Peel 'had not the spirit to oppose the motion on the principle [Newcastle observed after the debate] & in short wished to avoid all responsibility in the course which he took'.[37] Whilst Norman Gash described Peel's argument as 'very English, very pragmatic' and regarded his speech as 'cool and balanced', previous biographers, including Dalling and Doubleday, saw it as a likely indication of the certainty of defeat.[38] A week before the debate, Peel had privately confessed to Lloyd that 'the argument against repeal, for a popular assembly like the house of commons, is threadbare in the extreme' and later declared his aversion to delivering a self-fulfilling prophecy: if he had stated the indispensability of the acts to the preservation of the constitution in Church and state, and lost, it raised the potential for that very position to come true.[39] Peel failed to hold the ground on the basis of principle and, though Eldon afterwards attempted to do so in the house of lords, it is notable that the debates on repeal were, thereafter, almost entirely concerned, with 'the stability of society [rather] than with the abstract rights of man or the theoretical justification of political obligation'.[40]

The government subsequently went down to defeat on Russell's repeal motion by a majority of 44, with 237 votes given in favour; in the recriminations which followed, the blame was variously attributed to poor whipping on the part of the government, over-severe whipping on the part of the government and uncertainty as to whether it really was a government issue or a vote of conscience. However, at bottom, as Lord Hatherton observed and Lord Ellenborough confirmed, 'The debate was dull'; 'the Government spoke so feebly and all the arguments the other way were so ably put that it was impossible to resist and we all walked out with the Ayes'.[41]

An interesting aspect of Peel's position in the debate arose from the fact that he was not only speaking in his capacity as home secretary and leader of the house of commons but as MP for the university of Oxford. In introducing his speech, Peel made a good deal of the fact that he had received no specific instruction, petition or advice 'as to the course of conduct which [the university] desire their representative to adopt' and inferred from this silence that it was 'disposed to rely with confidence upon the

---

[35] *Committees*, ed. Davis, xxv.

[36] *Eldon*, ed. Twiss, ii, 200–1.

[37] *Unrepentant Tory: Political Selections from the Diaries of the Fourth Duke of Newcastle, 1827–1838*, ed. Richard A. Gaunt (Parliamentary History Record Series, 3, Woodbridge, 2006), 47; cf. *The Diary and Correspondence of Charles Abbot, Lord Colchester*, ed. Lord Colchester (3 vols, 1861), iii, 553.

[38] Gash, *Mr Secretary Peel*, 462; Lord Dalling and G. Bentley, *Sir Robert Peel: An Historical Sketch* (1874), 49; T. Doubleday, *The Political Life of the Right Honorable Sir Robert Peel: An Analytical Biography* (2 vols, 1856), i, 428–30.

[39] Peel, *Memoirs*, ed. Mahon and Cardwell, i, 66, 74–7.

[40] Hole, *Public Order*, 240–1.

[41] Arthur Aspinall, 'Extracts from Lord Hatherton's Diary', *Parliamentary Affairs*, xvii (1963), 20–1; Ellenborough, *Political Diary*, ed. Colchester, i, 42. With 435 MPs present, the division was the largest in the parliamentary session: *HPC, 1820–32*, i, 318.

judgement of this House'.[42] After the government's defeat, reports circulated that a 'strong disinclination was felt' to a petition against the measure by the vice-chancellor.[43] Wellington used this as one of the justifications for his government's subsequent about-face on the issue: 'The universities not only did not stir but large majorities of the heads of houses and the graduates at Oxford almost unanimously refused to concur in any address upon the subject'.[44] 'When we bear in mind Mr Peel's intimate connexion with Oxford, the orthodoxy of which city he may be considered to represent [the *Liverpool Mercury* observed], we deem the failure ... as amongst the favourable signs of the times, and as good presumptive proof that a "new era" is at hand'. 'In fact', the *Leicester Chronicle* concluded, 'intolerance must finally disappear there, just as certainly as Jacobitism has disappeared.'[45]

But, as Gash sardonically observed, 'Oxford was not England' and the government now faced a dilemma.[46] Wellington later maintained that the adverse parliamentary vote made the question 'hopeless in the House of Commons', for many who had voted with the government in the minority had 'declared their determination to vote for the repeal upon the next division'.[47] Peel's *Memoirs* also made play with what appeared to be 'decisive evidence of a change in public opinion' – as registered in the votes of MPs rather than the weight of petitions. It was no longer possible, as Eldon maintained, to use the massive majority against repeal in 1790 as the measure of sentiment on the subject, for that had now been eroded and turned into a majority in its favour.[48] Whilst the cabinet debated its course of action, given that the larger part of it was now regarded as favourable to repeal, Peel was faced with an immediate need to determine a response in the Commons. In formulating this, Peel remained mindful that a repeal measure would meet full-scale assault in the house of lords, bring the king's position into question and possibly lead to that wider assault on anglican privilege which an emboldened whig party and the organised efforts of dissenting opinion in the country might serve to provoke. Conversely, anything less than total repeal might enflame a delicate situation still further.[49]

As to the principle behind the acts, it is clear that, insofar as Peel is concerned, this had fallen victim to (if it was not already in full retreat before) the government defeat on the issue. In classifying the different positions of his cabinet colleagues, after the vote had passed, Ellenborough recorded Peel as being 'indifferent' to the acts' retention. Charles Lloyd had appeared to foresee this state of affairs when he advised Peel, a fortnight before, to oppose repeal 'this Session at least' before giving up the issue and staying out of the matter in order to save face.[50]

---

[42] Peel, *Speeches*, i, 551–6.

[43] *Diary*, ed. Colchester, iii, 552–3.

[44] Southampton UL, Wellington Papers [hereafter cited as WP], 1/930/39: Wellington to Montrose, 29–30 Apr. 1828; cf. Peel, *Memoirs*, ed. Mahon and Cardwell, i, 86.

[45] *Liverpool Mercury*, 28 Mar. 1828; *Leicester Chronicle*, 12 Apr. 1828.

[46] Gash, *Mr Secretary Peel*, 462.

[47] Southampton UL, WP1/930/39: Wellington to Montrose, 29–30 Apr. 1828.

[48] Peel, *Memoirs*, ed. Mahon and Cardwell, i, 100.

[49] Gash, *Mr Secretary Peel*, 461–2.

[50] Ellenborough, *Political Diary*, ed. Colchester, i, 46; Peel, *Memoirs*, ed. Mahon and Cardwell, i, 65; W.J. Baker, *Beyond Port and Prejudice: Charles Lloyd of Oxford, 1784–1829* (Orono, ME, 1981), 175.

However, as with catholic relief a year later, this last piece of tutorial advice proved impossible for Peel to subscribe to, although the pupil now took up the hint which his former master had thrown out not to concede the measure 'without consulting some of the heads of the church, and hearing their reasons – because in either case it may be of great importance for you to be able to say afterwards that you acted with their sanction'. Lloyd was clearly in favour of some form of declaration of Christian belief, as a substitute for the sacramental test, whilst Ellenborough felt that the bishops of London (William Howley) and Bath and Wells (George Henry Law) would agree to something similar, although whether as a declaration or an oath remained, as yet, unclear.[51]

In the interim, Peel flirted with another possibility which had been raised in the repeal debate by the back-bench MP, Sir Thomas Acland. Acland had suggested an annual suspension of the sacramental test as a fit method for proceeding; this would meet the dissenters' immediate grievance whilst deferring consideration of a permanent settlement until a future date. Ellenborough thought that Peel seemed 'to catch' at Acland's suggestion 'as a mode of getting out' of his difficulty, although it became increasingly clear to him that this would not satisfy the Commons.[52] In the words of the *Leicester Chronicle*, playing 'the game of suspension, instead of repeal [would] prove the intellectual littleness of an administration, who would stultify themselves and the nation by such mockery of legislation'.[53] Likewise, the United Committee addressed a resolution to Peel on 3 March specifically declaring: 'that they would be satisfied with nothing less than the outright repeal of the sacramental test laws and that they would not accept any other type of religious test for civil offices'.[54]

This point was brought home clearly enough two days after the vote on Russell's repeal motion. On 28 February, Russell moved immediately for legislation to repeal such parts of the Test and Corporation Acts as required the sacramental test and deflected Peel's suggestions for a necessary delay in which to consider the best manner of proceeding. Peel pointed out, fairly, that Russell's majority had been for a committee to 'consider the Sacramental provisions of the Test and Corporation Acts' and not for their total repeal; any such bill could only be introduced on the resolution of a committee of the House.[55] Lord Milton attacked Peel's 'pretences' at delay which he considered part of a determination 'to regain the vantage ground [the government] had lost, and . . . defeat the Dissenters'. This was 'warmly repelled' by Peel, who proceeded to leave the House, followed by a phalanx of about 100 supporters. Colonel Davies attacked Peel for allowing 'paltry, petty, and personal feeling to interfere with the broad path of [his] duty' and Sir George Warrender stated that 'if anything was likely to make him withdraw his support from the government it was the conduct of the Right Honorable Gentleman'.[56] 'It was not perhaps a line of conduct befitting the leader of the House', Gash observed, 'but Milton's . . . insult had rankled, and the plain fact was that

---

[51] Baker, *Port and Prejudice*, 175–6; Ellenborough, *Political Diary*, ed. Colchester, i, 47; *Diary*, ed. Colchester, iii, 550.

[52] Ellenborough, *Political Diary*, ed. Colchester, i, 43; Machin, 'Resistance', 125.

[53] *Leicester Chronicle*, 8 Mar. 1828.

[54] *Committees*, ed. Davis, 92.

[55] Peel, *Speeches*, i, 564–6; *HPC, 1820–32*, i, 296.

[56] Hansard, *Parl. Debs*, new ser., xviii, cols 816–33.

Peel could in no way control the proceedings.'[57] Though Peel subsequently returned to the House, claiming that he had left it to satisfy his hunger, rather than his anger, the incident gave rise to a good deal of critical commentary on Peel's highly-strung temperament and his sensitivity wherever a point of personal honour was concerned. Hobhouse noted that the drama had served to derail proceedings, because 'the chairman forgot to report on the bill and the object of the contest was lost' – an occurrence which the duke of Newcastle mistakenly took to be the signal for a counter-assault against the measure by Peel.[58]

Not for the first time, however, Newcastle was to be disappointed. Though the *Liverpool Mercury* felt that Peel was 'a sincere bigot, whose opposition to the claims of the Dissenters arises from his zeal for Mother church', they realized that his 'hostility to the measure [was] less distinguished than heretofore by dogmatism and inveteracy; and he recognises the respectability of the majority to which he was opposed'.[59] Peel now took the central role in formulating the government's response to the *fait accompli* of repeal by negotiating with the anglican hierarchy for a declaration which would satisfy their own desire for securities to the Church and facilitate the bill's passage through the house of lords without thereby enraging the dissenters. Russell prudently arranged a meeting between Peel and the United Committee, 'in order to allay any irritation' arising out of the last debate. From it emerged a promise, on Peel's part, not to oppose the bill 'in its present stage'. This allowed it to pass its second reading in the Commons, without division, on 14 March.[60]

3

By this time, the government's intended course of action in committee on the bill was becoming clear. Peel told Lloyd, on 4 March: 'I think Declaration in lieu of Sacramental Test – the latter being repealed – will be the measure; but we must not say so now.'[61] Both Wellington and Peel had consulted separately with the archbishop of Canterbury (Charles Manners Sutton) and the bishops of London, Durham (William Van Mildert) and Chester (Charles Blomfield) on the subject, but the crucial meeting occurred at Lambeth Palace on 15 March when, by the archbishop's invitation, Howley, Van Mildert and Blomfield were joined by the archbishop of York (Edward Venables Vernon) and bishop of Llandaff (Edward Copleston) to agree a 'form of declaration' with Peel.[62] Of those present, Van Mildert appears to have been the most reluctant to accede, a fact at which Peel subsequently expressed some surprise, given that the

---

[57] Gash, *Mr Secretary Peel*, 463–4.

[58] *Recollections of a Long Life by Lord Broughton: With Additional Extracts from his Private Diaries*, ed. Lady Dorchester (6 vols, 1910), iii, 246; *Unrepentant Tory*, ed. Gaunt, 47. For a further example of Peel putting his dinner first (28 Jan. 1832), see *HPC, 1820–32*, i, 409.

[59] *Liverpool Mercury*, 7 Mar. 1828.

[60] *Committees*, ed. Davis, 92.

[61] Peel, *Memoirs*, ed. Mahon and Cardwell, i, 73.

[62] Ellenborough, *Political Diary*, ed. Colchester, i, 47; W.J. Copleston, *Memoir of Edward Copleston DD Bishop of Llandaff with Selections from his Diary and Correspondence* (1851), 123; Peel, *Memoirs*, ed. Mahon and Cardwell, i, 74.

declaration which he introduced into the bill, on 18 March, was somewhat stronger than that agreed with the bishops: 'I [A B] do solemnly declare that I will never exercise any power, authority, or influence, which I may possess by virtue of the office of [X] to injure or weaken the Protestant church as it is by law established within this realm, or to disturb it in the possession of any rights or privileges to which it is by law entitled.'[63] Peel's wording was 'generally approved' at a 'full meeting of Bishops' on 21 March.[64] This led Blomfield, in correspondence with the dean of Peterborough, to declare that the Bill as it proceeded from the Commons:

> was strictly and literally a measure of the Bishops. The Dissenters acknowledge the concession, but consider it any thing rather than a triumph on their part. The more violent regard the proposed Declaration as a fetter, where there was none (in practice) before. Cobbett abuses Lord John Russell for acceding to such a security, and laughs at the dissenters for having been made fools of by 'sly old Mother church'.[65]

Wellington also placed most of the responsibility for the government's proceeding upon the bishops. According to the duke, the prelates were opposed to the occasional conformity currently practised in relation to the acts as an abuse of a religious rite and wished to avoid a clash between a house of commons supported by public opinion and the house of lords which might endanger 'the peace of the church'. Consequently, the government was in the position of deciding 'whether they would comply with the desire of the Archbishops and Bishops and others, and make an arrangement, or . . . urge them to concur in an opposition to the Bill in the House of Commons'. Significantly, Wellington stated that the declaration was 'concocted by the Archbishops and Bishops with Mr Peel'. However, when Peel introduced the declaration to the Commons, he stated that he had done so 'on his own view of the case' and without 'an opportunity of consulting any professional person'.[66]

Jonathan Clark and Boyd Hilton have argued that Peel 'beat the retreat' by helping to ' "orchestrate" the bishops' submission to what was technically a compromise, but actually a capitulation'. However, the two men differ in their interpretation of the cause and consequence of this retreat. Clark thought Peel insufficiently robust in resisting a pressure which he did not consider to be all that strong and misguided insofar as his solution promoted the very thing he was hoping to prevent – further inroads upon anglican constitutionalism. By contrast, Hilton thought Peel's compromise the inevitable consequence of the unexpected timing – and success – of Russell's motion.[67] However, there were plenty of contemporary critics who castigated Peel for his perceived surrender. For example, one correspondent to the *Morning Post* attacked Peel for sacrificing 'his

---

[63] *Diary*, ed. Colchester, iii, 555; Peel, *Memoirs*, ed. Mahon and Cardwell, i, 88.

[64] Copleston, *Memoir*, 123.

[65] A. Blomfield, *A Memoir of Charles James Blomfield, DD Bishop of London with Selections from his Correspondence* (2 vols, 1863), i, 138–9.

[66] Southampton UL, WP1/930/39: Wellington to Montrose, 29–30 Apr. 1828; Peel, *Speeches*, i, 581–5; *The Monthly Repository and Review of Theology and General Literature*, ii (1828), 279–80.

[67] Clark, *English Society*, 395; Hilton, *Mad, Bad*, 383; Hilton, 'Ripening of Robert Peel', 69.

own interest [and] the interest of his country [by joining] the ranks of his opponents, bearing his declaration as a cloak for his apostasy'.[68]

Yet, as Peel told the house of commons, in what was widely regarded as a 'conciliatory speech' introducing the government's measure, the alternatives to such a course of action were hardly more palatable. The Test and Corporation Acts could not be preserved as they stood; Acland's idea of suspension recognized the principle of a sacramental test (which had been decisively voted down by Russell's motion) whilst a simple, unqualified repeal of the sort Russell had introduced gave no corresponding security to the anglican Church.[69] By contrast, the proposed declaration was to be obligatory for all those chosen for office in corporations in England and Wales and at the discretion of the crown for holders of civil offices of trust and commissions under the crown. As the *Christian Observer* subsequently observed, the Church of England would 'at least, not be in a worse condition [under the declaration] than under the indemnity act, by which neither test nor declaration was required'.[70]

Whilst hostile to the idea of a declaration in principle, Russell had already expressed himself willing to accommodate it if it would facilitate the passage of the bill through the house of lords whilst satisfying the Church of England. As John Prest notes, Russell was willing to 'accept the irritation rather than lose the substance of the reform'; moreover, he persuaded the dissenters to do the same.[71] One overheated correspondent to the *Morning Post* complained that the declaration was accepted by the dissenters 'with a surly grace', whilst the *Leicester Chronicle* saw the declaration as 'so utterly nugatory' as to be little more than an 'expedient to [mollify] a certain class of high-church supporter, who regard this solemn kind of nothingness as the very perfection of statesmanship'.[72] However, the minutes of the United Committee for 21 March 1828 reveal a shrewder perspective:

> The Bill thus framed, abolished the Sacramental Test – enacts no penalties beyond loss of office – imposes no form of declaration on Protestant Dissenters, that is not equally imposed upon all classes of His Majesty's subjects – and, with regard to offices under the Crown, makes the declaration imperative only where it may be required by the competent lawful authorities. [Moreover], the declaration is not intended to bind the declarant, being a Protestant Dissenter, to abstain from that free expression of his opinion as an individual, and from those measures for the maintenance and support of his own faith and worship, in the use of which he is now protected by the law.[73]

Peel stated that he had 'reluctantly conceded' to bring forward the declaration himself, rather than cede the ground to either Acland or Russell. In doing so, he provoked some privately-expressed criticism from the 18-year-old Gladstone who, in his final term at

[68] *Morning Post*, 21 Apr. 1828.

[69] Gash, *Mr Secretary Peel*, 465; *Committees*, ed. Davis, 96.

[70] Quoted in *The Age of Peel*, ed. Norman Gash (1968), 20.

[71] John Prest, *Lord John Russell* (1972), 35; this rather calls into question Russell's subsequent discussion of the declaration in his *Recollections and Suggestions 1813–1873* (1875), 58.

[72] *Morning Post*, 17 Apr. 1828; *Leicester Chronicle*, 22 Mar. 1828.

[73] *The Monthly Repository and Review of Theology and General Literature*, ii (1828), 353.

Eton, wrote to a school friend declaring that Peel's conduct towards Acland was not 'altogether fair: I mean in taking the matter out of his hands'.[74] However, as Peel subsequently informed Lloyd, he had done so at the express desire of the bishops and especially the archbishop of Canterbury: 'Their wish was that I should propose the Declaration myself, or at any rate take a very prominent part in advising its acceptance.' Lloyd, moved to unusual epistolatory anger by the idea that his favourite charge should be exposed to public taunts of inconsistency, responded that he saw 'nothing but cowardice' in the bishops' advice.[75]

To that extent, the repeal measure bears out the argument promoted by Norman Gash and supported by Frank O'Gorman that Peel 'virtually took charge of' the bill at this stage of proceedings.[76] But if Peel had thereby framed the terms of the subsequent parliamentary debate, by focusing consideration upon the nature and wording of the proposed declaration, rather than the repeal of the sacramental test itself, he had just as obviously exposed himself to the objections to which the declaration gave rise.

Within days of Peel's speech, an alteration to the wording had been accepted, which inserted the terms 'power' and 'authority' in addition to what was regarded as the vague term 'influence'. This was conceded at the request of Edgar Taylor, a leading unitarian and member of the United Committee. Similar influence, conveyed from the committee to Peel through Lord Sandon, had already influenced the inclusion of the phrase 'by virtue of the office' before the declaration was introduced.[77] Beyond that, as Peel made clear to the Commons on 24 March, he was not prepared to go:

> I am satisfied with the security which this Declaration offers. I am not prepared to make any alteration in it to please the wishes of any party. All that has passed since I proposed it, confirms me in the sanguine hope that the present session will not close without our having every question satisfactorily arranged, with respect to Dissenters from the Church of England.[78]

However, it is clear that Peel's objection to further alterations arose from another consideration. The day after introducing the declaration, at a meeting with Russell and William Smith, the veteran campaigner for repeal and chairman of the United Committee, Peel:

> expressed it to be his earnest wish that the declaration should be so framed as that the House of Lords should not have any inducement to meddle with it; that if the Bill should pass the House of Lords without much observation, there would be no ill feeling in the country excited; that some opposition would most probably be raised but that he thought he had secured a satisfactory feeling in favour of the measure; that he thought the words now used would induce the leaders in the House of Lords to

---

[74] *Gladstone*, ed. Brooke and Sorensen, i, 203.

[75] Peel, *Memoirs*, ed. Mahon and Cardwell, i, 93, 95.

[76] Gash, *Aristocracy and People*, 137; Frank O'Gorman, *Voters, Patrons and Parties: The Unreformed Electorate of Hanoverian England, 1734–1832* (Oxford, 1989), 367. The same point was made contemporaneously by *Exeter Flying Post*, 17 Apr. 1828.

[77] *Committees*, ed. Davis, 96–7.

[78] Peel, *Speeches*, i, 592–3.

accede to the measure, but that he could not be answerable for the consequences if those words were altered.[79]

Peel said much the same in introducing the declaration to the Commons; a move which, as Eldon subsequently noted, 'made it impossible [for the house of lords] to resist with effect'.[80] However, for ultra-tories like Eldon and Newcastle, a principal ground for resistance arose from the fact that the declarant was 'not even required to acknowledge himself a Christian, so repugnant is that supposed to be to the liberal opinions of the present enlightened age'.[81] Likewise, a correspondent to the *Morning Post* complained that the declaration was 'too general and indefinite, and upon an occasion of too much personal interest, to be relied upon as an effectual restraint'. Dr Tournay, the warden of Wadham College, observed that the declarant did not 'declare generally that he will not destroy the church, but merely that he will not destroy her by means of his official power and opportunities', whilst Edward Irving attacked the declaration for asking 'a man to avoid doing what, as a subject, he was legally bound not to do'. Henry Drummond also regretted the lack of 'any reference to the divinity of the established church [which] thus reduced it to a mere object of mercenary gain'.[82] Amongst the tory press, whether government-subsidised or not, there was a general unity of feeling against repeal. *The Age* described the bill as an 'abortion' and Peel as a rat whilst the *Standard* proposed a substitute test, in place of the declaration, limiting office to christians.[83]

Important though these views were, they exercised little influence over Lords Winchilsea, Falmouth and Tenterden, who took a leading role in opposing the government's measure in the house of lords. Indeed, it is notable that discussion of the bill amongst the peers was dominated by issues arising from the absence or inclusion of particular words in Peel's declaration rather than the principle of repeal itself. To that extent, Peel's intervention and his subsequent handling of the bishops had helped move the debate away from territory which would have extracted embarrassing sentiments from ministers and exposed internal divisions on the catholic question (in a period when the Canningites still comprised part of the government) and on to the narrower ground of semantics. Viewed in this light, Peel's course of action was a shrewd political strategy which afforded important securities for the anglican Church.[84]

4

The progress of the Lords' debate is well attested in the published diaries of its leading participants (notably, those of Colchester, Ellenborough and Newcastle). The peers' treatment of the bill generated a good deal of public interest, being keenly read by Gladstone and stimulating the one caricature of significance to emerge from the repeal

[79] *Committees*, ed. Davis, 96.

[80] *Eldon*, ed. Twiss, ii, 200.

[81] *Unrepentant Tory*, ed. Gaunt, 49; also see Southampton UL, WP1/926/17: Westmorland to Wellington, 8 Apr. 1828.

[82] *Morning Post*, 21 Apr. 1828; Peel, *Memoirs*, ed. Mahon and Cardwell, i, 87; Machin, 'Resistance', 130–1.

[83] James Sack, *From Jacobite to Conservative* (Cambridge, 1993), 204; Machin, 'Resistance', 127–8.

[84] Hansard, *Parl. Debs*, new ser., xviii, cols 1571–1610; xix, cols 39–49.

campaign – William Heath's *Grand Battle of Lords Spiritual and Temporal or Political Courage Brought to the Test*.[85] Yet, in essence, the opposition to the bill may be summed up in two words: Lord Eldon. It was always likely that Eldon, drawing upon 20 years' worth of experience as lord chancellor and a sense of grievance borne of his exclusion from Wellington's cabinet, would constitute a formidable opponent. Throughout the debates, he was noted to have become proportionately more 'vehement and ill-humoured, as his chance of any sort of success in either defeating the dissenters or embarrassing his old associates became less and less'.[86] Lord Holland attempted to prepare for this eventuality by writing to Russell and the United Committee, in advance of the debates, to gain advice about the:

> omissions which Eldon pretends to have found & means to expose. This is material – for we should forestall all such as appear to be reasonable by avowing an intention to amend or supply them in Committee. You will observe these objections & omissions apply to the repealing Clause not to the declaration to your bill [and] not to Peel's part of it.[87]

Holland was to be disappointed in his expectation that the repeal clause, rather than Peel's declaration, was to be the object of fiercest consideration amongst the peers. In fact, most of the 20 amendments and 35 speeches which Eldon made, in the course of the Lords' debates, sought to improve the latter rather than prevent the former; either by turning the declaration into an oath or constituting it, through its wording, a more overtly protestant profession of faith which would provide greater protection to the 'practice, institutions and discipline of the church of England'.[88] After the contest was over, Harriet Arbuthnot considered that Eldon had fought 'like a dragon'; Eldon himself felt that he had 'fought like a lion, but my talons have been cut off'. He had conceded, even before the debates began, that those 'who oppose, shall fight respectably and honourably; but victory cannot be ours'.[89] Ellenborough thought Eldon had been allowed too much latitude in the initial stages of the debate, encouraging him to become 'more mischievous and grasping' as time elapsed. At one stage in the proceedings, Lord Chancellor Lyndhurst 'seemed rather unwilling to take upon himself the responsibility of [offering a legal] interpretation contrary to Eldon's', whilst the bench of bishops split on Eldon's amendment to insert the words 'I am a protestant' into the declaration for those admitted to corporation offices. Eldon subsequently gained George IV's support for this amendment, probably through the intervention of his brother, the duke of Cumberland, who returned from Hanover for the express purpose of opposing the repeal legislation. Only some deft manœuvring, on Wellington's part, deflected this

---

[85] *The Gladstone Diaries*, ed. M.R.D. Foot and H.C.G. Matthew (14 vols, Oxford, 1968–94), i, 170, 175; British Museum, Department of Prints and Drawings, 15530. This image provides the cover illustration to the present volume.

[86] *The Monthly Repository and Review of Theology and General Literature*, ii (1828), 354.

[87] TNA, PRO 30/22/1A, f. 197: Holland to Russell, 3 Apr. 1828; *Committees*, ed. Davis, 98–9.

[88] R.A. Melikan, *Lord Eldon, 1751–1838: The Duty of Loyalty* (Cambridge, 2000), 335–8.

[89] *The Journal of Mrs Arbuthnot, 1820–1832*, ed. Francis Bamford and the duke of Wellington (2 vols, 1950), ii, 166; *Eldon*, ed. Twiss, ii, 200, 203.

potential ambush. Nevertheless, the king's feelings on the measure are illustrated by his refusal to enforce obedience, or attendance, upon the household peers, during the bill's passage through the Lords.[90]

Ultimately, the union of whig and ministerial support and the attitude of the bishops ensured the bill's success. Indeed, in some respects, this represented a more united front than in the case of either catholic emancipation in 1829 or the English Reform Bill in 1832. Blomfield stated that: 'the Bishops took the lead, and were heard with great attention', whilst Ellenborough concluded triumphantly: 'We managed to keep the Bishops with us, to divide with a great majority, to resist successfully amendments which would have nullified the measure or converted it into a penal law, and to have all the grace of concession.'[91]

However, the bill emerged from the Lords with two major alterations to Peel's declaration. By an amendment which the house of commons subsequently accepted on 2 May, all 'Naval officers below the rank of Rear Admiral, military officers below the rank of Major-General in the army or of Colonel in the Militia, Commissioners of Customs, Excise, Stamps, and Taxes, and all officers concerned in the collection, management and receipt of the revenues' were exempted from the requirement to make the declaration upon admission to office.[92] More significantly, Copleston's amendment to insert the words 'upon the true faith of a Christian', which had the effect of preventing the possible extension of the act to jews and atheists, was accepted. Whilst William Smith told the Commons that it was not, in his opinion, 'of any great importance' whether the declaration existed or not, and John Wilson Croker correctly foresaw that the wording would not obviate the need for future Indemnity Acts, the alteration to the text of Peel's declaration provided a further barrier of admission.[93] Jews were only admitted to corporation offices, without the threat of prosecution, in 1845 (8 & 9 Vict., c. 52), and to the house of commons, after a compromise was reached with the house of lords – by which Lionel Rothschild took the oath on the old testament – in 1858 (21 & 22 Vict., c. 49). Whilst the Parliamentary Oaths Act of 1866 (29 & 30 Vict., c. 19) established the oath of allegiance to the crown and the protestant succession as the only required oath of office, the case of Charles Bradlaugh, the atheist MP for Northampton, raised a new difficulty for any freethinker objecting to the injunction 'so help me God'. Appropriately enough, in light of events in 1828, a solution to the parliamentary impasse that this created, resulting in the ability to make a 'solemn affirmation' under the Oaths Act of 1888 (51 & 52 Vict., c. 46), was provided by the critical intervention of the Speaker of the house of commons (and Peel's youngest son), Arthur Wellesley Peel.[94]

---

[90] Ellenborough, *Political Diary*, ed. Colchester, i, 88–92; *The Letters of George IV*, ed. Arthur Aspinall (3 vols, Cambridge, 1938), iii, 401.

[91] Blomfield, *Memoir*, i, 139; Ellenborough, *Political Diary*, ed. Colchester, i, 86.

[92] *Age of Peel*, ed. Gash, 20.

[93] Davis, *Dissent in Politics*, 248; *The Correspondence and Diaries of the Late Right Honorable John Wilson Croker*, ed. Louis J. Jennings (2 vols, New York, 1884), i, 385; Short, 'Indemnity Acts', 375.

[94] Frances Knight, 'The Bishops and the Jews, 1828–1858', in *Christianity and Judaism*, ed. D. Wood (Oxford, 1992), 387–98; Walter Arnstein, *The Bradlaugh Case: A Study in Late Victorian Opinion and Politics* (Oxford, 1965); Michael Wheeler, *The Old Enemies: Catholic and Protestant in Nineteenth-Century English Culture* (Cambridge, 2006), 3, 149.

5

It was never likely that Robert Peel's name would be on the lips of those who gathered to celebrate the achievement of repeal. A gala dinner of over seven hours' duration was convened at the Freemasons' Hall in London on Waterloo day, 18 June 1828. Henry Brougham and Robert Aspland lectured the assembly on the necessity of an imminent catholic relief, to which the presiding officer, HRH the duke of Sussex, retorted: 'thank you for the lecture which you have read my family, but I wish you to remember that I at least have not deserved it'.[95] For the dissenters, the achievement of repeal galvanised their energies for future campaigns – civil registration, church rates and university admission as well as parliamentary reform – and showed them a possible route for success. Yet the repeal of the sacramental test was insufficient, in itself, to guarantee the dissenters full access to corporations. As John Phillips argued, whilst the oligarchic structures of English local government were remodelled through the Municipal Corporations Act of 1835, dissenters could be made to feel 'painfully aware of their inequality [which was] reinforced by social interactions in church and chapel'.[96] Yet repeal also recognized the dissenting interest as an established political fact; the subsequent achievement of the £10 householder franchise as the basic qualification for the parliamentary vote in urban constituencies, under the terms of the 1832 Reform Act, necessitated that much of Peel's leadership of the Conservative Party in the 1830s be consciously constructed with an eye to conciliating it as a constituency of support. This was attested to privately by Peel in conversation with the duke of Newcastle in 1833 and publicly, through the prominence given to unresolved dissenting causes, in the Tamworth manifesto of December 1834.[97]

Repeal also had immediate consequences for the Church of England for it represented, in the words of *The Annual Register* for 1828, 'the first successful blow that had been aimed at the supremacy of the Established church since the [Glorious] Revolution'. Moreover, as Lord Holland observed, it had exploded 'the real Tory doctrine *that church & state are indivisible*'.[98] This is precisely what ultra-tories had understood at the time and what many others, less stridently, came to perceive thereafter. Historians of the Church of England have uncovered evidence of how widely such concerns came to be shared. For example, during the 1830s, John Keble 'clearly anchored tractarian protest to the reforms of 1828–9'. Meanwhile, Ian Machin has taken his cue from Geoffrey Best's immortal phrase that 'hardly a dog barked' at the passing of repeal, by contrasting the relative quiescence with which repeal passed onto the statute book with the sense of gloom and foreboding which followed fast upon its heels.[99]

---

[95] Robert B. Aspland, *Memoir of the Life, Work and Correspondence of the Rev. Robert Aspland of Hackney* (1850), 484.

[96] John Phillips, *The Great Reform Bill in the Boroughs: English Electoral Behaviour 1818–1841* (Oxford, 1992), 302.

[97] *Unrepentant Tory*, ed. Gaunt, 223.

[98] Gash, *Aristocracy and People*, 137; Clark, *English Society*, 532; cf. *Early Correspondence of Lord John Russell*, ed. Rollo Russell (2 vols, 1913), i, 272; Ellenborough, *Political Diary*, ed. Colchester, i, 44.

[99] William Gibson, *The Church of England 1688–1832: Unity and Accord* (2001), 12–18; Simon Skinner, *Tractarians and the 'Condition of England': The Social and Political Thought of the Oxford Movement* (Oxford, 2004), 87; G.I.T. Machin, *Politics and the Churches in Great Britain 1832–68* (Oxford, 1977), 20–1; Machin, 'Resistance', 115; cf. Hilton, *Mad, Bad*, 383.

As to Peel's role in these events, Lord John Russell was clear: he was 'a very pretty hand at hauling down his colours'. With more or less degree of sympathy, historians writing on the subject have tended to agree. For Norman Gash, 'the government had conducted a neat rearguard action', whilst Professors Machin, Davis and O'Gorman regard the ultimate success of repeal as having more to do with political circumstances and parliamentary arithmetic than (in Machin's words), 'long-term social trends or the rapid growth of dissent'.[100]

Whilst this hardly accords due weight to the long-term contribution made by dissenters to English public life, these historians are, nevertheless, correct in noting that the terms of the final repeal legislation owed much to the influence exerted upon it by Wellington and Peel, as leaders of their respective chambers. However, when compared with the repeal of the corn laws 18 years later, it is clear that the input of Russell and the United Committee to the final outcome was correspondingly greater than that exercised by Cobden, Bright and the Anti-Corn Law League in 1846.[101]

Unsupported by any significant degree of petitioning evidence to the contrary, any noticeable opposition from the universities, any clear signs of resistance from the bench of bishops as a whole and except for the principled (if vehement) opposition of the ultra-tory peers and the populist baying for ministerial blood of their representatives in the press, Wellington's government lacked any discernible appetite for a fight over the retention of the Test and Corporation Acts, during 1828. In these circumstances, Peel, in particular, must be credited for having intervened in the bill in a manner and at a point which served (in William Gibson's words) to 'insulate' and 'neutralise the source of the strife' to the extent that it salvaged something by way of security for the anglican Church.[102]

Peel's management of repeal also provided a precedent for his subsequent treatment of anglican Church questions during the 1830s. Indeed, a close parallel with Peel's strategy over repeal is provided in the formation of the Ecclesiastical Commission in 1835. By working with, rather than against, the grain of the anglican Church hierarchy, Peel, once again, helped in 'neutralising the source of strife' by creating a separate body which would debate the issues and propose legislative solutions for them. By attempting to isolate these discussions, as far as possible, from acrimonious debate in parliament, Peel helped to make the Church of England abettors in the solutions which legislators sought to provide.[103]

In later years, Peel himself was apt to elide the separate legislative enactments of the 'Constitutional Revolution' as being of apiece; hence the inclusion of the material upon repeal in the relevant volume of *Memoirs* concerned with the achievement of emancipation. However, whilst the achievement of repeal could not, necessarily, be divorced from the wider issue of emancipation, asking how repeal looks on its own terms, and what the motivations of key players such as Peel were when the event is thus isolated, remains a worthwhile activity. As Chester New observed in his biography of Henry

---

[100] Spencer Walpole, *The Life of Lord John Russell* (2 vols, 1889), i, 143; Gash, *Mr Secretary Peel*, 465; Machin, 'Resistance', 116; Richard W. Davis, 'The Strategy of Dissent in the Repeal Campaign, 1820–1828', *Journal of Modern History*, xxxviii (1966), 392; O'Gorman, *Voters, Patrons and Parties*, 367.

[101] Gaunt, *Peel*, ch. 6.

[102] Gibson, *Unity and Accord*, 107.

[103] Davis, 'Toryism to Tamworth'.

Brougham, over 50 years ago: 'it was said at the time [of repeal] and it has been repeated in all the books to this day that [repeal] was important only because it prepared the way for Catholic Emancipation. From that view Brougham [for one] strongly dissented'.[104] There was no expectation that emancipation would hurry along so quickly on the tails of the 1828 legislation as it did, though its supporters clearly believed that its achievement could not be long delayed. Tactically, this raised interesting questions. For example, the Catholic Association seriously considered suspending its rule of opposing all candidates pledged to support the government in parliamentary elections – a proposal which O'Connell himself supported.[105]

Given Peel's public declarations on the relationship between repeal and emancipation, and the tactical considerations raised by granting one before the other, it is likely that, when the time came, he expected repeal to succeed (rather than precede) emancipation. However, in neither case did he expect to play a leading role in their achievement. The speed and success of Russell's repeal motion changed that sequence of events, just as the need to respond decisively, whilst securing safeguards for the anglican Church, ensured that Peel assumed a decisive role in shaping the final legislation. To some extent, this was a foretaste of events the following year. Peel's indispensability to the government as leader of the Commons increased after the resignation of the Canningite ministers in May 1828. Likewise, Peel's view of a relief measure, stripped of wings or securities, proved to be decisive in ensuring the passage of catholic emancipation through the house of commons. The necessity of confronting repeal head-on formed a backdrop to that 'ripening' of Peel's views which commentators and historians have detected during this period.[106]

[104] Chester New, *Life of Henry Brougham to 1830* (Oxford, 1961), 322.
[105] Oliver MacDonagh, *O'Connell: The Life of Daniel O'Connell, 1775–1847* (1991), 248.
[106] Gaunt, *Peel*, ch. 2.

Index